Mrs. Virgil Goebel

PHYSICAL EDUCATION
FOR ELEMENTARY SCHOOLS

PHYSICAL EDUCATION
FOR
ELEMENTARY SCHOOLS

BY

N. P. NEILSON

*Chief of Division of Health and Physical Education,
State Department of Education,
Sacramento, California*

AND

WINIFRED VAN HAGEN

*Chief of Bureau of Physical Education for Girls,
State Department of Education,
Sacramento, California*

NEW YORK
A. S. BARNES AND COMPANY
INCORPORATED
1937

COPYRIGHT 1929 BY
N. P. NEILSON AND WINIFRED VAN HAGEN

COPYRIGHT 1930 AND 1932 BY
A. S. BARNES AND COMPANY
INCORPORATED

This book is fully protected by copyright and nothing that appears in it may be reprinted or reproduced in any manner, either wholly or in part, for any use whatever, without special written permission of the copyright owner.

PRINTED IN THE UNITED STATES OF AMERICA

ACKNOWLEDGMENTS

We wish to acknowledge the kind coöperation and assistance rendered by the following for permission to use material from their publications:

A. S. Barnes and Company
Dearborn Publishing Company
Benjamin H. Sanborn and Company
John C. Winston Company
Sherman Clay and Company
Recreation Training School of Chicago, Ill.

The manuals of physical education of other states and a few cities were available and some material was taken from these publications. Special acknowledgment is due the city of Oakland, California, for the use of portions of their courses of study; to Mr. Clark W. Hetherington and Dr. Herbert R. Stolz, whose philosophy and ideals have been a constant source of inspiration and guidance in our compilation of this volume.

We wish to express our appreciation to Mrs. Martha Anderson, who typed the manuscript; Miss Claire Colestock, who contributed the article on Posture; Mrs. Frances B. Toelle, Miss Lucile Czarnowski, Mrs. Mathilde E. Schuettner, Mrs. Belle Wentworth, and Mrs. Marjorie W. Leach, who assisted with the section on Rhythmical Activities; Miss Rosalind Cassidy, Miss Florence Weeks, Mrs. Jane Graves, Miss Helen Heffernan, Mr. Cecil Martin, Mr. Charles Hunt, Mr. C. L. Glenn and staff, Dr. Sven Lokrantz and staff, and members of the California Curriculum Commission, all of whom gave many valuable suggestions.

We desire to acknowledge our indebtedness to the members of the California State Board of Education for the permission granted to have the California "Manual of Physical Education Activities for Elementary Schools" published in revised form by a publishing company for general distribution.

FOREWORD

Accepted educational theory points out that the best road to all around development is participation. Physical education has acquired a broader connotation and correspondingly greater significance since it has come to be regarded as a *method of education* rather than a program designed for physical development alone. The physical education program is education by means of participation in the large muscle activities.

Health is only one of the major objectives of the physical education program. The development of the social qualities of courage, initiative, honesty, coöperation and self-confidence is concomitant. Play is a spiritual as well as a physical and social necessity for children.

Modern education strives to quicken the creative life of the individual. To many children, release of imagination and of latent artistic ability comes through rhythmic expression. Although the potential artists discovered may be few, all children are led to a cultural appreciation of rhythm and to a form of recreation that may have a therapeutic as well as an æsthetic value.

The field of physical education curriculum is comparatively barren of actual research studies. The authors of this volume have made a signally scientific contribution in bringing together activities which a considerable body of experience indicates to be sound. All available materials in the field were analyzed and tested against the judgment of well-qualified experts to form the program organized on the broadest conception of the function of physical education in the modern school.

HELEN HEFFERNAN,
Chief, Division of Rural Education
State Department of Education
Sacramento, California.

CONTENTS

	PAGE
ACKNOWLEDGMENTS	v
FOREWORD	vii
PREFACE	xiii

PART I

CHAPTER I—INTRODUCTION 1

CHAPTER II—OBJECTIVES.

Definition	6
Objectives	6
Effects of Muscular Activity	7

CHAPTER III—ORGANIZATION.

Physical Education Periods	8
Specimen Programs	9
Play Supervision	14
Achievement Tests	14
Classification of Children for Competition	15
Pupil Leadership	17
Incentives	17
Mass Athletics	18
Intramural Athletics	18
Track and Field Meets	20
Play Days	24

CHAPTER IV—CLASSIFICATION OF ACTIVITIES.

Athletic Games	27
Corrective Physical Education	27
Health Education	29
Hunting Games	30
Individual Athletic Events	30
Mimetics	31
Posture	31
Relay Races	35
Rhythmical Activities	36

CONTENTS

	PAGE
Story Plays	46
Stunts	47

CHAPTER V—PLAY AREAS, EQUIPMENT AND SUPPLIES.

School Sites	49
Surfacing	49
Laying out Grounds	49
Boundary Lines for Courts and Fields	52
Commercial Equipment for School Playgrounds	53
List of Play Areas and Equipment	60
List of Physical Education Supplies	61
Provisions for Safety	62

CHAPTER VI—SUGGESTIONS TO TEACHERS.

General Suggestions	64
Physical Education Books	66

PART II (Graded Program)

FIRST GRADE.

Story Plays	68
Rhythmical Activities	80
Hunting Games	89
Mimetics	92

SECOND GRADE.

Hunting Games	95
Rhythmical Activities	98
Story Plays	109
Relay Races	120
Mimetics	121

THIRD GRADE.

Hunting Games	123
Rhythmical Activities	127
Relay Races	140
Stunts	142
Mimetics	145
Athletic Games	146

FOURTH GRADE.

Athletic Games	151
Relay Races	163

CONTENTS

	PAGE
Hunting Games	166
Rhythmical Activities	172
Stunts	187
Mimetics	191

FIFTH GRADE.

Athletic Games	193
Individual Athletic Events	202
Relay Races	214
Rhythmical Activities	218
Stunts	228
Hunting Games	230
Mimetics	234

SIXTH GRADE.

Athletic Games	237
Individual Athletic Events	248
Relay Races	251
Stunts	254
Rhythmical Activities	258
Hunting Games	268
Mimetics	271

SEVENTH GRADE.

Athletic Games	274
Individual Athletic Events	297
Rhythmical Activities	300
Stunts	307
Relay Races	312
Hunting Games	315
Mimetics	316

EIGHTH GRADE.

Athletic Games	319
Individual Athletic Events	331
Mimetics	333
Rhythmical Activities	334
Stunts	346
Relay Races	348
Hunting Games	350

BIBLIOGRAPHY AND REFERENCE CODE	353
INDEX	357

PREFACE

Physical education activities give expression to the deepest instinctive tendencies of childhood, which are shown in the natural movements of running, jumping, climbing, striking and throwing. They are the chief means of developing motor coördination and control, and of training the emotions and social adjustments of the child. These activities have a special hygienic value during the period of growth and development because of their stimulative influence upon the vital organs and systems governing circulation, respiration, nutrition and elimination.

The child's interest in activities is spontaneous, but he requires adult supervision in the selection of them and in the guidance of the play spirit into wholesome channels. Lack of interest in an activity is usually due to poor selection, overuse, lack of skill, or to poor teaching. Given the opportunity, those who are athletically inclined are apt to find for themselves sufficient big-muscle activity; the weak, the undernourished, the underdeveloped, the backward and the crippled—these are the children most in need of physical education.

It is our hope that this book may serve as a basis for the physical education program in the elementary school. It is published for general distribution in response to the many requests for the "Manual of Physical Education Activities for Elementary Schools of California," on which this book is based. This book includes a graded program of activities which should be adapted to the school situation, the time of the year, and the individual needs of the child. Due to lack of space, a considerable number of activities have not been included but merely referred to and, therefore, the teacher should have available the recommended minimum list of books, and as many as possible of those listed in the bibliography.

In choosing activities for children of a given age, it is essential that those be chosen which have the greatest natural appeal for that age. As far as possible this has been done. There is no duplication of activities for the different grades because it is felt the progress of the student will be more rapid and his skills and interest more varied if the teacher is held to a definite content for each grade. This content should be taught first, then, if time permits, activities taught in any previous grade, if still interesting to the children, may be used as supplementary material. Throughout the manual where "boy" or "girl" is used in a description, it is not to be implied that the activity is necessarily unsuited to the other sex. The terms have been used only as a convenience.

Formal calisthenic exercises do not appear in the book. Being artificial movements, unrelated to child life situations, they are uninteresting to children and have very little, if any, carry-over value. The use of calisthenic drills (the "daily dozen") led by a phonograph is not acceptable as part of the physical education program. They are not adapted to the varying strength of children of different ages and are never used in the out-of-school play life of the child. Such mechanical teaching methods are not tolerated in any other subject and if continued will bring physical education back to the unenviable position it held a decade ago. There is neither mental content nor character training in such exercises. Formal exercises, when used as aids for correction of physical handicaps, should be given by persons trained in their use. As a rule, elementary teachers have in the past had little opportunity to secure such specialized training.

METHOD OF STUDY

The state Manuals of Health and Physical Education were secured from the states which have issued such manuals. A great many books published in the field bearing specifically upon the elementary school problem were also obtained. All these references were numbered for convenience in tabulating and studying the activities.*

The name of each activity was then written on an individual card and each card made to show all the available references upon that particular activity, also the grade placement, if given. As in many cases the same activity appeared under different titles, this duplication had to be eliminated.

After completing the tabulation of the activities, the cards were separated into groups dividing the field into story plays, mimetics, rhythmical activities, hunting games, relay races, stunts, athletic games and individual athletic events. Alphabetical lists were made showing the frequency with which each activity appeared in the available references with a distribution of its grade placement. This preliminary work gave us the practical advantage of reading all the material contained in our references on each activity at one time, thus saving us much time, making our work more efficient and helping us to select the description and grade placement which seemed most desirable.

The following criteria were kept in mind while the selection of material was made:

1. There should be no duplication of activities under different titles.
2. The activity should provide for the largest possible number actively participating at the same time in any one group.
3. There should be some activities for use in the schoolroom and a great deal for use on the playground.

---

* See Bibliography and Reference Code, page 353.

PREFACE

4. Some activities should be included which require no equipment except play space.

5. The description of each activity should be concise, accurate and complete.

6. Most of the activities selected should be vigorous in type.

7. Some of the less vigorous forms of activities should be included for handicapped pupils.

After making a selection of activities and arranging them by grades, a detailed study was made of each activity in order to determine whether it was clearly stated and whether all the essential points were covered. As a result of this analysis many of the activities were rewritten, either in part or entirety.

The following charts show the number of activities reviewed, number used, number referred to and number eliminated:*

Activities	Total Reviewed	Number Used	Number Referred to	Number Eliminated
Mimetics	109	52	...	57
Story plays	218	67	...	151
Rhythmical activities	1,180	83	119	978
Hunting games	...	98	54	...
	} 556	(153)	(65)	338
Relay races	...	55	11	...
Stunts	247	82	32	133
Athletic games	...	59	9	...
	} 351	(122)	(46)	183
Individual athletic events	...	63	37	...
Total	2,661	559	262	1,840
		(821)		

Activities		1	2	3	Grades 4	5	6	7	8	Total
Mimetics	U	5	7	7	7	7	7	6	6	52
	R	—	—	—	—	—	—	—	—	—
Story plays	U	34	33	—	—	—	—	—	—	67
	R	—	—	—	—	—	—	—	—	—
Rhythmical activities	U	10	12	13	11	11	10	8	8	83
	R	19	17	11	15	11	15	14	17	119
Hunting games	U	17	13	16	14	13	12	6	7	98
	R	6	6	13	7	9	5	5	3	54
Relay races	U	—	2	7	11	11	7	8	9	55
	R	—	—	2	—	2	3	2	2	11
Stunts	U	—	—	15	14	9	14	15	15	82
	R	—	—	—	5	5	5	7	10	32
Athletic games	U	—	—	4	13	11	10	13	8	59
	R	—	—	—	2	2	3	2	—	9
Individual athletic events	U	—	—	—	—	29	13	12	9	63
	R	—	—	—	—	9	12	10	6	37
Total	U	66	67	62	70	91	73	68	62	559
	R	25	23	26	29	38	43	40	38	262
										(821)

U—Used.
R—Referred to.

* These charts refer to the original study. For this book they should be slightly modified.

PHYSICAL EDUCATION
FOR ELEMENTARY SCHOOLS

PART I
CHAPTER I
INTRODUCTION

Physical education has had a most interesting history. Its nature and status at different times have been determined by the religious, political, economic, and social conditions in society. Primitive man was educated physically because it was necessary for him to obtain food and defend himself against his enemies; the Chinese, because of their policy of isolation, suppression of individuality, and absence of a universal language paid little attention to physical development; India, the land of the caste system, religious and mystic philosophies, was against progress, sanitation, and physical education; and Persia, under Cyrus the Great, believed education needed to be moral and physical, and that boys should have military training.

The Greeks and Romans were the first to give physical education an important place. It formed a major part of their educational program, and its utilitarian value in times of war was beyond question. Many of the present philosophical ideas controlling our modern programs date back to this early era. When the Teutonic barbarians invaded, Rome fell and Christianity appeared. The early Christians had little use for physical education. They believed that life should be spent in prayer, that the spirit and soul should be exalted, and that life should be lived for the world to come. Sometimes they tried to accomplish this by neglecting, punishing, and degrading the body.

The renaissance was a transition period between the middle ages and modern times. Records of life in Greece and Rome were re-studied. Progress in the sciences caused the health reason for physical education to gain in prominence, and with the sponsoring of the kindergarten by Froebel the third reason for physical education, "education through play," was introduced. Throughout history, the military, the health, and the educational reasons for physical education have been made plain.

The program in America has been affected by foreign systems of physical education. The Colonists brought with them the activities familiar to childhood, yet they did not include physical education in their school program because pioneer conditions provided much physical activity and their sober religious conception of life gave little place to recreation. Later, Beck, Follen and Lieber came over from Germany and introduced "German" gymnastics; Nisson and Posse brought with them the Ling system of Sweden; esthetic dancing, esthetic gymnastics, physical culture, psychophysical culture, harmonic gymnastics, and dynamic breathing all tried for a place. Physical education in this country has developed upside down and inside out. It began in the universities and landed in the elementary school; it emphasized athletics for the few instead of for the many; it tried to fit the individual to a system instead of utilizing natural activities and adapting them to the educational and health needs of the child. The military motive and physical training as a muscle developer have played all too great a part.

The need for physical education in the school program is now apparent. Civilization has shifted the burdens of the race. The industrial revolution with its attendant growth of cities has changed the activities of people from those requiring the large muscles of the body to those requiring peripheral muscles and mental activity. Indoor life has replaced outdoor life to a large extent. The physical restraints of the schoolroom, the improper adjustment of seats and light, tend to develop postural defects and careless habits in sitting, standing and walking. Play activities may be useful in counteracting these tendencies.

The rise of a machine dominated society which does less strenuous work, but work which creates great mental strain because of its monotony; transportation by machine rather than on foot; over-emphasis of adults on economic interests; concentration of population in large cities; crowded residential districts; homes contracted in size; families not only having no back yards, but having smaller rooms and fewer of them; the disappearance of occupations called "chores" which in early times were assigned to childhood; and often the actual elimination of child play in or near the home; these conditions are creating an environment conducive to physical inactivity. Biologically, man must have physical activity for growth, development, and maintenance of physical and mental health. Just as manual training and home economics have been transferred as a responsibility of the school so is the play of childhood being accepted as an educational problem.

Physical education is not a fad or a fancy, but is fundamental to all educational development. Physical education activities are educational activities and deserve a fair share of school time. Play is not wasted time, but serves a great purpose if properly conducted. Through muscular activity all the metabolistic functions are affected. Adults check the growth of children by keeping them still in school. Properly selected, properly organized, and properly taught activities serve to relieve the physical and mental strain incident to academic class instruction and are a real asset to the teacher in the adjustment of disciplinary problems. Increased attendance, improved mental attitude and better pupil-teacher response often follow as results of a good physical education program.

The idea has been too prevalent that physical education consists of gymnastic and calisthenic drills, setting-up exercises, and marching, taught in formal manner for improvement of health, posture and discipline. These formal activities are an outgrowth of European systems designed to prepare persons for military service. They are adult invented, adult given, and should be confined to adult use except where individual prescription is made for a specific purpose.

Formal drills are a bore to children and teachers alike. Teachers who themselves are enthusiastic and go through the motions vigorously often say their students enjoy these formal activities. Their judgment is based on the outward submission and not on the inward rebellion of their pupils. Children, when free to choose, do not select mechanical arm, leg and trunk movements in preference to the game activities which have a natural appeal. The physical education problem faced by each state is to set up a program of natural activities suitable for child life development to meet the conditions of our time, rather than to continue the use of formal and artificial drills mechanically executed, done in rhythm to command and having little, if any, basic value for child growth needs.

Theories have been advanced that play is due to surplus energy, to the need for recreation; that it is instinctive, inherited memory; that it is growth. Practically, we are least interested in what causes play, and are most interested in the results accruing from play. We are recognizing that play, properly conducted, results in the physical, mental, and social development of the child. The older conceptions, that physical education was a preparation for the military, that drills and mass formations were the means of developing obedience and discipline, and that it was a relief from mental tasks, have given way to the modern point of view. Physical education is now considered to be a way of education, not to produce soldiers, big muscles, or gymnastic posture, but to secure the educational development of individuals with the resultant by-products of health, neuro-muscular skills, attitudes, and proper social conduct.

Physical education is usually included in school programs as the result of the passage of a law or the establishment of rules. It is believed that physical education laws passed in the United States have reduced by a generation the time necessary to attain our present accomplishments toward the universality of physical education. To date, thirty-six states have passed laws making physical education compulsory in the schools. A few states have made provision for it by action of their state boards of education.

The responsibility for establishing a good physical education program rests with the school administration. The typical teacher tries to carry out the program sponsored by her superior officers. It should be the duty of the board of education of each school district in the state to prescribe and enforce through its administrative officers suitable courses of physical education for all the pupils enrolled in school. Pupils in elementary schools should be taught physical education activities daily during an instructional period which should be no less than twenty minutes in length. In addition, other free periods should be utilized for supervised play in the activities learned during the instructional period.

Play must be organized, taught and supervised. There is no time when play at school should be unsupervised. The teacher becomes the play instructor and play supervisor. Whenever the number of pupils and teachers in a school district warrants, the district should employ a competent supervisor of physical education. This supervisor should be experienced in supervision, and should advise teachers and school officials as to the best methods of improving the quality of the physical education work offered. Supervisors are generally more essential in rural communities than in the larger cities.

The aims and purposes of the courses of physical education should be to develop organic vigor, provide neuro-muscular training, promote bodily and mental poise, correct postural defects, secure the more advanced forms of coördination, strength and endurance, and to promote such desirable moral and social qualities as appreciation of the value of coöperation, self-subordination and obedience to authority and higher ideals, courage and wholesome interest in truly recreational activities; to promote a hygienic school and home life, secure scientific supervision of the sanitation of school buildings, playgrounds, athletic fields, and the equipment of them.

In order to protect the child, the parents, and the school authorities, each pupil should have a physical examination whenever it seems necessary to determine his fitness for participation in an activity program. A child, parent or guardian who objects to such an examination should be permitted to file annually or semi-annually with the principal of the school in which the child is enrolled a statement in writing, properly signed, stating the objections to the physical examination. When such a statement is filed, school employees should exempt the child from physical examination, but should not excuse the child from participation in the physical education program.

Whenever a parent asks to have his child excused from physical education on the ground of physical disability he should not at the same time demand exemption from a physical examination. In such instances the parent should be told that the school can not exempt a pupil from physical education activities without such physical examination as the school may deem necessary to determine the extent of such disability. Disability may be temporary or permanent. It should be understood that individuals who are injured or ill are entitled to temporary excuses, but there is no child able to attend the school regularly who will not benefit by some form of properly adapted physical education procedure. It is, therefore, recommended that no excuses from physical education for a term be granted unless the instructor in charge of physical education is unable to adapt a program to the individual's needs, or a local physician, who can make proper recommendations, is not available. This assumes that there may be cases organized in physical education ranging all the way from the regular program of activities down to rest and a specially prescribed hygienic regimen.

If physical education is to be extended to the great majority of children in the elementary schools of this country the general classroom teacher, in most instances, will have to do the work. This means that thousands upon thousands of teachers now in service must through encouragement, through supervision, and in some cases almost through compulsion, become acquainted with and prepared in physical education activities and methods of teaching them to children. It also means that the oncoming generations of teachers now in teacher training institutions, or yet in the elementary or high schools of the nation, must be not only exposed to, but become thoroughly familiar with the physical education content materials so essential to children's physical, mental, and social development.

CHAPTER II
OBJECTIVES
DEFINITION

Physical Education is education by means of physical activities. It is concerned with the big-muscle activities and related factors which influence the development of the child and the physical and social efficiency of the adult.

GENERAL OBJECTIVES

The general objectives of Physical Education are:
1. The development of organic vitality.
2. The development of many specific neuro-muscular skills.
3. The development of proper ideals and attitudes toward physical activity.
4. The establishment of desirable habits of conduct.

SPECIFIC OBJECTIVES

Some of the specific objectives of Physical Education may be stated as follows:
To—
1. Prevent handicaps and improve physical efficiency.
2. Improve the individual's posture.
3. Decrease mental strain and improve mental health.
4. Develop symmetry, control and grace of bodily movement.
5. Develop ability to meet physical emergencies.
6. Develop alertness and quick response.
7. Develop an active response to rhythm.
8. Develop courage, self-control, self-sacrifice, courtesy, kindness, loyalty, obedience, honesty, coöperation and initiative.
9. Create in youth an intelligent and healthful interest in physical activity and give to him a fund of activity material for use in leisure time.
10. Create an interest in the physical welfare of others.
11. Promote the desire for wholesome associations and recreation.
12. Develop the proper spirit toward victory and defeat.
13. Develop good character.
14. Develop the qualities inherent in leadership.

EFFECTS OF MUSCULAR ACTIVITY *

Circulation is increased throughout the entire body, or through the part exercised. This circulatory activity increases carriage of food to the tissues, removal of wastes, distribution of the endocrine secretions and equalization of the water and heat content of the body.

Big-muscle activity increases the demand for oxygen and thus causes an increased respiratory activity with the resulting increase in the rate of oxygenation of the blood, increased rate of elimination of the carbon dioxide and increased oxygen supply to the tissues. This increased respiratory activity is the result of the demands made by the exercise, and deep breathing without the bodily exercise will not have the same results. During increased activity the respiratory apparatus naturally responds by frequent and deep respirations.

Exercise stimulates the excretory system and increases the elimination of waste through kidneys, lungs, intestines and skin.

Digestion is improved and assimilation is accelerated by exercise. Digestion is not only a chemical but a muscular process. If the musculature of the alimentary canal is flaccid, digestion is retarded and impeded. Peristaltic movements are more vigorous when the muscle tone of the alimentary canal is good. Exercise is essential in keeping the muscles in good condition. The constipation resulting from sedentary life is in large part due to inadequate muscular activity.

Big-muscle activity stimulates growth and for the growing child is absolutely essential.

The heart is strengthened by the exercise of the skeletal muscles of the body. The best known way in which some types of weak heart can be made strong is by gradual and increasing amounts of physical work of the skeletal muscles. Exercise for the person with a weak heart should be arranged by skilled specialists; it should not be prescribed by an untrained person.

The muscles of the body are directly developed by physical activity. This is of great importance for health as regards the muscles of the trunk; the abdominal muscles must be in good condition for the maintenance of the upright posture which is necessary for the best position and functioning of the abdominal and pelvic organs and therefore of great importance for health.

Rational exercise results in increased neural activity and in neuromuscular control which develops skill, accuracy, endurance, agility and strength.

---

* Report of the Joint Committee on Health Problems in Education of the National Education Association and the American Medical Association, pages 50-51.

CHAPTER III
ORGANIZATION
PHYSICAL EDUCATION PERIODS

Instructional period. This is the period usually required by law, and should be exclusive of noon and recess periods. It should be programmed daily as one period coming either in the morning session or in the afternoon. The division of the period into two periods destroys its usefulness for instructional purposes. It is the period when new types of activity are taught and practiced. The teacher takes the initiative and actually teaches the graded material which is to be practiced in the other play periods. The instruction should be scheduled definitely, the attendance of pupils regular, and the attitude full of purpose and enjoyment. Competition should not be the primary factor during this period, or the timid and poor performers will quickly lose interest. The teacher should explain to pupils that the purpose of the period is to learn the game and develop habits of good form in skills.

Relief periods. A relief period of two minutes in length should be given when needed. The purpose of these relief activities is to counteract the ill effects of sitting long periods at school desks, stimulate the vital organs, relieve fatigue, equalize and stimulate circulation, give postural change, exercise the large muscle groups and give mental relaxation. The activities used should be those previously learned during instructional periods. Running in place, running around the room, running around the schoolhouse, mimetic exercises, short games and story plays are well adapted to furnish relief. Formalized exercises to command are fatiguing and should not be used. The following points should be kept in mind:

The activity should be conducted by the regular class teacher.

If the class remains in the schoolroom, windows should be opened during the period.

No time should be wasted in getting class into action.

Coats and wraps should be removed before exercise.

The activity must be vigorous in type to be effective.

Supervised play periods. The periods before school, morning recess, noon, afternoon recess and after school should be considered as physical education periods and require constructive leadership and supervision by teachers. These periods offer an opportunity to extend the educational influences of the school into the play life of the child. The child here has the chance to practice the activities which are taught in the instructional period. Children need a great deal of vigorous activity for growth and development and need definite supervision of the right kind in order that their activities may contribute to their improvement. Intramural athletics should be emphasized in these periods.

SPECIMEN PROGRAMS

The importance of making out programs in advance can not be overemphasized. In planning a program the teacher should select activities of the various types, so as to give a well-balanced development. Activities, after being taught by the teacher, should be practiced frequently by the pupils until satisfying skills are acquired. The specimen programs which follow merely suggest a method which may be used.

A—YEARLY PROGRAM FOR INSTRUCTIONAL PERIOD (FIRST GRADE)

Activities	September	Oct.	Nov.	Dec.	Etc.
Story Plays	Playground Day in the Country Sleeping Princess Circus Cutting the Grass Autumn in the Woods Etc.				
Rhythmical Activities	The Camel Cats and Rats Did You Ever See a Lassie Farmer in the Dell Mulberry Bush Etc.				
Hunting Games	Brownies and Fairies Chase the Animal Around the Circle Crossing the Brook Jack Be Nimble Leader and Class Etc.				
Mimetics	Rabbits Birds Ferry Boat Cats Horse Galloping Etc.				

B—WEEKLY PROGRAM FOR INSTRUCTIONAL PERIOD (FIRST GRADE)

Activities	Monday	Tuesday	Wednesday	Thursday	Friday
Story Plays	Playground, The	(Review)	Sleeping Princess Playground, The	(Review)	Cutting Grass Sleeping Princess
Rhythmical Activities	Did You Ever See a Lassie	(Review)	The Camel Did You Ever See a Lassie	(Review)	Farmer in the Dell
Hunting Games	Brownies and Fairies	Chase the Animal Around the Circle	(Review)	Magic Carpet	(Review)
Mimetics	Rabbits Birds	(Review)	(Review)	Ferry Boat Cats	(Review)

C—WEEKLY INTRAMURAL PROGRAM FOR SUPERVISED PLAY PERIODS

(For schools equipped with a free play area, two playground baseball diamonds and the following courts: (Two) Basket ball, volley ball, captain ball, kick ball, and long ball; (One) End ball, bat ball, hand ball, horseshoe, tether ball, tennis, paddle tennis, and a soccer field.)

MONDAY

Grade	Recess Boys	Recess Girls	Noon Boys	Noon Girls
8	Soccer Horseshoes Individual Athletic Events	Volley Ball Hit Pin Baseball Tennis Stunts	Basket Ball Volley Ball Stunts Hunting Games	Speedball Horseshoes Individual Athletic Events
7	Volley Ball Tether Ball Stunts	Nine-court Basket Ball Stunts Individual Athletic Events	Basket Ball Tennis Paddle Tennis Stunts	Hit Pin Baseball Captain Ball Tether Ball Hunting Games
6	Captain Ball Paddle Tennis Stunts	Baseball—Diamond I Net Ball Hunting Games	Net Ball Captain Ball Hunting Games	Baseball—Diamond I Stunts Individual Athletic Events
5	Captain Ball Hand Ball Stunts	Long Ball Individual Athletic Events	End Ball Captain Ball Individual Athletic Events	Captain Ball Hand Ball Stunts
4	End Ball, Triangle Ball, Hunting Games, Stunts, Baseball—Diamond II		Long Ball, Baseball—Diamond II, Hand Polo, Hunting Games, Stunts	
3	Hand Polo, Kick Ball, Hunting Games, Dodge Ball, Apparatus		Kick Ball, Dodge Ball, Prisoner's Ball, Hunting Games, Apparatus	

ORGANIZATION

TUESDAY

Grade	Recess Boys	Recess Girls	Noon Boys	Noon Girls
8	Baseball—Diamond I Tether Ball Hunting Games	Nine-court Basket Ball Hunting Games Individual Athletic Events	Basket Ball Tennis Stunts	Baseball—Diamond I Tether Ball Hunting Games
7	Hit Pin Baseball Horseshoes Hunting Games	Volley Ball Tennis Paddle Tennis Stunts	Basket Ball Hand Ball Captain Ball Hunting Games	Hit Pin Baseball Horseshoes Individual Athletic Events
6	Rotation Soccer Stunts Hunting Games	Net Ball Hand Ball Captain Ball Individual Athletic Events	Field Ball Captain Ball Paddle Tennis Stunts	Net Ball Baseball—Diamond II Stunts
5	Baseball—Diamond II Individual Athletic Events	Captain Ball Stunts	Long Ball Kick Ball Hunting Games	Long Ball Hunting Games Individual Athletic Events
4	Bat Ball, End Ball, Long Ball, Apparatus, Hunting Games		Prisoner's Ball, Bat Ball, Triangle Ball, Hunting Games, Apparatus	
3	Kick Ball, Hand Polo, Dodge Ball, Hunting Games, Stunts		Boundary Ball, Kick Ball, Dodge Ball, Hunting Games, Stunts	

THURSDAY

Grade	Recess Boys	Recess Girls	Noon Boys	Noon Girls
8	Volley Ball Tether Ball Stunts	Speedball Hit Pin Baseball Stunts	Soccer Horseshoes Individual Athletic Events	Nine-court Basket Ball Volley Ball Tennis Individual Athletic Events
7	Basket Ball Tennis Paddle Tennis Individual Athletic Events	Baseball—Diamond I Horseshoes Hunting Games	Hit Pin Baseball Stunts	Nine-court Basket Ball Volley Ball Tether Ball Stunts
6	Net Ball Captain Ball Individual Athletic Events	Hunting Games Stunts	Captain Ball Paddle Tennis Individual Athletic Events	Baseball—Diamond I Net Ball Individual Athletic Events
5	End Ball Captain Ball Stunts	Hand Ball Hunting Games	Bat Ball Hand Ball Captain Ball Stunts	Kick Ball Hunting Games
4	Baseball—Diamond II, Hand Polo, Long Ball, Triangle Ball, Stunts, Hunting Games		End Ball, Triangle Ball, Apparatus, Baseball—Diamond II, Long Ball, Stunts	
3	Bat Ball, Dodge Ball, Kick Ball, Hunting Games, Apparatus		Kick Ball, Hunting Games, Hand Polo, Dodge Ball, Apparatus	

ORGANIZATION

FRIDAY

Grade	Recess Boys	Recess Girls	Noon Boys	Noon Girls
8	Basket Ball Tennis Individual Athletic Events	Baseball—Diamond I Horseshoes Hunting Games	Hit Pin Baseball Horseshoes Hunting Games	Nine-court Basket Ball Baseball—Diamond I Hunting Games
7	Basket Ball Tether Ball Volley Ball Hunting Games	Hit Pin Baseball Hand Ball Stunts	Basket Ball Tether Ball Individual Athletic Events	Volley Ball Tennis Paddle Tennis Individual Athletic Events
6	Hunting Games Net Ball Captain Ball	Field Ball Paddle Tennis Baseball—Diamond II Hunting Games	Rotation Soccer Hand Ball Stunts	Net Ball Captain Ball Hunting Games
5	Long Ball Captain Ball Hunting Games	Long Ball Stunts	Baseball—Diamond II Hunting Games Stunts	Captain Ball Stunts
4	Prisoner's Ball, Bat Ball, Stunts, Apparatus		Bat Ball, End Ball, Hunting Games, Apparatus	
3	End Ball, Bat Ball, Hunting Games, Dodge Ball		Kick Ball, Hand Polo, Dodge Ball, Hunting Games, Stunts	

PLAY SUPERVISION

The playground may become a serious liability to the school organization unless supervision is provided. Some teachers do not fully realize what happens where play is unsupervised. Children tend to learn undesirable language and form many objectionable habits of conduct. Older boys and girls often mislead those of younger ages. Unsupervised play usually develops into roughness where teasing, tripping and fighting predominate. Such forms of activity lack all the ideals of true sportsmanship which is so necessary for proper social development. On the unsupervised playground the aggressive children usually usurp all the privileges, the timid children being neglected because they are not recognized as equals by their classmates. The purpose of supervised play is to provide a program of wholesome activity which will give all the pupils an equal chance for development through participation.

ACHIEVEMENT TESTS

The purpose of testing elementary school pupils for activity skills attained should be primarily to determine individual improvement rather than for comparisons with performance by other pupils. In such tests the competition should be between the pupil's past and present records, each measured by an adequate scoring scale. Most of the individual athletic events and game elements can be organized as achievement tests by developing standardized scoring scales.

Many scoring schemes have been devised to encourage athletic activity and to stimulate an interest for improvement of performance but, as yet, none of them have proven entirely satisfactory. The great difficulty has been to arrange a satisfactory scheme of student classification in order to give just scores for performance. The entire field of achievement testing for physical education activity skills of elementary school pupils, therefore, awaits the establishment of an adequate classification scheme for placing students into comparable groups as to age, height and weight factors. In the meantime, the testing program in the upper grades may be carried on by using the classification scheme suggested in this book.

After the pupils have been classified into groups, the performance records in any given event may be arranged, for a class group, into a frequency distribution. Points may be allotted to scores at unit distances each side of the median performance record thus giving each pupil a corrected score in terms of the performance of a group of children having very nearly the same age, height, weight factors.

In giving tests, these suggestions should be observed:

1. The procedure in giving a test should be carefully thought out by the teacher so there will be no waste of time.

2. Do not keep large groups of pupils lined up and waiting while one person at a time is taking a test; while one team is taking the test other teams under the leadership of their captains should be playing.

3. Students may be used to assist the teacher when necessary.

4. Scoring the test should be done by the teacher.

The athletic badge tests for boys and girls adopted by the Playground and Recreation Association of America are a form of achievement tests. It is important to note that all requests for certification blanks and badges or for additional information should be sent to the Playground and Recreation Association of America, 315 Fourth Avenue, New York City, which will continue to supply badges and to handle all the details connected with the badge tests. The pamphlet "Athletic Badge Tests for Boys and Girls," Physical Education Series No. 2, 1923, may be secured from the United States Department of Interior, Bureau of Education, Washington, D. C.

CLASSIFICATION OF CHILDREN FOR COMPETITION

At present children in the school system are organized by grades. Each grade contains children of widely varying mental, chronological and physiological ages. For purposes of competition in physical education activities the grade system of classification is inadequate.

Before ten years of age, sex differences may be ignored. As a general principle of safety girls and boys should be in separate groups after ten years of age.

Children should be classified in different groups according to their capacity to enter into different levels of graded activities. This capacity can best be determined by the aid of a physical examination and skill tests. For fairness and safety, individuals must also be classified in all competitive events according to limits in age, height and weight, or a combination of these factors. Any one of these factors used by itself has been found unsatisfactory.

*A suggested scheme for classification of pupils for competition in activities is here given:

---

* By permission from Oakland Course of Study (14G).
NOTE—The name "Playground and Recreation Association of America" has been changed to: National Recreation Association, Incorporated.

CLASSIFICATION CHART
Boys and Girls

Exponent	Height	Age	Weight	Exponent	Sum of Exponents
1	50–51	10–10–5	60–65	1	9 and below A
2	52–53	10–6 10–11	66–70	2	
3		11–11–5	71–75	3	
4	54–55	11–6 11–11	76–80	4	10–14 B
5		12–12–5	81–85	5	
6	56–57	12–6 12–11	86–90	6	15–19 C
7		13–13–5	91–95	7	
8	58–59	13–6 13–11	96–100	8	20–24 D
9		14–14–5	101–105	9	
10	60–61	14–6 14–11	106–110	10	25–29 E
11		15–15–5	111–115	11	
12	62–63	15–6 15–11	116–120	12	30–34 F
13		16–16–5	121–125	13	
14	64–65	16–6 16–11	126–130	14	35–38 G
15	66–67	17–17–5	131–133	15	
16	68	17–6 17–11	134–136	16	39 and above H
17	69 and over	18 and over	137 and over	17	

EXAMPLE:
A pupil whose height is 54 inches—exponent for height is...... 4
A pupil whose age is 12 years, 8 months—exponent for age is... 6
A pupil whose weight is 83 pounds—exponent for weight is..... 5

Sum of exponents is 15
Pupil is in Class C.

PUPIL LEADERSHIP

Teachers will greatly facilitate their work if they develop leaders to assist in conducting the physical education program. Pupils may act as leaders in all phases of activity in all grades. The teacher should encourage the desire to lead and develop it by careful instruction. Make it an honor to lead and change leaders often enough to give every one a chance. Special meetings may be held where instructions to leaders are given. The practice of allowing children to choose squad leaders in class work is conducive to the development of fine qualities of active leadership which often have carry-over value for recess and other play periods.

INCENTIVES

Children derive much pleasure in receiving symbols which represent achievement in activity. Individuals usually experience a keen sense of satisfaction in wearing emblems or badges which signify some accomplishment. This no doubt is due to the desire for social approval which is a fundamental human trait. Modern educational philosophy indicates that the giving of expensive rewards, such as medals, articles of clothing, jewelry of various kinds, money, trips and dinners is unsound and psychologically indefensible. The joy which comes from success in the activity should be adequate reward. It is especially unwise for schools to solicit or accept awards from outside organizations.

Point system. If a school letter or other emblem is given as an incentive a point system may be used as a basis for awarding under the following conditions:

(*a*) The point system should not be so involved that it will require extensive bookkeeping.

(*b*) Points should be awarded on a basis of real achievement so the child will feel the school letter is something he has to earn the privilege of wearing.

(*c*) The conditions to be fulfilled should not be so difficult to meet but that a fair proportion of the children in a school could earn letters.

(*d*) The conditions should require wholesome participation in all or a large part of the school program, rather than excellence in any one specific phase of it. For example: Points may be given in the following fields, 200 points being necessary to secure the first award:

	May earn	Must earn
Scholarship	50	30
Attendance	50	30
Character	50	30
Athletic activities	50	30
Other school activities	50	30
	250	150

(e) The plan should provide for a continuing interest beyond the immediate earning of the school letter. Add a star each time an additional award has been earned.

Suggestions. Judge scholarship in the light of the child's ability.

Require a certain minimum number of days of attendance before allowing points.

Assign leaders to keep the record of points for a given group.

Allow groups of students, with the guidance of a teacher, to set the standards and render the judgments on character within the group.

MASS ATHLETICS

In mass athletics the object is to obtain a team score which will represent the total effort of the entire group. Each individual's effort is a contribution to the final score. This method places the individual events, such as running, jumping, etc., on a similar basis to team games. The usual school plan emphasizes special team training and individual athletic performance. It is desirable to organize athletic activities on a basis that will bring all the pupils into the activity. While team and individual excellence are well worth developing within reasonable limitations, it is even more important to provide opportunities for improvement of every child and enable all to contribute something toward the final score. Strive to give an opportunity for all rather than place the emphasis on one winning team.

INTRAMURAL ATHLETICS

Intramural athletics are generally considered to be athletics conducted between groups of students within one school. Intramural athletics should be emphasized in the elementary school. Adult leadership with student management is the pivot around which the success of the scheme revolves. A successful intramural program depends on equality between competing teams. It is, therefore, necessary to classify the students according to some plan, taking into consideration the factors of age, height and weight or strength. (For classification scheme, see page 16.)

Club organization. The participation of children in games during their free time can be vitalized by the organization of two or more school clubs, or color groups, the primary purpose of which shall be to make more effective intramural competition. The membership of each of the clubs should include boys and girls from the fifth, sixth, seventh and eighth grades. Each club should then furnish teams to compete in different events with other clubs within the school.

It would probably be wise for the principal and teachers, in the beginning, to assign all the boys and girls to one or another of the clubs, the aim being to make the clubs as nearly equal as possible for competition regardless of the known preference of certain groups who always wish to play on the same team. Each boy or girl thereafter is a member of a particular club until he or she leaves the school.

Crippled or incapacitated children should be assigned to clubs. They may be organized to compete against one another in games suitable for their needs, such as horseshoes, croquet, center club bowls, bean bag board, target toss, etc. They need the discipline of games quite as much, if not more, than other more active children. They should be eligible to hold office, trained to officiate as referees, judges, etc., and, in so far as possible, be made to feel that they are important and valuable members of their clubs and schools.

It is recommended that the presidents or captains of the clubs, at the beginning of each term, meet as a committee and select for their club membership the incoming fifth grade pupils. New upper grade students may be assigned to a club by a committee of teachers always with the object of securing the fairest competition between clubs. It will doubtless be best to have the members of each club select their own officers for the term, such as president, secretary, official keeper of the record (score), executive committee, etc. Duplicate records of club activities should be kept, one copy being on file in the principal's office.

Students should act as umpires, referees, judges, scorers, etc., the qualities of good sportsmanship and good judgment being the result of practice and experience. Alternate the best players as well as the poorest ones for this phase of the club work.

Each club should select (by lot) one or more teachers who will act as advisers, patrons or club directors. It is recommended that:

1. Every teacher of the school be a member of one of the clubs.

2. The teachers be with their groups each day for at least a few minutes during the play period to encourage, inspire and direct the attitude of their groups toward clean play, group and school loyalty and the finest kind of sportsmanship.

3. The captains or squad leaders of each team should post daily their score, regardless of whether the game was won or lost. Whichever

team is ahead at the end of the playing time wins. Credit a team two points for winning, one point for a tie and zero points for a loss. Decide on a penalty for delaying the start of a game, such as, the offending team to give one point to the opponents for each minute the game is delayed by them.

It is recommended that schools do not use the daily instructional period for the playing of intramural games.

It is desirable to develop a few group "songs" and "cheers" keeping in mind good sportsmanship, including the qualities of courtesy, kindness and generosity.

TRACK AND FIELD MEETS (15B)

When organizing a track and field meet certain details must be cared for in advance of the day selected, so that the events may be run off smoothly and expeditiously. Planning for, or the neglect of, seemingly unimportant details often spells success or disastrous failure.

The general announcement of the track meet should contain the following:

1. Date, place, time and definition of the meet.
2. Classifications determined upon for competition.
3. Special rules as decided upon. For example, spiked shoes not to be allowed.
4. Eligibility requirements, such as scholarship, citizenship, etc.
5. Selected events listed with space underneath each event for writing names; the number of entries in a given event and substitutes allowed; the number and type of events each individual may enter.
6. A statement to be signed by the person vouching for the entrants, giving his position and school represented.
7. The method of scoring should be designated, such as 5, 3, 1, or 5, 3, 2, 1, when the winner of fourth place is to be determined. Also a statement should be made relative to awards if such are to be given.
8. The date (not later than one week prior to the meet) upon which entry blanks must be returned to the chairman.

ORGANIZATION

ENTRY BLANK (Suggested Sample)
ANNUAL TRACK AND FIELD MEET

Elementary schools of ....
Classifications to compete ....
Place of meet................Day..............Month..............Hour........
Please enter the following pupils from the .... in events
listed below: (Name of School)
              (...................Classification)
40 yard dash   High jump
  1. ....   1. ....
  2. ....   2. ....
Sub. ....   Sub. ....
Running broad jump   Relay (4 boys, 40 yards each)
  1. ....   1. ....
  2. ....   2. ....
Sub. ....   3. ....
                                            4. ....
                                           Sub. ....
                                           Sub. ....
              (...................Classification)

(List events as above for all following classes.)
I certify that these pupils are in good standing in my school and eligible to compete.
                        Name...
                        ....
                                Principal or Teacher (Position)

Rules (Suggested)
1. Each school shall enter pupils in all events.
2. Each school may enter two pupils for each event.
3. No pupil may be entered for more than two events; the relay counts as one event.
4. Substitutes' names must be listed.
5. Each pupil entered must have been in training previous to the meet for .... weeks.
6. Pupils are to be classified two weeks before the meet.
7. No spiked shoes will be allowed.
8. Entry blanks must be in a week previous to the meet.
9. Three (four) places will be scored.

OFFICIALS

Officials should be selected and their duties made clear to them before the day of the meet by personal conference or written instruction including the rules governing their special event.

The list of the officials and their duties follow:

Games Committee: The games committee should select the officials, make general plans for the meet and pass on eligibility. The committee should not interfere with the appointed officials who shall carry out their duties as assigned by the rules. Elementary school meets should be conducted under rules similar to those in official track and field handbooks. The rules may be simplified as needed.

The Referee: The referee is the head official. He shall decide all questions in regard to the conduct of the meet not definitely assigned to other officials.

Inspectors: Two or more who shall stand at places assigned by the referee and assist him but they may not make independent decisions.

Judges of the Finish: For the dashes and relays there shall be at least four judges, one acting as head judge. They shall pick by assignment 1st, 2d, 3d or 4th places. A fifth judge should watch for the fifth runner, and the record recorded, to be used in case one runner is disqualified. In case of disagreement the majority shall rule. After picking their runner the judge should secure his name, school and classification, and give this information with his placement in the event, to the scorer. The judges shall then make out a list of all the heat winners and the schools represented by them and give the same to the starter. They shall make out the records in the finals on official blanks and send them to the chief scorer.

Clerk of the Course: The clerk of the course and his assistants shall notify competitors to appear at the starting line. They shall have charge of heats, drawings for lanes, etc., for all the runs and relays.

Scorer: The chief scorer shall record from information received from all judges and other officials, the order in which competitors finish, together with the record or score made.

Timekeepers: There shall be three timekeepers for each track event. The time of the majority shall rule. If all stop watches disagree the watch giving the middle time shall be official. If only two stop-watches get the time the lower shall be official. Time shall be taken from the flash of the gun, not from the report.

Starter: The starter shall have complete control of the contestants at the starting mark. He shall start all races by the report of a pistol or by use of a whistle after the preparatory commands: "Get on your mark," "Get set," are given.

22   PHYSICAL EDUCATION FOR ELEMENTARY SCHOOLS

Marshal: The marshal and his assistants shall have full police charge of the field and shall prevent any but officials and actual competitors from entering or remaining on the field.

ORGANIZING THE PROGRAM

The names of the entrants sent in on the different entry blanks must be rearranged previous to the meet under the headings of the different events. For example, where large numbers are entered for the runs it requires the arrangement of a series of heats. The number of lanes available determine the number that can run in a given heat. If there are eight lanes and sixty-four entrants, run eight heats, select the winners and have them run in the final heat. Where there are six heats, select the six winners, and, in addition, the two fastest seconds to run in the finals. The heats should be listed on the program or typed copies prepared to give to the starter, clerk of course, judges, scorer and referee.

Field Events should run continuously from the beginning except that the field events of any special classification should be stopped while that class has its run trials.

Facilities: The person in charge should think through the whole meet, every event—the needs of participants, officials, spectators, and check up every item. Previous to the day the track surface should be cared for; lanes for runs and relays, starting and finish points for the different events and balk lines should be marked; sand or shavings secured for the jumping pits. Where many are competing a pit should be prepared for each classification and the runways for the jumps fenced off by low wire or rope fences.

Equipment: High jump standards, high jump bars, rakes, shovels, takeoff boards for the standing and running broad jump, stop watches (at least three), gun and blank cartridges, finish tape (cotton yarn is best), official badges, megaphones, large scoreboard, tables and chairs for scorers, pencils, paper, safety pins, scales, first-aid kit, numbers for marking contestants, rope and stakes in sufficient quantity to make it possible to keep spectators off the field. An "information desk" should be established; also a lost and found bureau. Both should be conspicuously marked. The starts, relay divisions, high and broad jump pits for the different classifications, and all locations used for other events should be designated by large signboards or placards placed on high standards. A checking system for clothes and lunches is important. Valuables should be put in a separate envelope, sealed and the name of the owner and school written on it. Each contestant must be marked either by a large number pinned on the clothing, or by having the classification stamped on the arm with a rubber stamp just before the meet begins. A physical examination of all contestants previous to or on the day of the meet should be scheduled and carried out. A written statement by parents giving their consent to have their children enter the meet should be secured, if such seems advisable. Dressing rooms and toilets should be labeled. Adequate drinking water facilities should be installed.

SCORE SHEET FOR TRACK EVENTS
(Heats and Semi-Finals)

Meet of .... Place............... Date ....

Classification............................Event ....

First heat:

   Winner ....Time ....

   Second ....

   Third ....
(Continue this form for all heats.)

Signed......................

Head Judge.

Select two extra places, as a runner may be disqualified. Return this blank to the starter.

SCORE SHEET FOR TRACK EVENTS
(Finals)

Meet of .... Place............... Date ....

Classification............................Event ....

   Winner ....Time ....

   Second ....Time ....

   Third ....Time ....

   Fourth ....

   Fifth ....

   Sixth ....
(Continue this form for all events.)

Signed............... Head Judge.   .... Head Timer.

Select two extra places, as a runner may be disqualified. Record time of the 1st, 2d, and 3d places. Deliver in person to chief scorer.

ORGANIZATION

SCORE SHEET FOR FIELD EVENTS

Meet of .... Place .... Date ....
Classification .... Event ....

Mark as follows: S, successful trial; P, passed trial; O, failure of trial; F, foul trial; B, balk.

Contestant's number	Name	School	Height of bar	Handicap (if any)	Final measurement
....	....	....	....	....	....
....	....	....	....	....	....
....	....	....	....	....	....

(Continue as needed.)

	Name	School	Height or distance
Winner	....	....	....
Second	....	....	....
Third	....	....	....
Fourth	....	....	....

Judge .... Referee ....
Judge ....
Judge ....
Deliver this sheet to the chief scorer.

SCORER'S BLANK

Meet .... Place .... Date ....

Classification and events	School A	School B	School C
40 yard dash (Class A).........	(1) 5	(2) 3	(3) 1
High jump	....	....	....
Running broad jump (Class B)....	(1) (2) 8	....	(3) 1
160 yard relay	....	....	....
Totals.......................	....	....	....
Grand totals.................	....	....	....

METHODS IN TRACK AND FIELD EVENTS

1. **Straight-away method:** (Example) In the standing broad jump No. 1 of team A jumps, No. 2 of team A toes No. 1's heel mark and jumps in the same direction, etc. Team B, starting from the same given line, jumps in the same manner. The team which covers the greatest distance wins.

2. **Shuttle method:** (Example) In the broad jump, two teams, A and B, face each other. No. 1 of team A toes a starting line and jumps forward. No. 1 of team B toes the heel mark of No. 1 of team A and jumps back. No. 2 of team A toes the heel marks of No. 1 of team B and jumps forward. This is continued until all have jumped. A member of team B has the final jump. If this jumper fails to reach or jump across the starting line, team A wins.

3. **Matching method:** (Example) No. 1 of team A jumps. The captain of team B chooses a man from his team to match this jump. The winner scores one point and jumps first in the next trial. This is continued until all have jumped. The team with the highest number of points wins.

4. **Survival method:** This applies to events which require one or more trials to scale a bar at each of several increasing heights. There are three ways in which, without measurement, jumps or vaults can be scored.
   (a) Elimination on failure and scoring points for each survivor at each height.

(b) The same process, but trials at three successive heights, all failures being scored against a team.

(c) The standard height method, which sets a series of heights with point values, and scores points for the number of contestants on each team who succeed in scaling each height.

PLAY DAYS

Play days are community get-together days. They should not be held to determine interschool or individual championships where only the best from each school are chosen to compete. Their primary purpose is to permit mass participation in athletic games, stunts, rhythmical activities, hunting games and individual athletic events. A serious effort should be made to include the adults of the community in types of activities suited to their needs.

Play days may be organized for all the children (1) within a school; (2) for two or three neighboring schools combined; (3) for schools within a geographical district or districts; (4) for a whole county. The latter organization means an interesting spectacle and often a delightful entertainment for adults but much stress and strain for administrators, teachers and parents. The use of small play days organized at the close of the fall, winter and spring program in physical education offers the incentive for teachers and children to plan and carry on a systematized progressive program from week to week and month to month. At the play days a selection from all the types of activities as outlined for the elementary grades should be used. This eliminates the necessity of working up special feature numbers with the resulting breaks in the daily program of the school for rehearsal. Every child present should have an active share as a participant in the activities or as an official assigned to special duties.

Each school should be instructed to bring its own play supplies, such as balls, bats, paddle tennis rackets, nets, hit pin bases, etc. These should be clearly marked with the name of the school.

Preliminary Plans.

Some weeks before the play day the hostess school should appoint a committee in charge of general organization. This committee should appoint other committees, being careful to distribute responsibilities; (1) a program committee including representatives from each school to select activities and manage the details; (2) a committee in charge of the preparation of the necessary facilities; (3) other committees on transportation, checking of lunches and valuables, refreshments, first aid, etc.

It is advantageous to secure the interest and coöperative assistance in meeting the financial problem involved in transportation and refreshments—of civic organizations such as: luncheon clubs, women's clubs,

P. T. A.'s, chambers of commerce, boards of trade, farm bureaus and the grange.

At least three weeks previous to the day itself entry blanks outlining the activities selected should be sent to the schools. On these blanks the schools should check the activities in which their pupils wish to participate with the number and names of students entering. The blanks should be returned to the hostess school not later than one week before the play day so that necessary scheduling arrangements for competition may be made. The preliminary schedule permits additional practice in the activities selected.

For competitive purposes the children may be assigned to color groups before arriving at the school grounds. Teams within each color group then score points which count toward the final rating of the entire color group. It is not necessary to keep the membership of a team strictly limited to one school. Small rural schools may combine forces where their own groups are too small. The hostess school should be prepared to use members of their own school to fill in any shortage of players among visiting groups. Children in the lower grades should be scheduled under assigned leaders for story plays, dramatizations, singing games, hunting games, a story hour, and the supervised use of playground apparatus.

If field and track events are to be used a previous classification of pupils for fairness in competition should have been made and entry blanks sent in. See page 21.

It may be of particular interest to program a final contest between the winners of individual athletic events previously held in each individual school.

It is most helpful to give to each visitor and group leaders a stenciled plan of the school ground showing the location of the courts, field and other play areas.

An opening session to include mass singing, salute to the flag, pledge of allegiance, possibly followed by a posture parade in which all the children take part, makes for a feeling of mutual understanding and solidarity. School musical organizations may provide entertainment at this time or later in the day. Following the opening exercises and necessary announcements there may be informal mass participation in play activities by schools, by classes or by color groups.

If a pageant is to be given a special time for it must be scheduled; either the period immediately following the opening session or immediately following luncheon seems the most desirable.

The practice of awarding prizes of value should not be tolerated. If some emblem of achievement seems desirable, colored paper ribbons, certificates or inexpensive silk ribbons may be used. These do not tend to develop a professional attitude. Inexpensive banners or plaques are a satisfactory means of giving recognition for group achievement.

Preparation of Facilities.

Previous to the day itself the lines for needed playing courts and fields should be plainly marked with whitewash or lime or lightly trenched.

Provided track events are to be used, an adequate number of running lanes should be marked. Jumping standards and pits should be provided in sufficient number to run off the field events expeditiously. Play courts and fields should be numbered and placarded so the visitors may find their places quickly. The school grounds should be put in the best condition possible. Parking space should be provided for automobiles. Dressing rooms, rest rooms, checking rooms, and lavatories should be plainly marked. For a large play day, a nursery room with a matron in charge gives opportunity for many parents to have a period of freedom. Areas should be reserved for luncheon festivities. Hot and cold drinks, sandwiches and other refreshments may be served and, if sold, a source of revenue is secured to help defray necessary expenses. Such concessions should be entirely under the control of the schools. If a considerable number of spectators are to be present it is very important that they shall not be allowed on the fields during the activities. A roped off area for spectators should be provided.

Play Supervisors and Officials.

It is probable that all teachers present will be assigned duties. Their responsibilities, however, do **not** end with the completion of any given assignment. Those in charge should be experienced in handling children, should be familiar with organization procedures and with the rules of play activities. Student officiating should be encouraged. At times high school students can be used. Officials may be recruited from the alumni, colleges and teacher training institutions. These officials should be thoroughly instructed concerning the general program and their specific duties. It is desirable to give each official a sheet of paper on which is listed his duties, and if in charge of a given game, the rules governing that activity. There should be on hand extra whistles, needles, thread, pins, paper and pencils, a first aid kit, tape measures, hammers, nails, cord, marking material, rakes, etc.

CHAPTER IV
CLASSIFICATION OF ACTIVITIES
ATHLETIC GAMES

Athletic games are competitive team games in which an organized group scores as a unit through coöperative effort against another similar group. They exhibit rivalry in intense form and exercise the original tendencies involved in all social struggles. Team play is the highest form of play. Its value lies in the coöperation of the players working toward a common end, the players thinking more of what is best for the team rather than using their efforts for individual glory.

Every normal child wants competition. Without some definite plan for placing boys and girls in groups where they may compete with others of equal age, weight, height, or strength and ability, athletic competition becomes sport for the few who are favored with natural ability, while the majority, or the ones who most need the active play, are eliminated early from the contest.

Athletic games bring into use the "big muscle" groups in the natural movements of running, jumping, climbing, throwing, and striking. The vigorous use of these fundamental muscles has a profound influence on the growth and development of the vital organs—heart, lungs, digestive and other important systems—resulting in improved health and increased vigor.

During the preadolescent and early adolescent stage each pupil experiences a period of rapid bodily growth. The heart also grows rapidly in size, the veins and arteries much more slowly, thus putting a great strain on the heart. Especially at this time long distance running and over-played basketball games are types of activity that may strain and permanently damage the heart and, therefore, much care should be exercised in their use.

CORRECTIVE PHYSICAL EDUCATION *

Some children have structural or functional defects which are handicaps to them and which may be corrected by special exercises. For example: infantile paralysis and other paralytic conditions often lead to part or complete paralysis of muscles and muscle groups. Usually

---
* Material contributed by Dr. Sven Lokrantz, Medical Director, Los Angeles city schools.

this is the case with the foot and leg. Many abnormal positions of the foot may result from paralyzation of the pronator muscles, the supinator muscles and dorsal flexor muscles of the leg.

Children having physical defects must be handled as individual cases so far as corrective procedures are concerned. In many cases they need the vigorous activities more than some other children. The exact program for each child must be determined after a physical examination. Individual corrective exercises can then be attempted upon the advice or recommendations of the family physician, school physician or health official.

Aims. We should strive through the use of corrective procedures to eliminate physical defects and produce a better physique in children who are thus handicapped, whether the defects be congenital or acquired. This can be accomplished best through the services of well trained people working with proper facilities and equipment. The greatest emphasis on a prevention program should occur in the elementary school. This will permit the corrections when the child's body is most susceptible and amenable to such correction and it will also lessen the amount of work necessary in the secondary school. This prevention program can be effective only when **"causes of defects"** are found and steps taken to **eliminate** or **minimize** them.

Scope. Cases requiring corrective procedures may be organized into classes under the following headings:

1. **Postural Conditions.** Forward head, round shoulders, kyphosis, scoliosis, lordosis (hollow back), and improper balance.

2. **Foot Conditions.** Structural and postural.

3. **Heart Conditions.** Functional, minor lesions, organic lesions well compensated, and organic lesions where compensation is poor.

4. **Overweight.**

5. **Underweight.**

6. **Nerves.** Chorea, speech defects, infantile and other types of paralysis.

7. **Menstrual (girls).** A modified activities program, or rest, during menstrual period.

Procedures. Some of the procedures in corrective work are (a) corrective gymnastics; (b) rest; (c) diet; (d) massage; (e) adaptation of clothing; (f) home exercises; (g) home lessons; and (h) general hygiene.

Equipment for Corrective Room.

Low plinths	Body mats	Weighing scale
High plinths	Mirror (6' x 4')	Horizontal ladder
Stall bars	Spirometer	Square hair pillows (18″)
Stools	Stethoscope	Hospital screen (3 wings)

Corrective Centers. Corrective centers should be established to which the children with the most pronounced defects can be sent. In sparsely settled school districts where transportation is difficult or financial circumstances do not permit, a traveling teacher for corrective work might be employed.

Suggestions.

a. Teachers should not attempt corrective physical education unless specially trained, and then only under the direction of a physician.

b. Examination of the child is necessary for diagnosis of conditions.

c. Corrective procedures in any given pupil's case should be advised by people responsible for medical service.

d. Work out an adequate follow-up system of individual cases.

e. Coöperate with the parents of children needing corrective work.

f. Structural conditions should be handled by a private physician or a clinician.

g. Medical treatment must be left altogether to the discretion of the family or clinic physician.

h. In regard to the foci of infection, provision for eradication should be made through inspections by school physicians and nurses who report findings to parents, to be transmitted to the family physician.

i. In all that you do keep a positive attitude; avoid the suggestion of invalidism. It is a great mistake to make a hypochondriac of any child or adult as a hypochondriac or a neurotic is a burden to himself and to society.

j. For detailed help in corrective procedures the teacher should refer to "Corrective Physical Education for Groups," by Lowman, Colestock and Cooper, and to "Preventive and Corrective Physical Education," by Stafford. Both these books are published by A. S. Barnes and Company, New York.

HEALTH EDUCATION

Health education in schools is usually considered to have three general divisions: **health service, health supervision** and **health instruction.** Health service includes the duties of physicians, nurses, dentists and oculists; health supervision includes the lighting, heating, ventilation and sanitation of school buildings, health inspection and supervision of the students' health habits and environment; while health instruction has to do with the teaching of health information and the creation of health ideals and attitudes.

Health is indispensable to success and enjoyment of life. It should be the aim of every good citizen to promote health in the individual, the family and the community.

The aims in health teaching are definite but in the development of methods of attaining these aims every teacher must be a pioneer. Boys and girls have little interest in health for health's sake but every girl desires to be beautiful and every boy desires to be strong and athletic. The wise teacher will build on these natural interests. She will discover what information has been imparted in the teaching of hygiene, home economics, science and civics and will attempt to test the functioning of this knowledge in behavior.

The end to be attained is not alone information but action; not alone knowledge but habitual maintenance of standards in behavior according to health laws with respect to: developmental activities, nutrition, sleep and rest, avoidance of infection, sanitation, avoidance of stimulants and drugs, and the care and control of sex functions and emotions.

In this book there has been no attempt to include subject matter pertaining to either health service, health supervision or health instruction.

HUNTING GAMES

"Hunting games are largely traditional, social games arising out of the hunger for activity and the hunting and protective responses." They all have an enemy or "it" or "tag" element and a number of combinations of such elements as hunting, chasing, striking, tagging, dodging, hiding and fleeing.

These activities occupy a prominent place in the book because they have a special appeal to the elementary school child. Due to their simple organization these games are usually quickly learned and, therefore, require that a greater variety and number be taught than of activities more highly organized. The hunting type of game is used less often as the child grows older, being supplemented by the simple team games.

INDIVIDUAL ATHLETIC EVENTS

Individual athletic events are those elements of athletic games which can be performed and scored without dependence upon one or more other players. They can be measured definitely as to time, distance, or number, and can thus provide competition between individuals, between groups, between an individual and scoring tables based on standards of group achievement, or between the individual and his own previous record. The specific advantages of these activities are:

1. They carry the spirit of individual rivalry, and thus furnish incentives to improvement.
2. They are easily adaptable to most conditions of time, organization and facilities.
3. They give training in game elements.
4. They can be practiced individually after being learned.
5. They permit each pupil to be taught and observed as an individual.
6. They present an opportunity to set up definite standards of achievement.

MIMETICS

Mimetic exercises are imitative movements of well-known activities without the usual equipment. They are very closely related to story plays except that they are more formal and more attention is paid to the way in which the exercises are performed.

These exercises are well suited to classroom work. They may be used to teach the form of different athletic events to large numbers of students at the same time. If so desired, when used for relief periods, the exercises may be performed in rhythm or to music.

POSTURE *

Posture affects the circulation, respiration, digestion and elimination of the human body. It is closely related to health and to personality. Habitually poor posture indicates weakness of important muscles and faulty coördination between different groups of muscles. Conditions which cause poor posture should be eliminated and a consciousness of good posture inculcated in the child at the earliest possible age.

Correct posture may be defined in terms of the relation of the position of the body segments to each other, and to their external environment. It is not possible to define a correct position of the body segments so definitely that it may be made to apply to all individuals alike. Individual differences as to gravity lines of the body, balance, and physiological types must be considered. A practical method of defining and checking correct posture is to note the position of the body segments in relation to the gravity or weight lines of the body—anteroposterior line, lateral line, and the foot and leg line. It is urged that in training for good posture, bones, joints, muscles and nerves must be considered, and in treating faulty posture, bone and joint conditions must be corrected, weak muscles strengthened and neural strain lessened.

Standing postures are illustrated by charts issued by the American Posture League, 1 Madison Avenue, New York City, which state: "In

---

* Material contributed by Miss Claire Colestock, Pasadena city schools, California.

correct posture, the neck and trunk form a straight vertical line; in incorrect posture, the neck and trunk form a zigzag line."

"Correct standing posture is defined briefly as one in which the different segments of the body, namely: the head, neck, chest and abdomen, are balanced vertically one upon the other so that the weight is borne mainly by the bony framework, and a minimum of effort and strain is placed upon the muscles and ligaments." *

The position of the body segments in correct sitting, standing and walking is as follows:

Sitting Position, "Rest" or "Reading." Head high, chin in, abdomen flat, hip—knee—ankle—a right angle bend (may be larger than a right angle at hip joint, dependent upon the backward slope of the back support), feet parallel, lower back and upper back in contact with back support, shoulders relaxed.

Sitting Position, "Rest" and "Relaxation." Same as above, except cross feet (not knees) at the ankle joint. Rest the feet on the floor, holding the outer border in contact with the floor. This position is recommended as a variation to relieve the strain of holding one position too long.

Sitting Position, "Active" or "Work." Same as in "Rest" or "Reading," except the trunk is bent forward at the hip joint. Lean forward at the hip joint keeping the back flat.

Standing Position, "Attention." Head high, chin in, neck back, abdomen flat, back with normal physiological curves, i.e., hips pulled down by tightening the buttocks, arms hanging naturally at sides, but not stiff, feet parallel and one or two inches apart with weight on outer border.

Standing Position, "Relaxed" or "Rest." Same position as for "Attention," except the feet should be separated (side stride position) one or two feet. Feet should be parallel with weight equally divided, arms at sides.

Walking Position. Head high, chin in, abdomen flat, feet parallel, arms swinging naturally at the sides. In walking the feet should be pointed straight ahead. The foot strikes the floor, heel first, very lightly, outer border of the foot second, ball of the foot third and finish with a push from the toes. The step should be light and graceful. Correct alignment of the body segments should be maintained.

To stimulate pupils to assume improved positions in standing and walking the following posture cues are suggested: Head high, chin in, neck back, abdomen flat, back straight, flatten lower back, shoulders relaxed (not stiff or thrown back), knees straight, feet parallel with

---

* Definition accepted by American Posture League.

weight on outer border, stretch as tall as possible, stand tall, walk tall, think tall. To stimulate improved positions in sitting, similarly: head up, chin in, neck back, abdomen flat, sit tall, etc.

The most common faulty postural conditions among school children are foot conditions and the traditional "fatigue posture." Improved position of the feet and legs, strengthening of the external abdominal muscles, control of the tilt of the pelvis are important factors in securing correct alignment of the body segments. Emphasis in all posture instruction should be placed on exercises to control the tilt of the pelvis, on abdominal and low back exercises, and on foot exercises. It is important to emphasize correct "fundamental" or "starting" positions for all exercises. Emphasize correct body alignment in starting positions during each position of exercise and proper mental attitude at all times.

Exercises for kindergarten and elementary grades, adapted to classroom, playground or gymnasium for large and small groups, may be found in "Corrective Physical Education for Groups," by Lowman, Colestock, Cooper.*

Posture work should be undertaken by the grade teacher only after she has become familiar with the fundamental principles of good body mechanics, and the exercises, either by personal instruction or thorough study.

Causes of Poor Posture. Some of the causes of poor posture are:
1. Structural defects.
2. Poor muscular development and tone.
3. General conditions such as poor nutrition, growth handicaps (tonsils, adenoids, etc.), rapid growth, overwork, bad lighting and ventilation of schoolroom or home. acute illness, and general lack of exercise.
4. Defective vision which is uncorrected.
5. Defective hearing.
6. Carrying weights improperly.
7. Ill fitting clothes.
8. Ill fitting school furniture; wrong kind of school seats; improper seat adjustments.
9. Too long sitting in one position without relief.
10. Habitually incorrect positions assumed while standing, walking, sitting and sleeping.
11. Lowered vitality due to loss of sleep, worry and other conditions of strain.
12. Fatigue.

* Lowman, Colestock, Cooper, "Corrective Physical Education for Groups," published by A. S. Barnes and Company, 67 West Forty-fourth street, New York City.

Posture Tests.*

The Vertical Line Test. In good posture the long axis of the trunk is a vertical line and the long axis of the neck and head taken together is also a vertical line. An imaginary line from just in front of the external ankle bone through the center of the lobe of the ear will parallel the long axis of these segments of the body. In poor posture these axes do not form one continuous vertical line but are broken into several zigzag lines.

Triple Test for Posture.

1. **Standing Test.** Inspect your class in profile and judge the posture of each child rapidly. Form two groups; group 1 made up of those that have good posture, and group 2 made up of those that have not.

2. **Marching Test.** Apply this test to the pupils in group 1 above. Have them drill on marching tactics for a few minutes. "It will be found that as the march proceeds old muscle habits will reassert themselves and many pupils who could hold a correct position for a few minutes of quiet standing will fall into habitually faulty attitudes as they march." Pupils showing these faults should be taken from the line.

3. **Exercise Test.** Apply this test to the pupils that pass both the standing and the marching test. Observe these pupils for a few minutes while they are going through a formalized drill and using the arms in upward positions. As the muscles of the neck, shoulders and back weaken, faulty postures will appear. As such faults of execution appear the pupils exhibiting them should be dropped from the line. The pupils passing all three tests should be classed in group 1; those that do not should be recorded in group 2.

The triple test standardizes posture so that it is possible to rate a pupil or a class. Each child should keep his individual rating on posture and the teacher should have the posture rating of the whole class. Habitual sitting positions are, of course, of much importance and should be considered in any rating of pupils for posture. The class percentage should be computed each month when the triple test is made and a systematic record kept, both on the blackboard and in permanent form. A separate book is preferable as it gives room for the names of pupils with their individual monthly ratings (A, B or C) in addition to the class percentage. When placed on the blackboard this record rouses the pride and interest of the class so that they work to raise the percentage from month to month. The class should always

---

* Quoted from Syllabus for Physical Training in the Elementary and Secondary Schools of the State of New York, which quotes "The Posture of School Children," by Jessie H. Bancroft.

CLASSIFICATION OF ACTIVITIES

know its percentage and whether it is gaining or losing, or marking time from month to month. To omit this is to fail of using one of the most potent psychological elements in the situation—the one that, coupled with personal desire for promotion from division 2 to division 1, relieves the teacher of the necessity for continual nagging about posture.

The triple test is merely preliminary to the teacher's real work for posture—the corrective teaching, through which alone those pupils deficient in posture may receive the development they need. This development lies in two distinct lines: (1) training the muscular sense whereby the child knows whether or not he is in the correct position and is able voluntarily to assume it; (2) strengthening by exercise those muscles in which weakness allows lapsing into poor posture. Little can be done for posture until the child knows how it feels to stand correctly.

Suggestions to Teachers.

1. Know what good posture is.
2. Be a good model yourself.
3. Notice often the posture of each pupil and determine what improvement is necessary.
4. Show the pupil how to correct defects in his posture.
5. Insist on good posture in and out of the classroom while sitting, standing and walking.
6. Try to eliminate conditions which cause poor posture. (See "Causes of Poor Posture.")
7. Try to secure the coöperation of parents in the factors which influence the posture of their children.
8. To stimulate interest in posture use such devices as a health club, a posture week, awarding posture emblems and the making of posters on posture.
9. Refer serious cases of foot defects and all structural defects to reputable orthopedic surgeons for advice and treatment.
10. Secure "Posture Exercises" from the United States Department of Labor, Children's Bureau, publication No. 165.

RELAY RACES

The popularity of relay races makes it desirable for the teacher to give special attention to the methods that make them most successful. They are governed by the same general procedure used in any group game, but for saving time and success in general, the following suggestions are given:

1. Explain how the relay is played, then illustrate by having a few players perform while the others watch.
2. To increase activity value have only four to six players in each relay line.
3. When lines are not equal use extra pupils as helpers, or have a pupil in each short line run a second time to equalize numbers.
4. Have the starting and finish points definitely understood.
5. Allow no players to start ahead of an agreed starting time and line. Impose a penalty if they do.
6. While relays are being run in the schoolroom insist that players seated at the desks keep their feet out of the aisles.
7. Use a whistle sparingly, but give all signals sharply.
8. Show an interest in the race and comment on the pupils' conduct.
9. Be careful to be correct in naming the winning team.

RHYTHMICAL ACTIVITIES

A rhythmical program which is rightly led under educational guidance in a wholesome environment cultivates tastes, habits and ideals which protect young people from the desire to participate in unwholesome forms of rhythmical expression in undesirable surroundings. Participation in rhythmical activities gives training in self-control, poise and posture. To secure these results leadership of the right sort must be provided by institutions responsible to the state for the education of its young people. Pupils must be prepared to use their leisure time in an intelligent, wholesome and profitable manner.

Many persons feel that for the boy, interest and the desire to take part in rhythmical activities after the third or fourth grade begins to decline because of his nature. This is not true. Wise enthusiastic leadership and teaching will carry the boy (1) through the self-conscious awkward age quite as successfully as it does the girl; (2) will enlarge his physical education experiences which too often are limited to types of activities usable only out of doors and charged with rivalry; (3) will give him a feeling of self-mastery and accomplishment; (4) will definitely train him to take his place with ease in the social life of his home, his school, and his community.

Classification of Rhythmical Activities.

Rhythmical activities fall into certain well defined groups, such as: singing games, folk dances or games, gymnastic dancing, natural dancing, and social dancing.

(a) **Singing Games** are valuable during the early years of child life because they require little technical skill and give training in cadence and rhythm.

CLASSIFICATION OF ACTIVITIES

(b) **Folk Dances or Games** follow as a natural sequence in the education of the child. A folk dance is a game form set to music, and hence folk dances are often spoken of as folk games. Among the chief factors that make folk dances so appealing to children and adults are their easy and simple movements; their compelling rhythm and vigorous action; the sociability inherent in their organization together with the realization that a mastery of highly technical skill is not needed to thoroughly enjoy the activity. Folk dances may be taught in connection with the social science subjects and literature as a means of illustrating social customs or of interpreting racial characteristics. Similarly rhythms in the kindergarten and primary grades may well be outcomes of stories.

(c) **Gymnastic Dancing** appeals to the many because of the stunt element that is usually present. Boys in the upper grades often develop a keen interest in these forms of vigorous activity and experience tremendous satisfaction in doing them.

(d) **Natural Dancing** has to be omitted in many schools because of the dearth of trained leaders in this field of rhythms. Where leadership is possible this form of dancing should be included as an integral part of the physical education program.

(e) **Social Dancing** includes the wholesome and artistic forms of dancing used for recreative purposes by society. Definite instruction and practice in the basic steps used in different forms of social dancing should be a part of the school program.

Formations Used.

1. "Single circle facing in." Players face inward toward the center of the circle.

2. "Single circle, partners facing each other." Players face each other with their backs toward their neighbor.

3. "Double circle, partners facing each other." Those in the inside circle have their backs to the center of the circle.

4. "Double circle, both partners facing inward." Partners stand one behind the other and all face the center of the circle.

5. "Circle formation facing clockwise." Direction taken is that direction in which the hands of the clock move.

6. "Circle formation facing counter-clockwise." Is the reverse of No. 5.

7. "Line formation." Players face front of room, singly, with partner, or in groups of threes.

8. "Double column formation." (a) Partners side by side, all facing in one direction; (b) partners facing each other. Boys may be in one line, girls in the other.

9. "Plain quadrille formation." A square formed by four couples, one couple on each side. Also known as "a set." Position of players: (1) head couple; (2) foot couple (opposite the head couple); (3) side couple on the right of the head couple; (4) side couple on the left of the head couple. If boys and girls are in the same formation the boy stands on the left side of his partner "next the lady's heart."

Changing Partners.

A frequent change in partners is desirable and should be made possible by using one of the following methods:
1. If in "single circle partners facing," give your right hand to your partner, pass to the left of your partner and move forward to meet the first person facing you.
2. If in "double circles partners facing each other," either the members of the inside circle may move one place to the right or left and meet a new partner, members of the outside circle standing still in place; or, the members of the outside may do likewise, the members of the inside circle standing still; or, both circles may move one step to their own left or to their own right and so meet a new partner.
3. If in "double circles both partners facing in the line of direction" (counter-clockwise or clockwise), members of the inside or outside circle may step forward or backward to meet a new partner.

Names of Steps and Descriptions.

Music: 2/4, 4/4, 6/8, 3/4.
 2/4 time always counted: "one-and-two-and."
 4/4 time always counted: "one-two-three-four."
 6/8 time always counted: "one-and two-and."
 3/4 (waltz) always counted: "**one**-two-three."
 3/4 (mazurka) always counted: "one-**two**-three" (slide)-(cut)-(hop).
 3/4 (minuet).

1. **Balance Step.** 3/4 or waltz time. Step L forward—**one**; bring R foot forward to L, close heels and rise on toes—**two**; lower heels—**three**. Continue, starting R and alternate thereafter.

2. **Bleking Step.** 2/4 time. Hop on L foot, placing R heel forward, toes turned up; at same time push R arm forward to extended position, shoulder high; draw L elbow back, shoulder high, twisting body slightly to L, weight on L foot—**one-and**; jump, reversing feet and arms—**two-and**; repeat same three times, doubling the speed in quick succession, holding last position through counts **two-and**. Repeat the whole.

3. **Buzz (Pivot) Step.** 2/4 time. Step L foot in place—**one**; step forward on ball of R foot—**and**; put down L foot on the same spot as

CLASSIFICATION OF ACTIVITIES

before—**two**; step forward on ball of R foot—**and**; continued usually for eight measures. With this step a partner is swung around in a small circle very vigorously.

4. **Change Step.** 2/4 or 6/8 time. Step forward L—**one;** bring R just behind L heel and transfer weight to R—**and;** step forward L—**two;** hold during—**and;** continue, starting R and alternate thereafter.

5. **Cut Step.** 2/4 or 4/4 time. A cut step means a quick replacing of one foot by the other. Begin with weight on R foot, L raised forward. Quickly and simultaneously the L leg takes the weight as the R is extended backward. Counts, **one-and.** Now reverse the movement by again taking weight on the R leg and extending L forward, **two-and.** The step may be varied by raising free leg in different directions forward or sideward; also by adding a short hop on supporting leg immediately after the cut has been taken.

6. **Draw Step.** 6/8 or 3/4 time. Step sideward with L foot and draw the R heel toward the L foot. There should be an outward rotation of the R leg the toes of the R foot pointing in the opposite direction to that of the direction of the draw. Weight is kept on the L leg except at the instant when the weight must be transferred on to the R in order that the L leg may be free to take the next step sideward.

7. **Glide Polka.** Slide, close, slide, close, polka. A modified form is: Slide and close, slide and close, stamp, stamp, stamp, in place. The stamps may be used in turning to change direction. Sometimes a slight hop precedes the first slide. (See Polka Step.)

8. **Grand Chain (Grand Right and Left).** Single circle partners facing; giving R hand to partner each passes forward to the side of the free hand (L), right shoulders adjacent. Give L hand to advancing person and pass on free side (R), left shoulders adjacent. Continue, alternating in and out, or out and in, as the case may be, until you meet your original partner, or until you return to your original position.

9. **Heel and Toe Polka.** 2/4 or 6/8 time. Touch L heel forward—**one-and;** touch L toes backward—**two-and;** next polka step: hop R—**one;** step forward L—**and;** bring R to L—**two;** step forward L—**and.** For younger children instead of the polka step, have them take three running steps forward, L, R, L and hold—**one-and-two-and.**

10. **Hop Waltz.** 2/4 time. Step L foot to side—**one;** hop on L, at same time swinging R leg sideways knee bent, bend body toward L side—**and;** step R to side—**two;** hop on R raising L leg sideways knee bent—**and.** Usually done with partners facing, arms on each other's shoulders, or hands grasped and extended sideways shoulder high, a turn being made forward or backward as desired. When done

with partner, they begin the step, one with the R and the other with the L foot.

11. Ladies' Chain. Two couples face each other, ladies on the right side of their partners. Gentlemen stand still. Ladies advance, join R hands, pass each other to the L side, drop each other's hands and give L hand to opposite gentleman. Without releasing her L hand, each gentleman puts his R hand under the left elbow of the lady and "hands" her around in place; gentleman turns backward in place, lady walks forward and around the gentleman, until they both face the other couple. Each lady is on the opposite side from her original position. All this is done in 8 steps (four measures), 4 steps to cross, 4 steps to turn. Same is repeated, the ladies returning to their own partners who turn them in place; 8 steps (four measures).

12. Mazurka Step. 3/4 (Mazurka time). Slide L foot diagonally forward—**one**; replace the L by the R (cut) at the same time extending L diagonally forward—**two**; hop once on R foot and at the same time bend the L knee sharply—**three.** Continue in the same direction with L foot leading. For a balanced practice use a series such as this: Three mazurka steps to L, then stamp L, R, L; three mazurka steps R, then stamp, R, L, R. Accented beat is always on count two (one-**two**-three).

13. Minuet Courtesy and Bow. 3/4 (minuet time). Two measures (six counts) needed.

For the COURTESY, the GIRL steps sideward right—**one**; draws left foot back behind right foot, starting to bend both knees just as left foot passes right foot—**two**; (the left foot passes through first position (heels together) as it moves from the left up to the right foot and then back behind the right foot. In dancing, never move the foot from an open position to an open position without passing through a closed position. "First position" is standing with heels closed or together); continue to bend knees deeply, gradually transferring weight to the rear or left leg—**three**; rise slowly, straightening both knees and, since the weight is on the rear or left leg, the right foot, if kept in proper position, will be pointing forward with the ball of the foot resting lightly on the floor—**four, five**; close the right foot to the left foot, either by placing right heel in front of left toe, or by closing heels—**six.** ARMS— either hold skirts out at both sides or use the following arm movements: Arms in second position (sideward)—**one**; Arms in first position (forward), hands slightly closed, palms down—**two**; Arms in first position (forward), hands opening, palms up (offering her compliments)—**three**; hold position—**four**; slowly and gracefully lower arms to starting position at sides—**five, six.** As you execute the courtesy, look into the eyes of the person or persons to whom you are bowing.

For the Bow, the Boy steps left—**one;** closes the right foot to the left, and executes a stately bow by bending only the upper trunk very slightly forward and looks into the eyes of the person to whom he is bowing—**two, three;** straightens trunk, still looks at the partner or the person to whom he is bowing—**four;** hold position—**five, six.** Arms: gracefully raise right arm sideward—**one;** move right hand to chest, over heart—**two;** move right hand forward, as if offering heart and hand—**three;** hold position—**four;** slowly lower the right arm to right side—**five, six.** If carrying hat, raise right hand, carrying hat, sideward right with a sweeping though dignified movement—**one;** with a similar movement, move the right hand to chest, placing hat over heart—**two;** move the right hand, with hat, forward—**three;** hold position—**four;** slowly move right arm down to starting position at right side—**five, six.** Left arm remains at left side throughout.

14. **Peasant Courtesy.** 4/4, 2/4 or 6/8 time. Step sideward with L foot—**one;** cross R foot in rear of and close to L foot, and bend knees—**two.**

15. **Polka Step.** 2/4 or 6/8 time. Hop R—**and;** slide L—**one;** cut right—**two;** leap left, bending right knee, with right foot in rear of left ankle—**three;** hold—**four.**

Directions for developing polka step:
1. Children stand still and clap hands to music—**one-two-three-hold; one-and-two-and.** Stamp with L foot three times and hold; stamp with R foot three times and hold; alternate feet in stamping L, R, L and hold; gradually make sound lighter by getting up on the toes when stamping. Advance around the room with three running steps and hold. Continue alternating. Then practice polka step as described.
2. Single circle, hands joined. Proceed in line of direction with slides forward, R foot leading for a long phrase of the music (16 or 18 measures) then, continuing in same direction, change and have L foot lead for another long phrase of music. Change to R for a shorter phrase (4 measures) and then same with L leading. When the phrase is again broken to two measures alternate the feet each two measures. Then execute two slides and a polka step with right foot leading; same left; continue, alternating.

The polka can be danced in such a variety of ways that it proves the source of much pleasure. In combination with skips any number of combinations can be made.

Polka Series: (Individual or with partner.)

A. Four polka steps forward; four polka steps back to place; four polka steps across to R; four polka steps across to L.

B. Four polka steps followed by eight skip steps in any direction. Repeat.

C. Same as A, but two polkas in each direction.

D. Two polkas, four skips, turning in place. Repeat, turning in other direction. Repeat all.

E. Face to face, and back to back.

Different positions that may be taken with a partner:

1. Partners standing side by side, inside hands joined. Free hands on hips.

2. Partners facing each other, R or L hands joined. Free hand on hip.

3. Partners facing each other, hands clasped and arms extended sideways, shoulder high.

4. Partners side by side, both hands joined forward in front of body L in L, R in R, skating position.

5. Partners facing. Girl with hands on shoulders of partner, boy with hands on hips of partner.

In executing the polka step, while in position No. 1, each partner begins with a hop on the inner foot. Thus the first polka will bring them facing, arms of clasped hands extended backward. The next polka will bring them back to back with arms of clasped hands extended forward in direction of movement.

16 (a). **Schottische (modified form).** 4/4 time. Slide L foot diagonally forward—**one**; bring R foot up to rear of L and transfer weight—**two**; slide L diagonally forward—**three**; hop on L foot, swinging R foot backward or forward—**four**. One of the best ways to teach the schottische step is for younger children to use three running steps and a hop gradually working into the slide. There is the possibility of adding endless combinations of step swings and step hops. Example: Series A—Four schottische steps; eight step hops, four forward, four turning. Repeat in other direction. B. Two schottische steps forward; four step hops forward; two schottische steps backward; four step hops backward. N. B.—With partners facing each other, both hands joined, they could combine both parts of B at one and the same time.

16 (b). **Schottische.** 4/4 time. Slide, cut, leap, hop. Slide right foot forward—**one**; bring the left foot up to the right, forcing the right foot off the floor (cut)—**two**; leap forward onto the right foot—**three**; hop on the right foot, bending the left knee in the rear and bringing the left foot back of the right heel—**four**. Step may be executed forward, sideward or backward.

17. **Skip.** 2/4 or 6/8 time. Step L—**one**; hop on L bringing R leg forward either straight or with knee bent—**and**; step R—**two**; hop on R bringing L leg forward in same fashion—**and**.

CLASSIFICATION OF ACTIVITIES

18. **Slide or Gallop Step.** 2/4 or 6/8 time. Slide L foot sideward—**one**; close R foot to the L foot—**and**; slide L foot sideward—**two**; close with R to L foot—**and**. Continue in the same direction. Can be executed forward with prancing step similar to that of horses. 6/8 time especially good for this form of execution.

19. **Step Hop.** 2/4 or 4/4 time. Step L forward and raise R foot and leg backward—**one**; hop once with L foot (R leg and foot remain in the rear)—**and**; step R forward and raise L leg backward—**two**; hop with R—**and**.

20. **Step Swing.** 4/4 or 3/4 time. When 4/4 time is used, step L forward—**one**; swing R leg forward and at same time hop on L in place—**two**; step R forward—**three**; swing L forward and at same time hop on R—**four**. When 3/4 time is used, step L—**one**; swing R leg forward and slightly across in front of L—**two**; hop on L foot—**three**. Repeat to R.

21. **Three-Step-Turn.** 4/4 or 3/4 time. Moving sideward to L, step L, R, L, executing a whole turn to the left—**one-two-three**;—hold position —**four**. May be executed in any direction. Fourth count may be varied by pointing free foot forward, sideward or in rear; or by closing heels. In 3/4 time, two measures are required to complete this step, unless it is used as a part of a dance phrase, in which case the fourth count may be omitted.

22. **Touch Step.** 2/4, 3/4 or 4/4 time. Point L foot forward, toes touching—**one**; step forward on L—**and**; point R foot forward—**two**; step forward on R—**and**.

23. **Waltz Step.** 3/4 time. "Step, slide by, close." Step L foot forward—**one**; slide R foot beyond the L—**two**; bring L to R and transfer weight to L foot simultaneously freeing R foot to begin new step —**three**. Repeat, beginning with right foot. The step is always taken on the accented beat or first count of the music. (**One**-two-three-**four**-five-six.) In the waltz the feet are never together on the second count as in the two-step, the sliding foot always passing beyond the weight bearing foot. Waltz steps may be taken forward and backward. When done sideways they constitute a waltz turn for which two waltz steps are necessary to complete the turn. Never forget that in a waltz the lady always begins with a forward step with the right foot, the gentleman always starting with a backward step with the left foot.

List of Children's Books.*

To more fully appreciate and feel the spirit of a folk dance, a study should be made of the country wherein the dance originated. This can

---
* Contributed by Effie Shambaugh, University of California, at Los Angeles.

be done by correlating the student's reading, art, history and geography along the desired lines. A brief list of children's books valuable as references to enrich the background for folk dancing in the elementary grades is here given:

American Indian. (a) "My People the Sioux," by Chief Standing Bear. Houghton, Mifflin Company. 1927.
    (b) "American Indians and Their Music," by Frances Densmore. Woman's Press, New York. 1926.
    (c) "Indian Music and Customs in Publications." National Government Printing Office, Washington, D. C.
Austria. "Boy Travelers in Central Europe," by T. W. Knox, New York. 1893.
Czechoslovakia. "Fairy Tales," by Filmore Parker. Harcourt, Brace and Howe, New York.
Denmark. (a) "A Little Journey to Denmark," by G. M. George.
    (b) "Peeps at Many Lands: Denmark," by M. P. Thomson, London. 1910.
England. (a) "Peeps at English Folk Dancing," by Vilet Alford, London. A. and C. Black, Ltd. 1923.
    (b) "Dictionary of British Folk Lore," by Alice Gomme, London. D. Nutt. 1894.
Finland. "Land of Long Night," by Paul DeChailu. Scribner's. New York. 1899.
France. (a) "Home Life in France," by Betham-Edwards. McClurg and Company, Chicago. 1907.
    (b) "French Life in Town and Country." G. P. Putnam's Sons. 1905.
Germany. (a) "German Life in Town and Country," by Danson. G. P. Putnam's Sons. 1905.
    (b) "Peeps Into Many Lands: Germany," by Mrs. Sedgwick, London.
Ireland. (a) "Peeps at Many Lands: Ireland," by K. Tynan, London. 1909.
    (b) "Kathleen in Ireland in Little People Everywhere," by McDonald and Dalrymple, Boston. 1916.
Italy. (a) "Italian Life in Town and Country," by Colin Coote, New York.
    (b) "Our Little Italian Cousin," by H. Wade. L. C. Page and Company, Boston. 1903.
Japan. "The No Players of Japan," by Arthur Waley. Alfred Knopf, New York. 1922.
Netherlands. (a) "Story of Little Jan the Dutch Boy," by H. C. Campbell. International Education, Publishers. 1905.

CLASSIFICATION OF ACTIVITIES 45

  (*b*) "Little Journey to Holland," by M. George and Dean, Chicago. 1902.

Norway. (*a*) "Peeps at Many Lands," by Mockler, Ferryman, London. 1909.

  (*b*) "Our Little Norwegian Cousin," by M. C. Wade, Boston. L. C. Page and Company. 1903.

Poland. "Polish Peasant in Europe and America," by Thomas and Znaniecki. University of Chicago Press. 1918.

Russia. (*a*) "Russian Folk Tales," by E. Magnus. E. P. Dutton and Company, New York. 1916.

  (*b*) "Our Little Russian Cousin," by M. C. Wade. L. C. Page and Company. 1901.

  (*c*) "Songs of Russian People," by W. R. S. Ralston. Old Book.

Scotland. (*a*) "Donald, Our Little Scotch Cousin," by McManus, Boston. 1906.

  (*b*) "Peeps at Many Lands: Scotland," by W. Smith, London. 1908.

Sweden. "Swedish Life in Town and Country," by Heidenstam. G. P. Putnam's Sons, New York. 1904.

Switzerland. (*a*) "Little Journey to Switzerland," by M. George, Chicago. 1912.

  (*b*) "Peeps at Many Lands," by J. Finnemore, London. Black, Ltd. 1915.

Suggestions.

  1. Keep the spirit of play! Does the class finish a rhythm with audible laughter or spontaneous clapping to show their approval? That's the test!

  2. Bear in mind the end in view, i.e., joy for the children rather than pleasure and amusement for spectators!

  3. Have all children participate—"good, bad or indifferent,"—not just a selected group of those most skillful.

  4. Let the participants learn by doing.

  5. Whenever possible rhythms for younger children should be given out of doors.

  6. When a dance has been learned it should be used often as a form of play.

  7. Before singing the words of a game their meaning should be thoroughly understood.

  8. Use the music period, when possible, for the mastery of the words and melodies of singing games and folk dances.

  9. The melody should be carefully pitched within the proper range of voices. Use a pitch pipe.

  10. When using a phonograph note that there is almost always an

"Introduction" during which the pupils stand quietly in place. Use a signal to warn the pupils when activity is to begin.

11. Urge county librarians to buy phonograph records of rhythms for the use of the schools.

12. If a musician or phonograph can not be secured let the pupils sing, hum, whistle or clap their own rhythm.

13. More difficult steps, such as the polka, schottische, waltz and mazurka should be taught separately, preferably in lines formation, before they are presented in the dance.

14. A series of fairly difficult steps can be given as a "Rhythm Test" in the upper grades. When used as a test, the student is graded and awarded points on (a) accuracy of phrasing, (b) correctness of rhythm, (c) accuracy of the dance step.

15. For boys in the upper grades having instruction by themselves, select those rhythmical activities whose steps have a stunt element or very vigorous action.

16. Use the rhythms learned—at class parties, "fun nights," at P. T. A. and community meetings.

STORY PLAYS

Story plays are a valuable form of physical education for little children. In grades one and two they take the place of the more formal gymnastics. They have a universal appeal if the activities are natural, spontaneous, and related to early childhood. In these activities the child imitates and impersonates incidents he has seen. He is a soldier, farmer, blacksmith, Santa Claus, or sailor, as the play demands.

Story plays have a twofold aim: First, to give a child a well balanced exercise; second, to help develop his dramatic ability. Much of the child's play centers about the home activities and the surroundings near the home. The plays involving bodily movements such as throwing, running and jumping are the most attractive to small children. The story play lends itself especially to dramatizations in connection with state and national holidays, such as Halloween, Thanksgiving and Christmas. Material will be found in the manual for dramatizing events in connection with each of these holidays.

In teaching story plays the following points should be kept in mind:

1. The teacher should work out and adapt story plays of her own based on stories already familiar to the children.

2. The movements should be suggested sometimes by the children and sometimes by the teacher.

3. The whole body should be brought into the movements if possible. Movements should be large and free.

4. The story should be vividly portrayed.

CLASSIFICATION OF ACTIVITIES

5. The story play may be related to other school work.
6. Story plays should be chosen according to the season of the year.
7. Emphasis should be laid upon vigorous action.
8. No formal commands should be used.
9. A circle formation is preferable both in the schoolroom and outside.

STUNTS *

Stunts are forms of play arising from the desire to test one's ability. They stimulate the powers of coördination, suppleness of body, and the formation of such virtues as courage, self-confidence and determination. Stunts provide an excellent form of exercise, are easily organized for practice, are economical of space and equipment, and are adaptable to many age periods. They lend themselves especially well to group organization, and give opportunity for student leadership. Because of their appeal they are continued during home play periods.

To make stunts popular and easy to conduct introduce the spirit of rivalry. The interest in competition may be stimulated by keeping a record of the relative accomplishments of the various pupils. Children should be encouraged to bring in stunts of their own which should then be tried by other members of the class.

Teachers should see that stunts do not involve a serious strain. Designate certain periods each month as stunt periods. Many stunts can be done indoors and are, therefore, suitable for stormy day physical education periods. It is usually desirable to separate the boys and girls in all grades for this work. Girls should wear bloomers and all pupils should remove their street shoes. For safety and cleanliness it is desirable to have certain facilities. A turf plot, a sawdust filled jumping pit, tumbling mats, individual straw mats, mattresses, strips of canvas, sheets of heavy paper or other substitutes may be used.

---

* Note.—For methods of organization of stunts and for additional material, see Martin Rodgers, "A Handbook of Stunts," copyright 1928, by Macmillan Co., publishers.

48   PHYSICAL EDUCATION FOR ELEMENTARY SCHOOLS

STUNTS	CHAIR VAULT	JUMP THE STICK	WOODEN MAN	BACK SPRING	HEAD STAND	KNEE DIP	BEAR DANCE	MEASURING WORM	FORWARD ROLL	FROG HAND STAND	NAME OF PUPIL
											Virginia W.
											Jack P.
											Herbert B.
											Charlotte S.
											Elbert V.
											Maude W.
											George S.
											Helen V.
											Arthur W.

Classroom Chart Showing Progress in Stunts

CHAPTER V

PLAY AREAS, EQUIPMENT AND SUPPLIES

In order to secure for children the development of organic vigor and those social and moral qualities which may be gained through well directed physical activities, certain space, equipment and supplies are necessary. It is the duty of boards of education and school trustees to provide a quantity of such articles as are necessary to make teaching and student practice effective.

SCHOOL SITES

Small rural elementary school sites should contain a minimum of three acres of level land. Consolidated, urban and city schools should have a minimum of five acres of level ground. In places where it is impossible to secure school sites which are level, grading should be done to provide a level area for playing games. Loss of balls, which results in delaying games, may be minimized by providing fences. The area needed for school sites should be based upon the requirements needed for various types of activities in the physical education program rather than upon a certain number of square feet per child.

SURFACING

The playground areas should be as level as possible, free from stones, graded to a slope of four inches to one hundred feet for rapid drainage and not subject to flooding during the rainy season. The surface may be dirt treated with a saline solution, grass, oil macadam or asphalt. For tennis and handball courts concrete should be used. When the ground is rocky or very sandy the only remedy is to haul in a covering of better soil and pack it down. Rock screenings may be used if properly rolled in, but loose screenings, pebbles or coarse gravel, give a poor footing and lead to accidents. The ground, sawdust, shavings or sand beneath the horizontal bars, horizontal ladders, at the foot of the slide, and in the jumping pits, should be dug up frequently to lessen the chance of injury from a fall.

LAYING OUT GROUNDS

In planning the school playground the needs of separate groups of children should be considered.

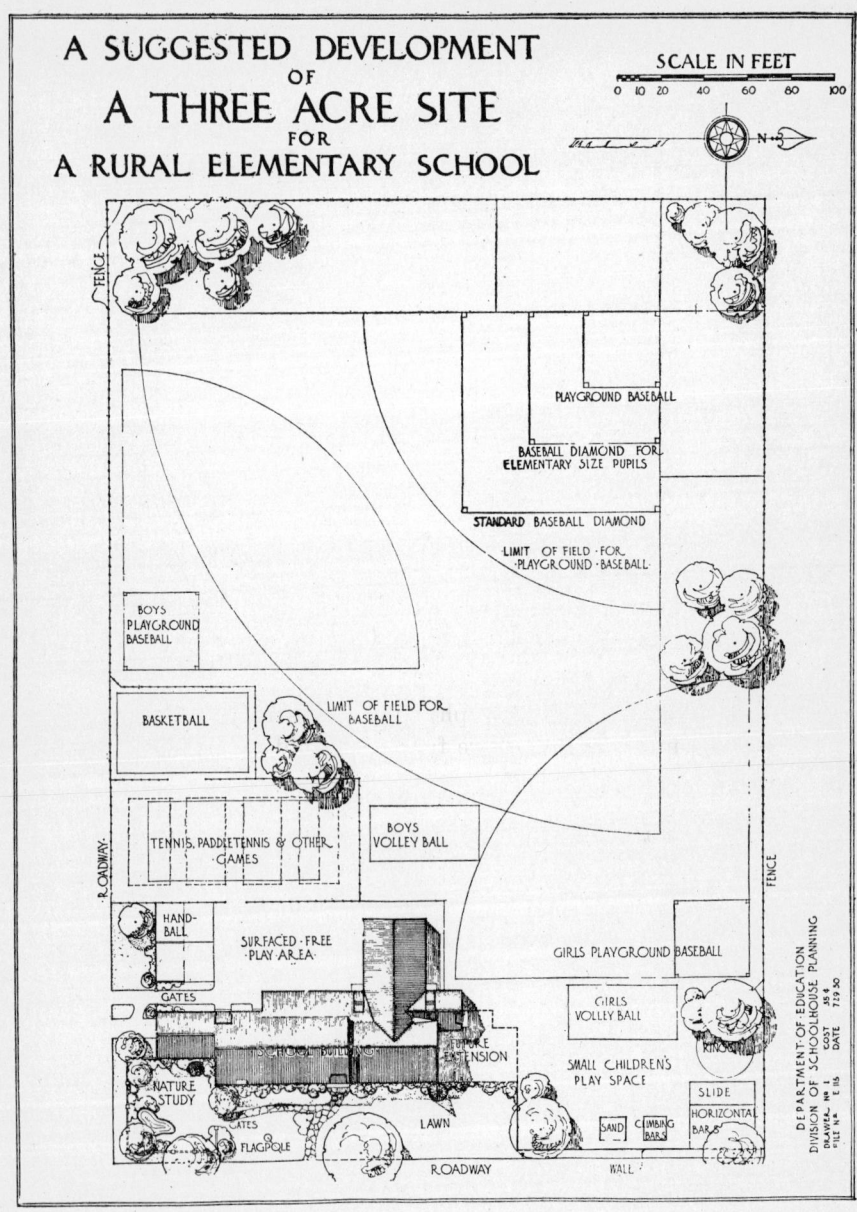

NOTE—The two plans showing the suggested development of school sites were contributed by Andrew P. Hill, Chief of Division of Schoolhouse Planning, State Department of Education, Sacramento, California.

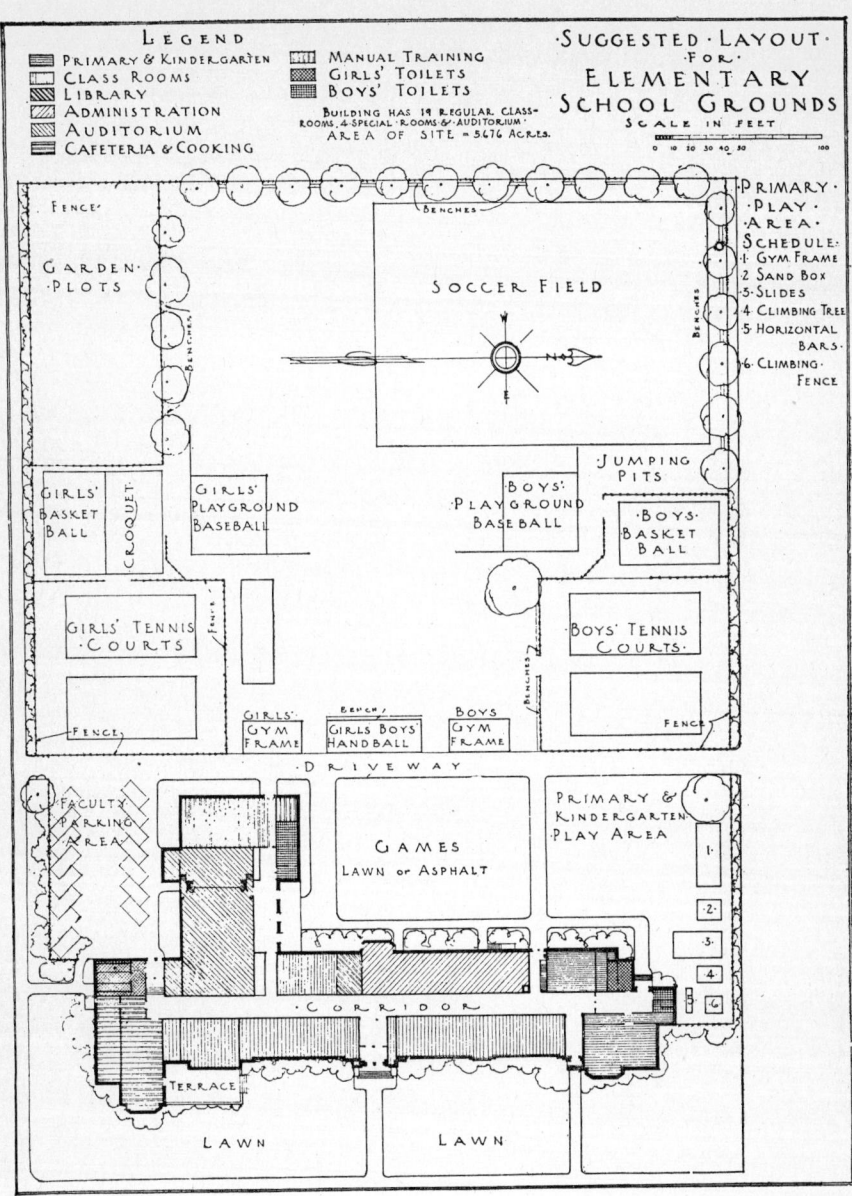

(a) The children under ten years of age should have a play space near the schoolhouse and so situated that they will not be interfered with by the older boys and girls. They should have their own permanent stationary apparatus.

(b) The boys ten years of age and older should be, at times, restricted to a definite part of the school yard for their games; otherwise the tendency is for them to usurp more than their share of the space and facilities.

(c) Boys and girls of older ages should use diamonds, fields and courts on a rotating schedule and should at times be scheduled to play together in the different game groups.

Shade is particularly desirable for the school playground but trees and shrubs should be planted along the outer borders and never in the middle of clear open spaces.

Whenever possible, courts should be laid out to run north and south so as to avoid the glare of the sun in the eyes of the players. Baseball diamonds should be laid out so that the homeplate is in either the northeast or the southeast corner of the diamond.

BOUNDARY LINES FOR COURTS AND FIELDS

To teach children obedience to law in games is one of the important aims of the physical education program. When the courts and fields are not plainly marked out it is not possible to distinguish between "out" and "in" and under these circumstances the rules are apt to be disregarded and, thus, the training loses much of its value.

For elementary schools it is almost impossible to keep all the courts properly marked with either dry lime or wet lime. On oil macadam or cement surface the lines may be painted. Certain types of grounds may be marked by digging a shallow v-type groove which serves as a line. For all other types of surface the most practical method of marking is by burying two-inch planks end to end so that the exposed edges are flush with the surface of the ground. The exposed edges can be painted white and thus afford permanent and satisfactory boundary lines. Volley ball courts, basket ball courts and the small fields needed for other games should be marked out in this way.

For convenience in marking grounds it is well to make all bases, corner marks, range marks, and location marks permanent by sinking in the ground at the proper places bricks, large stones, wooden or concrete blocks. These are easily found when the regular line markings become obliterated and save the trouble of making remeasurements. Wooden pegs are not satisfactory as they are not always easy to find. Markers should be just flush with or slightly below the level of the ground so that people will not stumble over them.

PLAY AREAS, EQUIPMENT AND SUPPLIES 53

Lines should be two inches wide. For liquid marking whitewash or cold water paint may be used. A very desirable whitewash can be made by adding to each eight quarts of unslaked lime, while it is slaking, a pound of tallow and two quarts of strong brine. Thin as needed and apply with a brush or marker. It is well to keep a supply of whitewash on hand in a galvanized iron ash can, strong cask or a large crock. A watering pot with the nozzle pinched partly shut is excellent for distributing the liquid. For dry marking use slaked lime. In the interest of economy the grounds should be kept marked by custodians or other service employees.

COMMERCIAL EQUIPMENT FOR SCHOOL PLAYGROUNDS *

Elementary school playgrounds should be provided with the following equipment:

Equipment	Minimum area required for installation	Recommended for grades
Safety climbing tree	10' x 10' = 100 sq. ft.	K, 1, 2
Safety platform slide	15' x 30' = 450 sq. ft.	1, 2, 3
Horizontal bars (graduated)	20' x 25' = 500 sq. ft. (Low)	K, 1, 2, 3
(Installed in sets of three)	(Int-High)	4, 5, 6, 7, 8, 9
Parazontal bars	20' x 30' = 600 sq. ft.	4, 5, 6, 7, 8
Horizontal ladder	15' x 25' = 375 sq. ft. (Low)	3, 4, 5,
	(High)	6, 7, 8
Stationary travel rings	25' x 25' = 625 sq. ft.	3, 4, 5, 6, 7, 8
Giant stride (rope or wooden rungs)	35' x 35' = 1225 sq. ft.	4, 5, 6, 7, 8
Junglegym	15' x 12' = 180 sq. ft.	all grades

All permanent equipment should be installed around the outside of the school grounds so as to leave unbroken play space for games. In general, horizontal ladders, parazontal bars, horizontal bars, and slides should parallel the fence. Permanent apparatus should be locked up and not used during periods when there is no supervision.

---
* Cuts loaned by courtesy of Patterson-Williams Company, San Jose, California; and A. G. Spalding and Bros., Chicopee, Mass.

Junglegym. The Junglegym can be purchased in either wood or steel and in varying sizes. This piece of equipment has particular value for children in the kindergarten and lower grades. If provided for children in the upper grades a larger size should be installed. A large number of games and stunts have been devised and adapted for use on the junglegym.

PLAY AREAS, EQUIPMENT AND SUPPLIES

Safety Climbing Tree. Nearly all children like to climb. This piece of equipment is especially adapted for kindergarten, first and second grades.

Safety Platform Slide. It is constructed with a platform ten inches below the top of the slide bedway which makes the top of the slide a railing in front of the child insuring safety from falling or being pushed off.

Horizontal Bars. These bars should be nonadjustable. The ground beneath the bars should be kept dug up or covered with eight inches of sawdust, shavings, or damp coarse sand. Do not use redwood sawdust. They should be installed in sets of three in different parts of the playground. The diameter of the cross-bar should be suited to the size of grip of the children using them.

Height of Horizontal Bars. Fifty children in each grade were taken in a group and arranged in line according to height of finger tips from ground with arms extended upward. The height in inches of the child at the tall end, the short end, and in the middle of the line is here given. These figures should be useful in helping to install horizontal bars, parazontal bars, horizontal ladders, and stationary circle travel rings at proper heights for the children who are to use them.

GRADES

								Girls			Boys	
Children	K	1	2	3	4	5	6	7	8	9	7	8	9
Shortest child.	48¾	48½	54	56	60½	61	65	67	72¼	74½	70	70	75
Middle child..	51½	57¼	62	65	65	67½	74	75½	78	79	77	80½	84½
Tallest child..	59¼	62¾	65¾	74	74	76½	87	85¼	85½	86	90	86	91¼

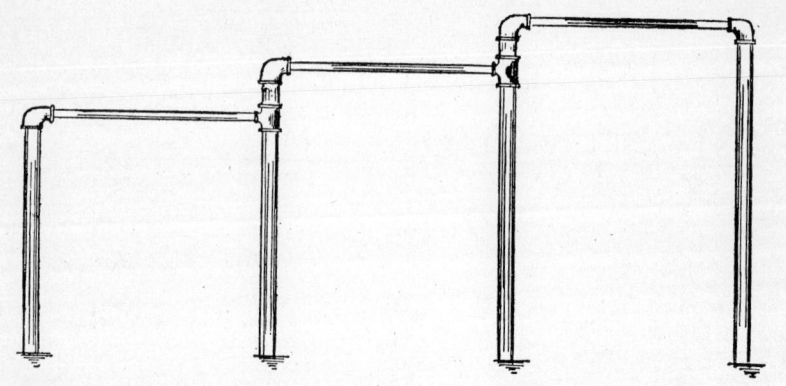

* This research was completed by Charles H. Hunt, Long Beach city schools.
 Set I. For grades K, 1, 2, 3, should be 52", 58" and 65" from the ground.
 Set II. For grades 4, 5, 6 should be 65", 68" and 74" from the ground.
 Set III. For grades 7, 8, 9 should be 76", 79" and 84" from the ground.
 The distance between posts should be five feet.

PLAY AREAS, EQUIPMENT AND SUPPLIES 57

Parazontal Bars. This piece of equipment consists of two acting bars, ten feet of inclined horizontal ladder and ten feet of inclined parallel bars. It accommodates twelve or more children at a time.

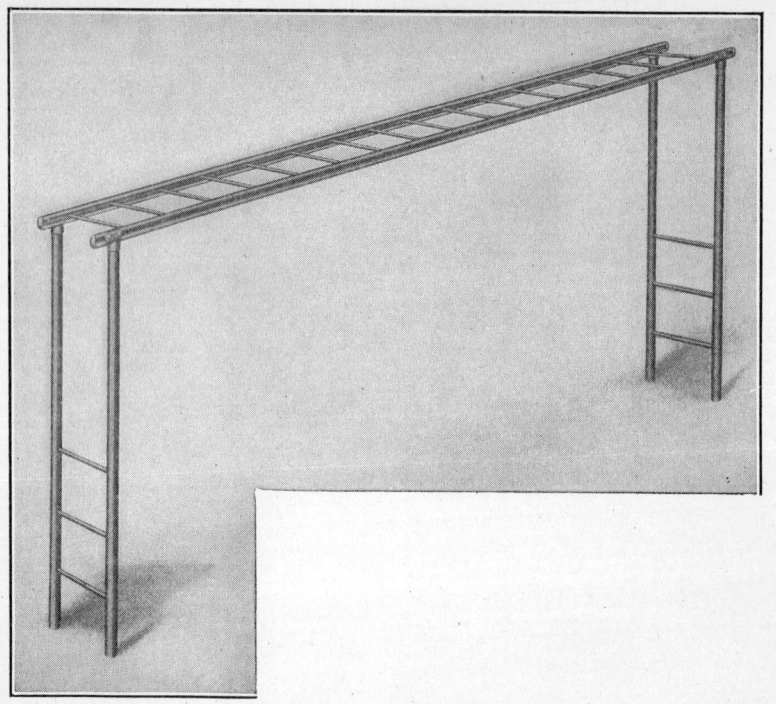

Horizontal Ladder. The ladder is sixteen feet long and has three rungs placed in the uprights to aid children in reaching the ladder. The ground beneath should be kept dug up or covered with eight inches of sawdust, shavings, or damp coarse sand.

For grades 3, 4, 5 ladder should be 5½′ from ground.
For grades 6, 7, 8 ladder should be 7′ from ground.

Stationary Circle Travel Rings. This apparatus does not revolve but permits the children to swing from ring to ring pulling, stretching and developing their arms, shoulders, back and abdominal muscles. The distance from the rings to the ground should be less when used by younger children. An inclined board should be furnished so shorter children can reach the rings.

60 PHYSICAL EDUCATION FOR ELEMENTARY SCHOOLS

Traveling Ring Outfit. Rings are steel forgings, jacketed with aluminum and hung by steel chains from roller bearing fixtures that are drop-forged.

Giant Stride. All pupils should be taught how to use the giant stride. Children wishing to stop while others continue around the circle should go to the pole taking their ladders with them and remain there until all have finished. The rungs should be made of rope or wood, rather than iron. The giant stride should always be located in areas where children do not play games.

LIST OF PLAY AREAS AND EQUIPMENT

Area, Unobstructed Play
  (For Primary Grades).
Area, Unobstructed Play
  (For Upper Grades).
Backstops, Baseball.
Backstops and Goals, Basket Ball.

Bars, Graduated (Horizontal).
Bars, Parazontal.
Beams, Balancing.
Courts, Basket Ball (Boys).
Courts, Bat Ball.
Courts, Captain Ball.

PLAY AREAS, EQUIPMENT AND SUPPLIES

Courts, Dodge Ball.
Courts, End Ball.
Courts, Hand Ball.
Courts, Hand Tennis.
Courts, Horseshoes.
Courts, Nine-court Basket Ball.
Courts, Paddle Tennis.
Courts, Pin Basket Ball.
Courts, Tennis.
Courts, Volley Ball.
Diamonds, Baseball.
Diamonds, Hit Pin Baseball.
Diamonds, Kick Ball.
Diamonds, Playground Baseball.
Field, Soccer.
Field, Field Ball.
Field, Speedball.
Frames, Baseball Throw for Accuracy.
Giant Strides.

Ladders, Horizontal.
Linograph.
Mats, Tumbling
  (Canvas, 3' x 5'—5' x 7').
Phonograph.
Phonograph Records.
Piano.
Pit—Broad Jump.
Pit—High Jump.
Poles, Climbing.
Posts, Tennis, Volley Ball, etc.
Posts, Tether Ball.
Rings, Traveling.
Ropes, Climbing.
Scales (with height attachment).
Slide.
Standards, High Jump.
Standards, Volley Ball.
  (Portable).
Track—100 yard (straightaway).

LIST OF PHYSICAL EDUCATION SUPPLIES (83)

Awl (Speedy Stitcher for repairing balls).
Bags, Bean.
Balls, Base (Hard).
Balls, Basket.
Balls, Beach.
Balls, Bounce (Large).
Balls, Hand.
Balls, Health
  (12" and 15" diameter).
Balls, Playground Base
  (9" and 12").
Balls, Soft Rubber (5").
Balls, Soccer.
Balls, Tennis.
Balls, Paddle Tennis
  (Sponge Rubber).
Balls, Tether.
Balls, Volley.
Bars, Cross.
  (For high jumping).

Bases, Baseball.
Bases, Hit Pin Baseball.
Bats, Baseball.
Bats, Playground Baseball.
Books, Physical Education.
Charts, Posture.
Charts, Age-Height-Weight.
Clubs, Indian.
Cord, (100'—for Marking).
Gloves, Baseball.
Horseshoes.
Kit, Repair.
Kit, First-aid.
Lime (For lines).
Mask, Catcher's.
Needles, Lacing.
Nets, Paddle Tennis.
Nets, Tennis.
Nets, Volley Ball.
Paper Cambric, Colored
  (To designate teams).

Protector, Catcher's.
Pump, Air.
Quoits.
Rackets, Paddle Tennis.
Rackets, Tennis.
Rake.
Ropes, Jumping (7' and 16').
Sets, Croquet.
Shovel.
Tape (100' steel or cloth).
Tape (25' steel or cloth).
Thread.
Wands.
Watches, Stop.
Whistles, Playground.
Yarn (Cotton and Wool).

PROVISIONS FOR SAFETY

Skill, strength and courage can be developed in vigorous games or on the apparatus without undue risk of accident if the school trustees and the teachers share the responsibility for taking all reasonable precautions to prevent such accidents. If the following suggestions are carried out there should be few injuries and the school district will not be held liable for damages for those accidents which do occur.

(a) *Protection of younger children.* Provide adequate play space exclusively for the younger children. Do not permit the use of hard baseballs within range of the space used by the younger children.

(b) *Choice of apparatus.* Purchase apparatus which by its use will give the most development. Avoid swings, teeters, and other sensational types.

(c) *Proper installation of apparatus.* See that all upright posts are firmly planted in concrete. Iron posts for standards should be used rather than wood which tends to rot. Carefully regulate the height of traveling rings, horizontal bars, and horizontal ladders so they will be appropriate for the children who are to use them. See that all horizontal bars are so fastened that they do not turn and can not come out. The ground beneath all apparatus should be free from rocks and stumps, and be kept dug up, even when covered with a cushion of sawdust, shavings or damp sand.

(d) *Instruction in use of apparatus.* Teachers should see that every pupil is given rudimentary instruction in the proper use of the apparatus upon which he or she is permitted to play. The older boys and girls, through demonstration, are usually quite able to assist the teacher to give such instruction.

(e) *Safety inspection of apparatus.* Once each month, or more often, the school principal should examine the playground and apparatus to discover any signs of wear which might lead to accident and should report the inspection, with recommendations, in a written statement to school officials.

(f) *Fencing.* For safety, the play areas of school grounds should be fenced with a good quality of material.

(g) To prevent the development of nasal and sinus infections the dust problem should be earnestly studied and action taken. Conditions may be improved by resurfacing the grounds; by planting grass adapted to soil conditions; by having municipal or county watering departments soak down the grounds frequently; by installing sprinkling systems; or by the use of a saline solution sold commercially for this purpose.

CHAPTER VI

SUGGESTIONS TO TEACHERS

GENERAL SUGGESTIONS TO TEACHERS

1. Keep in mind the objectives of Physical Education.
2. Emphasize character and sportsmanship values.
3. Do not tolerate profanity, cheating or bullying.
4. Plan a yearly, seasonal, monthly and daily program.
5. Keep a record of activities taught each month.
6. Save indoor activities for use on days of inclement weather.
7. Correlate the activities with other school subjects.
8. Select and adapt activities for the physically handicapped pupils.
9. Guard from overexertion the child who returns to school following an absence due to illness.
10. Do not let any child overstrain.
11. Teach children to await their turn when using apparatus.
12. Teach children how to use apparatus properly.
13. Be resourceful in adapting games to prevailing conditions.
14. Vary the size of the playing space if necessary.
15. Assign to each game the smallest number necessary to make it a success.
16. Increase the number of runners and chasers or balls in a game if conditions warrant.
17. Watch closely for waning interest.
18. When interest wanes, change to a new game.
19. Know the game yourself before you attempt to teach it.
20. Make explanations as simple and concise as possible. Lengthy explanations create rapid loss of interest.
21. Remember that children want action.
22. As little time as possible should be used in getting ready to play a game.
23. Teach children to play (as a rule) without coats and sweaters, and to wear shoes with low, broad heels.
24. Do not permit certain children to monopolize the game.
25. Play with the children at every opportunity.
26. Once rules are established for a given condition they should be observed.
27. When officiating, make quick, accurate and just decisions.
28. Impress upon children that decisions rendered by officials are final and are to be accepted cheerfully and courteously.

SUGGESTIONS TO TEACHERS

29. Children should be assigned to, and be held responsible for, the duties of officiating, scoring, timing, etc.
30. Have crippled or disabled children learn the rules of games.
31. Keep a record of injuries but do not coddle children who have been hurt.
32. Children who have been retarded in school because of language difficulties or other causes should be assigned to play with groups of children of their own age or size.
33. Use pupil leaders whenever possible.
34. Have pupil leaders responsible for care of game equipment.
35. Have all necessary equipment ready before beginning a game.
36. Stuff old casings with straw, paper or rags, and use in relays, etc.
37. Always have whistles available for use.
38. Blow the whistle only when necessary.
39. When the whistle is blown demand immediate and absolute attention.
40. Whistles should be kept in an antiseptic solution when not in use.
41. Remember that play outdoors when possible is preferable to that indoors.
42. When playing indoors have windows opened and have children remove extra wraps.
43. Use initiative in adapting activities for use during relief periods.
44. As a rule, have separate groups for boys and girls for grade 5 and above, but occasionally combine them.
45. Whenever possible arrange competing teams so they are nearly equal in strength and skill.
46. Designate team membership by using color bands or other distinguishing emblems.
47. In the upper grades discuss rules of games with children and give written tests on rules.
48. Have children keep a "game notebook," including in it the rules of games as given by the teacher.
49. Do not allow long distance running under competition for elementary pupils.
50. Do not use individual races over seventy-five yards as contests.
51. Girls should not compete for records in the high and broad jumps.
52. Do not permit "American football" as a game in the elementary school.
53. Know that it is doubtful whether interscholastic championships for elementary schools are of much value.
54. Plan semiannual play days or demonstrations of the different phases of your program.
55. Develop a strong intramural program in your school.

56. Encourage children to use this and other books in their study of games.

57. Teachers wishing to use material other than that presented for a given grade should use material from lower grades rather than from higher grades.

PHYSICAL EDUCATION BOOKS

Minimum List of Books Recommended for Elementary Schools

An Athletic Program for Elementary Schools. Leonora Andersen. A. S. Barnes & Co., New York. 1927.

Book of Games for Home, School, and Playground, The. Forbush and Allen. John C. Winston Company. 1927.

Corrective Physical Education for Groups. Lowman, Colestock and Cooper. A. S. Barnes & Co., New York. 1928.

Dramatic Dances for Small Children. Mary S. Shafter. A. S. Barnes & Co., New York. 1927.

Folk Dance Book, The. C. Ward Crampton. A. S. Barnes & Co., New York. 1909.

Folk Dances for Boys and Girls. Effie Shambaugh. A. S. Barnes & Co., New York. 1929.

Folk Dances from Old Homeland. Elizabeth Burchenal. G. Schirmer Co., New York. 1922.

Games for the Playground, Home, School and Gymnasium. Jessie Bancroft. The Macmillan Company, New York. 1921.

"Good Morning." Old-Fashioned Dances Revived. Mr. and Mrs. Henry Ford. Dearborn Publishing Company, Dearborn, Michigan. 1926.

Health by Stunts. Pearl and Brown. The Macmillan Company, New York. 1921.

Individual and Mass Athletics. S. C. Staley. A. S. Barnes & Co., New York. 1925.

Natural Rhythms and Dances. Gertrude Colby. A. S. Barnes & Co., New York.

Outline of Physical Education for the First and Second Grades, An. Andersen and McKinley. A. S. Barnes & Co., New York. 1930.

Physical Education. Wild and White. Iowa State Teachers College, Cedar Falls, Iowa. 1924.

Rhythmic Action Plays and Dances. Irene Moses. Milton Bradley Co., Springfield, Mass. 1916.

Rhythms and Dances for Elementary Schools. Dorothy LaSalle. A. S. Barnes & Co., New York. 1926.

(NOTE.—Elementary schools and city and county libraries should purchase these books and as many others listed in the bibliography as is possible.)

PART II (GRADED PROGRAM)
FIRST GRADE

	PAGE
Story Plays	68
Rhythmical Activities	80
Hunting Games	89
Mimetics	92

The teacher should refer frequently to Part I of the book as it contains many suggestions in regard to the various activities. For example, the material presented in Part I under "Posture," "Corrective Physical Education," and "Health Education" applies to all grades and should be reviewed frequently.

The activity classifications in each grade have been arranged in sequence according to judgments of their appeal and importance to the children who will use them. In situations where all the content appearing in this grade can not be taught, the teacher should make selections from each classification rather than attempt to teach all the activities found in any one classification.

STORY PLAYS

Playground, The

1. Run across street to playground—Run around the circle.
2. Going down the "slippery slide"—Climb up the ladder. Raise opposite arm and leg, then continue, alternating. To slide down the ladder, do slow deep knee bending about ten times.
3. Throwing and catching ball—Individually or with a partner.
4. The giant stride—Each group run around in a circle, both arms raised high as if holding on to rope. Occasionally give a leap.
5. The seesaw—Three lines for each "seesaw." Children in lines 1 and 3 face each other. Those in middle line act as the support, and stand facing front with arms extended toward lines 1 and 3. Children in lines 1 and 3 bend knees and stand erect, alternately, as line 2 does sideward bending.
6. Skip rope on way home—Around the room to desk.

Day in the Country, A

1. Run to trolley car—Run in place.
2. Play conductor—Stop and start car, etc. Collect fares.
3. Get off car and walk to farm—Walk around the circle.
4. Change to play clothes—Pull on overalls.
5. Run to barn to gather eggs—Run about hunting for eggs.
6. Pick berries and apples—Stoop for berries and reach to basket. Stretch for apples and place in basket.
7. Go swimming—Use arm motions of breast stroke.
8. Skip stones over the pond—Throw with sideward, underhand movement.
9. Jump fences on way home—Jump over seats.
10. Tired—Sit down to rest and relax.

Sleeping Princess, The [*]

1. Approach the forest. Chop down trees—Chopping movement, a vigorous oblique downward swing of the arms with twisting and forward bending of the body.
2. Run around castle walls to the gates—Run with light step, in place or around the circle.

---
[*] Contributed by major students in Physical Education at the University of California, Berkeley.

FIRST GRADE

3. Reach for golden ring that opens gates to castle and pull the same—Reach up as far as possible, grasp ring and pull down, assuming squat position.
4. Swim across the moat—Swimming motion.
5. Walk over sleeping court, careful not to awaken them—Step slowly with high knee bending.
6. Run up the long flight of marble stairs—Run with high knee upward bending.
7. Discovers beautiful princess—Leans over slowly and awakens her with a kiss. Bend one knee, and lean forward at the same time.
8. Great rejoicing—Jump up and down. Clap hands.

Circus

1. Chariot Race—All face side of room. Even rows stand with arms stretched out driving. Odd rows grasp hands across and gallop in place.
2. Feeding Elephants—One-half of class are elephants, the other half, children. Elephants and children face each other. Children have peanuts in large bag on floor. Stoop down, get a handful of peanuts and throw to elephants. Repeat several times. Elephants form trunks by clasping hands extended in front. As peanuts are tossed they swing trunks high up in the air, catch peanuts and carry them to mouth.
3. Ringmaster and Horses—One child is chosen "ringmaster"; other children are horses. Ringmaster snaps whip. Horses gallop. Second time whip is snapped, trot; third time, high step.
4. Circus Band—Two rows beat drums; two rows play fifes; two rows play trombones. Each group marches around a circle, all keeping in step with music.
5. Circus Clowns—All imitate some clown's trick, such as balancing stick on chin, juggling balls, walking tight-rope.

Autumn in the Woods

1. Skip to the woods.
2. Climb into tree to look into bird's nest—Reach high with alternate arm and foot.
3. All run and jump over brook—Make two chalk lines on floor for brook.
4. Throw stones into brook—Stoop and secure stone, throw and jump back from splash.
5. Shake tree branches to see leaves fall.
6. Walk, rustling the leaves.
7. Gather leaves and toss into pile.
8. Run and jump into pile of leaves.
9. Hop home.

Cutting the Grass

1. Running lawn mower—Walk around, pushing lawn mower with both hands and making "Br-r-r" to imitate sound it makes.
2. Raking grass—Face front of room. Reach forward and to either side with long strokes. Rake grass into piles.
3. Gathering grass—Pick up big armfuls and put into wheelbarrow.
4. Dumping grass—Run with wheelbarrow to large pile of grass.
5. Emptying wheelbarrow—Take out large armfuls and throw onto the pile.

Halloween

1. Jump over the fence into the field where the pumpkins grow—Jump over seat into next aisle.
2. Bend over and hunt for big pumpkin for your jack-o'-lantern—Bend forward and downward.
3. Stoop down and lift one up—Run home with it. Stoop, lift pumpkin and run in place.
4. Make lantern—Sit down, cut off top, take out seeds, and light candle.
5. Playing with lantern—Run to window. Hold lantern high up to the window. Hear some one coming, so stoop down quickly to hide. Creep along to the next window. Can hardly reach this window, so have to stretch up on toes.
6. Run home—Softly on tiptoes.
7. Blow out candle in lantern.

Brownies

1. Brownies come out at sunset—Creep out of their desks, which are their houses in trunks of trees.
2. They exercise their legs which are cramped from inactivity—Skip around.
3. Creep very quietly into the woods to see if any one is near. If they hear any one coming they stoop quickly.
4. Peep into the windows of an old hut—Stretch high.
5. See poor old lady asleep with house in disorder—Tell each other of their surprise. Decide to help.
6. Brownies help—Gather wood, sweep floor, wash soiled clothes, wring them out, hang them up to dry, wash dishes, wash windows.
7. Day breaks—Brownies skip home to trunks of trees.

Nutting

1. Run to the woods, carrying over the shoulder a bag in which to put nuts.
2. Climb over stone wall—Climb over seat or substitute.

FIRST GRADE

3. Walk through the carpet of leaves—Lift knees high.
4. Jump over a little brook, for the trees are on the other side.
5. Reach up and shake branches, standing on tiptoe.
6. Throw things at the trees to make more nuts drop.
7. Stoop and bend to pick up the nuts. Place nuts in bag.
8. Lift the bags up, balance them on the head, and walk home with them.

Preparing for Thanksgiving

1. Get flour—Dip into flour barrel (under seat) and pour into bowl on table.
2. Sift flour—Both hands forward as if holding a sieve. Shake from side to side.
3. Stir mixture—Circular motion of arms, alternating.
4. Roll out crust—Push forward and backward.
5. Put pies in oven—Bend over and open oven door. Get pie from table. Put pie in oven. Get another pie.
6. Run out to play while the pies bake—One or more groups run around in a circle.
7. Take pies out of the oven.
8. Blow on fingers—Fingers are burned while taking pies out of oven.

Coming to This Country

1. Row out to large boat—Sit and row.
2. Climb ladder to get into big boat—Reach one hand up and lift opposite knee high; bring arm down and put foot on floor; at same time stretch other arm and raise other foot. Continue alternating movement.
3. Pull up anchor—One foot forward; stoop and pull first with one hand and then with other.
4. Hoist sails—Reach up high with one hand and grasp rope. Pull down, then reach up with other hand and pull. Continue movement.
5. High waves make boat go up and down—Rise and sink on toes, and when it gets very rough bend the knees.
6. Row to shore.

How Animals Get Ready for Winter (3)

1. Squirrel gathers nuts and buries them—Jump on toes, get nuts, put in mouth, stoop down, dig hole, put in ground.
2. Birds fly south—With arms shoulder high, fly about.
3. Bear looks for cave—Walk around, swaying from side to side; find and crawl into own cave (seat).
4. Deer in north woods make tracks in snow—Run, making a zigzag trail.

5. Pony is shod—Hammer horseshoes. Every other child pony and blacksmith.

6. Pony breaks loose and runs away—Gallop around free areas.

7. Snake wiggles slowly into hole—Glide toward a hole and wiggle into it.

Firemen (6A)

1. Firemen asleep—Heads on desks, faces toward open windows.

2. Gong! Gong! The fire bell goes!—Pupils jump out of seats and make motions of dressing quickly.

3. Slide down the pole—Stoop and stand several times to imitate many firemen sliding down.

4. Drive to the fire—Run around in a circle and back to place.

5. Unwind the hose—With hands clasped together, both arms, describe large circles in front.

6. Playing hose—Teacher points to a corner and says, "There is the blaze." Children grasping hose, work arms up and down, throwing streams of water. Make soft hissing sound. Teacher points to different places saying, "There is smoke," or "There is another blaze." Children play the hose on it. Have some of the blazes in the ceiling.

7. Raise the ladder—Both hands pushing up.

8. Climb the ladder—Alternate raising of arms and knees.

9. Wrap valuables in a sheet and throw them out of window.

10. Climb down ladder—Same as climbing up, except with deep knee bending.

11. Wind up the hose—Reverse of unwinding.

12. Drive home—Same as driving to fire.

Clever Wood Mice [*]

1. The wood mice run out to find tall dry grass—Run lightly and quickly twice around an open space.

2. With sharp teeth they bite the grass over their heads, and hold it with their paws—Throw heads back. While walking slowly, with high knee bending, make motion of drawing bunches of grass to chest and biting them.

3. The mice run back to their holes and line them with the soft sweet grass—Run lightly to and wriggle into hole (seat); with feet and hands make motion of spreading grass around.

4. Tired out, they take a nap—Eyes closed. Quiet for a moment.

5. All wake up and stretch—Good stretching, arms above heads.

6. They run out to play and climb a bush to look around—Form a circle, then climbing action, looking around alertly.

---

[*] Contributed by major students in Physical Education at the University of California, Berkeley.

7. The breeze blows gently; the slender stalks sway; the mice hold tightly—Standing on tiptoe, arms stretched forward, hands and feet together, body sways from side to side.

8. Mice see remnants of a picnic; climb down and run to food—Action of climbing down and running to center for food (if out of doors), or around room (if inside).

9. They eat hungrily—Crouched on heels, bend forward for food, using paws to assist. Old cat appears and pounces on one. The others run home. Run swiftly.

10. Little mouse escapes and comes home; all gather round, sniff him up and down, and decide the cat must be belled. One is chosen to do it—Standing around mouse, bend forward deeply and up. Heads together for discussion. One volunteer is chosen.

11. Mouse with bell tiptoes to place where cat sleeps, followed by the others. He puts bell around cat's neck—Pantomime action. All tiptoe.

12. Mice dance for joy until warned by tinkle of cat's bell—Move around circle with high knee bending, arms raised sideward-upward alternately. At tinkle of bell all run home.

13. Old cat cannot find them, so goes home—Children crouch on heels, backs straight.

14. Mice, overjoyed, return to play—Dance same as No. 12, with higher leaps.

Cowboys

1. Lasso the pony—Twirl lasso over head in large circles, with right hand about eight times. Throw lasso; lean well forward, arm stretched out, then pull back. Repeat with left hand.

2. Gallop on ponies—Each group around the corral.

3. Cowboy's trick—Throw a ball up in the air. Pull out revolver, aim and shoot, saying, "Bang!" as trigger is pulled.

4. Gallop and pick up handkerchief—At signal from teacher, all stoop while still galloping, pick up a handkerchief and wave it in air until they reach the hitching fence.

5. Stretch after long day in saddle.

Play in the Snow

1. All are sleepy—Heads on desks.

2. Wake up and sit straight, stretching arms as though just waking. What shall we do to make us lively? Go out in the snow and play.

3. Pull on rubber boots, first right and then left.

4. Pull cap over ears, elbows kept out and back.

5. Run out into snow and play tag.

6. Very cold day. Arms must be warmed—Arms out at side. Fling them across chest and slap opposite shoulders.

7. Stoop down, pick up handful of snow and make snowball—Throw snowball at some spot with right arm. Repeat all with left arm.

8. Walk through snowdrift with hands on hips, lifting feet and knees high with each step.

9. Run home.

Skating (10)

1. Put on sweater, cap and mittens. Reach up to get skates from shelf.
2. Get sled and run to lake, giving little brother a ride.
3. Snow on ice—Clear a place to skate, using shovel and broom.
4. Put on skates. Make simple skating movements.
5. Remove skates.
6. Very cold—Warm hands. Find some wood and build a fire. Heap on wood to make it burn faster.
7. Dance and play around the fire—Use a rhythmical game learned previously.
8. Skip home.

Snow Fort (15A)

1. Walk through field of deep snow—With shovel held over one shoulder, bring knees up high.
2. Groups shovel snow into big piles to make forts.
3. Pat the snow down hard on top with shovel—This is done up high and around in a circle as if fort surrounds them.
4. Snowball fight—One-half of group against other half. All make snowballs, then one-half throw them at others, while the latter dodge them or drop down within their fort.
5. Repeat. The first side dodging and the second side throwing.
6. Walk home on snowshoes through deep snow.

Dear Old Santa (5)

1. Santa makes toys—Children seated go through motions of hammering, pasting, sewing and painting.
2. Toys finished—Santa stretches and stands.
3. Packing the toys—Stoops to right and left to gather toys for pack.
4. Santa runs to the barn for his reindeer—One group at a time runs and returns to place.
5. Reindeer prance and shake their heads—Place thumbs on heads with fingers spread like antlers. Shake heads and dance from one foot to the other.
6. Put the pack into the sleigh—Bend to gather the pack, then slowly rise as if the pack were heavy; stretch hands over head, and standing on tiptoe give a little jump as if pushing the pack into the sleigh.
7. Santa rides away—Same as number 4.

Christmas Tree

1. Put on coats and hats.
2. Run to barn for sled and hatchet—When secured, children run out to the woods.
3. Chop down trees—With one foot forward, swing ax over other shoulder. Chop and stoop forward several times to one side and then to the other.
4. Place tree on sled. Drag sled home. Hands behind as if holding ropes.
5. Walk rapidly to secure boards, hammer, nails and saw. Make stand for tree.
6. Decorate tree with presents, ornaments and candles.
7. Dance around Christmas tree—Use a game previously learned.
8. Blow out candles on tree.

Christmas Toys (15A)

1. Jack-in-the-Box—Teacher makes downward motion with hand as if closing lid of box and all children stoop down. Hand is raised quickly and children jerk up to standing position.
2. Wooden Soldiers—March, beating drums.
3. Each group forms a train of cars—First child in each group has his hands on his hips. Those behind place hands on shoulders of child in front. Short steps around on toes, making "choo-choo" sound of engine.
4. Jumping Jacks—Teacher makes motion as if pulling a string. Children jump into air with feet apart; bring them together when they land. Arms are brought straight out to side and down again while jumping. Repeat.
5. Rocking Horse—One foot well in front of other, hands on hips. Stiff wooden legs. Rock forward, lifting back foot. Rock backward, lifting front foot.
6. Jointed Doll—One child may be the leader and show the class the variety of positions the doll can assume. Head, arms and legs. As each new position is demonstrated the leader says, "Like this" and the class imitate the same position.

Washington's Cherry Tree (6A)

1. Pull on sweater—Take several pulls to get sweater over head. Then push arms up into sleeves. Finally give two or three pulls to get it down from shoulders.
2. Run out with hatchet—Two lines are drawn on the ground to represent a brook. As children come to the brook they jump over it.
3. Chop down cherry tree.

4. Hurry home—This time they come to a log fallen across the brook and have to walk over it very carefully. Draw a long line. Extending arms out at sides, walk the line without stepping off it.

Building a House

1. Start for work—Put on coat and hat and briskly walk to work.
2. Digging cellar. Break up ground with pickax—One foot forward, swing pickax high over one shoulder and then to ground. Shovel dirt. Throw over shoulders. Alternate.
3. Climb ladder out of cellar—Lift knees high.
4. Putting up house—Saw lumber, plane boards, bore holes. Stoop down to raise beams and then place high over head. Drive nails.
5. Painting house—Stoop, dip brush in pail, reach high up and make strokes from side to side.
6. Walk home from work, buying groceries on the way.

Gathering Wood for Fire

1. Walk into woods to get wood. Climb fence.
2. Chop down trees and saw wood with help of brother.
3. Hand wood over fence to brother. Haul wood home.
4. Split into kindling, and carry upstairs.

Betsy Ross Making the Flag (5)

1. Tear cloth for the stripes—Hands meeting in front. Arms flung to the sides as if tearing strips. Do this seven times for the red stripes and six for the white.
2. The stars—Jump with feet apart and arms swung upward to represent a five-pointed star, the head being the fifth point. Do this thirteen times for the stars in the first flag.
3. Sewing the flag—Hold material in left hand and sew with right hand throwing arm high as if sewing with long thread.
4. Waving the flag—Run around waving the flag first with right arm and then with the left.
5. Carry flag to flagpole—March in a soldierly manner to position facing the flagpole.
6. Hoist flag to top of pole—Pull down to squat position.

March Winds (2)

1. Tops of trees bowing to the wind—Bend forward and backward slowly. Sideward right and left slowly. Repeat.
2. Trees bending trunks to the wind—Feet sideward. Place hands on hips. Bend body right and left slowly. Repeat.
3. The windmill—Raise arms sideward shoulder high. Lower right, raise left. Reverse movement. Repeat.

FIRST GRADE

4. Weathervanes—Hands on shoulders, elbows shoulder height. Twist body right and left. Repeat.

5. The dancing leaves—Light running steps in place, run around in place several times, hop on one foot, then on the other.

6. Wind blowing limbs of trees to the ground—Bend and stretch knees.

7. Skip home out of wind.

Birds Learning to Fly

1. Mother bird and little birds all stretch their wings.
2. Look at sky to see if it is a pleasant day.
3. Fly around, then hop on ground.
4. Pick up crumbs scattered by children.
5. Birds fly back to their nests and rest.

Toy Shop, The (2)

1. Reach for toys on high shelf.

2. Jack-in-the-Box—Bend the knees deeply with arms folded and held high in front. On the word "up" jump up in place stretching the arms sideward.

3. Monkey climbing a stick—Bend the knees upward, alternating, and stretch the arms upward as if climbing.

4. Dolls—(a) Walking. With a jerky step keeping the knees stiff and arms bent at the elbow, walk four steps forward and four steps backward. (b) Bow (boys). With hands at sides and heels together, bow, bending trunk forward. Raise trunk at once without command. (c) Courtesy (girls). Holding skirt with both hands and placing toe of right foot behind left heel, courtesy by bending and stretching knees quickly.

5. Riding a bicycle—Run in place, lifting the knees high in front, arms stretched forward with hands closed grasping handle bars.

6. Jumping Jack—Jump so feet are apart and the arms raised sideward. Jump bringing feet together and arms to side.

7. Train of cars and engine—With hands on shoulders of the child in front, march or run in step in a circle.

8. Whistling Balloon—Place hands before the mouth and whistle to represent the whistle of a balloon.

Aëroplanes

1. Reach up, grasp propeller with both hands, and with vigorous downward pull crank aëroplane, first to the right and then to the left.

2. First one in each group jumps on aëroplane, squat position. Others in the group have to push it to get it started. To do so they push against desks with both hands while running in place.

3. All jump on aëroplane—With hands on desks swing forward and jump to squat position on the floor.

4. Breaks down over a lake—All swim to shore and then walk home through plowed field.

At the Seashore

1. Ride to seashore—Represent horses and drivers.
2. At seashore—Skip to bathhouse. Put on bathing suits.
3. Play in sand—Dig holes, throw stones, etc.
4. Race with waves—Run to meet wave, turn and race it back.
5. Jump over waves—Join hands along the beach. At given signal all jump into a big wave. Repeat several times.
6. Swim around in the ocean—Make swimming motion with arms.
7. Racing on sand—One child from each group might compete at the same time.
8. Skip to bathhouse—Change clothes. Drive home.

Playing in the Wind (6A)

1. Skip out to play—Two rows may form one circle and skip.
2. Look up and point to wind clouds—While skipping.
3. Weathervane—Stretch arms out at sides. Slowly twist trunk to right and left.
4. Flying kites—Toss kite into air, run back a few steps, pull string and watch the kite. Haul it in and wind string.
5. Windmill—Stretch right arm overhead. Let arms describe motion of windmill.
6. Trees swaying in wind—First the fluttering of leaves (fingers), next the bending of branches (arms), and finally the swaying of the entire tree (body).
7. Toss some light object into air, as feather or leaf—Watch the wind carry it away. Run and blow to keep it floating.
8. Mother calls—Run into the house.

Gathering Flowers

1. Start out to gather flowers—Skip vigorously.
2. Climb over the gate and jump down on the other side—Climb over seat, jumping into next aisle.
3. Stoop and pick a few flowers, putting them in the basket.
4. See some prettier flowers. Run quickly and stoop to pick them.
5. Jump over logs to pick some violets on the other side—Draw two lines to represent a log.
6. Little brook. Many flowers on other side. Cross carefully on stepping stone—Walk chalk line.

7. After the baskets are filled, climb over a stone wall and skip home.
8. Sit down and arrange the flowers into bouquets.

May Queen (15A)

1. Pick daisies for a chain—Each group runs about in its own field. After every five or six steps stoop and pick a few daisies and put in basket hanging on left arm.
2. May Queen is chosen and sits in chair in front of room.
3. Honoring May Queen—The members of one group run or skip and lay flowers at queen's feet as they pass. The other groups follow.
4. Wind the maypole—Each group dances around its own maypole, raising the hand nearest the center as if holding a streamer.
5. At finish of dance all bow to Queen. Queen bows to children.
6. All skip by the Queen, holding daisy chains high over heads.
7. All play games—Use those already known.

At the Beach

1. Dig a hole in sand—Take shovel in both hands, lift one knee, place foot on shovel, push it down with foot, throw sand to right. Repeat, using other foot to push shovel. Continue until there is a deep hole.
2. Jump into hole—Jump forward.
3. Bury feet in hole with sand—Bend body forward from waist and with hands scoop the sand and cover feet with it.
4. Lift feet out of sand—Hands on hips. Stand on one foot and lift other foot out of sand, very slowly. Shake foot vigorously to get sand off of it. Same, standing on other foot.
5. Pick up pebbles—Deep knee bend. Pick up several pebbles, place them in pail. Stand, take one or two steps, pick up more pebbles. Repeat. Run to edge of water.
6. Throw pebbles into water—Throw first with right hand, then with left. Skip stones by throwing underhanded.
7. Going near the water—Take three or four long steps forward on toes. When a big wave comes, run backward quickly so that feet will not get wet. Repeat several times.
8. Wading—Take long steps, raising knees high.

RHYTHMICAL ACTIVITIES

The Camel *

MARY MORGAN MOSHER

The camel lives in the desert drear,
There is no food or water near;
Sometimes trees make a pleasant place
Where he can rest a little space.

And then he goes upon his way,
Patient, kind, the live-long day;
But, oh, how glad when home he sees,
For he is tired and wants his ease.

To be played rather slowly. The words are sung by the teacher alone, or by the children and teacher together.

Some children represent the camel and several are scattered around the room to represent trees. The trees stand with arms outstretched

---

* From Shafer and Mosher, "Rhythms for Children." Copyright 1921. By permission of A. S. Barnes and Company, publishers.

for the branches. For the first two lines the children slowly walk around the room with head and shoulders bent forward and arms folded across the back to represent the hump of the camel. They make a slight up and down movement of the head to show how the camel's head has a different motion from that of other animals.

At the words "Sometimes trees make a pleasant place," the camel goes under a tree and either stands still for the next line, or lies down under the tree to rest.

Then he slowly gets up and again walks quietly around the room until the end of the music when he may again lie down, or stand waiting, trying in this manner to show he is glad to be home again.

Did You Ever See a Lassie *

Did you ever see a lassie, a lassie, a lassie,
Did you ever see a lassie do this way and that?
Do this way and that way, and this way and that way,
Did you ever see a lassie do this way and that?

(Columbia: 10008D)

Formation: Single circle, all facing left with hands joined. A leader stands within the ring.

* From Crampton & Wollaston's "The Song Play Book." Copyright 1917. By permission of A. S. Barnes and Company, publishers.

Lines 1 and 2. Players walk forward around the circle. At the words "do this way and that," the one within the ring demonstrates some movement which the others are to imitate.

Lines 3 and 4. Players stand in place facing center and perform with the one in the center the movement shown.

The leader chooses another child to succeed him in the ring and joins the circle.

Suggestions: Activities of the household, of the farm, gymnastic exercises, dance steps, imitations of animals, street games, athletics and industrial activities may be used. Make movements vigorous.

Ducks *

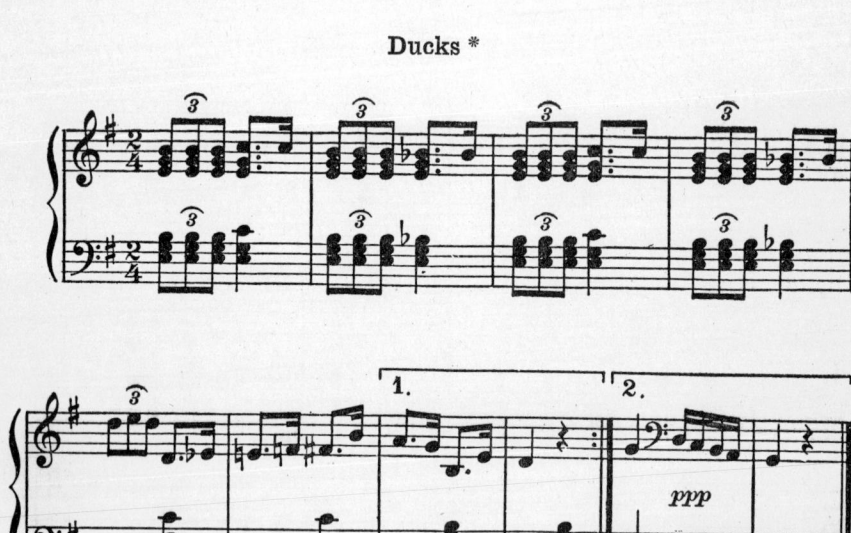

Some little ducks a walk did take
Down the yard and past the gate
Into the pond as you shall learn
And out they pulled a worm.

Quackity quack, quack, quack, quack, quack
Quackity quack, quack, quack, quack, quack
Into the water down they go
Just so!—

This music is to be played rather slowly. The little ducks may come down the farm yard in single file, or they may come in groups of two or

* From Shafer and Mosher, No. 1, "Rhythms for Children." Copyright 1927. By permission of A. S. Barnes and Company, publishers.

FIRST GRADE 83

three. The children walk forward slowly in full squat position, hands are on hips and the arms are used to represent the wings of the duck. At the words "Out they pulled a worm," their heads go down to the floor and they tug at, and pull out a worm and swallow him. This first part is usually sung by the instructor. All the children say the "quackity quack" words together in a soft voice.

At the words "Into the water down they go, Just so!" the little heads disappear again, and the hands and arms are thrust backward and upward to represent the feet of the duck sticking out of the water as he searches for worms.

The Farmer in the Dell (15A)

One child is chosen to be the "farmer" and stands in the center of the ring, while the rest join hands and circle around him singing:

The first child chooses and leads to the center of the circle a second one; the second chooses a third, and so on, while the rest sing the following verses:

> The farmer takes a wife,
> The wife takes the child,
> The child takes the nurse,
> The nurse takes the dog,
> The dog takes the cat,
> The cat takes the rat,
> The rat takes the cheese,
> The cheese stands alone.

The "cheese" may be "clapped out," and must begin again as the "farmer."

Variations: (a) The game may be ended in this way: After the children sing, "The cat takes the rat," they continue with, "The cat

84 PHYSICAL EDUCATION FOR ELEMENTARY SCHOOLS

chases the rat,'' and during the rest of the verse the farmer's family join the circle. When the verse is finished the "cat" chases the "rat" in and out and around the circle of children, who keep their hands tightly clasped, and by raising and lowering them try to help the "rat" and hinder the "cat."

(*b*) The last verse may be, "We'll all chase the rat," who breaks through the ring, and is followed by the players eager to catch him. If one succeeds he becomes the next farmer. This variation is especially good for outdoor play.

French Doll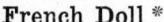

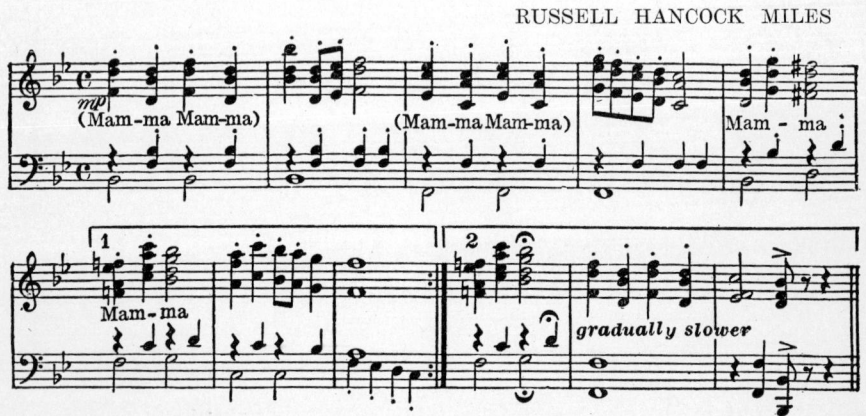

RUSSELL HANCOCK MILES

Here comes our little French Dolly
In laces and ribbons, oh so fine
She's just as stiff as stiff can be
And she walks so jerkily.

Her head she nods, and says, "Mamma."
Both arms move, and she says, "Mamma
I'm as tired as tired can be,
Mamma, Mamma, Mamma, Mamma, Ma----."

DOROTHY HINMAN.

When the spring runs down she can no longer walk or even stand erect so she topples over in a heap.

Music.—The music is moderately fast with the notes very staccato. The unwinding of the spring is suggested by a succession of notes working down to a lower pitch.

* From Andersen and McKinley, "An Outline of Physical Education for the First and Second Grades." Copyright 1930. By permission of A. S. Barnes and Company, publishers.

FIRST GRADE

How D'ye Do, My Partner *

(Swedish)

How d'ye do, my partner, how d'ye do today?
Will you dance in the circle? I will show you the way.
CHORUS: Tra, la, la, la, la, la, etc.

Formation: Double circle, partners facing each other.

Verse

Line 1. Children in the outside circle make a low courtesy to partners.

Line 2. Children in the inside circle return the courtesy.

Lines 3 and 4. Partners join right hands, then left, and turn in order to skip side by side.

Chorus

Couples skip in a circle.

At the close, children in the outside ring step forward, face a new partner, and the game is repeated.

Variations: (a) Both bow twice simultaneously; (b) single circle partners facing. At "Show you the way," all join hands in the big circle and skip or slide in line of direction.

* From Crampton & Wollaston's "The Song Play Book." Copyright 1917. By permission of A. S. Barnes and Company, publishers.

Looby Loo

(Victor: 20214; Columbia: 10008D)

(Introduction and chorus after each verse.)

(Chorus)
Here we dance looby loo,
Here we dance looby light,
Here we dance looby loo,
All on a Saturday night.

(Verses)
1. Put your right hand in,
   Put your right hand out,
   Give your right hand a shake, shake, shake,
   And turn yourself about.
2. Put your left hand in, etc.
3. Put your right foot in, etc.
4. Put your left foot in, etc.
5. Put your head 'way in, etc.
6. Put your whole self in, etc.

Formation: Single circle, all facing left with hands joined.

Introduction and Chorus

Players dance around the circle to the left with skipping, sliding, walking or running steps.

* From Crampton & Wollaston's "The Song Play Book." Copyright 1917. By permission of A. S. Barnes and Company, publishers.

FIRST GRADE

Verses

Players stand facing the center. The action suggested by the words of the song is given in pantomime. The children should be encouraged to make large and vigorous movements.

Round and Round the Village (10)

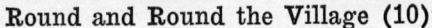

Go round and round the village,
Go round and round the village,
Go round and round the village,
As we have done before.

Go in and out the windows,
Go in and out the windows,
Go in and out the windows,
As we have done before.
Now stand and face your partner, etc.
Now follow me to London, etc.

The players form a circle, clasping hands, with one or more players outside the circle. In this game the circle stands still and represents the houses of a village. During the first verse the outside players walk, skip or run around the village while all sing. On the second verse, "In and out the windows," the children in the circle raise their clasped hands and the outside player (or players) passes **in** under one arch, **out** under the next and so on. At the beginning of the third verse, outside player chooses a partner and stands before him. Verse four, the partners join hands and walk, skip, or run around the inside of the circle. At the same time the outside circle skips in the opposite direction.

Shoemaker's Dance (3)
(Danish)

(Victor: 20450. Columbia: A3038.)

See the cobbler wind his thread,
Snip, snap, tap, tap, tap,
That's the way he earns his bread,
Snip, snap, tap, tap, tap.
So the cobbler blithe and gay,
Works from morn to close of day,
At his shoes he pegs away,
Whistling cheerily his lay.

Double circle, facing partners.

Measures 1–2: Arms shoulders high, hands clenched, roll one arm over other three times.

Reverse and roll over three times.

This represents winding the thread.

Measure 3: Pull hands apart by jerking elbows backward and upward twice. This represents pulling the thread tight.

Measure 4: Clap hands three times.

Measures 1–3: Repeat.

Measure 4: Hammer fists together. Driving the peg.

Measures 5–8: Join inside hands, outside hands on hips. Skip or simple polka step around room.

Repeat from beginning.

Additional Rhythmical Activities

Here We Go Round the Mulberry Bush...........Ref. No. 17, p. 50
Kitty White ....Ref. No. 19, p. 274
Muffin Man, The (Victor: 20806)................Ref. No. 19, p. 282
Cats and Rats..................................Ref. No. 26, p. 177
Here We go Round the Christmas Tree...........Ref. No. 26, p. 157

FIRST GRADE

Hickory, Dickory, Dock (Victor: 20621) (Columbia: 10006D) ....Ref. No. 26, p. 173
Little Miss Muffet............................Ref. No. 26, p. 189
Raindrops ....Ref. No. 26, p. 129
Fairies ....Ref. No. 31, p.   9
Little Ducks ....Ref. No. 31, p. 46
My Dog ....Ref. No. 31, p. 22
Rabbit in the Hollow..........................Ref. No. 31, p. 51
Trotting Horses ....Ref. No. 31, p. 12
Baa, Baa, Black Sheep (Victor: 20987)..........Ref. No. 34, p. 57
Little Jack Horner (Victor: 20212).............Ref. No. 34, p. 12
I'm Very Very Tall............................Ref. No. 40, p. 18
Look out ....Ref. No. 40, p. 22
This Is the Way My Dolly Walks................Ref. No. 40, p. 24
Goosy, Goosy, Gander..........................Ref. No. 47, p. 54
Here We Go on a Merry-go-round................Ref. No. 47, p. 38
Playing Train ....Ref. No. 47, p. 36
Wee Willie Winkle (Victor: 20621).............Ref. No. 47, p. 27

HUNTING GAMES

Brownies and Fairies (6A)

Draw two lines about 40 feet apart for goals. The players in two equal groups stand behind the goals. One group (fairies) turn backs, while the others (brownies) creep up as quietly as possible. One fairy is watching, and when they are near calls, "Look out for the brownies." The fairies then chase the brownies to their goal and tag as many as they can. All who are caught are fairies. Then brownies turn backs and fairies come up quietly, etc. The side having the greater number at the end of six chasings, or of available time, wins.

Cat and Mice

A cat hides behind the teacher's desk. A number of mice creep up to the desk and scratch on it. Immediately the cat gives chase to the mice, who run for safety to their holes (seats). Any mouse caught becomes cat for the next game.

Chase the Animal Around the Circle

The leader presents an object to the children to be given an animal's name. The "animal" is then passed around the circle and back to the leader who starts him around again, this time sending another animal (the children's choice) out to chase him. The game is made progressively difficult by increasing the number of objects sent around the circle, by making them varied as to shape and size, and by changing the direction of the pass. By calling bean bags or other objects animals, a passing game, which otherwise is stupid and objectless to the small child, becomes lively and interesting.

Crossing the Brook (17) *

Two lines are marked off one foot apart to represent the "brook." Each child runs and tries to jump across the "brook." If he can do this, he turns around and makes a standing jump back. Any one who fails to make both jumps is out. Wider places in the "brook" are marked for those who have been successful, and the one wins who makes the longest jump both ways. Children may be divided into groups according to size, and the width of brook varied. A two-by-four board, or balance beam, may be used as a "bridge," which the players must walk along without stepping into the water.

Huntsman

Choose a leader. This leader marches around in any direction he wishes and announces, "Who would like to go with me to hunt ducks?" (or bears, rabbits, foxes, etc.). All the players fall in line behind him and march as he does. When the leader sees that all are in line and away from their seats, he calls "Bang," when all scamper for their own seats. The first one to be seated in his own seat may be leader next time.

Jack Be Nimble

Any object, about 6 or 8 inches high, placed on the floor may represent a candle. On signal the players, in single file, run and with feet together jump over the candle, repeating the rhyme:

"Jack be nimble, Jack be quick,
And Jack jump over the candlestick."

Players who knock down the candle must replace same.
Variations: 1. Several candles may be used in various positions. 2. Each row may run separately, while those seated repeat the rhyme.

Leader and Class

A leader is chosen for each group of from four to eight players. The players stand side by side in a line with the leader eight or ten feet away. The leader tosses the ball or bean bag to the players in turn, beginning at the head. Any player missing goes to the foot. If the leader misses he goes to the foot and the one at the head becomes leader. If the ball goes twice around and the leader does not miss, he

---

* From Forbush and Allen, "The Book of Games for Home, School and Playground." Copyright 1927. By permission of John C. Winston Company, publishers.

goes in the line just above those who have missed and the head player becomes leader.

Magic Carpet

Draw one or more squares on the floor. Children holding hands and following a leader, skip or run through the squares which are magic carpets. At signal all stop. Those caught on magic carpets are eliminated. This may be done to music. The signal to stop may be sudden cessation of music or clapping hands or blowing whistle.

Railroad Train (10)

Each player is named for some object on a train, as engine, baggage car, etc. One person is trainmaster or starter, and tells a story naming all the articles. The player bearing each name runs, as named, to the starter and lines up behind him, putting his hands on the shoulders of the one in front. When all are on the train the starter gives the signal for going, and the whole train moves on its journey. For large groups make up two or more trains.

Run, Rabbit, Run (16)

One group, rabbits, are safe in their homes. The other group, foxes, walk through the woods. The old mother rabbit takes her young ones out to play in the sunshine and look for food. They go softly because they fear old fox may see them. Suddenly the leader of the foxes cries out, "Run, Rabbit, Run!" at which all the rabbits try to reach their homes before the foxes catch them. All who are caught become foxes and on venturing out next time help catch the remaining rabbits.

Skip Tag (4)

All players but one form a circle. The odd one skips around on the outside of the circle and tags another player. The one tagged skips after the tagger, trying to catch him. If he is caught, he must be "It" again, but if he reaches the vacant place first, he is safe, and the other player becomes "It" and skips around the circle and tags some one else.

Squirrels in Trees

Two-thirds of the players stand in couples with hands on each other's shoulders, forming hollow trees. The trees are scattered about in no set formation, with considerable space between them. Place inside each tree one of the remaining players, representing a squirrel. There should be in addition, one (or more) odd squirrel who is without a tree. The teacher or leader claps her hands, or blows a whistle, when all of the squirrels must run for another tree and may not return to the tree they have just left. The odd squirrel tries to secure a tree. The one who is left without a tree becomes the odd squirrel.

Stop and Start

Children run in the direction pointed out by the teacher and stop immediately when the whistle blows. Then the teacher may point in another direction and give the command "fly," "hop," or "skip," etc. Children who do not stop or follow directions immediately are assigned to a second group. The object of the game is to see who will be the last player in the original group.

What to Play (2)

Stand beside desks. The teacher calls one child to the front to be the leader. As the child is coming forward the class sings—

Mary (any name can be used) show us what to play,
What to play, what to play,
Mary show us what to play,
Show us what to play.
(Tune, "Mary Had a Little Lamb.")

When the class stops singing, the leader who is facing the class says, "Play like this," and then makes some motion with her arms, legs, trunk, etc., and the class imitates until the teacher says, "Stop." This child then takes her seat and another child is called to be the leader. Encourage originality and vigorous action.

Additional Hunting Games

Puss in the Corner..................................Ref. No. 17, p. 28
Charley Over the Water.......................Ref. No. 19, p. 65
Do This, Do That................................Ref. No. 19, p. 75
Frog in the Middle..............................Ref. No. 19, p. 96
Hide the Thimble................................Ref. No. 19, p. 104
Slap Jack ....Ref. No. 19, p. 178
Squirrel and Nut.................................Ref. No. 19, p. 184

MIMETICS

Animal Imitations

Rabbits—If music is used, slow 6/8 time. Stoop down and hop on all fours, or the hopping may be done on the feet with the thumbs held at the head, fingers extended upward, to imitate rabbits' ears.

Ducks—Slow 4/4 time. Sit down on the heels, place the hands on the knees, waddle slowly forward.

Horse Galloping—Fast 6/8 time. Right or left foot leads all the way.

High-stepping Horses—6/8 time. Bring knees up high in front.

FIRST GRADE

Birds—Fast 3/4 time. Run lightly on the toes, waving the arms up and down.

Butterflies—Fast 3/4 time. Quick running, with slow, gentle movement of arms over head and down to the sides.

Cats—Move quietly on all fours.

Bears—Hands on floor, close to feet, knees straight, slowly lumber from side to side.

Frogs—Hands on floor, arms between knees, jump forward, kicking legs to rear.

Elephants—Hands clasped in front of body, bend forward and walk, swinging from side to side. Reach out and up with trunk.

Building Stone Wall

With feet apart, stoop and bend down as if picking up stone, then straighten up and thrust hands forward as if placing stone on wall.

Ferryboat

Feet apart, arms raised sideward. Holding arms in position bend trunk first right then left several times.

Follow the Leader

Members of class follow a leader repeating his actions, such as clapping hands, skipping, etc.

Scooping Sand

Stand with the feet apart, gather up sand with both hands and throw into sand pail.

SECOND GRADE

	PAGE
Hunting Games	95
Rhythmical Activities	98
Story Plays	109
Relay Races	120
Mimetics	121

The teacher should refer frequently to Part I of the book as it contains many suggestions in regard to the various activities. For example—the material presented in Part I under "Posture," "Corrective Physical Education," and "Health Education" applies to all grades and should be reviewed frequently.

The activity classifications in each grade have been arranged in sequence according to judgments of their appeal and importance to the children who will use them. In situations where all the content appearing in this grade can not be taught, the teacher should make selections from each classification rather than attempt to teach all the activities found in any one classification.

HUNTING GAMES

Back to Back

Players are arranged in couples, back to back. One odd player who is "It" starts the game by commanding "Change!" At this signal each player must seek a different partner with whom he stands back to back. The one left without a partner is the new "It," who in turn gives the command "Change!"

Bird Catcher

Two corners are marked off at one end of the playground or the classroom; one serves as a nest and the other as a cage. A mother bird is chosen, and enters the nest. One or two other players taking the part of bird catchers stand midway between nest and cage. In the schoolroom the remaining players sit in their seats; on the playground they stand behind a line which is called the forest. All players should be named for birds. Each bird should be represented by several players. In the classroom each row may choose its name, after which the players should all change places, so that all of the robins or orioles will not fly from the same locality. The mother bird calls the name of a bird, whereupon all players who bear that name run from the forest to the nest, while bird catchers try to catch them. In the classroom the birds called should run to the rear of the room, and only then may the bird catchers start chasing them. Birds caught go to the cage. A bird is safe if it once reaches the nest. The players should run and dodge in different directions, instead of going in a simple, straight line for the nest.

Cat and Rat

Choose a cat and a rat. The other players join hands and form a ring, with the cat on the outside and the rat in the center. The cat tries to catch the rat. The players favor the rat, and allow him to run in and out of the circle under their clasped hands; but they try to prevent the cat from following him by lowering or raising their hands. When the rat is caught, he joins the circle. The cat becomes rat, and chooses a new cat from the players. When there are a large number of players, form more than one circle, or three cats may be chosen to chase three rats. In this case the cats are distinguished by handkerchiefs tied on their arms.

Changing Seats (5)

All the players are seated. The leader gives command, such as, "Change right!" "Change left!" "Change front!" "Change rear!" all players moving in the direction of the command. The players who are forced into the aisles, next to the side or rear walls or the front of the room, run to the vacant seats at the opposite side, front or rear of the room. Variations: Pupils skip or hop to seats.

Double Circle

The class is arranged in two concentric circles, one having one more member than the other. On signal they begin to skip around in opposite directions until a whistle is blown or the music stops, when each player endeavors to secure a partner from the other circle. One player is left without a partner.

Flowers and the Wind

The players are divided into two equal groups, each group having a goal marked off at opposite sides of the playground, with a long neutral space between them. One group choose the name of a flower which they represent, such as daisy, lily, lilac, etc. They then skip over near the goal line of the opposite group. The opposite players representing the wind stand in a row back of their goal line, ready to run, and guess the name of the flower chosen by their opponents. When the right flower is named, the group turn and run home, the wind chasing them. Players caught by the wind before reaching their goal become prisoners and join the wind. The remaining flowers repeat their play, taking a different name each time. This continues until all of the flowers have been caught. Each group may alternate in being flowers.

Hound and Rabbit

Players stand scattered about, but in groups of two with their hands on each other's shoulders. The two players thus make a small circle representing a hollow tree. A player who takes the part of a rabbit is in each tree. There should be one more rabbit than the number of trees. One player is chosen for a hound. The hound chases the odd rabbit, who may take refuge in any tree, but no two rabbits may lodge in the same tree. Therefore, as soon as a hunted rabbit enters a tree, the rabbit already there must run for another tree. When the hound catches a rabbit, they change places, the hound becoming rabbit and the rabbit hound. The chase continues. All should have the opportunity to be rabbits or hounds. This may be done by stopping the game and changing players.

Midnight

One player is the fox and the others are sheep. The game starts with the fox in a den in one corner of the play area. The sheep are in a sheepfold marked in the diagonally opposite corner. The fox leaves his den and wanders about the meadow (playground), whereupon the sheep also come forth and approach as close as they dare. They keep asking him, "What time is it?" Should he say, "Three o'clock," or "Eleven o'clock," etc., they are safe, but when he says "Midnight!" they must run for the sheepfold, the fox chasing them. Sheep caught become foxes and assist the first fox. When there is more than one fox they should hold up their left hands while chasing. The last sheep caught becomes fox for a new game.

Moving Day

Two adjacent rows play a game together. The first of May is moving time, and the seats are houses. The seats not occupied and one more must be marked and not used in the game, so that there will always be one person without a house. One player chosen to be "It" walks up and down the street between the two rows. The residents along the street change houses before and behind him. He tries to get a house while it is vacant. If the people do not move often enough the one who is "It" may call "Change!" whereupon all must move to a new seat.

Puss in a Circle

Mark a large circle on the ground or floor. One player, who is Puss, stands in the center of this circle; the other players stand outside of the circle surrounding it. These players may be tagged by Puss whenever any part of them is inside of the circle. They tease Puss by entering and leaving the circle. Any one whom Puss touches becomes Puss. When the circle is cleared, the game is repeated. Those who persist in trying to be caught should for a time stand outside the circle by the leader and watch the children who are skillful in not being caught, but who at the same time are daring.

Ring Call Ball

Players form a circle, with one in the center. This player throws a ball in the air, at the same time calling the name of one of the circle players. The one called runs forward and tries to catch the ball before it bounces more than once. If he catches it, he returns to the circle. If he does not catch it, he changes places with the thrower. There should be a ball for each group of eight players.

Spider and Flies

Two goals are marked off, one at each end of the play area. The players form about a circle, which is drawn an equal distance between the two goals. One player is chosen to be the spider, and sits very still in the middle of the circle, while the flies walk or skip around, clapping their hands as they go. When the spider jumps up and chases them they run toward either goal. If the spider tags them before reaching the goal, they become spiders and must go into the circle, sit down with the first one and must not run to help tag until the original spider again gives the signal. The last fly caught becomes the first spider for a new game.

Additional Hunting Games

Black Tom ....Ref. No. 17, p. 157
Circle Ball ....Ref. No. 19, p. 356
Drop the Handkerchief ....Ref. No. 19, p. 80
Letting Out the Doves ....Ref. No. 19, p. 129
Mother May I Go Out to Play ....Ref. No. 19, p. 134
Wee Bologna Man ....Ref. No. 19, p. 204

RHYTHMICAL ACTIVITIES

Chimes of Dunkirk *

(Columbia: A3061.)

Formation: A single circle. Partners face each other, with hands on hips.

Description:

Measures 1–2: Stamp three times; right, left, right.

Measures 3–4: Clap three times.

Measures 5–7: Join hands with partner, arms extended to side; start

---

* From Crampton's "The Folk Dance Book." Copyright 1909. By permission of A. S. Barnes and Company, publishers.

with the left foot and turn round to the left in place with quick running steps.

Measure 8: Change partners by running forward on the last measure.

Measures 9-16: Sixteen running steps moving counter-clockwise all hands joined in a single circle. Partners may be changed on the last measure by having partners face each other on count 14, joining right hands; then advance to new partner on counts 15 and 16.

Variation: Double circle, partners facing. After turning the partner in place, with seven light steps, each player in each circle moves or jumps to his own left to meet his new partner. The first part of the figure is repeated with each new partner. In this variation the run is omitted.

Danish Dance of Greeting (27)

(Victor Record No. 17158)
Clap, clap, bow;
Clap, clap, bow;
Step, step;
And turn yourself about.

Formation: Single circle players facing the center with hands on their hips.

Measures 1-2. Clap hands twice. Turn to partner and bow. Clap hands twice, turn and bow to neighbor.

Measure 3. Stamp right, stamp left.

Measure 4. Turn in place with four running steps.

Repeat measures 1-4.

Measures 5-8. All join hands in a circle. Take sixteen running steps to the right.

Repeat measures 5-8. Sixteen running steps to the left.

Repeat the entire dance

A-Hunting We Will Go *

Oh, a-hunting we will go,
A-hunting we will go,
We'll catch a fox and put him in a box,
And then we'll let him go,
CHORUS: Tra, la, la, la, la, la, la, etc.

Formation: Two parallel lines of six players each, facing each other.

Verse

Lines 1 and 2. The first (head) couple join crossed hands and skip down between the ranks. The other players stand in place and clap hands in rhythm.

Lines 3 and 4. The couple face about (turning inward without losing the grasp), and return in the same manner.

Chorus

All join crossed hands and skip to the left in a circle, following the leaders. When the head couple reach the place previously occupied by the last couple, they form an arch under which all the others skip.

The second couple now become the head. The game is repeated until all have regained their original positions.

* From Crampton & Wollaston's "The Song Play Book." Copyright 1917. By permission of A. S. Barnes and Company, publishers.

Marusaki (10)

1. Marusaki (1) lives in far Japan,
   She wears a long dress and waves a fan.
   When (2) she makes a bow, she bends so low,
   She (3) sits on a mat on her heels just so.

2. She (4) learns to do writing with a brush,
   Always very careful, never in a rush.
   She (5) makes a low bow and bids us come (6),
   To see the fête of chrysanthemum.

3. Then (7) away we'll haste to fair Japan,
   Each one with a sunshade and a fan.
   When the visit's over, home we'll come,
   Each one bringing home a chrysanthemum.

Notes: Stand in aisle, or in a circle.

1. Point to far away place. Make gesture to long dress and wave a fan.
2. Begin Japanese bow by placing one hand on one knee and drop to floor, then the other hand and knee; drop head at "low."
3. Sit back on heels and remain until note 5.
4. Through eight measures hold one hand as if holding a paper, and make printing motions with other hand.
5. Rise to knees and bow heads.
6. Stand, use hands as in note 1.
7. Move forward for the first line of stanza 3, backward for second line, etc., with short steps on toes; two steps to a measure.

102   PHYSICAL EDUCATION FOR ELEMENTARY SCHOOLS

Oats, Peas, Beans (86)

Oats, peas, beans and bar-ley grow, Oats, peas, beans and bar-ley grow; Can you or I or an-y-one know How oats, peas, beans and bar-ley grow?

(Victor: 20214.)

2. Thus the farmer sows his seed,
   Thus he stands and takes his ease;
   He stamps his foot and claps his hands,
   And turns around to view the land.

3. Waiting for a partner,
   Waiting for a partner,
   Open the ring and choose one in,
   While we all gaily dance and sing.

4. Now you're married, you must obey,
   You must be true to all you say,
   You must be kind, you must be good,
   And keep your wife in kindling wood.

Verse 1.   Circle walks around farmer who stands in center.
Verse 2.   Actions follow words.
Verse 3.   Farmer chooses a partner from players in circle, who continue to walk around as in verse 1.
Verse 4.   All skip.

SECOND GRADE

Old Roger Is Dead (3)

Old Rog-er is dead, and gone to his grave; Hm, ha, gone to his grave.

Traditional North Carolina Folk Game:

1. Old Roger is dead and lies in his grave,
   Hm! Ha! Lies in his grave.

2. They planted an apple tree over his head,
   Hm! Ha! Over his head.

3. The apples were ripe and ready to drop.

4. There came an old woman a-picking them up.

5. Old Roger got up and gave her a thump.

6. Which made the old woman go hippity hop.

Circle, hands joined. Choose Old Roger, who lies down, in center, arms folded over chest.

Verse 1. Players sing and march around circle.

Verse 2. Child representing apple tree enters circle with arms stretched out shoulder height, fingers extended.

Verse 3. Tree moves fingers (apples falling).

Verse 4. Child representing old woman comes in and picks up apples.

Verse 5. Roger gets up and chases old woman.

Verse 6. Roger lies down, old woman limps around circle.

Each child then chooses another to take his place and game is repeated.

Popcorn Magic *

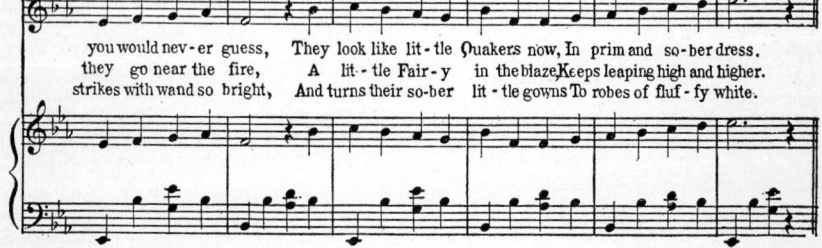

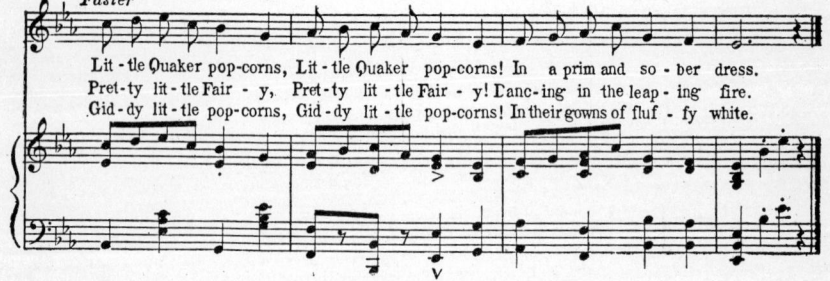

Formation—Boys in a circle; girls in the middle.

Boys—

Measures 1–8: Shake popper. Primary accent, arm extended. Secondary accent, arm in.

Measures 9–12: Shake popper. Four movements to each measure.

Girls—

Measures 1–4: Stand still.

Measures 5–8: Jump once to each measure. Half or a designated number.

Measures 9–12: All jump, four movements to a measure.

* From Jones-Dorrett, "Rhythmic Stunts and Rhythmic Games." Copyright 1927. By permission of Sherman Clay and Company, San Francisco, publishers.

Pussy Cat, Pussy Cat (13C)

(Victor: 20621)

Formation: Hands joined in a single circle. One player in the middle for the cat.
1. "Pussy Cat, Pussy Cat, where have you been?"—Four slides to the right.
    "I've been to London to visit the Queen."—Four slides to the left, and at word "Queen," all courtesy.
    "Pussy Cat, Pussy Cat, what did you there?"—Those in the circle walk toward the Pussy Cat pointing their fingers at her.
  Pussy Cat sings:
    "I frightened a mouse from under her chair."—As Pussy Cat sings she whirls around and swings her arms toward those in the circle, who scamper back.
2. Chorus:
    "Tra, la, la," etc. Repeat music.
Measures 1–2: Hands joined in the circle, take three slides to the right and swing left leg forward.
Measures 3–4: Repeat to the left.
Measures 5–6: Four walking steps toward the center of the circle.
Measures 7–8: Three walking steps backward, ending with a jump, feet together.
Variation—Formation: A double circle, partners facing, No. 1's in inside circle, No. 2's in outside circle.

No. 1. "Pussy Cat, Pussy Cat"—Shake finger at partner. No. 2 standing still.

"Where have you been?"—Clap hands four times. No. 2 standing still.

No. 2. "I've been to London to visit the Queen."—Courtesy. No. 1 standing still.

No. 1. "Pussy Cat"—Same as above.

"Pussy Cat"—Same as above.

"What did you there?"—Same as above.

Nos. 1 and 2. "I frightened a little mouse under her chair."—Nos. 1 and 2 clasp hands and slide around in place, circling to the right.

The whole is repeated with No. 2 asking the question and No. 1 courtesying.

Sleeping Beauty *

The children form in a large circle in the middle of which stands Sleeping Beauty, while in a small circle about her are the courtiers.

The King's son and the fairy are outside of the large circle.

1. Both circles move around in opposite directions.

"The princess was so beautiful, beautiful, beautiful,
The princess was so beautiful, beautiful."

2. The children stand still and lift the forefinger warningly at the princess.

"Oh, little princess, have a care, have a care, have a care,
Oh, little princess, have a care of a wicked fay."

3. The fairy breaks through the circle and proclaims a curse.

"Then came a wicked fairy there, fairy there, fairy there,
Then came a wicked fairy there, and she said,"

4. The princess kneels down and covers her eyes, the courtiers all do the same.

"Princess! sleep for a hundred years, hundred years, hundred years,
Princess! sleep for a hundred years, and all of you."

5. The children in the outer circle take hold of hands and raise them high to form a hedge.

"A great hedge stood up giant high, giant high, giant high,
A great hedge stood up giant high to guard them all."

---

* From Caroline Crawford, "Folk Dances and Games." Copyright 1908. By permission of A. S. Barnes and Company, publishers.

6. The King's son breaks through the circle.

"There came a prince unto this place, to this place, to this place,
There came a prince unto this place, and said to her,"

7. The prince sings alone.

"Oh, little princess, lovely maid! lovely maid! lovely maid!
Oh, little princess, lovely maid, awake! arise!"

8. The prince lifts up Sleeping Beauty, the courtiers form in couples, and those in the outer circle drop the arms and step backward.

"The little princess then awoke, then awoke, then awoke,
The little princess then awoke to be his Queen."

9. The kingly pair walk around the circle followed by the attendants.

"They held a splendid marriage feast, marriage feast, marriage feast,
They held a splendid marriage feast, marriage feast."

10. The prince and princess with the attendants dance in the center, while those in the circle gallop first to the right, then to the left around them.

"The people all made merry then, merry then, merry then,
The people all made merry then, through all that land."

The Swing (27)

(Victor: 20744.)

Words:

> How do you like to go up in a swing,
> Up in the air so blue?
> Oh, I do think it the pleasantest thing,
> Ever a child can do.
> Up in the air and over the wall,
> Till I can see so wide—
> Rivers and trees and cattle and all,
> Over the countryside.
> Till I look down in the garden green,
> Down on the roof so brown;
> Up in the air I go flying again,
> Up in the air and down.

Formation: Groups of three; groups forming a circle around the room. Two children join inside hands to form a swing—the third pushes the swing.

Measures 1–8: Place the right foot forward, sway forward, raise heel; lift the left foot from the floor and swing the arms forward and upward. Sway back to the left foot and swing the arms down and back. Repeat, swaying forward and back for seven measures. On the eighth measure, the child who is swinging drops hands, runs under the raised arms of the two remaining in the group, goes to the next group and swings there.

Measures 9–16: Same as above in new group.

Additional Rhythmical Activities

Rig-A-Jig-Jig .... Ref. No. 17, p. 81
Soldier Boy (Victor: 20806) .... Ref. No. 17, p. 86
King of France .... Ref. No. 19, p. 273
London Bridge (Victor: 20806) .... Ref. No. 19, p. 278
I Want to Go to London Town .... Ref. No. 26, p. 159
Let Us Wash Our Dolly's Clothes .... Ref. No. 26, p. 158
Otto and the Crow .... Ref. No. 26, p. 188
Roman Soldiers .... Ref. No. 26, p. 182
Snowball Game .... Ref. No. 26, p. 167
Elephants .... Ref. No. 31, p. 57
Running .... Ref. No. 31, p. 8
Santa Claus Will Come Tonight .... Ref. No. 34, p. 32
Hey Diddle Diddle (Victor: 20212) ..... Ref. No. 47, p. 144
Hippity Hop to the Barber Shop .... Ref. No. 47, p. 75
Oh, Where, Oh, Where Has My Little Dog
  Gone? .... Ref. No. 47, p. 42
Pancake Man .... Ref. No. 47, p. 31
Seesaw .... Ref. No. 47, pp. 53, 69, 92
Twinkle, Twinkle, Little Star .... Ref. No. 47, p. 126
I See You .... Ref. No. 54, p. 16

SECOND GRADE

STORY PLAYS

Swimming

1. Jump over waves—Join hands along the beach. Teacher calls, "Splash!" as a signal that a wave is coming. All the children jump.
2. Swim around the raft—Make swimming motion with arms.
3. Climb on raft—Jump to kneeling position on seat.
4. Jump noiselessly into water—Jump either backward or forward.
5. Hop, skip and jump on beach to get warm—All move forward, then turning around return to place.

The Fire

1. Fire whistle blows—Breathe deeply and make whistling sound.
2. Crank engine, climb into the machine quickly, release the brake—Stoop keeping body almost erect and swing arm in circular motion five or six times (change arms). Take two or three upward knee bendings as if stepping up and then push forward with the right hand, as if releasing a brake.
3. We must go very fast for the fire is a long way off—Run around in a circle three times.
4. Arriving at fire, climb down, lift heavy ladder from machine and raise it against the house—Do two deep knee bendings, then reach up and lift down heavy object to the ground. Stoop over and pick the ladder up slowly. Go through motions as if leaning it against a building.
5. Climb up the ladder. Rescue a little girl who is shut in her room—Climbing movement. Step through window, bend over. Stoop, pick up object, and put over shoulder.
6. Come down the ladder. Give the little girl to her mother. With one hand holding object, and one hand on the ladder, carry the child to the ground—Do a very slow deep knee bend.
7. Break into a room in the building. Chop away the burning parts—Walk a few steps and then do a swinging movement over shoulder and down between knees.
8. The fire is out. We are tired—Stretch several times.
9. Return to fire house—Slow jog trot.

Indians

1. Paddle in canoe to woods—Kneel on left knee, move arms from front to rear on left side.
2. Walk through woods—With one hand shielding eyes, look all around among shrubs as if scouting.
3. Shoot a bear—Kneel on one knee, stretch arms and aim bow and arrow. Draw one arm back. Make soft, hissing noise as arrow goes through air.

4. Run four or five steps forward to bear.
5. Stoop and pick up bear. Throw bear over shoulder.
6. Walk back to canoe. Paddle home.

Automobiles

1. Pump up the tires—Bend and stretch, working arms up and down. Make sound of "sh" as you pump.
2. Crank the automobile—Join hands in front and make a big circle by swinging arms.
3. Engine starts—Run in place, hands on hips. Increase speed gradually.
4. Shower coming, put up the top—Reach down, arms extended, and pull up.
5. Rain comes down—Raise arms high, fingers move to represent raindrops. Go to squat position.
6. Wipe the rain from the car—Use up, down and side movements.
7. Take a friend for a ride—One child puts hands on shoulders of the child in front and they move forward. Stop occasionally for traffic signals.

Countries

1. Make the windmills in Holland—Children stand by twos back to back with right arms stretched diagonally upward, left arms diagonally downward. As they bring their right arm outward and downward the left arm goes up. The movement is continued.
2. Venetians poling gondola—While walking slowly reach arms forward and then bring them back on the right side twisting the body as if pushing or poling a gondola. Repeat on left side.
3. Scotchmen playing bagpipes—Walk around taking deep breaths and playing some tune.
4. Swiss climbing the mountains—Walk with high steps using mountain stick to help.
5. Japanese walk—With short, quick steps.

In the Barn

1. Race to barn—One group at a time around the circle and back to place.
2. Climb ladder to hay loft—Raise opposite arm and leg. Continue movement.
3. Jump from rafters into the hay—Stand on chairs. Jump to floor. Encourage landing on toes, reminding them that feet make no sound in the hay.
4. Play in the wheat bin—Bend forward to get scoopful. Stretch high and pour it back.

SECOND GRADE

5. Feed the fowls—Each group moves around the circle and back to place swinging arms as if scattering grain.

6. Jump over barrels—Vault seats.

Toys' Jubilee, The *

1. The toys on the shelf wake up—All are asleep with heads on arms. Gradually all waken and stand up breathing deeply while stretching.

2. Tin soldier marches down—March twice around room in military manner.

3. Jack-in-the-box jumps out to the floor and up and down for joy —Jump from deep knee bending with hands crossed between knees, to erect position with arms stretched diagonally upward. Repeat.

4. Ballet dancer trips lightly from her place of honor—Run lightly around room on tiptoes with arms out to side.

5. Rocking horse rocks back and forth—Kneel on both knees in circle formation. Rock back on heels and up again to erect position. Repeat.

6. Animals march out of the ark two by two, the elephant and the kangaroo—Two groups march out at a time. Go once around the circle as elephants walking slowly with body bent forward, hands clasped in front and hanging down to make trunk. Swing arms from side to side and sway lightly while walking. Next jump forward like a kangaroo with bent knees and with arms bent and hanging loosely from the elbow in front of body.

7. Top spins round and round—Two children join hands and spin around.

8. The cock crows. All the toys run back to their places on the shelf—Stop and listen, then toys run lightly back to their places.

Farm Chores

1. Run from house to barn. Pump cool water from well.

2. Feed chickens—Left arm holds box. Right hand takes grain from box and throws it over high fence.

3. Climb ladder into hay loft.

4. Pitch hay into stall below—With one foot forward lift hay with pitch fork and thrust forward into chute. After repeating several times run pitch fork hard down chute to be sure hay goes down to stall.

5. Climb down ladder.

6. Skip into house.

Maple Sugar

1. Put on coats, hats, gloves and boots.

2. Tramp to the woods—Jump over ditches and over logs.

* Contributed by major students in Physical Education at the University of California, Berkeley.

3. Select tree and drive several spouts into the maple tree.
4. Stoop and lift six pails up and hang them on tree.
5. Run home and go to sleep while pails fill.
6. Return to woods and empty contents of pails into barrels.
7. Horses draw barrels of sap away to the camp where it is poured in iron kettles for boiling.
8. Gather wood and build fire.
9. Stir sap as it boils, and then carry sugar home.

Day at the Playground, A

1. Roller skate to playground—Do a skating movement sliding first on one foot, then on the other.
2. On the teeters—Two pupils face each other. One pupil bends knees as other rises on toes. Continue action.
3. Playing hop-scotch—Hop first on one foot around the circle and back on the other.
4. Playing ball—Make a throwing movement. Jump up and reach as if to catch the ball. Repeat several times.
5. On the swings—Place one foot forward and balance back and forth with a swinging movement. Hold hands up as if grasping a rope.
6. Riding home on train—With knees bent place hands on shoulders of person in front. All start forward on same foot. Twist the shoulders as arms move with a backward and forward motion like the piston rods on wheels of a train. Make a chug-chug noise while moving.

Thanksgiving

1. Run to the woods and hunt for turkeys.
2. Carry turkey home—High stepping so as not to fall over logs.
3. Hang turkey up high and pick feathers—Stand on tiptoe to reach.
4. Roll pie crust, stoop to put pie in oven.
5. Set the table for dinner. Shake the cloth before placing on table. Reach in cupboard for dishes, glasses, etc.
6. Run out to play while dinner is cooking—Make a circle. Play a game.
7. Play with the leaves—Stoop gathering leaves. Stand and throw leaves over head. Repeat several times.
8. Return to house—Run to seats.

Pilgrims

1. Cabins must be built. Winter time and snow on the ground—Run to woods dragging sleds. Hands behind as if holding rope.
2. Chop down and trim trees—One foot forward, swing ax over opposite shoulder, then chop, stooping over as you do so.

SECOND GRADE

3. Lift logs on sled—Every other child faces back of room and both stoop together. Pick up logs and place on sled at side.
4. Drag sled home—First child drags sled stooping forward slightly when walking, hands held behind back. Next child, about three feet behind, stoops and pushes.
5. Want fire to cook, so must saw wood before starting to build fire—Every other one faces a partner. One child puts right foot forward and holds arms forward. The one facing him puts left foot forward and bends arms. As first child pulls arms inward and sways back the one facing him stretches arms forward and sways forward.
6. Build walls of cabin—Use hammer, pegs and saw.
7. Run to swamp to get rushes for roof.
8. Use sickle and cut rushes—Take a stride position. Twist body to the right, then stoop low and swing body to the extreme left. Stand erect and repeat movement.
9. Arms full of rushes, run back and place rushes on roof.
10. Dig post holes for fence—One foot on spade, hands on handle, push down. Stoop, straighten and toss dirt over shoulder.
11. Setting in posts—Take post, lift high with both hands, and bring down. Stamp in dirt. Repeat.

Newsboy

1. Run from school to store to get papers.
2. Reach up and take papers down one at a time. Each child counts to himself and puts papers in a neat pile on floor.
3. Walk from house to house folding papers and throwing them onto porch.
4. Skip home.
5. Reach up and place pennies one at a time into a bank on shelf.

Modes of Travel

1. Riding a horse—Gallop about as space permits.
2. On street car—Crowded car so reach up high to hold strap. Conductor rings up fares. Show the correct way to step from a street car.
3. On bicycle or motorcycle—Run in place.
4. In automobile—Run and stop for traffic signals.
5. On steam train—Ring bell, blow whistle, have arms describe motion of piston, and make sound of escaping steam while running around room.
6. In aëroplane—Turn propeller blade rapidly. Climb into aëroplane quickly. Use high knee action.
7. In row boat—Bend forward and backward, extending and bending arms to describe big rowing movements.

8. Use some of the travel suggestions to introduce competition between individuals and groups.

Building an Eskimo Home

1. Eskimos walk through wet snow to site of new home—High knee action.
2. Draw circles with bone to show where wall is to be built.
3. Cut blocks of ice and snow.
4. Lift a block, carry to circle and lay in position—Repeat several times.
5. Stamp down first layer of blocks—Jump with both feet together.
6. Place other segments of the wall.
7. Stoop and look into new home and then run around it.
8. Crawl into house.

Washing Clothes

1. Washing clothes in a stream—Kneel or squat on heels. Forward downward movement of trunk, making a rubbing motion with hands.
2. Some of clothes float down stream—Run in circle once or twice occasionally stooping to catch clothes.
3. Use wash board and soap—Rubbing motion with hands and arms with forward bending of trunk.
4. Run upstairs and get more clothes, come down with arms full—Run with high knee action. Use slower motion when coming down stairs.
5. Use hand washing machine—Motion of turning hand washing machine.
6. Electric washing machine—Twist, with arms horizontal, to imitate modern washing machine.
7. Hang clothes on line to dry—Reach downward to get clothes and upward to hang on line.

The Eskimos

Tell briefly where the Eskimo lives, about his house, how he hunts. etc.

1. Eskimos go out of their igloos to feed the dogs—To leave igloos stoop walking with bent knees. Use high knee action to get through the snow. Throw meat to dogs with sideward motion of the arm.
2. Seal hunting expedition—Skip around circle twice.
3. Cross the blocks of ice toward the seals—Jump from block to block landing lightly.
4. Creep up softly so as not to frighten the seals—Walk without making any sound.

SECOND GRADE

5. Raise harpoon and strike—With arms raised overhead, swing forward and downward in spearing fashion.
6. Drag seal to sledge—With hands behind back bend forward and take slow steps.
7. Seal is large, load it on sledge—Lifting motion.
8. Drive dogs home to the igloos—Run.

Santa Claus' Visit

1. Driving reindeer—Sit on heels and walk forward, backs straight, arms stretched out in front, hands holding reins. Alternately pull in and release reins. Say "whoa" as you pull in.
2. Warming feet—With hands on hips run in place on tiptoes.
3. Santa Claus reading names on stockings—Hold pack over back. Bend forward from hips. Look up and read names. Suggest names. Stand up straight.
4. Place presents in stockings—Reach to pack on back. Bend knees and stoop forward to deposit present. Repeat.
5. Jump up the chimney—High springs into the air, knees stiff.
6. Drive home.

Mining Coal

1. Going down mine elevator—Slowly bend knees to stoop position with knees apart and back erect.
2. Boring to dynamite—Both hands clasped in front, make large circular movements.
3. Swinging pickax—Place left foot forward and both arms raised over right shoulder. Bend trunk forward and strike at rocks. Repeat in reverse order.
4. Shoveling ore into car—Right foot forward, trunk bent forward, arms extended downward, hands grasping shovel. Raise trunk and shovel ore over right shoulder.
5. Push car to elevator—Grasp desks or lean forward, hands against a bench, and run in place.
6. Freight train carrying ore away—Each group represents a train of cars by placing hands on the shoulders of the one in front. The groups move slowly around in circles with tiny steps.
7. Train stopping on siding—Escape of steam shown by saying "choo," at regular intervals.

Coasting with New Christmas Sled

1. Drag sled up steep hill.
2. All push sled and jump on—Face seat and push it with both hands while running in place. At signal one hand is put on desk and

one hand on back of seat, children jump so that they sit on seat with feet out in front of them facing side of room.

3. Hold ropes taut with straight arms. Pull first one arm and then other, as if to steer around corner.

4. Jump off—They jump off into next aisle. Turn, face seat and coast down hill again. Repeat.

5. Toes cold, so jump in place.

Ice Play

1. Reach up high for cap, coat, mittens, and put them on.
2. Run to the lake. Jump over a log on the way.
3. Put on skates—Skate singly and by twos.
4. Saw blocks of ice, and haul onto sleds with pulleys.
5. Warm hands and arms—Swing arms across and let hands strike opposite shoulders. Haul ice to ice house.
6. Warm feet—Hop in place. Skip home.

George Washington (3)

1. A great soldier—Stand very erect while walking.
2. Mounting his horse—Raise one foot high putting it into the stirrup, with hands high holding saddle. Repeat same with other foot.
3. Riding his horse—Each group gallops once around the circle.
4. Crossing the Delaware with his soldiers—Head erect. Place right foot a long step forward. Raise and lower heels making the motion of a boat.
5. Soldiers looking for enemy—Bend body right, shade eyes with right hand, look far away. Same, bending left.
6. Raising the American flag—Reach up first with one hand, then the other and pull the rope. Bend knees with arm movement.
7. Saluting the flag—Look up at high flag and salute.
8. Giving the bugle call—Hold imaginary bugle with both hands near mouth and give a bugle call.

Repairing Roads (10)

1. Harness horses—Good opportunity for reaching and stretching exercises.
2. Lead horses to well and give them a drink—Pump water.
3. Hitch horses to wagon, climb on seat and drive to a bad section of the road.
4. Chop old concrete with pickax.
5. With shovel load broken pieces into wagon. Stoop to lift heaviest pieces.
6. Drive wagon away. Dump load by pushing lever.
7. Get a load of sand and bags of cement on return trip.

SECOND GRADE

8. Shovel material into mixer. Start engine.
9. Carry concrete and fill holes in road.
10. Climb into wagon and drive home.

Moving Day (3)

1. Select a few children to represent moving van with one child as driver—At given signal have driver bring van to front of room.
2. Load van with furniture—Some children can carry things to front of room while others pack them in van.
3. Stoop to roll up rugs. Climb on ladder and reach to get pictures.
4. Shake curtains and small rugs.
5. Get barrels from the basement and roll them out to the van.
6. All loaded. Climb on van and drive to new house—Skip around circle.
7. Unload van—Repeat some of the above and let children add other items.

Lumbering

1. Run into the forest.
2. Chop trees—Put right foot forward and swing arms over left shoulder as if grasping an ax. Fling arms downward, bend trunk forward as if chopping close to ground. Repeat with left foot forward and arms raised over right shoulder.
3. Sawing with cross-cut saw—Right foot forward, arms stretched forward, hands touching. Throw weight on back foot. Bend elbows bringing fists close to chest. Repeat.
4. Roll logs—Crouching position. Swing both arms forward as if pushing log. Return to standing position. Push right foot forward as if pushing log. Repeat with left foot.
5. Rafting down the river—Walk slowly pushing with pole, first on one side then on the other.
6. Ride the rapids—Run in place with high knee action.

Wind, The

1. Wind whistles—Let children make sound of "sh" on inhalation and whistle on exhalation.
2. Running against the wind—Run around room and back to place, chests and heads high.
3. Wind blows the blossoms—Lift arms high and move fingers to imitate fluttering blossoms.
4. Wind blows the branches—Arms swing from side to side, trunk bending faster and faster, now slower as the wind dies down.
5. The weather vane—Raise arms at sides to shoulder level. Twist trunk to right and left without moving feet.

6. The windmill—Swing right arm making as large a circle as possible. Swing left. Swing both.

7. Wind blowing waves on the water—Feet apart, rock from side to side. Bend right knee and swing both arms to right side as high as head. Repeat to left swinging arms low in front and high at side.

8. The wind blows hats off—Run after hats.

Flower Play (12)

Let the child who stands the straightest choose a flower to be represented.

1. Chase winter away—All run to the rear of the room and with arms extended push winter away just as hard as possible. Then all run on tiptoe so he will not hear any footsteps.

2. The rain knocks at the earth to wake up the flowers—Each child reaches up high, then brings arms slowly to floor. Showers continue.

3. The flowers grow up—Bend the knees and sit on heels. Rise slowly and stand as tall as possible.

4. Greet the sun by raising arms high, and dance.

5. The flowers sway in a strong breeze—Raise arms sideward, swaying from side to side, bend at waist and touch finger tips to floor, first one side, then the other.

6. Children run to pick flowers—Run in place. Stoop and rise several times. Gather several big bunches of flowers.

7. Take some flowers home to mother—Skip or run around circle once or twice and stop at own seat.

Spring Play

1. Roll hoops—Run, striking hoop with stick.

2. Spin top—Hands on hips, whirl around in place to right.

3. Play marbles—Throwing marbles. Place one foot a little in front of the other, bend body forward and throw marbles. Repeat, right and left.

4. Jump rope—Run two or three steps, then jump two or three times in place, run three or four steps more. Repeat.

5. Fly kite—Look at kite up in air. Turn head left, bend head backward, look up. Same right.

6. Squat tag—Stoop quickly, then come to standing position. Repeat.

7. Blow feather in air—Bend head backward, blow imaginary feather. Walk around keeping feather in the air.

Cleaning House

1. Open windows—Reach up to pull top ones down. Push up lower ones.

SECOND GRADE

    2. Roll up rugs—Stoop and walk forward a few steps as you roll rugs.

    3. Carry rugs out of doors. Shake small rugs.

    4. Beat large rugs—Kneel on one knee. Use beater in right hand and then in left hand. May use beater in both hands.

    5. Wind carries dust away—Skip around room.

    6. Run into house and sweep floors.

    7. Get rugs and replace them on floor.

    8. Wipe furniture with cloth—Reach up high to clean shelves.

    9. Welcome guests and entertain them. Play a game.

Making a Garden (6A)

    1. Reach up to get spading fork and rake from shelf.

    2. Put them over shoulder and walk to garden.

    3. Spade up earth. Turn each fork over and strike dirt hard to break up large pieces.

    4. Rake garden. Pick up stones and throw them into a pile.

    5. Run to get a wheelbarrow.

    6. Stoop to pick up stones and put them into wheelbarrow. Wheel them to corner of garden and dump in a pile.

    7. Plant seeds—Walk slowly, stooping and rising.

    8. Blow up seed bags. Break them between hands and say "bang!"

Motorcycle

    1. Pump up tires.

    2. Push motorcycle and jump on—Facing seat with one hand on seat and one on desk, as if grasping handles, run in place. Jump through and sit on seat with feet out in front facing side of room.

    3. Sitting, pump up and down with feet to start motorcycle.

    4. Go for ride—Run, steering the machine.

Windmills at Park, The *

    1. It is such a nice day let's go to the park to see the windmills—Skip around in a circle.

    2. The man says we may go up into one and see how it works—Climb up the ladder. Alternate arm stretching upward with opposite knee upward bending.

    3. The wind blows and the windmills turn—Two children stand back to back with feet apart and arms side horizontal. Each bends to his own left, then over to the right, gradually increasing speed.

    4. The beach is right below us, we'll go down and play in the sand.

---

    * Contributed by major students in Physical Education at the University of California, Berkeley.

Climb down the ladder and run out to the edge of the water—Do deep knee bending several times, then run.

5. Race with the waves—Skip toward the water. As big waves come in run back with leaping steps. Repeat several times.

6. Pick up handful of pebbles and throw them out into the ocean—Stooping over, pick up a handful, then throw with big arm sweeps twisting the body to the side.

7. Return home.

Policeman (6a)

1. At a given signal (whistle) all run to report at headquarters (an assigned place).

2. Go to posts of duty—Traffic squad, patrolmen, mounted police, pedestrians.

3. Traffic squad—Give signals. Whistle and stop traffic. Give directions to pedestrians.

4. Patrolmen—Help blind man across the street.

5. Mounted police—Catch horse running away.

6. March back to headquarters.

7. Salute police captain as you pass him on street—One child elected to represent captain.

RELAY RACES

Aisle Pass Relay

Players sit facing aisles. The first player in each row has an object to be passed. At the leader's command he passes it back, in the aisle with his left hand, to the pupil seated beside him, who, in turn, passes it on with his left hand and so on to the end of the row. The last pupil in the row changes the object to the right hand and then passes it forward to the next pupil. The row getting the object back to the starting point first, wins.

Variations: 1. Pass several balls, books, Indian clubs or other objects in quick succession. 2. The first pupil receiving the object with his left hand from player No. 1 changes it to his right hand, then passes it to the next pupil, who receives it with his left, changes it to his right hand and then passes it on. Continue to the end of the row. The object is then sent forward in like manner.

Automobile Relay Race (17) *

Two or more short files of children line up, side by side, behind a starting line which is from thirty-five to forty feet from its own goal.

---

* From Forbush and Allen, "The Book of Games for Home, School and Playground." Copyright 1927. By permission of John C. Winston Company, publishers.

Each file or team chooses the name of an automobile. At a signal, the first one of each line runs forward, around the goal and back, and touches the right hand of the next player on his team this one having moved up to, but not over, the starting line. The first runner then runs to the foot of the line while the second runner repeats his play, and so on until every one on his team has played and the first player is back again at the starting line.

MIMETICS

Bell Ringing (5)

Separate the feet and at the same time extend the arms diagonally forward and upward with hands closed as if taking hold of a rope. Keeping the back erect and heels tight on the floor, bend and separate the knees and pull the arms down in front bending the elbows. Return to starting position.

Climbing Ladders

Left knee bent upward, right hand raised overhead, left arm bent, elbow at side. Change to right knee bent, right arm bent, and left arm overhead. Continue in quickened rhythm.

Elevator

With feet slightly apart and hands on hips, do deep knee bending and stretching in slow rhythm.

Snowballing

Deep knee bending to pick up snow. Rise and press snow into a ball. Move the right foot back, raise right arm to a position for throwing and throw with force. Repeat several times with each arm.

Rooster

With arms bent, raise elbows sideways, rise on toes, and move head backward. Lower elbows and heels.

Toad Jump

With hands on hips and knees bent until sitting on heels, hop forward keeping knees bent.

Weather Vane

Stand with feet apart, hands on shoulders, elbows up. Trunk twisting from side to side.

THIRD GRADE

	PAGE
Hunting Games	123
Rhythmical Activities	127
Relay Races	140
Stunts	142
Mimetics	145
Athletic Games	146

The teacher should refer frequently to Part I of the book as it contains many suggestions in regard to the various activities. For example—the material presented in Part I under "Posture," "Corrective Physical Education," and "Health Education" applies to all grades and should be reviewed frequently.

The activity classifications in each grade have been arranged in sequence according to judgments of their appeal and importance to the children who will use them. In situations where all the content appearing in this grade can not be taught, the teacher should make selections from each classification rather than attempt to teach all the activities found in any one classification.

HUNTING GAMES

Ball Passing

Divide players into two teams, but in a single circle. A basket ball is passed around from player to player. The teacher keeps introducing more balls until five or six, or even more, are rapidly passing around the circle. The balls may be of different sizes and weights; basket, medicine, tennis or playground baseballs. When a player drops a ball it scores against his team.

Ball Puss (10)

Each player chooses and occupies a home or corner. The players beckon to one another to exchange places, and as they run, "It" tries to hit them with a soft ball. Any one hit changes places with the one who is "It." Divide players into small groups.

Bean Bag Box (12)

Fasten box No. 1 inside No. 2, which is inside No. 3. Box No. 1 should be about six inches square. There should be six inches between the sides of the boxes. This should be set up at a slight incline, a definite distance from a throwing line. Each player provided with five bean bags takes his place in turn on the throwing line, and throws all five bags, one at a time. Whoever throws a bean bag into the smallest box scores fifteen points; one into the middle box ten points; and into the outside box five points. The one who first scores a hundred points wins. Bags which remain on edges of partitions do not score.

Bean Bag Circle Toss (4)

All players form a circle, separated from each other by a space. Every other player should have a bean bag. At a signal, each player turns toward his right hand neighbor, tosses his bag to him, turning at once to receive the bean bag which is coming to him from the left. The game should move rapidly, as the aim is to develop quickness and skill. When the tossing has gone once or twice around the circle to the right, the direction should be changed to the left. It is well to have one of the bags a different color from the others, so as to know when the circle has been completed. When the players become proficient in this form of the game, more bean bags may be added, until all players but one have a bag.

Double Tag

Players are in couples. One couple is separated. One player becomes tagger and the other is chased. If the one being chased joins a couple, it forces the third member to be runner. If the tagger catches the runner, the runner becomes tagger and the tagger, runner.

Exchange Tag

Players seated. One chosen to be "It" stands in front of the room. The teacher calls the names of two players who must try to exchange seats before the one who is "It" can tag either of them. The one tagged becomes "It." If neither of them is tagged, two other names are called with the same one "It." The game may be played in circle formation standing.

Fire Engine

Divide the class into small groups. Each group is given a number. The players are stationed in any order back of a line thirty feet from a goal line. The fire chief who stands in front at some distance from the players, gives an alarm by clapping his hands or jumping in the air. The number of signals given indicates the group which runs to the goal line, and back, starting when the chief calls, "Fire!" The first player back becomes chief. If the chief calls, "General alarm—fire!" all run.

Floor Tag (16)

A small group of players form a circle, placing right or left hand on the floor as the leader indicates. Player who is "It" stands in the center. At a signal, the players rise and move around the circle. The player who is "It" attempts to tag one of the others before he gets his hand on the floor. If he succeeds, the one tagged becomes "It" and the game proceeds.

Flying Dutchman

Single circle, all holding hands. One set of partners are runners. The two runners run around the circle, keeping hold of hands. While running, one of the runners tags the joined hands of two players standing in the circle. The ones tagged, retaining their hand clasp, start around the circle in the opposite direction. The two sets of partners attempt to gain the vacant place. The set failing becomes "It" and continues the game. Runners should always pass each other to the right.

Follow the Leader

The children form a single line behind a leader. They must try to do everything he does. He may jump, touch things that are high up, walk backwards, or walk along the top of a narrow board, etc. Any one who fails goes to the foot of the line.

Forest Lookout (14B)

Form in double circle with all players facing center. Those on the inside represent trees. Each member of the outside circle takes his place behind one of the "trees." The one selected as "lookout" takes his place in the center and says, "Fire in the mountains! Run! Run!" and begins clapping. All on the outside circle behind the "trees" begin running to the left. When they have gone around the circle once or twice, the "lookout" suddenly stops clapping and takes his place in front of a "tree." The runners do the same. The one that can find no "tree" becomes "lookout" and the former "trees" are now runners.

Ocean Is Stormy, The (14B)

Arrange all but two players in pairs in scattered positions about the playing area. Have each pair draw a circle three feet in diameter about its position. Have each pair join hands and secretly choose the name of some fish. Appoint the extra players "whales" and place them in the center of the playing area holding hands. At signal the "whales," continuing to hold hands, walk about the playing area calling the names of fish. Each pair that has the name of the fish that they have adopted, called, falls in behind the "whales" and follows after them. When the "whales" can think of no more fish, they call, "The ocean is stormy" and all run for the empty circles. The pair left without a circle become the "whales" for the next game.

Statues

Arrange players along a starting line. The leader, with back toward the players, stands some distance in front, on a finishing line. When the leader says, "Come," the players advance; but when the leader gives a signal then suddenly turns and faces the players, all must remain immovable, like statues. Those caught moving must return to the starting line, and advance as before. Continue playing until half the players have crossed the finishing line. The player crossing the finishing line first becomes leader for a new game. The game may be varied by having players advance by different methods such as hopping or jumping with both feet.

Stoop Tag

One player is "It." Other players try to escape being tagged by squatting on heels. Any player may squat not more than five times, after which he may resort only to running to keep from being tagged. A player when tagged becomes "It."

Three Around

One player is "It." In two concentric circles the remaining players stand, one behind the other, facing the center. "It" starts running around the outside circle to the left. He tags an individual and continues running. The pupil tagged immediately tags the player in front of him. These individuals leave their positions and run around circle to the right striving to reach the space formerly occupied before "It" can arrive. The last pupil reaching said position is "It" and the game continues. To vary game, have pupils walk, skip or hop. If desired, form three concentric circles, thus making four around.

Additional Hunting Games

Hill Dill ....Ref. No. 17, p. 159
I say "Stoop!"...Ref. No. 17, p. 109
Ball Chase ....Ref. No. 19, p. 324
Bean Bag Board..Ref. No. 19, p. 304
Chinese Chicken ....Ref. No. 19, p. 68
Fox Trail ....Ref. No. 19, p. 93
Have You Seen My Sheep?.................................Ref. No. 19, p. 102
Jumping Rope I..Ref. No. 19, p. 118
Lame Fox and Chickens...................................Ref. No. 19, p. 124
Old Man Tag...Ref. No. 19, p. 142
Schoolroom Tag ....Ref. No. 19, p. 172
Weathercock ....Ref. No. 19, p. 204
Who Goes Round My Stone Wall?...........................Ref. No. 19, p. 206
Wood Tag ....Ref. No. 19, p. 209

THIRD GRADE

RHYTHMICAL ACTIVITIES
Bean (Pease) Porridge Hot (12)

Pease porridge hot, pease porridge cold,
Pease porridge in the pot nine days old;
Some like it hot, some like it cold,
Some like it in the pot nine days old.
CHORUS: Tra, la, la, la, tra, la, la, la, etc.

(Victor: 20621.)

Formation: Double circle, partners facing.

Verse

Line 1. Clap both hands to thighs; clap own hands together; clap partner's hands. Repeat.

Line 2. Clap thighs; clap own hands; clap right hands only; clap own hands; clap left hands only; clap own hands; clap partner's hands.

Lines 3 and 4. Repeat action from the beginning. (Counts 1, 2, 3; 1, 2, 3; 1, 2, 3, 4, 5, 6, 7.)

Chorus I

All raise arms sideways (hands joined), and take sixteen sliding steps around the circle to the left; then sixteen in the opposite direction. During the last measure all move to the right and take new partners. Repeat from the beginning with the new partner.

Chorus II

Join right hands and change places, with two polka steps (1-2-3, 1-2-3). Facing partner, clap own hands together (1-2-3) stamp three times, shaking head (1-2-3). Four measures. Repeat to place.

When used in a classroom containing seats permanently fastened to the floor, have the students form a single circle around a row of desks or around all of the desks. For a class with a large membership form two circles with a row of desks separating the two circles. Partners in the single circle face each other and clap hands, as described for the verse. During the chorus have all face inward, join hands forming a single circle or circles; take 16 slides to the right, 16 slides to the left. To secure a new partner, locate third person from you as you face and look over your partner's shoulders. This person will be facing you. Give your right hand to your partner, move forward passing to the left side of partner (to the side of your free hand) and meet the third person. Stop there. Repeat the dance. For Grand Chain or Grand Right and Left, see page 39.

Carrousel *

(Victor: 20432; Columbia: A3036.)

Little children, sweet and gay,
Carrousel is running,
It will run till evening;
Little ones a nickel,
Big ones a dime,
Hurry up, get a mate
Or you'll surely be too late.

Chorus:
Ha, ha, ha, happy are we,
Anderson and Peterson and Henderson and me!
Ha, ha, ha, happy are we,
Anderson and Peterson and Henderson and me!

Formation: Double circle, all facing center. Players in the inner circle join hands; those in the outer circle place hands on the shoulders of the one in front.

Verse

Lines 1 to 5. Circles move to the left with a slow "follow-step" sideward (step-close).

Lines 6 and 7. The step is shortened and the time quickened.

---

* From Crampton and Wollaston, "The Song Play Book." Copyright 1917. By permission of A. S. Barnes and Company, publishers.

Chorus

Lines 1 and 2. The time is doubled. Players continue moving sideward, now using a sliding follow-step on toes.

Lines 3 and 4. Change direction, that is, sliding step, right.

Players in the two circles exchange places and repeat from the beginning.

Hot Cross Buns (2)

Double circle formation, facing line of direction.
1. "Hot Cross Buns."
    Step forward with outside foot, swinging joined hands back. Step forward with inside foot, swinging joined hands forward. Step forward with outside foot, swinging joined hands back. Point inside foot forward and hold.
2. "Hot Cross Buns."
    Change hands, swing around and repeat "1," going in opposite direction.
3. "One a penny."
    Face partner. Point right foot forward. Hold up first finger of right hand to partner and put left hand on hip.
4. "Two a penny."
    Change to left foot forward, two fingers of left hand up, right hand on hip.
5. "Hot Cross Buns."
    Both hands on hips. Quick change of right foot front, left foot front, then right foot front, pointed.
6. "If your daughters don't like them."
    Girls put hands on hips and shake head "no." Boys hold out both hands to partners, palms up, and bow.
7. "Give them to your sons."
    Girls extend hands, palms up. Boys nod heads, "yes."
8. "One a penny, two a penny, Hot Cross Buns."
    Repeat 3, 4, 5.

Repeat music without singing, and dance face to face and back to back polka, moving in a circle. At end of dance each player moves to his own left and meets new partner. Repeat whole dance.

Indian War Dance*

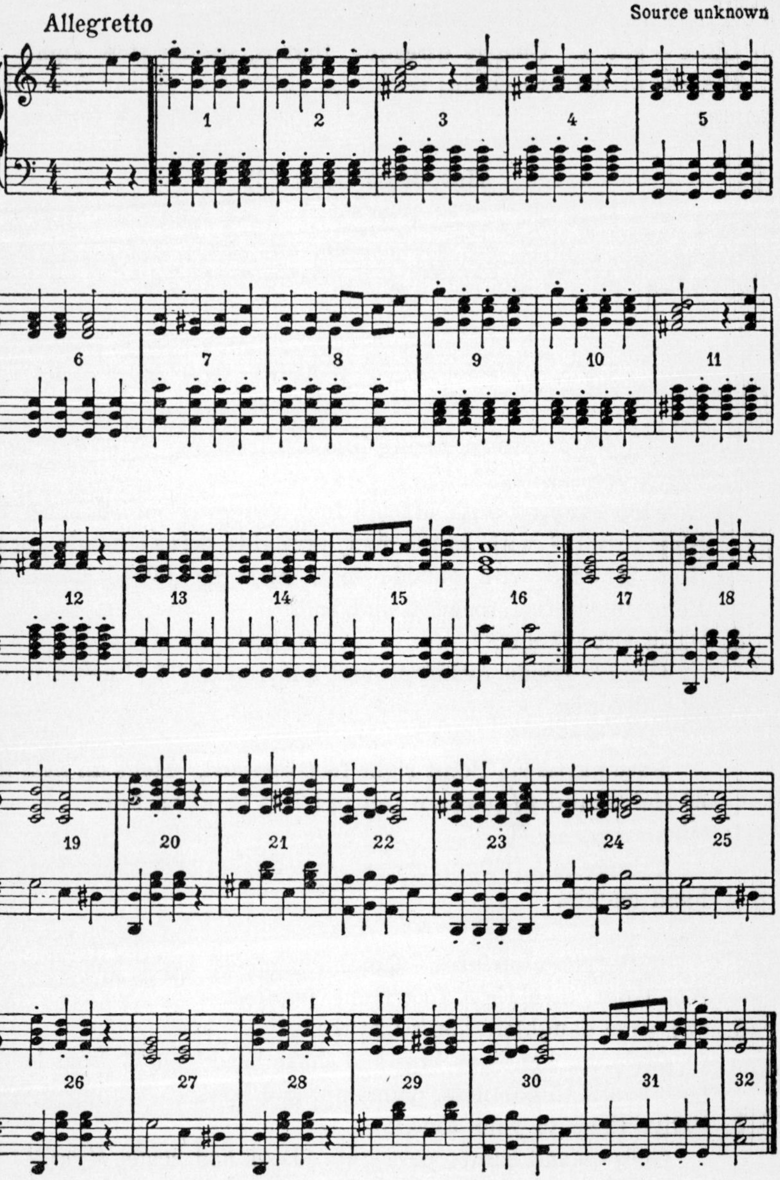

*From Lydia Clark, "Physical Training for Elementary Schools." Copyright 1918. By permission of Benj. H. Sanborn and Company, publishers.

THIRD GRADE

Formation: Seated cross-legged in a single circle, to offer prayer to the Great Spirit and to smoke the pipe of peace.

Pantomime. Measures 1–4: Raise the arms overhead and sway the body forward. Raise the trunk. Repeat, bending and raising twice.

Measures 5–8: Repeat, bending right and left.

Measures 9–12: Bring arms down to the side and raise them slowly overhead. Repeat twice.

Measures 13–16: Smoke the pipe of peace four times. An imaginary pipe is passed from one to the other. Jump up on the last count, fling the arms straight up over the head and yell, "Wow!"

Dance: Face in circle and advance counter-clockwise with Indian step.

I. Measures 1–16: Crouch forward. Leap on the right foot, and swing the left up at the back. Leap on the left foot, and swing the right up at the back. On the second measure take three quick running steps, right, left, right. The arms are bent at the elbows and are moved sharply up and down as the steps are taken. Repeat for sixteen measures alternating right and left.

II. Measure 17: Squat down. Slap the floor with the right hand. Repeat with the left hand.

Measure 18: Right hand over the mouth and yell, "Wow, Wow, Wow."

Measures 19–20: Repeat above to the left.

Measures 21–24: Repeat Indian step twice.

Measures 25–32: Repeat all, ending with "Wow!"

132   PHYSICAL EDUCATION FOR ELEMENTARY SCHOOLS

(Victor: 20214; Columbia: A3078.)

Formation: A double circle, partners facing in the same direction, with left sides to the center and inner hands joined. One odd player stands in the center of the circle.

Description: All march or skip forward around the circle while singing the first three lines. At the last line, those in the outer circle step forward and those in the inner circle step backward, thus changing partners. The game is repeated as often as is desired. When the children have learned this well, the extra player standing in the center

THIRD GRADE

when the change is made, endeavors to secure a partner. If he is successful, the one left without a partner must take his place.

Variation: The two circles walk forward together until words "right skips forward and the left skips back." At the word *back* have the right or the outside circle of players continue to skip forward and the left or inside circle of players about face and skip in the opposite direction. All continue to skip until the music stops or a signal is given, when every one tries to get a partner, including the odd one in the middle.

Little Bo-Peep (13C)

134 PHYSICAL EDUCATION FOR ELEMENTARY SCHOOLS

"Little Bo-Peep has lost her sheep,
And can't tell where to find them,
Leave them alone and they'll come home
Bringing their tails behind them."

"Then up she took her little crook,
Determined for to find them.
What was her joy to behold them nigh
Wagging their tails behind them?"

(Victor: 20212.)

Partners in single circle.

Line 1. Hands at waist. Three skips forward, right, left, right, and feet together.

Line 2. Shake heads, right, left, right, left.

Line 3. Three skips back to place, right, left, right, face partners.

Line 4. Nod heads up and down to partners three times and on last nod bow to partner.

Second verse. Repeat 1–4.

Chorus: Repeat music. Single circle, hands at waist; sixteen skips, change partners.

Repeat entire dance.

Nixie Polka *

A little while we linger here,
With many a joy and many a fear;
Hey! little Brownies, come and frolic,
Let us always be merry.

Formation: Single circle, all facing center, with hands on hips. One child stands in the center.

Lines 1 and 2: The center (A) stands in front of a player (B) in the circle, inviting her to dance. On the words "while," "here,"

* From Crampton & Wollaston, "The Song Play Book." Copyright 1917. By permission of A. S. Barnes and Company, publishers.

"joy" and "fear" all dance the Bleking step four times, alternating left and right. (Bleking step—hop on the left foot, bending the left knee, and place the right heel forward.)

Lines 3 and 4: At "Hey" all clap hands; A then faces about with hands on hips; B places hands on A's shoulders and they run twelve steps to another player (C). At the same time those in the circle take twelve running steps in place.

Lines 1 and 2: Repetition of verse. In this position all dance four Bleking steps.

Lines 3 and 4: A and B both face about on "Hey." Thus B is the leader. A places hands on B's shoulders; C places hands on A's shoulders, and all three run in line to another player (D).

The game continues in this manner until all have been chosen from the circle and have entered the running line. The first runner now grasps the shoulders of the last girl, thus making a complete circle. Lines 3 and 4 may be repeated several times while players continue running in circle formation.

Old Dan Tucker I (3)

(Victor: 20447.)

North Carolina Folk Game, early 18th century. For music see page 303.
  I. Verse: In couples, double circle, march around circle. Chorus: Single circle, facing center, all hands joined. Four steps to center, four back to place. Face partner, join hands and swing.
 II. Verse: Eight slides (or running steps or skips) around to left, single circle, all hands joined; same to right. Chorus.
III. Verse: Face partner, single circle, right hand joined with partner; grand right and left around circle until end of verse, then *chorus* with new partner faced at end of verse. Chorus.

Sandal Polka *

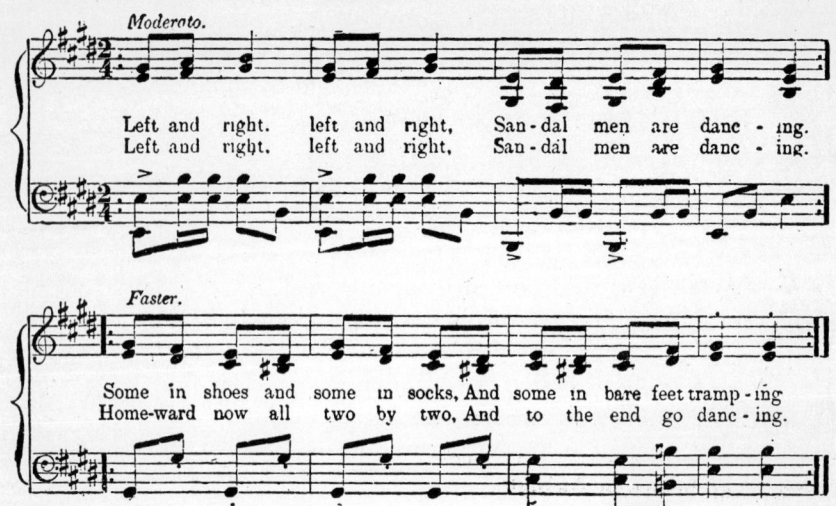

Formation: Double circle, partners facing line of direction. Inside hands joined, outside hands on hips.

Measure 1. Step sideways with left foot and close with right foot.

Measure 2. Repeat.

Measures 3-4. Both hands on hips. With four running steps make a half turn to the left to face in opposite direction.

Measures 1-2. Same as measures 1-2 above.

Measures 3-4. With half turn to the left face in line of direction with four running steps.

Measures 5-8. Inside hands joined and outside hands on hips. Skip sixteen steps around circle.

* From Crampton's "The Second Folk Dance Book." Copyright 1916. By permission of A. S. Barnes and Company, publishers.

THIRD GRADE

Taffy Was a Welshman (10)

A

Two straight lines, boys on one side, girls on other, facing each other.

Measure 1. "Taffy Was a Welshman." Face right, take three strong steps forward, left, right, left, arms swinging (1, 2, 3). Left about turn on 4. (Lines move in opposite directions.)

Measure 2. Sneaking steps back to place, right, left, right (1, 2, 3), face partners on 4.

Measure 3. Three strong steps to center, right, left, right, and feet together on 4. Make a straight line down center, girls facing one way, boys the other, partners' right shoulders together.

138 PHYSICAL EDUCATION FOR ELEMENTARY SCHOOLS

Measure 4. Back to places with quick, little backward steps; arms in circle in front of chest as though holding something (1, 2, 3, 4).

Measure 5. Forward with three skips, right, left, right, and together on 4. Form straight line as in 3.

Measure 6. Bend forward and look right (1, 2), look left (3, 4).

Measure 7. Four sneaking steps around partners to face original places.

Measure 8. Quick, little running steps; forward to original places; arms as in 4.

B

Quicker music, no singing, head couple leads down center to place, all following. Step right, left, right (1, 2, 3), extend left foot forward and hop on right (4). Same, beginning with left foot. Continue through eight measures.

Ten Little Indians (13C)

Arranged by E. B. GORDON

Formation. Part I: Single circle facing center. One player stands outside the ring.

Words: 1. One little, two little, three little Indians,
Four little, five little, six little Indians,
Seven little, eight little, nine little Indians,
Ten little Indian boys (girls).
Chorus: Tra, la, la, la, la, la, etc.

2. Ten little, nine little, eight little Indians,
Seven little, six little, five little Indians,
Four little, three little, two little Indians,
One little Indian boy (girl).

First verse. The child outside the circle runs around, touches and numbers ten players, who immediately step into the ring and join hands in a small circle.

Chorus. Players in the outer circle join hands and slide to the left. Those in the inner circle join hands and slide in the opposite direction.

Second verse. Those in the center return to the outer circle in reverse order on the words "ten, nine, eight," etc.

Chorus. All join hands in a single circle and slide to the left.

Formation. Part II: Each child has previously been given a number from one to ten. They scatter about the room.

1. Music played, no singing. All move in to form a circle with long steps Indian fashion, crouching, shielding eyes, etc. When circle is reached all crouch down.

2. On first verse, as each child's number is sung he springs up and does Indian step in place. When all are up they fall forward and do Indian step around circle, yelling as they sing the chorus. (See Indian Dance.)

3. Facing center in a circle, sing the second verse, each number crouching in turn. When all are crouched the music is played again while the Indians steal away and hide.

The Merry-Go-Round (3)

Traditional North Carolina Folk Game. Use music "We Won't Go Home Till Morning," page 267.

In couples, all hands joined, facing center of circle, odd player in center.

1. Eight slides to left; eight slides to right.
2. Face partner and join both hands; four slides to center, four out.
3. Give right hand to partner, and take "grand right and left" around circle until music stops, when each player tries to retain partner he then has, as odd player in center is now trying to secure a partner.

Additional Rhythmical Activities

Ride a Cock Horse	Ref. No. 18, p. 163
Nest Making	Ref. No. 26, p. 201
Santa Claus and the Reindeer	Ref. No. 26, p. 184
The Hobby Horse	Ref. No. 26, p. 203
Three Little Mice	Ref. No. 26, p. 169
Yankee Doodle	Ref. No. 26, p. 179
Barnyard Squabble	Ref. No. 31, p. 35
Old Woman Who Lives in a Shoe	Ref. No. 31, p. 36
Polka	Ref. No. 31, p. 15
Our Little Girls	Ref. No. 42, p. 42
Swiss May Dance	Ref. No. 44, p. 44
Mistress Mary	Ref. No. 47, p. 139

RELAY RACES

Around the Row Relay

The game starts with all players seated, and with an even number in each row. At a signal the last player in each row leaves his seat on the right hand side, runs forward, continues around his own row and enters his seat on the right hand side. Score a point for the winning row. Then signal those sitting in next to the last seat to run, etc. The row scoring the most points is declared winner.

Bean Bag Passing Relay (17) *

The children stand side by side in lines, with not more than eight to a line. Each line passes a bean bag as rapidly as possible, from the head of the line to the foot and back again. There may be different rules for passing; the bag may be passed only by the right hand, or by the left hand, or by both hands, or it must be touched to the floor by each player before being passed, etc. The line which passes it down and back first wins. If the bean bag is dropped or is not passed according to the rules, it must go back to the head of the line and be started again.

Bean Bag Ring Throw (10)

The players are divided into teams of equal numbers, which compete against one another. Circles 12 to 18 inches in diameter are drawn on the ground or floor, one ring opposite each team of players lined up in single file. Each group has five bean bags or other objects for throwing. At a signal the leader of each row, standing behind the starting line, throws each of his bags in succession toward the circle. One point is

---

* From Forbush and Allen, "The Book of Games for Home, School and Playground." Copyright 1927. By permission of John C. Winston Company, publishers.

scored for each bag that lands within the circle. Any bag that touches the circle line does not count. The player then takes up his bags and runs to the rear of the line, giving the bags as he passes to the first player in the row. The players all throw in turn until the leader comes again to his original place. The row having the highest score wins. Points may be awarded for the team finishing first.

Cross Over Relay (14B)

Formation is the same as for simple form of relay. The leader of each team holds a basket ball, volley ball, soccer ball, or baseball behind a starting line. On signal, he runs to a designated goal line opposite his team, turns to face his team (feet behind the goal line), and throws the ball back to the second player on his team who has stepped up to the starting line. The second player, on catching the ball, runs as the first one did, stands in front of the first player, and throws the ball to the third player. The race proceeds in this way until every player has caught the ball and crossed to the opposite side. The team which has all its members on the opposite side first, wins. If the player to whom the ball is thrown fumbles it, he must recover it and return behind the starting line to begin his run to the goal line. If the player at the goal line throws the ball so inaccurately that the waiting player cannot reach it, the thrower must recover the ball and throw it again from the goal line. As the players' skill increases, the distance from the starting to goal line should be increased.

Eraser Relay

Equal number of players in rows across the room. Place an eraser on floor beside each child of an outside row. At signal each child picks up eraser beside him, changes it from one hand to the other *above head* and puts it down on floor in aisle between him and the next child, who repeats. Row that gets eraser across room first wins.

Relay Race

Mark off a starting line and, at whatever distance is decided upon, mark off a goal line. Teams with an equal number of players line up, each team in single file behind the starting line. On signal the first player in each file runs to the goal line, touches it, runs back again, tags the hand of the second player, and goes to the end of the line. The tagged player runs to the goal line in the same manner. Continue until all the players have run. When a runner starts, his file moves forward and the waiting player toes the starting line. The team wins the race whose last runner first crosses the starting line on his return.

Stoop and Stretch Relay

A chalk line is drawn across the front of the room. Alternate rows play at the same time. Rows not playing remain seated. Players stand by desks facing forward with an equal number in each row. The leader of each row stands on the line holding a bean bag in both hands shoulder high. At the word "go" from the teacher the leader raises the bean bag over his head and drops it back of him. The next child stoops, picks it up, raises his hands over his head and drops it back of him, and so on down the line to the last player, who runs in the empty aisle to the front, toes the line and continues the game. Each time the last player runs forward the players move back the distance of one desk. When a leader returns to the head of his line the race is ended. The players of the row finishing first raise both hands and say, "We win." Clothes pins may be used instead of bean bags. Each player must move back to another desk, or the line will be too crowded. A child not running should watch each row to see that there are no errors.

Additional Relay Races

Lineball ....Ref. No. 19, p. 384
Tag the Wall Relay............................Ref. No. 19, p. 192

STUNTS

Duck Walk

Deep knee bend, hands on knees, walk forward in this position. Place hands behind back, palms together, fingers pointing backward to make a duck tail. Walk in this position.

Rabbit Hop

Deep knee bend, place hands on floor. Move hands forward and bring feet forward between the hands with a jump.

Crab Walk

From squat position reach backward and put both hands flat on the floor without sitting down. With head, neck and body in one straight line, and back toward the floor, walk or run.

Human Rocker

Lie face downward; grasp the ankles, and rock the body to and fro. A rigid curve of the chest and abdomen must be kept.

THIRD GRADE 143

Step Hop (14B)

Step weight on left foot; hop on the left foot as the right leg is swung forward and across to the left. Keep right knee almost straight. Repeat to right.

Dog Run

With both hands on the floor, and with knees kept slightly bent, imitate the gallop of a dog.

Gallop

Do a "follow-step" keeping left foot in advance, left knee raised high, back straight. This is done by standing on the right foot with left knee raised high in front. Step forward on left foot and bring up the right to the heel of the left. Then raise left knee and repeat. After leading with the left foot for some time, lead with the right.

Frog Hand Stand

Squat down with hands flat on the floor, elbows inside of and pressed against the knees. Lean forward slowly, transferring the weight of the body onto the hands and elbows, until the feet swing clear of the floor. Keep head well up and point toes backward. An additional stunt may be performed by leaning forward, touching the head to the floor, thus forming a tripod.

Forward Roll

Place the hands on the floor. With head bent forward, chin touching the chest, back round, roll forward on the neck and back, keeping body in the shape of a barrel. Grasp the ankles while coming up to position of attention. The roll may also be done without the use of the hands.*

* Illustrations drawn by A. J. Schuettner, Los Angeles Junior College, California.

Backward Roll

Standing straight, drop to squat position, then roll backward in a ball, keeping the head well forward during the roll to avoid bumping it. Use the hands to assist in completing the roll. Stand erect on the finish.

Measuring Worm

Place the hands on the floor, shoulder width apart, extend the legs to the rear, feet together, thus supporting the body on the arms and toes; arms straight and body in one straight line from head to heels. With hands stationary and knees straight, bring the feet up (by little steps) as close to the hands as possible. Next, keeping feet stationary, move hands forward with little steps until starting position is again reached. At no time should the body sag. Repeat several times, progressing forward.

Cart Wheel

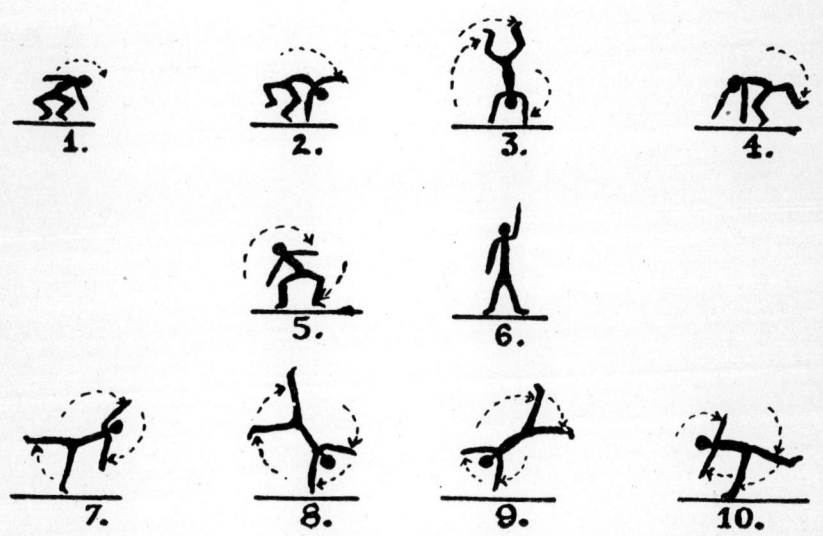

From the position of attention on the mat, jump to a sidestride position (heels about one foot apart sideways), swing left arm through the sideward position to upward, right arm remains at right side. Swing left arm to sideward position, right arm to upward position, bend trunk to the left swinging right leg sideward and upward. Support the body weight on left arm as left foot swings from mat. Continue the circle sideways, feet spread and overhead, supporting the body weight on right arm; then on right leg; then on both feet to erect position.

Bear Dance

Squat on one heel. Extend the other foot forward. With back straight and arms extended forward for a balance, rapidly shift the position of the feet.

Dog Collar

Two pupils on hands and knees face each other a foot or two apart. Two belts hitched together are placed around the back of their heads. At signal "Pull," each tries to pull the other across a line drawn on the floor between them. Hands must be kept on the floor.

Chinese Get Up

Two persons sitting on the floor back to back, lock arms. From this position they try to stand up.

MIMETICS

Bicycling

Alternate knee upward bending with hands held in front as if grasping handle bars. Hands on neck (riding without hands).

Bouncing Balls

Take three soft light jumps in place, turn to right on fourth jump. Repeat to right.

Cowboys Throwing Lasso

Feet apart, place left hand on hip and raise right hand above head; swing the right arm round and round in circles over head. At the end of eight turns throw the hand forward as if throwing a lasso. Repeat four times. Left arm four times.

Furling Sail

With feet apart, bend down and grasp sail between the feet with left hand (clenching fist). Straighten up, bringing left hand to the hip.

With left hand still on hip, reach down with right hand. Continue, alternating right and left.

Seesaw

Three children to a seesaw. The center, standing with arms stretched out at side, is the plank, and the two outer players, each holding with both hands to the end of the seesaw, are the riders. Center player bends right; rider on that side bends knees to sitting position; the other stands on tiptoes. Then the right hand player stands on tiptoes while the one on left bends knees. Continue movements. Players may be asked to change positions.

Skating

Use positions of hands clasped behind back, or hands raised in front as if holding a hockey stick. Slide diagonally forward right and diagonally forward left. Emphasize long steps with rear foot lifted high.

Striking the Anvil

Stand with feet well apart. Swing the right arm (elbow stiff) sideward upward, overhead, and down in front of body, and strike the left hand just over the left knee. As the arm swings downward, bend the left knee and twist to the left. Straighten knee, face front and continue swing of right arm to left side. Repeat with left arm.

ATHLETIC GAMES

Boundary Ball (14B)

Draw two parallel lines sixty feet long and sixty feet apart. Draw a center line halfway between these lines. Divide players in two teams of equal numbers and place each in opposite ends of the field facing the center. The line back of each team is that team's goal line. Give each team a ball (volley or soccer). At signal, each attempts to *throw* the ball so it will cross the other team's goal line. To cross the goal line fairly, it must cross on the bounce or roll across. Balls going across on the fly do not count. Each team tries to prevent the ball thrown by the other from crossing its goal line. The players may move about freely within their own ends of the field but cannot enter the opponents' half. After the first throw, the balls are thrown back and forth at will. The team which succeeds in throwing across the opponents' goal line first, wins.

Dodge Ball

Draw a circle. Players in a group are divided into two even teams. One team toes the circle. The other team is scattered about inside the circle. The circle men try to hit the center men with a ball, the center men dodging to escape being hit. They may jump, stoop, or resort to any means of dodging except leaving the ring. Any player hit by a fly ball on any part of his person, other than the head, at once joins the circle men. The last player in the center is individual winner. The teams then change places for the next game, the center men becoming circle players and the circle men going to the center. The team which eliminates all the center players in the shortest time wins the game. The center players do not at any time throw the ball, they merely dodge it. A circle player may leave his position to recover the ball. When recovered it should be thrown to a circle man and not carried back. When two center men are hit by one throw of the ball, only the first one hit leaves the center.

Kick Ball (14D)

Number on Team.—Five to twelve.
Materials.—Soccer ball or basketball, never a volley ball. Bases, 12" x 12".
Field.—Baseball diamond with bases thirty feet apart.
Pitcher's Box.—Fifteen to twenty feet from home plate. Box is 6" x 3'.
Rules.—Seven innings shall constitute a game. In match games the officials may shorten the innings to five, or lengthen to nine. In case of a tie, the game is continued until one side scores. The pitcher rolls the ball to the batter, who kicks the ball into the field. The general rules of baseball apply, with the following exception: The base runner shall be out if tagged out or "thrown out" before reaching first base, second base, third base, or home plate. A runner must be tagged *with* the ball held in the hand just as in baseball. "Thrown out" means that the base is tagged with the ball or touched by some part of body of baseman or fielder while the ball is in his hands, before the runner reaches the base.

Hand Polo (14B)

Size of Field of Play.—The field of play may be a basketball court or a space of approximately that size, the end and side lines of the court serving as boundary lines. The two end lines are known as goal lines. In the center of the playing field, a straight line about three feet long is drawn parallel to the end lines and called the center line. The object of the game is to push or roll the ball across the opposing team's goal line. Only one hand may be used and the ball must be struck with the open hand.
Ball.—Soccer, basket ball, volley ball or large gas ball.
Number on Team.—Nine players, i.e., three goalkeepers, one center and five fielders.
Position of Players.—At beginning of game, each team is stationed in its own half of court: the three goalkeepers placed at intervals directly in front of their own goal line, the five fielders scattered between their goal line and center field—center player astride center line facing opposing center player. Goalkeepers should rotate to center and field positions after each goal is made.
Serving.—The ball is placed on the center line by the referee, each center placing one hand on the ball. The ball is put into play when

the referee's whistle is blown, by each center's attempting to push or strike the ball to his teammates, who try to push it down the field over the opponent's goal. A goalkeeper may use one or both hands to bat the ball or to pick up the ball and throw it back on the ground away from his goal. If the ball is struck out of bounds (across a boundary line of the court), it is returned by a member of the opposite team. He rolls it back between both teams (fielders and centers), who line up inside the court facing each other about six feet apart.

Penalty for Using Two Hands and for Kicking the Ball.—A free bat on the ground for the opposite team where foul was made. Opposing team must be ten feet back.

Scoring.—A team receives one point each time the ball crosses the opponent's line. A time limit for playing may be established.

Tech Ball *

Field.—The field should be rectangular in shape, with two end walls extending the width of the field. (An enclosed tennis court makes an excellent field.) On the end walls designate goal lines six feet high. The spaces on the end walls below the goal lines are known as the goals. Ten feet from, and parallel to the end walls, draw guard lines across the field. The field between the guard lines is known as the center area. The two spaces between the guard lines and end walls are the guard areas.

Equipment.—Use a soccer football.

Players.—Twenty-four players are divided into two teams of twelve each. There are four guards and eight centers. The guards play in the guard areas and the centers in the center area.

Rules.—The object of the game is to kick the ball against the end walls within the goal areas. Begin the game in the center of the field with two opposing centers, each resting a foot on the ball. (The other centers must be at least ten feet away from the ball.) At a signal, the two center players kick the ball. All center players may handle the ball with any part of the body except the hands and arms. Guards may play the ball with the hands or any part of the body above the knees. A guard shall not hold the ball more than five seconds. Guards are permitted one pass within their guard area. A guard must put the ball back in play into the center area by rolling it in while touching the guard line. No player shall step beyond the lines of the area in which he is playing. A ball rebounding from side walls or the end walls above the six-foot line, is still in play.

Fouls.—Center players playing the ball with hands or arms.
Players stepping over the guard lines.

---

* Contributed by C. F. Martin, Pasadena city schools.

Guards holding the ball more than five seconds.
Guards making more than one pass.
Guards touching the ball with their legs below the knees.
Players pushing, tripping or being unnecessarily rough.

Penalties.—The penalty for a foul is a free kick awarded to the opponents at the point where the foul was committed. The defenders shall stand five feet from the ball until the ball has been kicked.

Scoring.—Field goal—two points. Penalty kick goal—one point. A point shall be awarded the opposing team when any player throws or kicks the ball over the side or end walls.

FOURTH GRADE

	PAGE
Athletic Games	151
Relay Races	163
Hunting Games	166
Rhythmical Activities	172
Stunts	187
Mimetics	191

The teacher should refer frequently to Part I of the book, as it contains many suggestions in regard to the various activities. For example —the material presented in Part I under "Posture," "Corrective Physical Education," and "Health Education" applies to all grades and should be reviewed frequently.

The activity classifications in each grade have been arranged in sequence according to judgments of their appeal and importance to the children who will use them. In situations where all the content appearing in this grade cannot be taught, the teacher should make selections from each classification rather than attempt to teach all the activities found in any one classification.

ATHLETIC GAMES

Bat Ball

A volley ball shall be used.

Field.—The field of play should be divided into two sections which shall be designated as Area A and Area B. Area A shall be thirty-six feet by sixty feet. One end line shall be used as a serving line, and the other as a base line. A base post or goal is placed on the base line at its middle point. Area B shall be determined by a line drawn twelve feet from the base line and parallel to it; the side lines of Area A shall be extended to connect with this line. (Modification of Area B may be made when necessary.)

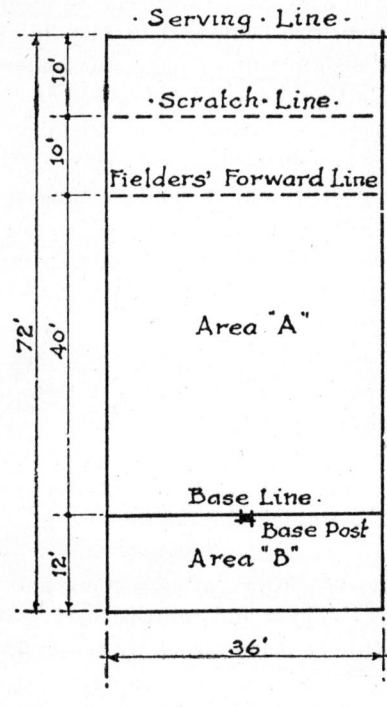

BAT-BALL COURT

Scratch Line.—Draw a line ten feet from the serving line, parallel to it and within Area A. For older players draw the scratch line fifteen feet from the serving line.

Fielders' Forward Line (see diagram).—This line may or may not be drawn.

Match Contests.—May consist of two out of three games, or may be played with a definite number of playing periods of equal length without regard to the number of outs made.

Officials.—For match contests there shall be two officials as follows: (1) A starter who shall also serve as scorer and referee; (2) a base referee.

Duties.—Both officials shall watch the hits, runs, fouls and outs. The base referee moves around, as necessary, to watch the play of the fielders.

Game.—Seven innings shall constitute a game. Three outs shall bring the other side to the battery. (See Match Contests above.)

Number on Team.—Seven players shall constitute a team. More or fewer players may be used by mutual agreement.

Position of Players; Battery.—The players shall be numbered and shall bat in rotation, as in baseball.

Fielders.—Fielders shall rotate field positions with the change of innings. Not more than two fielders shall play in Area B at the same time. When fielders' forward line is used, no fielder is allowed to cross the forward line until after the ball has touched the ground. This gives the batter a better chance to start his run. Fielders may leave Areas A and B when necessary to get the ball, and may run with it back to the boundary line, from which point it shall be thrown to another fielder.

Scoring.—Two points are given for a run—one point for a foul.

Serving.—In serving, the server must stand with both feet back of the serving line. The ball must be batted with the open hand, fingers extended. The ball to be *fair* must cross the scratch line and fall in Area A. Two trials are allowed each player to make a "fair hit," but if on the first service the batter serves the ball over the scratch line, and it lands outside of Area A, an "out" is made by the batter. Failure of the second service makes an "out" for the batter. A line ball shall be a "fair" ball. Not more than five seconds shall be allowed the batter to cross the scratch line after serving. Failure constitutes an "out."

Runs.—Each time the batter (after serving a fair ball) crosses the scratch line, encircles the base and returns to the scratch line (keeping within bounds and without being struck by the ball), a run is made for his side—two points. The batter must keep moving and must completely encircle the base before returning over the scratch line. To encircle the base the runner may try from either side. If a fielder in order to put a batter out, runs toward the batter and hits him with the ball, the batter does not continue his run, no out is made, but a foul by the fielding side and a run for the batter—three points for the batter. If the fielder misses the batter in his throw while running, the batter continues his run. One point is given to the batter for the foul.

Fouls.—Fouls made by either side during the play shall count as points for the opposite side. Such shall be noted as foul runs on the score card. Fouls are given for:

1. Failure of the batter to keep moving. (Play does not stop unless the batter makes the same foul twice during his run, when it shall be an "out.")

2. Fielders running with the ball; bouncing the ball; holding the ball more than five seconds; passing the ball between two players more than twice in succession; hitting the batter while the fielder is running with the ball.

3. A foul is awarded to the battery for each additional fielder over two in Area B at the same time.

4. A fielder hitting a batter before he crosses the scratch line after serving. The batter continues his run.

5. A fielder crossing the fielders' forward line before served ball has touched the ground.

Outs.—Outs are made when:

1. A ball is caught on the fly by a fielder.

2. Failure of the batter to encircle the base when making the run.

3. A ball hitting the runner when fairly played by a stationary fielder.

4. The runner stepping on or running outside the side boundary lines of Areas A and B.

5. The runner remaining back of the base line more than twenty seconds.

NOTE.—This does not prevent the runner from returning to any section of Area A and making further attempts to encircle the base to complete his run.

6. Failure to serve with the open hand, fingers extended.

7. Failure to serve the ball inside of Area A.

8. Stepping on or over the service line when serving.

9. Serving the ball over the scratch line and having it land outside of Area A.

10. Failure to cross the scratch line in five seconds after batting the fair ball.

11. Failure to serve a fair ball in two trials.

12. Batter standing still more than once during the same run.

End Ball (86)

Equipment.—Basket ball, volley ball, indoor baseball, soccer football, stuffed outer casing, bean bag, knotted towel, or a sponge.

Playing Area.—Twenty feet by thirty feet or an increased or reduced area when necessary to make an interesting game for available players. For all match games, teams shall agree on the size of the court and preliminary practice should be on the same sized court.

Number of Players.—Three to twelve on a team. One-third of the members of a team are end men, the others are fielders.

Position of Teams and Suggested Rotation.—1, 2, 3, and A, B, C are end men and opponents; 1, 2, 3, and the fielders, 4, 5, 6, 7, 8 and 9, belong to the same team.

```
        TO·9         ← 12' →←3↨
    ┌─────────────────────────┐ ↑
  ↑ │                          │ ┊
  1 │  I    D    6   ←7    C  │ ┊
    │                ↓         │ ┊
  ↑ │                    ↑     │ 20'
  2 │  H    E    5    8    B  │
    │            ↓             │ ┊
  ↑ │                    ↑     │ ┊
  3 │  G    F    ↙4   9    A  │ ┊
    └─────────────────────────┘ ↓
    ←--------- 30' ---------→
```

Rotation of Players.—Number the players of each team. Each time a team scores, that team only rotates, each player moving one place to a new position; an end man each time leaves the end area, goes into the field and becomes a fielder, while a fielder enters the end area and becomes an end man. During the rotation, the ball remains at the end where caught. It is put in play by one of the end men after the rotation of players has been completed.

Classroom Organization.—If played in a classroom with stationary desks, the opposing end men are stationed at opposite sides of the room in the aisles, next to the walls. The remaining aisles determine the playing areas of the fielders. The rotation of players indoors is the same as when played on an outdoor court.

Time of Playing.—Two halves of an agreed length of time, with a two-minute rest between halves. The referee may call for time whenever it seems wise. At the beginning of the second half, the teams shall change goals, players taking the corresponding positions to those held when time was called. This game gives excellent training in handling a ball. It is a valuable game as a preparation for captain ball and nine court basket ball.

Object of the Game.—The fielders on one side try to throw the ball to one of their end men. The opponents try to secure the ball and throw it to one of their end men.

Scoring.—A score of one point is made if any end man with both feet inside of his zone catches the ball on a fly without its having first touched the wall or any other inanimate object. The team having the highest score at the end of the second half wins.

To Start the Game.—Flip a coin or other object to determine which team shall put the ball in play. The ball is put in play by an end man trying to throw the ball to one of his fielders. The fielder immediately tries to return the ball to him or to one of the other of his end men, and so score.

Fouls.—It shall be a foul for any player, fielder or end man to step over any end, side line or into the opponent's territory with one or both feet. A ball so caught shall not score. It shall be a foul to carry the ball. It must be thrown from the place where caught. It shall be a foul to hold the ball more than five seconds. It shall be a foul to push or hold an opponent. It shall be a foul to snatch or interfere with the ball when held by another player.

Penalty for Foul.—If a player on either team makes a foul, the ball shall be thrown to the nearest fielder of the opponent team, and play shall continue immediately. In case of a double foul, the ball shall be put in play from the center between two opposing fielders who shall jump for the ball and attempt to tap it back to their teammates.

Out of Bounds.—If the ball is thrown or rolls out of bounds on the side lines, the nearest fielder gets it and passes it to the nearest fielder of the team who did not send it out of bounds. Play continues immediately. If the ball is thrown or knocked out of bounds at the ends, the nearest end man retrieves it, returns to his position and the play continues immediately.

Long Ball (86)

Equipment.—In match games, a nine-inch playground baseball shall be used unless lack of ground area calls for a twelve-inch playground baseball. Use a playground baseball bat.

Play Area.—The long base shall be sixty-five feet from the home plate. This base must be placed to right or left of pitcher's position to avoid collisions. The first and third bases are used only to designate and define "fair area." The long base may be a pole, large square drawn on the ground, etc. The pitcher's box is from thirty to forty feet from the home plate, or as agreed upon by the officials.

Players.—Two even sides of three or more players on a side. Pitcher, catcher, fielders. One of the fielders stays by the base. Players must run to "base" on anything that touches the bat—foul tips, fouls, or fair balls, etc. A player must continue at bat until a "touch" is made. If a foul tip or foul ball is made by the player he must run to the base and must remain at the base until a succeeding player makes a fair strike. If a fair strike is made by the player he must run to base and then run home if he can. All players held at base by previous foul balls may run home on any fair strike. Three outs change the sides. Outs are made by:

1. Any fly caught.

2. Any person thrown or tagged out at long base or tagged out at home.

3. Any person tagged running between bases or any person tagged off at base.

4. If all players on the batting side are held at long base this shall constitute a side out.

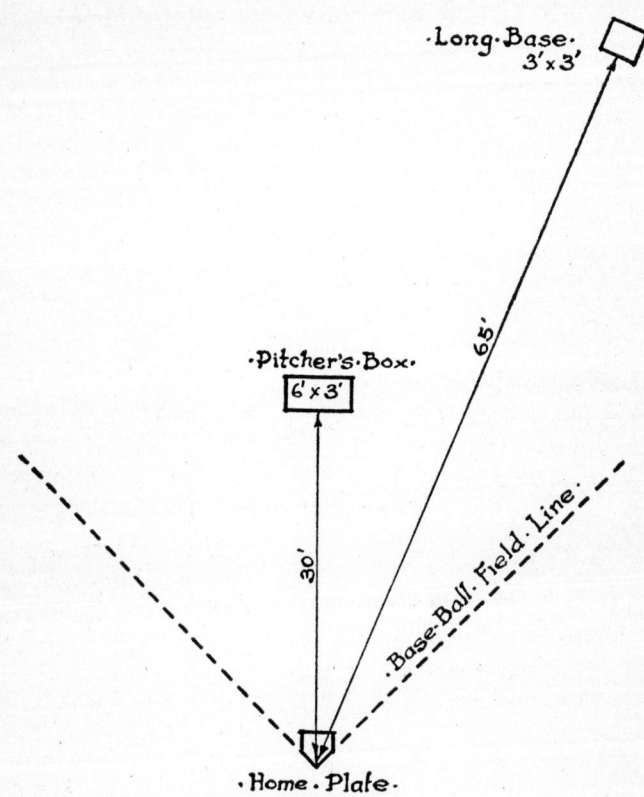

○ LONG ○ BALL ○

5. Any player who "slings" the bat when starting for the base.

Scoring.—A point is made for the side at bat each time a batter reaches long base and returns home again on a fair hit. Several players may be held at the base at the same time and all must wait until a "fair strike" before they can run home and score. (Note: All players returning home must tag the base.) For those not skilled in the knowledge of baseball, and for younger children, twenty-one points shall constitute the game, though a higher score may be agreed upon.

For other players, seven innings shall be the official number for a game. In case of match games the players shall not be less than five on a side and as many more may be used as agreed upon by the captains and instructor.

Elements.—Practice throwing, catching, batting and base running.
1. Throwing and catching between pitcher, catcher and fielders.
2. Catching batted balls in the field of play.
3. Batting practice: Holding bat; batting pitched balls and running to base against time; running to base and back against time.
4. Bunting practice: Holding bat; rest of practice is the same as batting practice.
5. Fielding and throwing: Catch and then throw a batted ball to long base or home.

One Old Cat

There is a pitcher, a catcher, and one batter. The rest are fielders. There is a home plate and one base. After a pitched ball, the batter is out if a fly is caught, if a foul is caught, or if a third strike has been caught by the catcher. When a hit is made the batter must run to the base, touch it and return to home before the ball can be returned to the catcher who must touch home base. When the batter is put out, each player moves up, that is, the catcher goes to bat, the pitcher becomes catcher, the first fielder, pitcher, and so on. The batter now becomes the last fielder.

Pin Soccer (33) *

Number of Players.—Two to ten.

Equipment.—Soccer ball; four Indian clubs or four pieces of wood, two by two by twelve inches each, whittled off at one end and each attached to a base four inches square so that it will stand on rough ground.

Playing Area.—Court thirty by forty feet with a goal area marked on each end line. The *goal area* extends sixteen feet along the end line (seven feet from either corner) and extends four feet into the playing area. Two Indian clubs or blocks placed sixteen inches apart are set in the center of each goal area.

Object of the Game.—To knock down a club of the opposing side.

Game.—The game is played in ten-minute halves. The ball is put in play in the center of the field. It is placed on the ground between two opposing players who stand with their left sides toward the ball. At signal each taps the ground with his right foot, then taps his opponent's right foot above the ball. This is done three times, after which

---
* From Leonora Andersen, "An Athletic Program for Elementary Schools." Copyright 1927. By permission of A. S. Barnes and Company, publishers.

each tries to get the ball away from his opponent. The ball may be dribbled, passed, or kicked down the field, each side trying to knock down the clubs of the opposing side. No player may play within the goal area. (If the game is played with no goal area, the players crowd too close to the clubs.)

Scoring.—Two points are scored each time a club is knocked down during regular play. One point is scored each time a club is knocked down by a free kick.

Out of Bounds.—Any ball passing over the side line, the end line, or into the goal area, is kicked in from the spot at which it left the field, by a member of the team opposing that which last touched it. No point may be scored on a kick-in. At least one other player must play the ball before a point can be scored. If only two are playing, the one

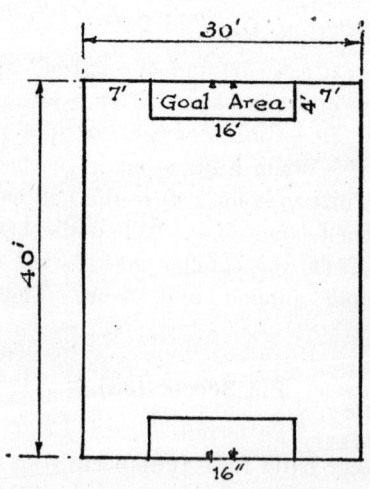

PIN·SOCCER·

who kicked the ball out kicks it in, thereby giving a slight advantage to his opponent who is already in the field of play.

Fouls.—1. Touching the ball with the hands. 2. Pushing, holding, or shoving an opponent. 3. Stepping into the goal area, except to retrieve the ball.

Penalty.—A free kick from the center given to the opposing side. No obstruction is to be offered to a free kick.

Playground Baseball (14B)

Size of Diamond.—Thirty-five feet between bases; thirty feet to pitcher's box. Note: Size of diamond may be increased for upper grades.

FOURTH GRADE

Team.—Two teams of nine players each.

Length of Game.—Seven innings shall constitute a game. In match games the officials may shorten the innings to five or lengthen to nine. Score shall be taken when each side has had an equal number of times at the bat. Three outs change the battery side.

Method of Pitching.—The overhand throw shall be used. The distance from home plate to pitcher's box should be adjusted to this method of throwing.

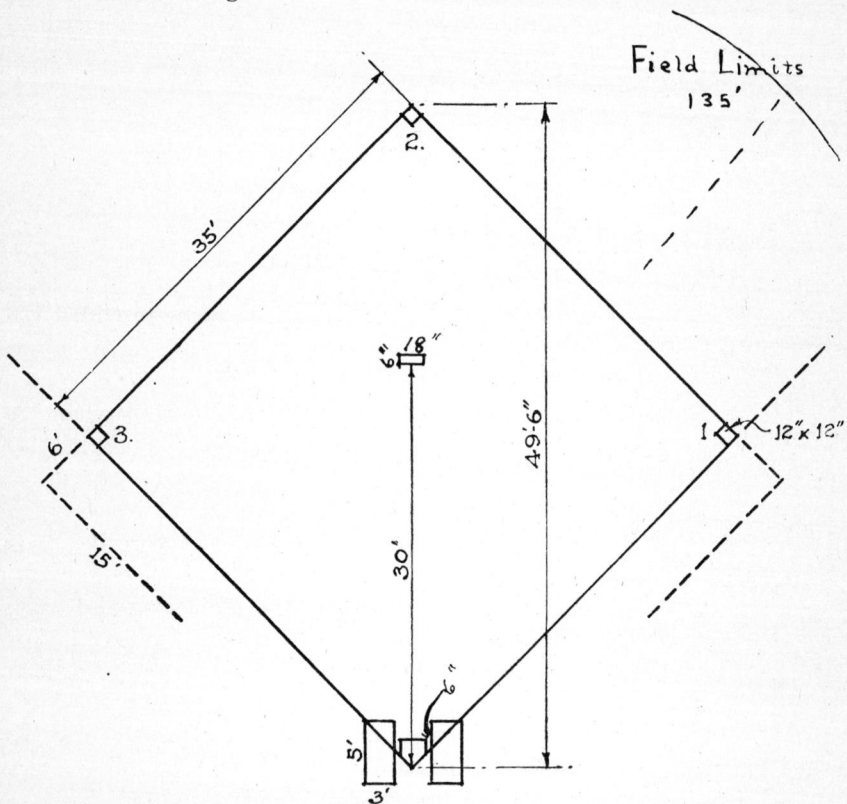

• PLAYGROUND • BASE-BALL •

Equipment.—Nine- or twelve-inch playground ball and playground bat.

Fair Ball.—A fair ball is a legally batted ball striking and remaining in the infield (between first and third bases), or striking into foul territory and rolling into fair territory. If the ball strikes on fair territory in the outfield and rolls out, it is considered a fair ball.

Foul Ball.—A foul ball is a legally batted ball that strikes out of fair territory or rolls out of the infield after striking in fair territory.

A foul ball hit not higher than the head of the batter is a foul tip, and counts as a strike, except on the third strike.

Strike.—(1) A strike is a legally pitched ball passing over home plate between the knees and shoulders of the batter; (2) a legally pitched ball struck at and missed; (3) any foul strike until the batter has two strikes.

Balls.—A legally pitched ball not a strike. (1) Any motion to pitch the ball to home plate, first, or third base without completing the throw; (2) Taking legal position on pitcher's plate without having the ball.

Batter Is Out.—1. On three strikes.

2. On foul tip legally caught on the third strike.
3. On foul fly legally caught.
4. On intentional interference with the catcher.
5. On being hit with a foul ball before it strikes the ground (third strike only).
6. On a fly ball legally caught.
7. On making an illegal hit.
8. On making a legal hit when batting out of turn, provided the error is discovered before the ball has been pitched to the next batter.
9. On bunting on third strike, if a foul ball.

Base Runner Is Out.—1. On running three feet out of base line to avoid being tagged.

2. On being hit by a fair ball.
3. On failure to tag bases when running.
4. On failure to return to base on a fly ball caught before the baseman secures the ball.
5. If the base is left before the ball leaves the pitcher's hand when delivering the ball to a batter.
6. On being tagged while off a base, except when returning to base after a foul ball.
7. On failure to reach first base after a fair hit. The base may be tagged instead of the player in this case.

The Batter Becomes a Base Runner.—1. After a fair hit.

2. After four balls have been called.
3. After being hit by a pitched ball.
4. After three strikes.
5. If interfered with by the catcher.

An Illegal Hit.—Batter hitting the ball while out of batter's box.

Dead Ball.—A pitched ball which hits batter's bat. Suggested that captain and umpire decide ground rules before game, i.e., one base on an overthrow, etc.

Prisoners' Ball (14B)

Size of Field.—A basket ball court or area of equivalent size. Divide playing field into three parts, a neutral territory in the center five yards wide, and two end courts. The two end courts may be enlarged to accommodate more children. The teams stand in their respective end courts, facing each other. A "prison," which is merely an extension of the neutral territory, is drawn from this territory to the left of each team.

Number on Team.—Nine players.

Ball.—Volley ball or soccer.

Service.—Players on each team are numbered and the play begins by number one on either side calling "number three" or any number of a player on the opposing team, and then throwing the ball into the opposite court. A member of the opposing team must catch the ball before it touches the ground, or the player with the number called becomes a prisoner. A member of the prisoner's team then throws the ball. Any one on a side may catch the ball and has the privilege of throwing it back to the other side, calling a number before so doing. The object of the game is for either team to get all members of the opposing team into their prison. If the ball falls in neutral territory or outside, it does not count, but is a "dead ball" and is thrown again by the opposite side. The play continues until one whole team is in prison. However, a team has the privilege of getting back its prisoners rather than putting the opponents out. This is done by calling "prisoner number five," or any prisoner's number, before the ball is thrown. If the opponents drop the ball, the prisoner returns to play with his team.

Soccer Dodge Ball (3)

Draw a circle thirty feet in diameter, and arrange the two teams as in Dodge Ball, one team outside the circle, the other scattered about inside. The outside team keeps the ball in play by passing it with the feet or head, or kicking it as in soccer, attempting to eliminate the players on the inside of the circle by hitting them with the ball. No player of the outside circle is permitted to touch the ball with his hands; penalty for this is his elimination from the game. Should any player of the inside team step outside the circle he is out of the game. The team eliminating the greater number of players in a given time is the winner. Players on the outer circle should keep their places; players on the inside team scatter within the circle to best avoid the ball. If the ball stops within the circle, the nearest player goes in and dribbles the ball out. Variation: Players are not eliminated when hit, but points scored against their team.

Triangle Ball

Equipment.—A playground baseball and bat is used.

Ground.—Triangle for home plate, three feet on each side, with the apex toward the pitcher's box. First base is placed in the usual position twenty feet from the triangle. The pitcher's box, three feet by five feet, is placed fifteen feet in front of the triangle. Any size of field may be used for the players.

Players.—The players are divided into two teams. One team is at bat, while the other fields. There is no catcher, but one player serves as a backstop. The fielders are scattered about any place on the field.

Object of the Game.—The batter tries to hit the ball thrown to him by the pitcher. In order to score he runs on a hit, fair or foul, and immediately back to the triangle, as in One-Old-Cat. The fielders try to get the ball as soon as they can. Whether caught or picked from the ground, they must throw it to the pitcher, who must throw it into the triangle before the batter gets home. An out is not counted if the ball hits the line of the triangle; it must light within or roll across it. When the batters have three outs they exchange places with the players in the field. The side having the largest score at the end of the playing time, wins. When only two play, they exchange places at each "out."

Volley-Tennis [*]

This game is very much like volley ball and therefore the teacher is referred to the rules of volley ball for descriptions of the game, number of players, size of court, ball, position of players, line ball, and scoring. The following exceptions should be noted:

1. The ball may hit the ground *once* before going over the net or before playing on it.

2. The top of net is 3'6" to 4'0" above the ground.

3. In serving, the ball must hit the ground once before bouncing over the net.

4. A served ball, after having bounced, may be assisted over the net by a player on the serving side.

5. Another trial is given server if ball hits net or does not go over net.

6. In returning the ball (a) the ball may hit the ground *once* before being played, (b) a ball may hit the ground *once*, strike the net and still be in play, (c) as many as five players may play the ball before sending it over the net provided the same player does not touch it twice in succession, (d) the ball hitting the ground twice in succession is an out.

7. Reaching over the net is a foul.

---

[*] Contributed by Laurence H. Purdy, Director of Physical Education, Pt. Loma High School, San Diego, California.

Work Up

Equipment.—A playground baseball and bat are used.

The Field.—Use a baseball diamond, thirty feet between bases; twenty-five feet to pitcher's box.

Players.—One, two or three batters according to number of players; the rest all out at field.

Object of the Game.—Each player tries to get into bat and to remain a batter as long as possible. Each player keeps his own score.

Rules.—The pitcher uses the overhand throw in pitching. Outs are made as in playground baseball. Baseball rules of baserunning, stealing, etc., apply. Whenever a batter or baserunner is put out, the players all work up one position nearer batter. The following is the order of advancement: An "out" goes to right field; right field to center field; center to left field; left to short stop; short stop to third base; third base to second; second to first; first to pitcher; pitcher to catcher; catcher in at bat. When there are more batters than one, and an "out" is made, the other batters stay in at bat or on the bases they are occupying, while the advancement is made. The baserunner nearest home is out if he does not reach home before the ball is held on home plate after the last batter has batted, it being a forced run home in order to have some one in at bat. It is the object then of every batter to get around the bases as fast as possible in order to stay in at bat. This encourages stealing bases, and taking big risks. A player who catches a fly ball becomes batter.

Additional Athletic Games

Bound Ball	Ref. No. 19, p. 336
Circle Dodge Ball	Ref. No. 19, p. 364
Square Ball	Ref. No. 19, p. 404
Schoolroom Dodge Ball	Ref. No. 19, p. 369
Fongo	Ref. No. 26, p. 85

RELAY RACES

Arch Ball Relay (17) *

The players are divided into equal teams. The first player of each team stands on a line, and the other players line up behind him, placing their hands on the shoulders of the person in front, arms outstretched. Each of the first players has a ball or a bean bag, and at a signal, passes the ball over his head with both hands to the player behind him, and so on to the last player. When the last player gets

---

* From Forbush and Allen, "The Book of Games for Home, School and Playground." Copyright 1927. By permission of John C. Winston Company, publishers.

the ball he runs to the front and passes the ball over his head. Each player, after he has passed the ball, at once places his hands on the shoulders of the person in front, so that the length of the rows will always be the same. The team wins when the first player again takes his place at the head of the line with the ball held high overhead.

Attention Relay

Divide players into teams. Arrange the players in lines, the lines six or eight feet apart, all teams facing the leader. If there are only two lines have them face each other. Number each group consecutively from right to left. Bring the groups to attention. Call a number. The players holding this number step forward and run around to the right, each making a complete circle about his own line, returning to his original position. The other players assume "at rest" as soon as the number is called. The player first standing at attention in his own position wins and scores a point for his team. Players are not allowed to touch end members of their own team in turning corners. As soon as the winner is determined, bring the players to attention again and call another number. This continues until all have run. The team scoring the most points wins. This can be arranged for the schoolroom, running around rows of seats.

Carry and Fetch Relay

Each team is provided with a bean bag. A circle about fifteen inches in diameter is drawn directly in front of each team from ten to fifteen feet away. At a signal the first pupil in each team runs forward, places the bean bag in the circle, and runs back to the rear of his row, tagging the first pupil in the row as he passes. This pupil runs forward, secures the bean bag and hands it to the third player as he passes. Continue until every pupil has run. The row which gets back in its place first, wins. If played in the classroom all players must remain seated, except the runner.

Farmer and the Crow Relay (14B)

The class is divided into teams. The first player on each team is the farmer, the second the crow, the third the farmer, the fourth the crow, etc. The farmer hops forward and plants seeds (bean bags or small, suitable objects) two feet apart along a straight line. He then returns and "touches off" the crow. The crow hops over each seed to the end of the line, turns around, changes to the other foot and hops back, picking up the seeds on his way. He then hands them to the next farmer, who imitates the first farmer's play. At the end of his turn each player goes to the end of his line. The team finishing first, with every one back in his original place, wins the race. If the game is repeated, the farmers and crows change places. For fairness, indicate by a mark the farthest point at which the last seed must be placed.

Home Base Bean Bag Relay (13D)

As many bags as there are players in the row are placed on the first desk in every row. A circle for home base is drawn on the floor in front of each row of desks as far away from the first desk as room allows. At a signal the first player passes a bean bag back over his head to the next player, who in turn passes it back to the next, and so on. When the last player in the row receives the bag he runs forward with it, and places it in his home base. As this player passes by the first desk in the row, all move back one seat leaving the first seat in the row ready for the runner when he returns from the home base. When seated he starts the second bean bag over his head to the next player and so on. The game is over when all the bean bags are at home base and the players are sitting in their original seats. The row wins whose last runner is seated at his desk first with both hands held high.

Hopping Relay

Bean bags or cardboards are placed on the floor in two rows. They should be arranged so the bags are fifteen inches apart and the rows three feet apart. There should be ten bags in each row. The players are divided into four equal teams—A, B, C and D. Two players—one each of teams A and B—toe the starting line two feet from the first bean bags. At a signal they hop over their bags on the right foot to the other end of the row and immediately hop back on the other foot. The player first crossing the starting line scores five points for his team; one point is deducted each time the player steps on a bag or touches the floor with the other foot. The team wins whose players score the most points. The players of teams C and D hop in like manner and the winner plays the winner of A and B for the championship of the room. Variations: 1. Jump with both feet. 2. Holding one foot. 3. Jump backwards (reduce the number of bean bags in each row).

Hurly Burly Bean Bag Relay

Players seated, rows even in numbers, a bean bag on each front desk. At signal, each front player takes bag and tosses it up and back over his head. The player behind him must catch it, or pick it up, then clap his hands before passing the bag to the next player. The rear player, on getting the bag, hops down the aisle on one foot to the front of the room, and there executes some movement previously agreed upon. While he is doing this, all the other players move back one seat. When he has finished the movement, the player from the rear takes the front seat and begins as at first. This continues until the player who was in the front seat reaches it again, puts the bag on the desk as in the beginning, and holds both hands high over his head. The row whose leader does this first wins.

Soccer Relay

Draw two parallel lines, the first twelve to twenty feet, and the second thirty-five feet from the starting line. Formation for play is the same as in simple relay. The leader of each team, holding a soccer ball, runs to and across the thirty-five-foot line, turns and runs back to the twelve-foot line, from which point he rolls the ball across the ground (as in kick ball) to the waiting player. If the ball is so inaccurately rolled that the waiting player can not reach it, the pitcher must recover it, return to the twelve-foot line and roll it again. A more difficult form would be to dribble the ball with the feet to the thirty-five-foot line, then back to the twelve-foot line, and from the twelve-foot line kick the ball to the waiting player.

Stunt Relay (14B)

The races are run as in simple relay except that each player must perform a stunt on the way to the goal, such as, bounce a ball, skip, gallop, bear walk, bunny hop, frog hop, cart wheel, jump rope, carry bean bag on head, etc. On returning from the goal after the stunt is performed, the child *runs*.

Walking Relay

Arrange the teams in files, not more than six members to a team, behind a starting line. Establish a goal or a turning point sixty feet in front of each file. At signal, the first player of each team walks forward and touches the goal, or walks around the turning point and walks back to the starting line. In walking, a player *must* place the heel of the advancing foot on the floor before the toe of the trailing foot is lifted. On reaching the starting line, the walker touches off the second player, who repeats. The team finishing first wins.

Additional Relay Races

Corner Spry Relay ....Ref. No. 19, p. 360

HUNTING GAMES

Barley Break

Divide a narrow strip of ground into three spaces, each measuring from ten to fifty feet square. The central one of these three spaces is called the barley field. In each of the three spaces are players in couples, one or more in each. The players in the center space must play with linked arms. The players in the end spaces advance, singly or in couples with linked arms, into the barley field, tramping the barley by moving around the field without being caught. When one of the players is caught, he must remain inactive in the barley field until his partner is also caught. When the two are caught, they become warders of the barley field, changing places with the previous couple, and any other individuals who have been caught return to their own field. The players owning the barley field may not step beyond its limits, nor may the players being chased take refuge in the field opposite to their own. Couples in the adjoining fields should venture far into the barley, taunting the couple who have linked arms by calling, "Barley Break!"

Bears and Cattle

Two goals, fifty feet or more apart, are marked off, one at each end of the play area. A den is marked off at the side of the field equidistant from the goals. The players (cattle) are divided into two groups who stand in the goals, while one player (the bear) stands in the den. The cattle run across to exchange goals. The bear runs out and tries to tag as many as he can. The cattle who are caught become bears, and go to the den. These bears join hands with the first bear, who is always at one end of the line, while the first one of the cattle caught is always at the other end. These end players are the only bears who may tag. Should the line break, the cattle may drive the bears back to their den. The last one of the cattle to be caught is the bear in the next game.

Boiler Burst, The (3)

Arrange the seats so there is one more player than there are seats. This extra player stands at the front of the room and begins a story. At its most dramatic point, the narrator says "and then—the boiler burst!" when all players must change seats, while the narrator tries to secure a seat for himself. The game continues with the odd player as "it."

Circle Chase (14B)

Arrange the group in a circle, players standing elbow distance apart, facing in. Have the group count off by fours. At a signal, call a number—any number from one to four. All players bearing the number, step back and run around the circle, each runner attempting to tag the player in front of him. Runners tagged are eliminated and withdrawn. Runners who tag a player continue about the circle attempting to tag another. Runners who are not eliminated, upon arriving at their starting point, step into it. Another number is called—these players run as before. Continue this until all numbers have been called. Reform the circle with those who have not been tagged and again count off by fours. Call each number as before, those eliminated withdrawing. Continue in this manner until all but four players are left—these are the winners. This game may be varied according to the number of players by having the players run two, three or four times around the circle, or by having the players count off twos, threes, fives or sixes.

Circle Race

Players first stand in a circle facing the center, arm's distance apart. They then turn right (around in single file in the same direction). At a signal all start to run around the circle, each trying to pass on the outside the runner next in front of him. Any player passed drops into the center of the circle and is out of the race. The last player wins. When a signal is given by the leader, the circle turns about and runs in the opposite direction. This reverses the relative position of runners and adds fun to the game.

Come Along

Players stand shoulder to shoulder. When a player is chosen the other players do *not* close in, but leave the area vacant. An odd player skipping around inside the circle pulls a player out, saying, "Come along." Keeping their hands joined, the second player pulls out another, the third, a fourth, etc. When the signal is given, or the music stops, every one skipping runs for a vacant space.

Gathering Sticks

Draw a line across the middle of the play area. A goal six feet by four feet is marked at each end of the play area and equidistant from the center of the middle line. Six sticks are placed in each goal. Two captains are appointed and sides are chosen. Distinguish the players on one side in some way. The two sides form in two rows facing each other, one on each side of the middle line. The captains may, if they wish, appoint some of their men as runners and some as guards for the goal. These guards must stand at least twelve feet from the goal, but if an opponent passes them on his way to their goal, they may, of course, chase him. The object of the game is to carry away all the sticks from the goal of the opposing side. A player may be caught as soon as he has both feet in the enemy's territory. If he reaches the goal without being caught, he may take one stick to his own side without being tagged. If he is caught he must stand in the goal as prisoner until rescued by some one from his own side. While he is prisoner, he may reach out towards the one who is coming to release him, but must keep both feet within the goal. After a player has reached him without being tagged, he and his rescuer may return to their own side in safety. While any member of one side is a prisoner, that side may not take any sticks from its opponents' goal. The prisoners must be rescued first. The game is won by the side which first carries away all of its opponents' sticks.

Inner Circle Ball (14B)

Arrange players in a double circle, each outer circle player standing four feet behind a member of the inner circle, all facing in. At signal, players of the inner circle pass the balls among themselves. Any player who is responsible for a ball striking the floor, either through a poor throw or a failure to catch the ball, changes places with the player in back of him. The ball is recovered and at signal the game continues. After the players become skilled, require those who are in the inside circle to keep both feet on the floor. In this case, moving either foot also forces a player into the outside circle. The players in the outside circle should not interfere with the players of the inside circle. If balls collide while being passed no exchange is made.

Last One Out

This game is played one row at a time, or alternate rows. The children in the row stand, and one more child joins them, making one more player than there are seats in the row. They start running around the row of seats. When the teacher claps his hands they all try to get a seat. The one failing makes the odd one when the next row runs.

Link Tag

Designate a base. Two players link hands and attempt to tag the other players. All players tagged take their places between the two first players, the chain growing longer with each new addition. The players being chased may break the chain if pressed too closely. If successful in this, those forming the chain must unite again before continuing the tagging. Players dropping out to rest must return to base and remain there until they reënter the game. Players may not return to base to escape being tagged. The last two players caught must begin the game anew.

Oyster Shell

Draw two parallel lines, three feet apart, across the center of the playground. This space is neutral territory. Forty to sixty feet beyond, and parallel to these lines, draw two lines. The space beyond this second line is a safety area for those playing on that side. Divide players into two equal teams which take their places, one on either side of the neutral territory, all members toeing their line with one foot. Each party chooses a color, light or dark, corresponding to the light or dark side of an oyster shell or some other small object which is used in the game. An odd player who acts as leader takes his place at either end or in the center of the neutral territory and tosses the "oyster" shell into the air. If sides are equal and no such leader is available, the teams may choose captains to toss the shell alternately. Throw the shell so it falls in the neutral territory. If the light side is upward, the members of that team must turn and run for their safety area, the other team chasing them. Any one tagged must return and play with the opposite team. Those chasing should tag as many as possible. The team wins which secures all the opponents, or has the largest number of players when the game is stopped.

Poison Seat

Children sit at desks. Place a book on each empty desk. Also place a book on one additional desk. At signal, all pupils change seats, trying to get one without a book, as the seats with books are poisoned. The player failing to get a seat goes to the back of the room. After each trial place a book on another occupied seat. Continue giving signal until all but two are eliminated. These are the winners. As a variation, seats may be raised instead of books being placed on desks. On changing seats, children may skip, run or march to phonograph music or to a melody sung by children who have been eliminated from the game.

Simon Says

The players stand. One is chosen leader, whom the others follow. The leader says, "Simon says, 'Jump,' " whereupon he begins jumping, as do all the players. He may say, "Simon says, 'Stop.' " All the players should then stand still. If he says only "stop," any players who stop are caught and must sit down or squat. Only Simon must be obeyed, so the words "Simon says" are necessary to start or stop any activity. The last player to remain standing wins the game. Many active movements, rather than passive ones, should be used.

Tip Cat

A piece of broom handle six inches long is sharpened at both ends, leaving two inches in the center unsharpened. This is called the "cat." A batter puts the cat in the center of a circle eighteen inches in diameter, and hits the end of the "cat" with a stick. The stick should be about one inch in diameter, eighteen inches long and sharpened like a blade at one end. As the "cat" flies into the air the batter hits it again with his stick and knocks it away if he can. If it falls inside the circle the batter is out. If it falls outside he guesses how many jumps his opponent can have from the edge of the circle to the cat. If the jumper fails to jump the distance in the number of counts allowed, the batter adds this number to his score. If the jumper succeeds he becomes batter. If a player can bounce the cat several times in the air before knocking it away, each bounce counts him one point. The one having most points after ten innings wins. The batter may hit the "cat" in the circle only once.

Two Deep

A group of players in single circle formation stand arm's length apart and face the center. Select one player as a runner and another as a chaser. The chaser attempts to tag the runner, who tries to escape by running around the outside of the circle and jumping in front of a player where he is safe. This should occur early in his run. The runner, plus the one in front of whom he has taken refuge, makes two deep. The player to the rear is now compelled to run to try to escape being tagged. If the chaser catches the runner, the runner becomes the chaser, and the former chaser the runner. Groups of six to fifteen may play in one circle. Above that number divide the class into two or three groups according to the number of pupils. When playing with a double circle the game becomes "three deep."

Additional Hunting Games

Bear in the Pit	Ref. No. 17, p. 119
Bull in the Ring	Ref. No. 17, p. 119
Animal Chase	Ref. No. 19, p. 46
Farmer is Coming	Ref. No. 19, p. 85
Home Tag	Ref. No. 19, p. 106
Jumping Rope II	Ref. No. 19, p. 119
Target Toss	Ref. No. 19, p. 315

RHYTHMICAL ACTIVITIES

Broom Dance (9A)

One, two, three, four, five, six, seven;
Where's my partner, nine, ten, eleven?
In Berlin, in Stettin,
There's the place to find him in.
Repeat with: "Tra, la, la, etc."

(Victor: 20448.)

Formation: A circle of couples, partners facing. An odd child stands in the center of the circle with a broom in his hand.

Measures 1–8: As the class marches around the circle, the child with the broom gives it to some one in the circle, at the same time taking his place. The one who receives the broom quickly runs with it to some one else, taking this new place, and so it goes around the circle. The one who has the broom as the last word of the song is sung takes it to the center.

Measures 9–16: While the remainder of the class skips gaily around the circle singing, "Tra, la, la," this one must dance alone in the center with the broom. He then starts the play the next time by passing the broom to another child.

Variation: Players form two lines. Lines face each other with broom man between them. Lines advance until "seven." Lines retreat until "eleven." Lines advance until "Stettin." Lines retreat until "in" when all rush for a partner including the broom man. When partner is secured, skip around the room, thereby disclosing the odd player. To form lines again one partner goes to one side and the second partner to the opposite side of the room. They should *not* remain together. The fun is lessened if the players rush forward before singing the word "in." Game is repeated with the new broom man in the middle.

FOURTH GRADE

Children's Polka *

(Columbia: A3052.)

Formation: Single circle. Partners face each other. Join hands, arms extended at sides, shoulder high.

Measures 1–8: Glide polka towards center—slide, close, slide, close, three running steps in place. Repeat moving outward two measures. Repeat the whole step four measures.

* From C. Ward Crampton, "The Folk Dance Book." Copyright 1909. By permission of A. S. Barnes and Company, publishers.

174 PHYSICAL EDUCATION FOR ELEMENTARY SCHOOLS

Measures 9-12: Clap thighs with both hands. Clap own hands in slow time. Clap partner's hands three times in quick time. Repeat.

Measures 13-14: Point right toe forward, place right elbow in left hand, and shake finger at partner three times. Repeat left.

Measure 15: Turn complete circle right, with four jumps.

Measure 16: Stamp three times.

Repeat from beginning.

Comin' Through the Rye (4)

Formation: Double circle, partners facing.

a. Measures 1-2: Step back left, step back right, step back left, bow, rise, bring right foot beside left.

b. Measures 3-4: Step forward left, step forward right, step forward left, bow, swaying weight forward on left, replace right foot.

c. Measure 5: Raise arm sideward, embrace partner, arm sideward, arm down.

Measure 6: Right face twice.

d. Measures 7-8: Step forward left foot and bring right foot beside it, looking over right shoulder at partner, repeat right, left, right, always bringing feet together on the even counts and looking over shoulder.

e. Measure 9: Turn around to left and run back to partner four steps, left, right, left, right.

Measure 10: Step sideward left and bow, same right.

f. Measures 3-4: Face line of direction and join inside hands.

Touch outside foot forward, same sideward, same backward, bending forward and looking at partner (the last count is a hold). Slide forward three times and hold.

Measures 5–10: Repeat f three times.

g. Measures 3–4: Touch outside foot forward, same sideward, same backward, bending forward and looking at partner. All face partners. On the third count of measure 4 the outside girl pretends to slap the inside one, while the inside one slaps her own hands low down.

h. Measure 5: Outside girl turns and runs three steps away, bringing feet together on fourth count. She stands in place and twists her shoulders disdainfully.

i. Measures 6–7: Inside girl turns and runs three steps to partner, bringing feet together on fourth count. She then tries to get the attention of her partner by poking her in the back four times.

j. Measure 8: Outside girl turns around and pretends to slap her, while inside girl slaps her own hands. Inside girl pretends to slap outside girl.

Measure 9: Repeat j.

k. Measure 10: Put left foot forward and turn scornfully from partner (outside girl puts right foot forward). Turn to partner and shake hands four times, put arms around each other and run off.

Dutch Couple Dance (13C)

(Music: Where, Oh, Where, Has My Little Dog Gone?)

Formation: Double circle facing counter-clockwise. Partners' inside hands joined.

Measures 1–6: Six Dutch steps forward. Step on the inside foot with a stamp (count 1). Swing the other foot across the body, brushing foot on the floor (count 2). Hop inside foot (count 3). Repeat five times.

Measures 7–8: Turn away from partner and face in the opposite direction with four light hops on both feet, holding last position for two counts.

Measures 1–8: Repeat measures 1–8 ending facing partner, in double circle, girls' backs to the center.

Measures 9–12: Four step hops away from partner.

Measures 13–16: Repeat measures 9–12, going forward toward partner.

Measures 17–22: Dutch waltz six times right and left as follows: Join both hands with partner, arms raised shoulder level. Step on the right foot (girls); hop and raise the left leg to the side. (Boys just the opposite.) The body is bent toward the side on which the hopping is done.

Measures 23–24: Four little hops on both feet in place, holding last position for two counts. End facing forward to repeat dance from the beginning.

178 PHYSICAL EDUCATION FOR ELEMENTARY SCHOOLS

Hansel and Gretel*

*From C. Ward Crampton, "The Second Folk Dance Book." Copyright 1916. By permission of A. S. Barnes and Company, publishers.

FOURTH GRADE

Formation. Double circle, facing partners.

Measures 1-2. Step away from partner and courtesy. Return to position.

Measures 3-4. Take partner's both hands.

Measure 5. Point forward toe to side, point forward toe in back.

Measure 6. Polka step in line of direction.

Measures 7-8. Same as in measures 5-6, but in opposite direction.

Measures 9-16. All partners skip sixteen steps around circle with inside hands joined, outside hands on hips.

Measure 17. Stand still.

Measure 18. Stamp three times, right, left, right.

Measure 19. Stand still.

Measure 20. Clap three times. Take partner's both hands.

Measures 21-24. Same as measures 5-8.

Repeat dance. At measure 18, nod three times. At measure 20, snap fingers three times.

180 PHYSICAL EDUCATION FOR ELEMENTARY SCHOOLS

Indian Hunters (Boys) *

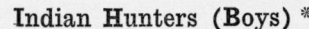

* From Jones-Dorrett, "Rhythmic Dances and Rhythmic Games." Copyright 1927. By permission of Sherman Clay and Company, San Francisco, publishers.

This description was written for a group of grammar grade boys. They transformed a large platform into a hunting ground. In the right-hand corner was massed a quantity of underbrush. At the back sufficient branches were placed cleverly, to conceal the approaching Indians. The boys wore Indian costumes and carried bows and arrows.

Measures 1–4: Chief appears, crawling slowly, cautiously, from beneath the branches at the back—moving in rhythm, one movement to each measure.

Measures 5–8: Chief stands erect, looks about, moves slowly, beckons to the others who (repeat) crawl from beneath the underbrush and branches.

Measures 9–19: Chief forms circle, using hop dance step.

Measure 20: Increase tempo suddenly.

Measures 21–24: All rush toward underbrush shooting into it; crawl out of sight.

Measures 25–32: Return with bear. Use high stepping skip step and form circle around the two carrying the bear.

Measures 33–42: All dance, using the war dance step.

(Repeat) On the repeat pick up bear and journey home.

(Hop dance—Two little hops on each foot, sway body from side to side. War dance—High stepping skip step; head and body move forward then back. Swing arms in rhythm—swing left arm forward and raise right foot; swing right arm forward and raise left foot.)

If the group is large it will be necessary to repeat measures 25–42.

Jump Jim Crow (13C)

Arranged by E. B. GORDON

Formation: A double circle, partners facing.
1. "Jump—Jump and Jump—Jim Crow—"
   Partners join hands and take two slow and three quick jumps in place.
2. "Take a little twirl and then away we go."
   Turn partner with light running steps.
3. "Slide, slide and stamp just so—"
   Players take two slides to the right and stamp three times.
4. "Then you take another partner and you jump, Jim Crow—"
   Join hands with new partner, turn four steps, finishing turn with three jumps. Repeat with new partner from beginning.

FOURTH GRADE

Minuet I (27)

MOZART

Formation: Couples. Partners' inside hands joined. Girl holds skirt with outside hand, boy's outside hand on hip. Should be danced in slow, courtly manner.

Action—Measures 1–6: Point outside foot forward—one. Lift slightly off the floor and point again—two. Step on outside foot—three.

Repeat six times in all.

Measures 7–8: Face partner, deep courtesy. Boy, heels together, makes a low bow. Girl steps in line of direction—one; facing partner, steps backward with inside foot, leaving outside foot pointed forward—two; courtesy—three; steps forward on outside foot—four; brings inside foot up to outside—five; rises on toes and lowers heels—six.

Measures 9–16: Face partner, joining right hands. Step forward right foot—one; rise on toes and sink—two, three. Step backward on the left foot—one; point the right foot forward—two, three.

Repeat. Three walking steps in circle around partner, right, left, right—one, two, three; point left foot forward—one, two, three.

Deep courtesy during measures 15–16.

Repeat with left hands joined.

Measures 9–16 repeated. Couple No. 1 faces about and joins right hands with couple No. 2 in star formation.

Take three walking steps, right, left, right—one, two, three; point left foot forward—one, two, three.

Repeat three times in all. Drop hands. Deep courtesy during measures 15–16.

Repeat all with left hands joined.

Measures 1–8: Repeat first step.

FOURTH GRADE

Pop Goes the Weasel I (10)

All around the vinegar jug,
  The monkey chased the weasel;
The teacher pulled the stopper out,
  Pop goes the weasel!

Penny for a spool of thread,
  Penny for a needle;
That's the way the money goes,
  Pop goes the weasel!

(Victor: 20151; Columbia A3078.)

Formations: Double circle. Partners holding inside hands, outside hands on hips.

Measures 1–2: Beginning with right foot, step, step, step, point left.

Measures 3–4: Beginning with left foot, step, step, step, point right.

Measure 5: Step right, place left foot behind, bend knees.

186 PHYSICAL EDUCATION FOR ELEMENTARY SCHOOLS

Measure 6: Step left, place right foot behind, bend knees.

Measures 7–8: Girl skips around under boy's right arm, which is held high. Sing "Pop Goes the Weasel."

Repeat the whole dance in the same direction. Boy skips under girl's left arm.

Secure a new partner.

Variation: Dance through once and then repeat dance in the opposite direction.

Formation: A double circle, partners facing each other.

Part I

Description:

Accents sharp, light and spirited.

Measure 1: Dancers stand in place.

Measure 2: All stamp left, right, left.

Measure 3: Stand.

Measure 4: Clap own hands three times.

Measure 5: Shake right forefinger at partner.

Measure 6: Shake left forefinger.

Measure 7: Spin completely around to the left.

* From Caroline Crawford, "Folk Dances and Games." Copyright 1908. By permission of A. S. Barnes and Company, publishers.

FOURTH GRADE

Part II

Dancers join hands and move around the circle with the old-fashioned slide polka, turning halfway around each time (slide, slide, step, step, step), as follows:

Measure 8: Two slides to the side, around the circle.

Measure 9: Three steps, turning around in place, so that partner who was outside, is now inside.

Measures 10 and 11: Repeat, beginning with the other foot and moving in the same direction.

Measures 12–15: Repeat.

Change partners and repeat the dance.

Additional Rhythmical Activities

Grandmother Will Dance	Ref. No. 18, p. 213
Christmas Dance	Ref. No. 26, p. 217
Swedish Ring Dance	Ref. No. 26, p. 222
Three Little Girls	Ref. No. 26, p. 207
Indian Corn Husking Dance	Ref. No. 31, p. 82
Money Musk (Victor: 20447)	Ref. No. 31, p. 87
Vineyard Dance	Ref. No. 31, p. 90
Klappdans (Clap Dance) (Victor: 20450)	Ref. No. 41, p. 26
English Harvester's Dance	Ref. No. 42, p. 8
The Rill I	Ref. No. 42, p. 46
The Rill II	Ref. No. 42, p. 69
Chain Dance	Ref. No. 44, p. 60
John Brown	Ref. No. 45, p. 60
Girls and Boys Come Out to Play	Ref. No. 47, p. 129
Today is the First of May (Columbia: 10009D)	Ref. No. 48, p. 69
May Pole Dance (Bluff King Hal) (Columbia: A3038)	Ref. No. 54, p. 66

STUNTS

Frog Hop (14B)

Deep knee bend, place hands on floor. Move hands forward and let feet follow with a jump, kicking legs out behind to imitate a frog.

Stooping Stretch

Place both heels against a line, and about one foot apart. With a piece of chalk held with both hands stoop forward, with knees straight, and mark the floor as far back as possible. The hands are stretched backward between the legs. Regain the erect position without removing the feet from the line or touching the floor with the hands. If impossible to touch the floor with both hands on chalk, try with either right or left hand.

Knee Dip (86)

(a) Stand at attention. Raise right arm sideward for balance. Raise left foot backward bending left knee, grasp left foot at the instep with the left hand. Bend right knee until the left knee touches the floor lightly. Straighten right knee. Execute with other leg. (b) Stand at attention. Raise left knee upward clasping both hands at the ankle of the left leg. Bend right knee deeply. Straighten right knee. Execute with other leg. (c) Stand at attention. Raise left leg and arms forward. Bend right knee deeply. Straighten right knee. Execute with other leg.*

Clown Tricks (14B)

Balance stick on chin or forehead. Lying on the floor with an object on the forehead, stand up, etc.

Coffee Grinder (14B)

With right hand on ground, arm stiff, body extended, without sagging, head well back, walk around in a circle using arm as a pivot. Repeat with left arm as a pivot.

Double Forward Roll

Make two complete forward rolls without a pause before coming to an erect position. The rolls must be made in a straight line.

Minuet Bow (14C)

Step right, circle left leg to rear, step on left foot, bending left knee and extending right foot front (knee straight). Keep head and chest

---

* Illustrations drawn by A. J. Schuettner, Los Angeles Junior College, California.

well up, back straight, sit on left foot. Come slowly to standing position without touching hands to floor.

Head Stand *

There are several methods of coming to the head stand. 1. From the frog hand stand position lean forward until the forehead touches the floor. Then shift the weight of the body forward, bringing the legs to the vertical position. Arch the back slightly and keep feet

together. 2. Kneel, place both elbows on the floor and the head in both hands. From this position push the legs to a vertical position. 3. Kneel, with arms folded, place the elbows on the floor, the head several inches in front of them and push the legs up as before. 4. Place the hands and head on the floor, forming a tripod. Then kick the legs up slowly to a vertical position.

Back Spring

One boy takes a position on the ground on his hands and knees. A second boy from the side throws his hands to the ground near the first boy, and turns a forward roll over the first boy's back. The boy underneath should raise his back slightly just as he feels the first boy going over him. This stunt may be used as preliminary training for the "handspring."

---
* Pictures illustrating stunts were taken at the River School, Butte County, California. Floyd Tarr, County Supervisor of Physical Education.

Leap Frog and Forward Roll

One player bends over and with knees slightly bent, places the hands on his knees or on the floor. A second player runs, places his hands on the first player's back and leaps over him. The second player then does a forward roll.

Centipede

Additional Stunts

Lath and Plaster.................................Ref. No. 19, p. 250
Lunge and Hop Fight..........................Ref. No. 19, p. 246
Wand and Toe Wrestle........................Ref. No. 19, p. 247
Fish Hawk Dive..................................Ref. No. 60, p. 96
Human Wheel ....Ref. No. 60, p. 103
Jumping Jack ....Ref. No. 60, p. 105
Stump Walk ....Ref. No. 60, p. 94
Wicket Walk ....Ref. No. 60, p. 93

MIMETICS

Archery

From the position of arms forward, fists clenched and facing and touching each other, step backward with right foot, turn body a quarter turn to the right, and sharply pull back right arm to forward bend position as if pulling back a bow string. Replace right foot, turn front and extend right arm forward. Repeat movement to the left, using left foot and arm.

Firecracker

Clap hands in front of chest—1. Clap overhead—2. Bend forward and slap knees, mid-leg and ankle in quick succession, keep knees straight—3. Rhythm is "1-2, 1-2-3."

Jack in the Box

Feet slightly apart. Bend the knees deeply on count one. On count 2 spring high in the air and land on toes. Repeat several times.

Jack Knife Bend (13B)

With feet widely apart, bend down quickly and touch the floor, keeping the upper back flat, knees straight, neck pressed back. Return immediately to starting position, striking thighs with hands.

Jumping Rope

Bend elbows and close hands as if holding a rope. Jump lightly and rhythmically as if turning and jumping a rope. Keep the trunk erect.

Sewing Machine

Running in place, hands on hips, start slowly and lightly and gradually increase speed.

Skating

Children skate in couples. Take hands as in skating, right hand takes partner's right, and left hand takes partner's left. Slide diagonally forward right, slide diagonally forward left. Skate forward. Turn around and skate back. If there is a victrola in the schoolroom, use a slow march for this exercise.

FIFTH GRADE

	PAGE
Athletic Games	193
Individual Athletic Events	202
Relay Races	214
Rhythmical Activities	218
Stunts	228
Hunting Games	230
Mimetics	234

The teacher should refer frequently to Part I of the book, as it contains many suggestions in regard to the various activities. For example —the material presented in Part I under "Posture," "Corrective Physical Education," and "Health Education" applies to all grades and should be reviewed frequently.

The activity classifications in each grade have been arranged in sequence according to judgments of their appeal and importance to the children who will use them. In situations where all the content appearing in this grade can not be taught, the teacher should make selections from each classification rather than attempt to teach all the activities found in any one classification.

ATHLETIC GAMES

Basket Ball Toss Up

This is a basket ball game played between two to eight players, all using one basket ball goal. The players are divided into two equal teams. A player throws the ball from the free throw line as when throwing a foul in regular basket ball. The free throw line is fifteen feet from the basket. If a basket is made, one point is scored for his team, and he continues to throw until he fails. When he fails to make the basket all players scramble for the ball and attempt to make a field goal, which counts two points. Twenty-one points is a game, and two games out of three a match. When a field goal is made, the player making it must be the next player to throw from the free throw line. The last point in the game can be made only by a field goal.

Variation.—Game may be played by tossing up ball between two players at the free throw line, as in basket ball. In this case only field goals would be made.

Captain Ball I

The court is marked as shown in the diagram:

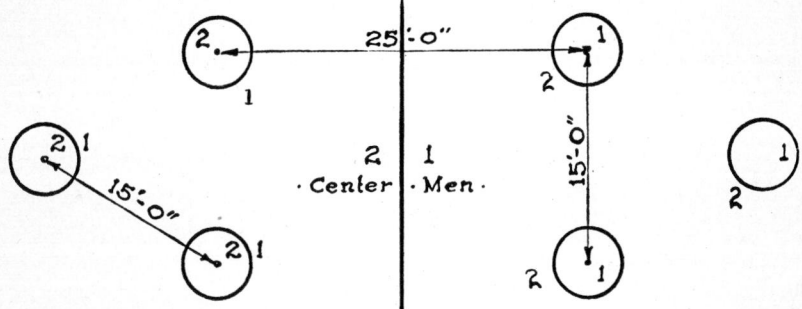

Each team consists of three circle men, three guards and one center player. The circle men are guarded by the guards. The circle man stationed in the circle farthest from the center of the playing area is known as the captain. The leader tosses up the ball between the two center players, who endeavor to bat the ball to one of the guards, and they in turn endeavor to throw it to one of their circle men. The circle man, if he secures it, tries to throw the ball to his captain. The guards, of course, intercept the ball, if possible, and throw it to their circle men. The circle men may place one foot outside the base, but at no time both feet; the guards must not touch the circles or the circle men; the players must not kick the ball, run with it, snatch or bat it from an opponent's hands, bounce it or hold it longer than three seconds. Any violation of the above rules entitles an opposing circle man to a free throw to his captain; the only player interfering is the captain's guard. One point is scored each time the captain catches the ball from a circle man. A point is not scored if a guard or center throws directly to the captain. The team wins that has the most points at the end of the playing period. There should be two ten minute halves. At the beginning of the second half, the circle men become guards, and guards become circle men. This changes the direction of throwing for each team. A ball which goes far afield is put in play again at the center. After each center ball, the center players play on their side of the field.

Circle Soccer *

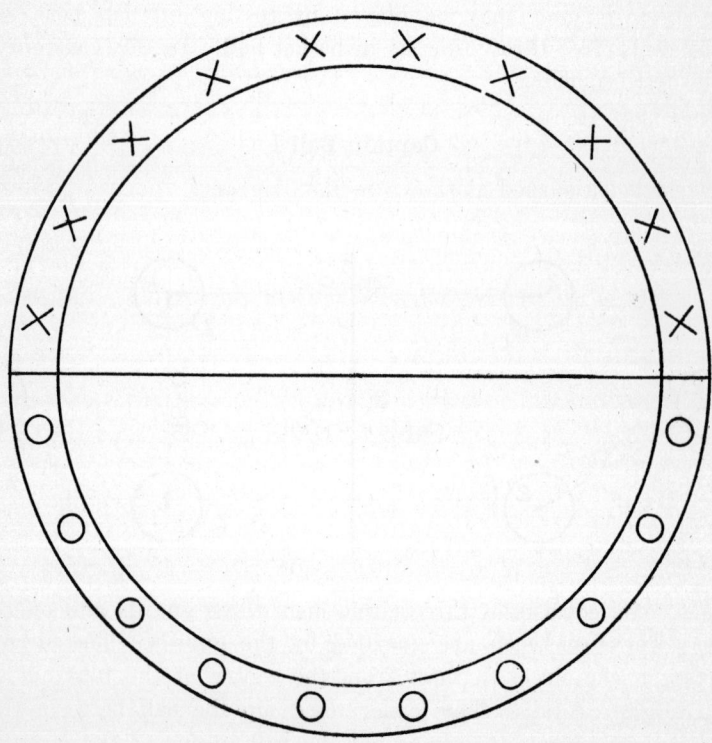

* Contributed by Theodore Treutlein, San Diego city schools.

Field.—A double circle. Outer circle twenty to twenty-five feet, depending upon number of players. Inner circle two feet smaller in diameter. Draw a diameter line through both circles.

Teams.—Players are divided into two teams which line up on the outer circumference of the larger circle, one team on each side of diameter.

Object.—The object of the game is to kick a soccer ball past the opponents lower than their shoulders.

Score.—One point is scored for a team whenever the ball is kicked across the opponents' outer circle line lower than the shoulders of the smaller player of the two players where the ball went through. Twenty-one points in a game.

Opponents score.—(1) If the ball is touched with the hands; (2) If player steps over inner circle when kicking; (3) If player backs up and lets ball get out of outer circumference; (4) If player kicks ball across his own team line; (5) If ball is kicked higher than shoulders of smaller player of the two players where ball went through; (6) If blocking puts the ball out.

Dead ball.—A ball stopping in circle beyond the kicking distance of a player. A dead ball belongs to the captain on whose side the ball stopped. When ball goes out of bounds it is put in play by the player on whose right side it went out. This is also true when the ball goes between the legs or over the head of a player.

Blocking.—Stopping the ball with any part of the body, except the hands and forearm, is called blocking. Blocking should be used whenever possible to prevent ball from going out.

Suggestions.—(1) Keep your eyes on the ball; (2) Kick ball low; (3) Step to the left or right, but never in front of a player; (4) Avoid dead balls; (5) Become an expert at blocking; (6) Never back up, but step toward ball as far as inner circle allows; (7) Avoid kicking through your own team.

Scorekeeper.—Each captain may keep score. In doing this, captains need not get out of game. If advisable, a special scorekeeper may be appointed. Game may be played in halves, with a definite time limit. After each half, sides should exchange places. There seems to be an advantage to be in the center of the team, and teammates should, therefore, rotate so end players have a chance to play in the center of the team.

Feather Ball (14B)

For one feather ball, five or six players on a side is enough. The two teams stand on opposite sides of a center line drawn across a court twenty by thirty feet. The feather ball is served to the opposite side.

It is batted with the open hand and returned to the side serving in the same manner. The object of the game is to keep the feather ball in the air. A "miss" on one side counts one point for the other side. The score is 21 points. Serving out of the court gives the ball to the other side. The game could be made more difficult by using net ball or volley ball rules. Feather balls may be purchased at a Chinese store, or shuttle cocks may be purchased or constructed. Feather balls or shuttle cocks should always be picked up by the cork end and never by the feathers.

Hand Ball

Court.—A satisfactory single service wall can be made eighteen feet wide, twelve feet high, with six feet of small mesh chicken wire on top. Side walls may be used. The service line should be thirteen feet back of the service wall and parallel to it. The rear or back line should be

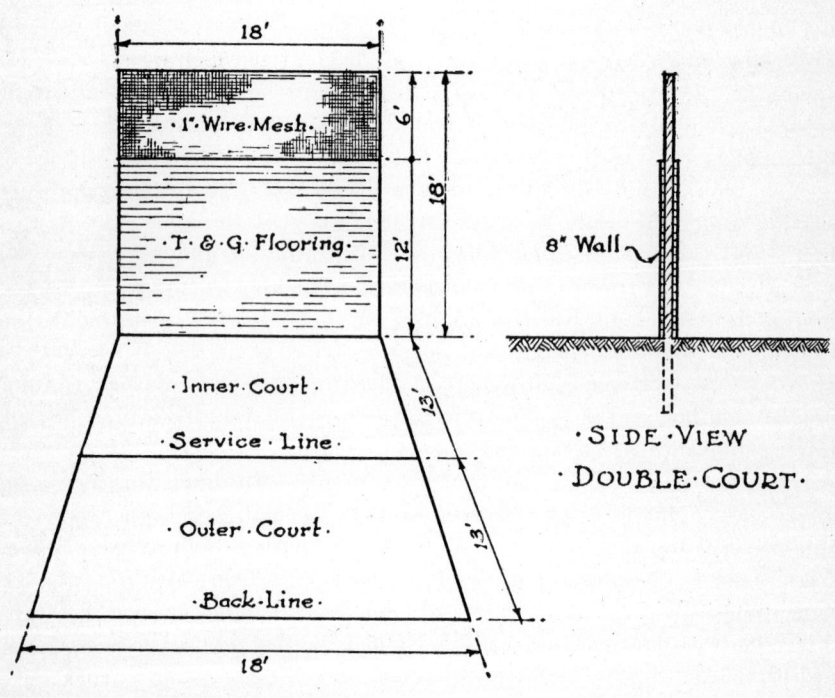

· HAND-BALL·COURT·

twenty-six feet from the service wall and parallel to it. A ball hitting the wire is in play as well as when it hits the wall.

The Ball.—Regular Irish hand ball or regular tennis ball.

The Game.—Consists of eleven or twenty-one points, and may be played by two or four players. The player serving the ball shall be called the "server" and the player receiving the ball shall be called the "receiver." The server stands back of the thirteen-foot line and near the side line. The receiver stands near the rear or back line. On the service the ball must be struck from a bounce on or in front of the service line, i.e., between the service line and the service wall; must hit the service wall and then land in the outer court between the service line, the rear line and the side lines. If the ball is within these limits the service must be accepted exactly the same as in tennis. The umpire may make allowances for a rough court and when the service is impossible to get on account of the court, he may require the service to be taken over. The server is allowed two trials. A failure of the server to properly serve or return the ball is known as a "handout," i.e., the other side receives the ball and has an opportunity to serve and score points. The serving side wins a point if the receiving side fails to return the service or the ball while in play. The receiving side does not score points. The server loses his service (1) if he serves two faults, i.e., does not get the ball within the outer court; (2) if he returns the ball in play so that it falls outside the field of play; (3) if in returning the ball it fails to strike the service wall. A ball hitting the line is good.

In a four-handed game the service is by sides, the two on one side serving and then the two on the other. In doubles there shall be two handouts in succession for the serving side, except at start, when the side winning the toss-up for service shall have only one handout. During service the partner of the server must stand outside and back of the twenty-six foot back line. If the ball, when served, strikes the server or his partner, the server shall be retired; if it strikes one of the opposing side the count shall be for the server. If the ball in play, before hitting the service wall, strikes a partner, it counts against the side playing the ball. If the ball in play, before hitting the service wall, strikes an opponent, it is a hindrance. Other hindrances are: (1) interference by a spectator; (2) when a player unintentionally interferes with the play though not trying to return the ball; (3) when a ball strikes any apparatus which is not higher than the service wall. A hindrance does not count and the ball is served again. The foot can not be used and only one hand at a time. The ball may be struck only once on the return.

During a match omit the playing for "game point." Playing for game point demands the securing of two points in succession to win, should both teams have a score of ten points each—same as playing off "deuce" in tennis. Only in cases of injury shall substitutes be allowed during match. A player must not play in both singles and doubles in league contests. A match shall consist of two eleven-point games, and a twenty-one point game, and may be played by two to four players.

Suggestions.—Learn to place the ball on the service as well as on the return. Learn to judge the ball so that you can hit the wall low. Play your own side of the court. A good hand ball player will have a good service. A valuable game for girls. The game may be played by the smaller pupils with a light volley ball.

Progressive Dodge Ball

The ground is divided into three adjacent courts, each thirty by twenty feet. Players are divided into three teams, each occupying a court. Give these teams names, such as A, B and C. When the game is played between boys alone or girls alone, a basket ball may be used.

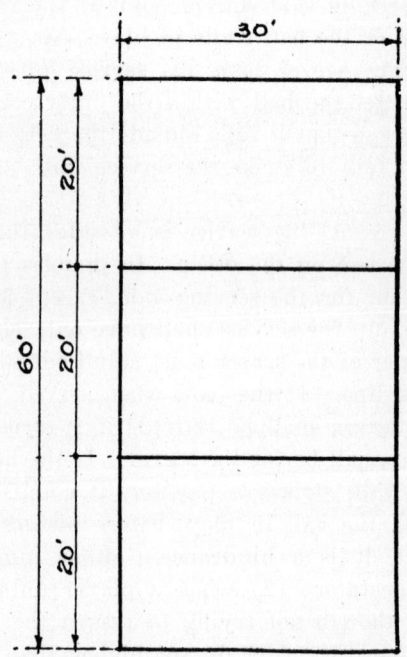

When it is a mixed class a volley ball or other light ball should be used to prevent injury. The game is played in three divisions of five minutes each. Scores are made by hitting the players of another team with the ball. No score is made if a player is hit after the ball has bounced. The umpire calls the name of the team whose player is hit and checks a point against it. Players stepping over their boundary lines add a point to their score. A player hit by the ball thrown by a player out of his court with either or both feet is not scored against. The team having the lowest score at the end of the three periods, wins. As soon as the ball strikes the floor or a player, the players in that section of the floor should try to get it before it rolls to another section of the floor, and throw at opponents. It is allowable to run up to the boundary line to throw, but not to step over it. Players not having the ball may run to the far side of their space and dodge in any way they please to escape being hit. When the first division of the time is up, the middle team changes places with one of the end teams, and at the end of the second division this second middle team changes with the other end team, so that each team plays in the middle for one period. When these changes occur the umpire must keep the names of the teams clearly in mind and not make mistakes in calling the score. A ball going out of bounds is secured by the nearest player who must return to his court before throwing the ball.

Variation.—Three courts—two teams. One team in the center court and the opposing team equally divided and occupying the end courts. The game is played in two halves, the players exchanging places.

Rotation Soccer (33) *

Number of Players.—Twenty-four to forty-eight.

Playing Space.—Forty-five by seventy-five feet.

Players.—The players are divided into two equal teams which are

---

* From Leonora Andersen, "An Athletic Program for Elementary Schools." Copyright 1927. By permission of A. S. Barnes and Company, publishers.

again divided into three equal groups and lined up as shown in the diagram.

Object of the Game.—To kick the ball over the opponents' goal line.

Game.—The game is played in two eight-minute periods. The ball (soccer ball) is placed in the center of the field and is put in play by a kick-off as in soccer. The forward line takes the ball down the field by dribbling, passing or kicking, and attempts to get it over the opponents' goal line. Forwards may not play back of the twenty-foot line on their own side. The halfbacks may follow the forwards to the twenty-foot line on the opposite side. The goal guards must remain within the goal area. All players must play within their own lanes up and down the field. As soon as a point has been scored, the forwards take the places of the goal guards; the goal guards take the places of the halfbacks; the halfbacks take the places of the forwards. Play is then resumed as described above, the kick-off being taken by the side opposite that which scored. If the game is continued for more than three or four minutes with neither side scoring, the referee should blow the whistle and have the players rotate, play being resumed at the spot where the ball was when the whistle blew. This shifting of players is a further safeguard against danger of over-exertion on the part of the forwards.

Fouls.—(1) Touching the ball with the hands or forearms, except on the part of the goal guards, who may catch the ball with the hands; (2) pushing, holding, shoving, or blocking an opponent; (3) overstepping the restraining lines; (4) kicking the ball over the heads of the goal guards.

Penalties.—(1) For fouls 1, 2, and 3, a free kick is awarded to the opposing team; (2) For foul 4, a throw-in is given to the opponents and the goal does not count. A free kick is executed as in soccer.

Out of Bounds.—Any ball kicked over the side lines shall be put in play by a throw-in, as in soccer.

Scoring.—One point is scored each time the ball is forced over the opponents' goal line, except as in 4 (under "Fouls"). No goal may be scored on the kick-off or on a free kick.

Six Hole Basket Ball

Six three-foot circles are made around the basket ball goal, as shown in the diagram. The players line up and take turns in attempting to throw baskets, starting on the left at circle number one. Every basket made advances the player one hole, and he continues to progress until he fails to make a basket. Holes two and four are marked safety. If a player overtakes another player in a hole not marked safety, the first player must return and start over again. The person wins the game who first makes the circuit of holes and returns to the starting point.

FIFTH GRADE

A player overtaken on his return goes back to hole number six, rather than hole number one.

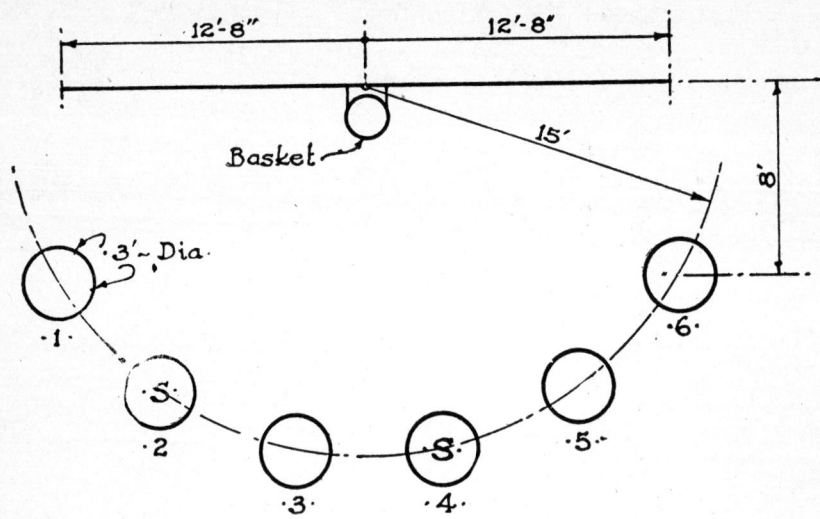

SIX HOLE BASKET BALL

Shinney (17) *

This is a simple form of hockey or polo, and, as usually played by boys, does not have very definite rules. The field may be any size and is marked off with goal lines and side lines. A small wooden ball or a hard rubber ball is desirable, but boys often play with nothing better than a small wooden block or a tin can. Regular shinney sticks or hockey sticks may be bought, or boys may whittle out their own sticks. The object of the game is to drive the ball over the enemy's goal line. One point is scored when this is done. The game is started in the center of the field as in hockey.

Soccer Keep Away

Field.—The field is twenty-five by fifty feet. Draw parallel lines across the field every ten feet, thus forming five zones.

Players.—Divide the players into three groups, A, B and C. One group occupies the middle zone, and the other two stand on the end lines of the end zones. The unoccupied zones form neutral territory. The object of the game is to have the center team try to intercept passes

---

* From Forbush and Allen, "The Book of Games for Home, School and Playground." Copyright 1927. By permission of John C. Winston Company, publishers.

made through the center zone. A stopped ball is returned to either end zone by the nearest player.

Rules.—The game is played in three shifts, each team being given the chance to play in the center zone to score points. The time should not exceed five minutes for each shift. The ball may be dribbled in the end zone, and then kicked through the neutral territory and center zone to the opposite team. Sides and players alternate in kicking the ball through the center zone.

Method of Scoring.—(1) The center team scores a point each time the ball is intercepted when passing through their zone; (2) center team scores a point whenever a player in the end zone steps into neutral territory; (3) center team scores a point when ball is kicked over their heads; (4) end teams score a point when a member of the center team steps outside the center zone; (5) opponents score a point when a team member touches the ball with the hands.

Square Soccer (33) *

One team is lined up on two adjacent sides of a thirty-foot square, and the other team is lined up on the other two sides. The object of the game is for any player who secures the ball to kick it from his line through the opposite team not higher than the players' heads. At no time may the ball be touched with the hands. It may be blocked as in soccer. The players may run out into the field to secure the ball. It should then be kicked or dribbled to a player in line, but all players must return to their places in line before the ball is again kicked. A point is scored each time the ball is forced over the opponents' line. A game of ten points may be played, or a time limit may be set. When the ball crosses a line it is put in play again at the point where it crossed.

Additional References

Drive Ball ....Ref. No. 19, p. 375
Corner Kick Ball..Ref. No. 26, p. 68
Line Ball ....Ref. No. 33, p. 93

INDIVIDUAL ATHLETIC EVENTS

Balancing Test (27)

A standard balance beam twelve feet long and two inches wide may be used, or a two by four-inch plank set on the two-inch side. The

---

* From Leonora Andersen, "An Athletic Program for Elementary Schools." Copyright 1927. By permission of A. S. Barnes and Company, publishers.

length shall be twelve feet. There is no time limit in this event. Two trials are allowed.

First Test.—The girl starts from the center of the beam, walks forward to the end, without turning walks backward to center, makes a quarter turn, and balancing with toes on beam, holding head up and body erect, makes a deep knee bend, coming to a full squat on heels. Rising, she completes turn, walks forward to end of beam, makes half turn and walks to center of beam, the starting point.

Second Test.—This is the same as the first except that the girl must throughout the test have a book balanced upon her head. For the sake of uniformity, this book should be five inches by seven inches, with stiff board covers, weighing from three-quarters of a pound to one pound. The girl's hair should not be arranged to assist in balancing the book.

Third Test.—This is the same as the second test, except that the girl must keep her hands on her hips throughout the test and must make three deep knee bends in succession in place of one.

Baseball Batting for Accuracy

Draw two diverging lines six feet apart at the point where the batter stands, and fifteen feet apart at a distance of ninety feet. From the batter's line, for scoring purposes, draw cross lines at sixty feet for the fifth grade, seventy feet for the sixth grade, eighty feet for the seventh grade, and ninety feet for the eighth grade. Each player tosses up the ball and tries to bat it. Ten trials are allowed. If the batted ball strikes the ground and rolls across the line for the player's grade, and within the side lines, or if a fly strikes within ten feet of this cross line and within the side lines, it is a perfect hit. The total number of perfect hits gives the score.

Baseball Fly Catching

Each player stands within the diverging lines at the assigned distance noted under Batting Ball for Accuracy. A fly ball is thrown so as to come within the space between the diverging lines, the cross line of the student's grade, and the next one beyond. The player must catch the ball. The total number of catches out of ten trials gives the score.

Baseball Throw and Catch

On a playground baseball diamond place a pitcher and three basemen. A player stands at home. This player must catch the ball delivered from the pitcher, throw to first, catch the return, throw to second, catch the return, throw to third, and catch the return. Thus the player must catch four throws and throw to each of the three bases, giving a possible seven errors. A throw by the player or to the player shall be judged as being good if both hands can be placed upon the ball by stretching with either foot on the base. In case of a bad throw to the player, the throw must be repeated. A bad throw by the player, or failure to catch the ball thrown by the pitcher or basemen, shall be an error. The number of errors subtracted from seven gives the score.

Baseball Throw for Accuracy (Boys)

Equipment.—Two official baseballs; a frame (inside dimensions) eighteen inches wide by thirty-seven inches high, set twenty-one inches off the ground. This same area may be marked on a wall if a frame is not available. A line is marked forty-five feet from the frame for fifth and sixth grades; a line is marked sixty feet from the frame for the seventh and eighth grades.

Rules.—Contestants must stand back of the line when throwing. Stepping on or over the line counts as a trial without score. The ball must be thrown with speed, not merely tossed. Each contestant shall have ten throws. Take position similar to pitcher; take three throws to warm up before beginning the test; take a step in throwing. The number of successful throws out of ten is the pupil's score. A ball hitting the frame is considered a successful throw.

Baseball Throw for Accuracy (Girls)

Equipment.—A frame (inside dimensions) eighteen inches by thirty-seven inches high, set twenty-one inches off the ground, or an area of equal size marked on a wall. This area represents the area in front of the batter into which a ball must be thrown to be a "strike"; twelve-inch playground balls; a "pitcher's box" thirty feet for fifth and sixth grades, and thirty-five feet for seventh and eighth grades is marked by a line.

Rules.—The ball is thrown from "pitcher's box" into the wooden frame or wall area. Ten trials are allowed. The ball must be thrown (overhand) with speed, not tossed. A catcher may stand behind the frame to catch thrown balls. The thrower must in all cases remain back of the line. Stepping on or over the line counts as a trial without score. The number of successful throws out of ten is the pupil's score. A ball hitting the frame is considered a successful throw.

Base Running

Use a baseball diamond. Stand on home base. On signal run around the bases, touching first, second, third and home base in the order named. Failure to touch any base invalidates the record. Use a watch with second hands, or a stop watch. The time needed to complete the run is the individual's record. One player runs at a time.

Basket Ball Foul Throw

This event is done on a basket ball court. The contestant stands behind the free throw line, which should be fifteen feet from the backstop, and tosses the ball at the basket as in foul shooting. Five, ten, fifteen or more trials may be used. Each fair throw going through the basket counts one. The total number of successful throws represents the contestant's score.

Basket Ball Pass for Accuracy

Equipment.—A circle of three feet radius, marked on a wall, center of circle five feet from the ground; line marked on the ground parallel to the wall, twenty feet from the wall; basket ball.

Rules.—The ball is thrown, left or right arm, at the circle from the line twenty feet from the wall. Ten trials are allowed. The number of times the ball hits inside the circle is scored. The player must not step over the line in throwing. For grades seven and eight, use thirty feet.

Practice Events.—Passing the basket ball, with one arm, to another player, using different styles of passing; the side pass with right and left arm; the underhand pass with right and left arm.

Basket Ball Throw for Distance

Equipment.—A basket ball; a one hundred foot tape line; a starting line.

Rules.—The contestant must stand behind the starting line to throw. He must not touch or step over the line with any part of the body until after the ball has struck the ground, as it invalidates the record. The side throw shall be used, i.e., balance the ball on the hand and forearm and use a full arm swing. Two trials shall be allowed, the better of the two being scored. The distance thrown shall be measured from the starting line at the point where the contestant stood to the point where the ball first struck the ground.

Suggestions.—Stand well back of starting line, side of body toward direction of the throw, one foot advanced, weight on rear foot, rear knee bent, ball resting on hand and forearm farthest from direction of throw. Swing round quickly, bringing weight forward as the ball is released. Throw the ball high.

Variations.—(1) Throw with left arm; (2) throw with both hands on the ball from overhead. Feet must not be moved except to raise the heels until after the ball strikes the ground; (3) throw with both hands on the ball from chest position.

Basket Ball Throw for Goal

Equipment.—Basket ball; backstop and basket. From a line perpendicular to the middle of the backboard, draw a semicircle with a radius of fifteen feet.

Rules.—Ten throws are allowed. The first throw is taken from any point outside the semicircle. Each of the remaining nine throws is taken from the point at which the ball is recovered after the preceding throw. Try to recover the ball before it hits the ground. If the ball rolls out of the court or beyond the semicircle, the next throw is taken from the starting point. The contestant must not take a step after recovering the ball. The ball may not be held more than three seconds. Any style of throwing may be used.

Practice Events.—Receiving a pass while running toward the basket and throwing for goal; receiving a pass while running away from the basket and throwing for goal; throwing for basket from a short distance and increasing the distance as each successful throw is made; throwing foul goals from the foul line; scooping the ball from the ground while running and throwing for goal in one motion; all styles of throwing for basket should be practiced.

Variations.—When timed, one minute allowed. Throwing is started from a line fifteen feet from the backstop. After the first throw the contestant may catch and throw from any spot. The object is to throw as many baskets as possible in one minute. Bouncing the ball wastes time. When not timed, throwing is started from a line fifteen feet from the basket and continued after the first throw until a failure is made. The thrower stands for the next throw at the point where the ball is recovered. If it goes out of bounds, return to the fifteen-foot line. This series of trials is repeated twice more—three times in all. The total baskets made in the three series is the score. It is a foul to step on or over the fifteen-foot line when throwing from behind the line. A basket made while doing this does not score, and counts as one of the series.

Eskimo Race (59) *

The contestant stands behind the starting line with feet together and knees stiff. Holding this position he travels forward by a rapid succession of toe springs. The knees should be held absolutely rigid. Any contestant who fails to travel in exactly the manner prescribed is eliminated. The race is started and judged as the straight-away run. From fourteen to thirty yards makes a good race.

* From S. C. Staley, "Individual and Mass Athletics." Copyright 1925. By permission of A. S. Barnes and Company, publishers.

Half Lever and Toes to Bar (15B)

The movement is one of the three fundamental movements involved in all stunts on the apparatus. It requires great abdominal strength, hence it should not be attempted until considerable ability is shown in the sit-up. Ability in it should also be developed through the lever series of exercises as follows:

Hanging:
- (a) One thigh and leg flexion (knee to chest).
- (b) One thigh flexion (knee straight).
- (c) Two thigh and leg flexion (knees to chest).
- (d) Two thigh and leg flexion, then leg extension to half lever and hold for a second.
- (e) Two thigh flexion to half lever, knees straight and hold for a second.
- (f) Two thigh and leg flexion (knees to chest) and extend legs, toes to bar.
- (g) Two thigh flexion, knees straight and toes to bar.
- (h) Two thigh and leg flexion, extend legs and thighs to bar.
- (i) Two thigh and leg flexion, extend legs and circle bar to rest.
- (j) Thigh flexion, legs straight and circle bar to rest.

Heel Run Race (59) *

The runner, traveling with short rapid strides, runs forward on his heels. The toes should be kept free of the ground throughout the race. Any runner violating this rule should be eliminated. The race is conducted as the regular straight-away. From twenty to forty yards makes a good race.

Hobble Race (59) *

The contestant stands on one foot, raises the other foot backward, grasps the instep of the raised foot with both hands and holds it against his buttock. Retaining his grasp on the up-raised foot he hops toward the finish line. Any contestant releasing either hand from his up-raised foot or falling over is immediately eliminated from the race. The race is started and judged as the regular straight-away run. From twenty to fifty yards makes a good race. Try hopping on the other foot.

Jump and Reach (Girls)

Equipment.—A yard stick or rule 2 feet long. Wall or vertical surface that can be marked. Piece of chalk 1 inch long.

---

* From S. C. Staley, "Individual and Mass Athletics." Copyright 1925. By permission of A. S. Barnes and Company, publishers.

Rules. The contestant stands facing and close to the wall, heels and toes on the floor. Reaching high with both hands held together, a mark is made with the chalk. Contestant then stands sideways to the wall. While swinging both arms vigorously, a jump is made. At the highest point of the jump a second mark is made on the wall with the hand holding the chalk. The distance between the two marks is the individual's record.

Leg Lifts

Lie flat on the back on the floor, legs together and extended, hands placed palm down on the floor under the hips. Raise the right leg to vertical position a number of times. Repeat the exercise with the left leg. Keeping legs together, knees stiff and extending the toes, raise feet until they reach an angle of ninety degrees or more from their original position, and then lower them to a point within two or three inches from the floor. Do this a number of times. This event is used to develop abdominal strength, and should not be used as a contest.

Mass Running

Two methods of conducting mass running may be used. In team competition, if the sides are unequal in numbers, one team may run at a time. Pupils take their places one behind the other *back* of the starting line. When the starter, who stands at the finish line, gives a signal by lowering rapidly something white held in the hand, the first runner starts. As this runner crosses the finish line the signal is again given and the second pupil begins running. This is continued until all pupils have run. The starter with a stop watch in hand records the time from the instant the first runner starts until the last runner crosses the finish line. This same procedure is used for the second team. The time consumed by each team is divided by the number of players on that team. The team having the lowest average running time, wins.

When the sides are even, two or more starters are used. The first runners of the teams begin running at the same time. The signals are given by each starter as explained above and the team wins whose last runner crosses the finish line first.

Potato Race

Two small potatoes or blocks are placed thirty-four feet and forty-two feet, respectively, from a starting point. Blocks should be placed in circular areas one foot in diameter marked on the floor or ground.

Rules.—Contestant starts back of a starting line, brings the blocks in successively, places them in a circular area one foot in diameter with the circumference tangent to, but back of, the starting line, returns the blocks to their original positions and recrosses starting line. This process requires two round trips from the starting line to each of the two circular areas. Failure to place blocks in the circular areas invalidates the record. The seconds consumed in the event are scored. In all cases, blocks placed in the circles must not touch the circumference. For practice purposes, reduce distances to seventeen and twenty-one feet.

Pull Up

Equipment.—A horizontal bar.

Rules.—The overhand grasp; i.e., back of hand toward face, thumbs under bar, hands shoulder width apart. The feet must clear the ground. Each contestant hangs from the bar with arms and legs straight, feet together. He must pull himself up so his chin is over the bar. He must lower himself after each pull-up until his arms are straight. Only a pull-up without snap, swing or kick, shall score.

Hints on Development of Ability.—Practice hanging and exercising in hanging position on bar, rings, horizontal ladder, etc.; climb rope.

Push Up *

CORRECT.　　　　　　**INCORRECT.**

This movement exercises the muscles of the arms, shoulders and abdomen. It is one of the three fundamental movements in handling the body on the arms. Stand at attention. Squat. Bend knees, turning them out at an angle of ninety degrees, and place hands on the floor, shoulder width apart, fingers forward. Jump the feet to the rear so the weight rests on the hands and the toes, arms straight, feet together, neck, back and knees in a straight line; i.e., avoid the "swayback" position, keep the hips high and the back flat. Bend the arms until the chest (not the chin, abdomen or knees) touches, or nearly touches the floor. This is the dip. Straighten the arms. This is the push-up. Repeat as many times as possible. Jump the feet to the squat-rest position, then stand erect. This completes the "push-up." *Practice event.*—Lean against the wall of a building or against a desk or other object, dip and push up.

Run (Girls 40 Yards—Boys 50 Yards)

Preparation.—The track should be measured and permanent distances marked at forty, fifty, sixty, seventy and eighty yards. If pos-

---

* Illustrations drawn by A. J. Schuettner, Los Angeles Junior College, California.

sible, secure a track without curves. Carefully lay off a starting and a finish line, parallel, and the required distance apart. Cotton yarn should be available for determining the winner at the finish line. A stop watch or a watch showing "seconds" should be used for timing. When an ordinary watch with a "second" hand is used for timing, the timer may also act as starter and should stand at the finish line. The race in this case is started by rapidly pulling down a handkerchief held in the hand when the "second" hand is at a convenient division.

Crouching Start.—The crouching start should be practiced and used, as it is faster than the standing start. Students take the places assigned to them behind the starting line. The left foot is placed about six inches from the line; the knees are bent; the right knee rests on the ground beside the instep of the left foot; the hands are on or just behind the starting line; arms straight, shoulder width apart; the muscles are relaxed. When the instructor says, "On your mark!" students take their positions as described above. When he says, "Get set!" the right leg is partly straightened, the knee is raised from the ground, and the weight is put well forward on the hands. The muscles are tense. On the word "Go!" push off with hands and right foot. Do not straighten the body too quickly. Remain crouching for the first few steps, and do not assume an upright position until after the fifth or sixth stride. Pick up the knees and run in a straight line down the course. Take short strides at first and lengthen them gradually.

Suggestions.—In all timed events, "jumping the gun" or starting before the signal is given, necessitates the recall of all contestants. The offender is penalized by being set back one yard for the first, two yards for the second and disqualified for the third offense. Do not run the full distance in competition without preliminary training. Students should learn to run on their toes, with feet pointing straight ahead, arms moving straight forward and backward, with elbows bent and held fairly close to the sides. Do not slow up as the finish line is approached, but cross it at full speed, slowing up gradually after it has been crossed. Never look backward while running. Practice the "start" running ten to twenty yards. Run one hundred and two hundred yards at moderate speed to develop form and endurance.

Running Broad Jump (Boys)

Whenever possible it is best to have a jumping pit. Toes may not project over the front of the "take-off" board, nor touch the ground in front of it, in making the jump. Each competitor is allowed three jumps, his best jump being taken as his record. All measurements shall be made from the front edge of the "take-off" board to the nearest point at which any part of the body touches the ground. In landing, boys should fall to the side or forward, and never backward. There is

FIFTH GRADE

no limit to the distance that may be run before making the jump, but short runs are preferable. If a competitor runs over the "take off" board it shall count as one of his three trials. Boys should practice so as to jump off the same foot each time.

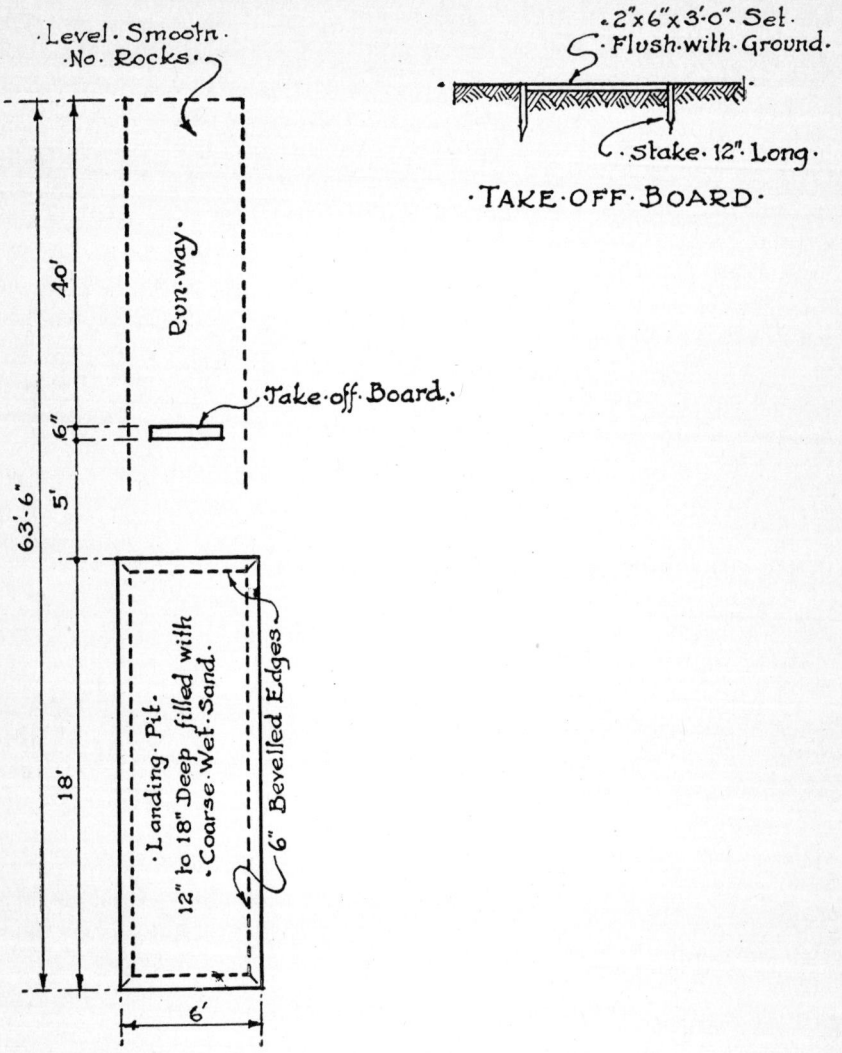

· BROAD JUMP ·

Run and Catch (27)

At a distance of thirty feet from the starting line and parallel to it, stretch a cord ten feet from the ground. At signal, the player runs from the starting line, tosses a basket ball or a volley ball over the cord, catches it, and runs back to the starting line. Three such trips are made, finishing at the starting line. In case of failure to catch the ball, it must be secured, tossed over the cord (either direction), and caught before running is continued. The starting line and the cord should both be well away from any obstruction. Total distance is sixty yards. The time taken to complete the run is the individual's record.

Running Double Broad Jump (Boys)

This event is similar to the running broad jump, except that the boy jumps off with both feet at the "take-off." Both feet must be together at the time of taking off. The mark is set and the distance measured as in the running broad jump.

Running High Jump (Boys)

In the running high jump three trials are allowed each boy at each height. The crossbar should be a thin stick, 1" x 1" x 14', and should

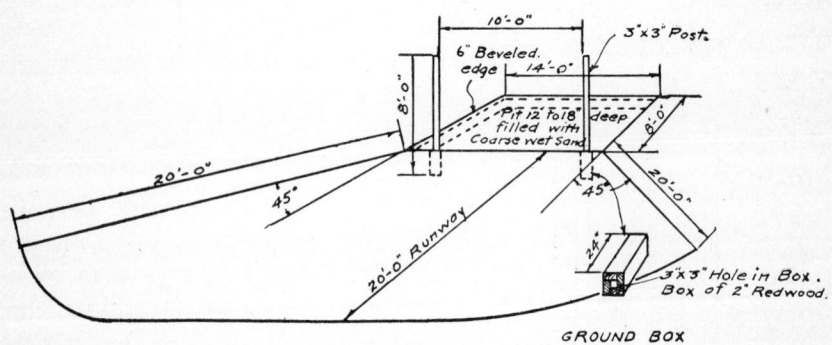

rest on pins which project not more than two inches from the uprights. When the bar is removed by a jumper, it constitutes a trial jump without result. The height is measured from the middle of the bar to the ground on a direct line. Running under the bar in making an attempt to jump is counted as a balk and three successive balks shall constitute a trial jump. Holes 3/8" in diameter should be drilled in the standards at one-inch intervals so the bar can be raised one inch at a time.

Sit-up

Equipment.—Clean space, floor or bench. Spread paper on the ground to prevent soiling the clothing.

Rules.—Lie flat on the back, feet held in position by a strap or an assistant. Rise to a sitting position slowly, without jerk, chest leading, head back, bending only at the hips. Resume the starting position slowly, back flat, head back. Arms should be placed across the abdomen. The back must be kept straight in this exercise. Discontinue the exercise before the abdominal muscles are severely strained. To avoid the danger of hernia, it is recommended that the child exhale while doing the sit-up and inhale while lowering the body.

Practice Events.—Lie on the back, raise one leg at a time to a vertical position and allow it to sink slowly. Raise both legs and allow them to sink slowly. Lie on the back, raise both legs and continue their movement until the toes touch the floor near the head.

Soccer Dribble (59) *

To conduct this event establish four posts in line, posts twenty feet apart. These may be boys, jumping standards, or Indian clubs. The contestant places the ball on a starting line twenty feet from the first post. On the signal "start" he dribbles the ball forward around the opposite side of each successive post to the last post, dribbles it around the last post, and dribbles the ball back to the first post in the same way. On rounding post No. 1 on the return trip, he kicks the ball across the starting line. The contestant must use only his feet throughout the performance. The time elapsing from the signal "start" to the moment the ball crosses the starting line is taken as the contestant's record. The event may be conducted by having the contestants make two or three round trips.

Soccer Kick for Goal

Equipment.—A soccer football. Two goal posts twenty-four feet apart with a crossbar eight feet from ground. If there are no goal posts, mark same area on wall or hand ball backstop, or indicate the twenty-four feet with two stones. Mark a point directly in front of the center of the twenty-four-foot goal line a distance of thirty feet for fifth and sixth grades, and thirty-six feet for seventh and eighth grades.

Rules.—The ball must be kicked from the ground at the place marked, and must pass between the goal posts, under the eight-foot bar, while a goal keeper attempts to prevent the ball passing between the posts. For the final test, the best goal keeper should be chosen by the teacher from each class, who shall guard the goal for each contestant. Each contestant is given ten trials.

---

* From S. C. Staley, "Individual and Mass Athletics." Copyright 1925. By permission of A. S. Barnes and Company, publishers.

Suggestions.—Keep eyes on the ball. A run of two or three steps will give more force to the kick. Kicking should be done with street shoes. Kick for goal from all angles.

Swimming

Due to a general lack of facilities for swimming in elementary schools, no attempt is here made to give rules or the technique of teaching the various strokes used. Where facilities are available, swimming should be taught. The teacher is referred to "Swimming Simplified," by Lyba and Nita Sheffield, published by A. S. Barnes and Company, 1927, or to other books on the subject.

Additional Individual Athletic Events

Hand Ball Drill I	Ref. No. 19, p. 379
Basket Ball Target Throw	Ref. No. 33, p. 115
All Fours Race	Ref. No. 59, p. 15
Baseball Target Throw	Ref. No. 59, p. 70
Baseball Throw for Distance	Ref. No. 59, p. 56
Batting for Distance	Ref. No. 59, p. 65
Hopping Race	Ref. No. 59, p. 9
Kangaroo Jump (Boys)	Ref. No. 59, p. 32
Running Double High Jump (Boys)	Ref. No. 59, p. 39

RELAY RACES

All-up Indian Club Relay (17) *

Directly in front of each aisle or row of players, and near the wall or boundary, draw two tangent circles eighteen inches in diameter. The circles should be so placed that if a line were drawn connecting the centers, the line would be parallel to the wall. In one of the circles place three Indian clubs in a standing position. Each row should contain the same number of players. At the leader's command the last player in each row runs up the right side of the row and changes the clubs, one at a time, to the other circle, using the same hand. The other hand is kept behind the back. He then runs down the left side of the row, going around to the right side, to his place. He touches the player in front of him, who runs in the same way, changing the clubs to the other circle. If a club falls over it must be placed in proper position before the player continues his run. The row wins whose front player in the row first returns to his place. Variation: Players hop to the circles and run to their places.

---

* From Forbush and Allen, "The Book of Games for Home, School and Playground." Copyright 1927. By permission of John C. Winston Company, publishers.

Arch Goal Ball Relay

Two or more baskets are placed on the floor or on hooks at any convenient height—a throwing line is drawn fifteen feet from each basket. Players of the different teams line up in single file behind the throwing lines facing the baskets. Each rear player has a basket ball, a volley ball, or a bean bag. Set length of time for play—three to five minutes. On signal the ball is passed forward with both hands over the heads of the players until it reaches the front, then the front player throws for goal. Whether he makes it or not the thrower gets the ball, runs to the rear of the line, and the play is repeated. The side having made the most goals when time is called, wins. This can be played out of doors by using basket ball goals or barrel hoops nailed to trees.

Blackboard Relay

The competing rows should be placed equidistant from the blackboard. Each row must have an equal number of players in it. The first player in each row has a piece of chalk. At a signal, this player runs to the board and makes a mark with the chalk. He then returns, sits down, and hands the chalk to the next player behind him, who runs to the board and makes his mark. This continues until the last player has made his mark and has returned to his seat. Later, players may be required to make a cross, capital letter, question mark, write a word, etc. The row wins whose last player first returns to his seat.

Bull Frog Relay

Pupils in file formation. Equal number of players in each file behind a starting line. The first runner for each team, with hands on hips and in deep-knee bend position, jumps forward around a given point for each team, then runs back. As he crosses the starting line the new player starts and performs in the same way. The first file to have its last player recross the starting line wins.

Kangaroo Relay

Divide players into two or more equal teams. Line teams up in single file behind a starting line. At the opposite end of room, or thirty feet distant, draw another line parallel to the starting line. The first player of each team places a volley ball (or whatever is used) between his knees and at the starting signal jumps to the line on the other side of the playing space, keeping the ball between his knees without touching it with his hands. If the ball falls out he must pick it up and replace it at the point where he dropped it. Upon reaching the line he takes the ball in his hands, runs back to the starting line, where he gives it to the next player on his team who should be toeing the line. He then takes his place at the rear of his team. Continue until all players have run. That team wins which first has each one of its members complete the run and is standing in a straight line at attention.

Over and Under Relay (4)

This game is a combination of arch ball and stride ball. The players are divided into equal teams and line up in files. The captains stand toeing a line drawn on the floor or ground. Each captain has a ball, Indian club, or other object, which at a given signal he passes *over* his head to the player behind him. This player passes the object *under* or between his feet to the next player, and so on, the ball going down the line, over the head of one player and between the feet of the next. When the ball reaches the end of the line, the last player runs with it to the head of the line and starts it back *over* his head. This is repeated until the captain is the last in line. He runs forward with the ball, places it on a mark fifteen or twenty feet in front of his line, and runs back to his original place at the head of the line. The team wins whose captain is the first to return to his original position.

Pass and Squat Relay

Arrange the teams in files behind a starting line. Place the captain of each team ten feet in front of his file. Give the captain a ball or bean bag. At signal the captain throws the ball to the first player in his file. The player catches it and throws it back to the captain. Immediately after passing the ball this first player squats. This continues until all have caught the ball and passed it back to the captain. Any player dropping the ball must recover it and return to his position before throwing it. Throws may be made in any manner. The team which finishes first with all members squatting, including the captain, wins.

Rescue Relay

Formation is the same as in the simple form of relay, except that a captain from each team stands facing his team at some distance from it. On the signal, the captain runs forward, grasps the hand of the first player on his team, and both run back to the captain's original place. The captain then stays there, but the one whom he took over goes back and gets the next player, and so the game continues until all have been brought over and a new line formed behind the captain. The team that is first rescued, i.e., that gets all its players to the new line first, wins.

Run, Toss and Catch Relay

Stretch rope, wire, or net eight feet above the ground. Thirty feet from, and parallel with the net, make a starting line. Line up teams in single file and at right angles to the starting line. Number from front to rear. At signal, No. 1, carrying a ball, runs forward, throws it over the net, catches it, and returns the ball by throwing, passing or handing it to No. 2. No. 2 receives the ball without assistance and must start his run with the ball in his possession back of the starting line. If runner fails to catch his own throw over the net, he must regain the ball without assistance, and throw again until a catch is made. The team whose last player returns first, carrying the ball across the starting line, wins. Two players holding a stick as high as they can reach may substitute for the stretched rope, wire or net.

Shuttle Relay (4)

There may be six, eight or more players on a team. Each team is numbered, then divided into two groups, even numbers in one group, odd numbers in another. The groups form lines, one player behind the other, and stand facing each other about fifty feet apart. At the word "Go," or at the whistle, the captain, number "one" of each team, runs forward and tags number two on his own team in the other group, who is opposite him; he then goes to the rear of that line. Number two then runs and tags number three. This continues until the two groups of each team have exchanged places. There may be any number of teams running at the same time; indeed it is better to have a number of teams than to have too many players on each team. A flag, handkerchief, bean bag, etc., may be given instead of the tagging.

Stride Ball Relay

Any kind of ball may be used. There must be one ball for each team. The players stand in rows with their feet wide apart. A ball is placed on the ground in front of each row of players. At the word "Go," the ball is rolled down the row between the legs of the players. The last one in each row takes the ball and runs forward along the left side of his team to the head of the line. Facing forward he rolls the ball between his legs and the legs of his team as before. Continue until each player has run to the front and passed the ball. The last runner on each team as he finishes holds the ball high above his head, so as to help the judge pick out the winner.

218   PHYSICAL EDUCATION FOR ELEMENTARY SCHOOLS

Additional Relay Races

Home Run Relay ....Ref. No. 19, p. 384
Potato Shuttle Relay ....Ref. No. 19, p. 154

RHYTHMICAL ACTIVITIES

Bleking (Swedish) *

(Victor: 20989; Columbia: A3037.)

Formation: A single circle, partners facing each other with both hands joined.

Part I

Description:

Measure 1—Hop, bringing the right heel and the right arm forward, elbow straight, right hand in front of partner's shoulder, and left arm

---

* From Crawford's "Folk Dances and Games." Copyright 1908. By permission of A. S. Barnes and Company, publishers.

well back with elbow bent (one, and). Hop, extending left heel and left arm in same manner (two, and).

Measure 2—The same changes made three times in quick succession, right, left, right.

Measures 3-4—Repeat, beginning with the left foot.

Measures 5-8—Repeat all.

Part II

With joined hands held straight out to the side, shoulder high, partners dance around the circle. The one with the left side toward the center starts forward with the right foot, the partner moves backward, starting with the left foot.

Measure 9—Hop twice on each foot, at the same time swinging arms up and down, windmill fashion, once in each measure. Right arm down when hopping on right foot; left arm down when hopping on left foot.

Measure 10—Use two of these steps to turn around.

Measure 11—Like measure 9, partners in reverse position.

Measures 12-16—Repeat.

Repeat dance from the beginning.

Csebogar*
Pronounced Ché-bo-gar (Hungarian)

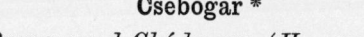

(Victor: 20992.)

Formation: Partner dance, single circle, hands joined.
Measures 1–4. Eight slides to the left.
Measures 5–8. Eight slides to the right.
Measures 1–2. Four skips toward center of circle.
Measures 3–4. Four skips back to place.
Measures 5–8. Hungarian turn.

Partners face one another. Place right arm around waist of partner.

Raise left arm above head. Hop right, step left, step right. Repeat three times, doing step four times in all.

---
* From Dorothy La Salle, "Rhythms and Dances for Elementary Schools." Copyright 1926. By permission of A. S. Barnes and Company, publishers.

FIFTH GRADE 221

Partners face one another, single circle. Boy places hands on girl's waist. Girl places hands on boy's shoulders.

Measures 9–12. Four draws toward center of circle.
Measures 13–16. Four draws back to place.
Measures 9–10. Two draws toward center.
Measures 11–12. Two draws back to place.
Measures 13–16. Hungarian turn. Finish with a shout.

Finnish Reel (Skvaller Ulla) *

(Columbia: A3062.)

Formation: Two parallel lines facing each other. Hands on hips.

Measures 1–8: Hop on left foot, and at same time touch top of right toe at side, leg twisted so heel is raised. Hop on left and touch right heel at side, toes turned up. Repeat to other side. Repeat whole step three times.

---
* From C. Ward Crampton, "The Folk Dance Book." Copyright 1909. By permission of A. S. Barnes and Company, publishers.

Measures 9–10: Step forward right. Stamp left, bringing heels together. Step backward left. Stamp right, bringing heels together.

Measures 11–12: With three running steps partners change places, passing on right side. Face the center on four.

Measures 13–16: Repeat measures 9 to 12, returning to former places.

Repeat from beginning.

The Land of Cotton (3)

(Victor: 20166.)

Music—"Dixie."

Partners around circle, girls, right shoulders to center, inside hands joined high; outer hands at hips.
1. (a) Beginning with outside foot, walk three steps forward and point inside foot, bending toward partner. Repeat, beginning inside foot and pointing away from partner.
   (b) Boy stands still as girl turns with four steps under raised arms; then girl stands as boy turns under raised arms.
   (c) Eight slides to left, away from partner; eight slides returning.
2. Repeat (a) and (b), of 1.
   (d) Join both hands and take eight slides forward around circle; eight slides returning.

Pop Goes the Weasel II *

For music see page 185.

Formation: Double circle, fours facing. No. 1 couples facing line of direction, No. 2 couples facing against line of direction. Partners inside hands joined, outside hands on hips.

Line 1—Skip forward four steps.

Line 2—Skip back four steps.

Line 3—Join hands in circles of four and skip around four steps.

Line 4—All couples No. 1 raise joined hands to make arches and skip forward while couples No. 2 skip under arches to meet new couples.

Repeat all.

Practice Polka (10)

Music: "Coming through the Rye," see page 174, or any 2/4 music.

Formation: Couples side by side with inside hands joined, outside hands on hips, facing around circle.

Polka step: After a preliminary hop on left foot, step forward with right foot—**one;** close left foot to right foot—**and;** step forward again with right foot—**two;** hop on right foot—**and.** (Measure 2.) Repeat same, beginning left foot.

---

* From Chester E. Marsh, "Singing Games and Drills." Copyright 1927. By permission of A. S. Barnes and Company, publishers.

Counts: **One-and-two-and.**
1. Polka three times forward, starting with foot away from partner.
2. Stamp three times; face partner.
3. Polka three times forward, at same time turning toward partner, then away, then toward, letting arms swing well back, then forward and then back.
4. Clap three times; partners face.
5. Polka three times (see number 3).
6. Stand still three counts (facing partner).
7. Point right toe forward, place right elbow in left hand, shake finger at partner three counts.
8. Repeat left.
9. Polka once, each one turning in place with hands on hips.
10. Stamp three times.

Repeat from beginning.

224 PHYSICAL EDUCATION FOR ELEMENTARY SCHOOLS

Ritsch, Ratsch *

Ritsch, ratsch, filebom-bom-bom,
Filebom-bom-bom, filebom-bom-bom;
Ritsch, ratsch, filebom-bom-bom,
Filebom-bom-bom, filebom.

Miss Henderson, Miss Henderson, Miss Henderson,
Miss Henderson, and little Ann Marie;
They washed themselves in ocean water, ocean water, ocean water;
Washed themselves in ocean water, ocean water clear.

* From Crampton & Wollaston, "The Song Play Book." Copyright 1917. By permission of A. S. Barnes and Company, publishers.

FIFTH GRADE

Formation: Groups of four. Players stand on the corners of a square, all facing center. Partners stand on diagonal corners. Hands are on hips. For convenience in teaching, number children 1, 2, 3 and 4.

Line 1. All clap hands twice; then hop on the right foot and place left heel forward.

Line 2. Hop on left foot and place right heel forward; hop on right foot and place left heel forward.

Lines 3 and 4. Repeat action of lines 1 and 2.

Line 5. As "Miss Henderson" is sung the first time, numbers 1 and 2 bow, bending from the hips with the heels together. At the same time their opposites 3 and 4 courtesy (touch right toe behind the left heel and bend both knees). As "Miss Henderson" is sung the second and third time in quicker rhythm, numbers 1 and 2 courtesy and 3 and 4 bow.

Line 6. As "Miss Henderson" is sung, numbers 1 and 2 bow, and 3 and 4 courtesy as at first. At the words "Little Ann Marie" clap hands three times.

Lines 7 and 8. All face left. Beginning with the left foot dance seven polka steps forward. Finish facing center, stamping on the word "clear."

Virginia Reel (Sir Roger de Coverley) *

* From Mr. and Mrs. Henry Ford, "Good Morning; Old Fashioned Dances Revived." Copyright 1926. By permission of Dearborn Publishing Company, Dearborn, Michigan, publishers.

Reel (Mrs. Mc Leod)

D.C. Reel until March

March (John Brown's Body)

(Victor: 20447; Columbia: 50018D; 33048F.)

FIFTH GRADE

Form in two straight lines, six couples in each set. Do not walk through the changes, but use a light, springy, trot step, with plenty of action from the toes and ankles. The head lady and the foot gentleman begin all movements in the first period, and are immediately followed by the head gentleman and foot lady who execute the same change. The music and dancers start together.

Head lady and foot gentleman forward and back—4 bars. Both advance forward four steps, meet, bow and courtesy, and return to place, each moving backward.

Head gentleman and foot lady forward and back—4 bars.

Head lady and foot gentleman swing with the right hands—4 bars. Head lady and foot gentleman advance four steps, join right hands, "shoulder high" make one complete turn, drop hands, and return to place moving backward.

Head gentleman and foot lady swing with the right hands—4 bars.

Head lady and foot gentleman swing with the left hands—4 bars. Both advance and swing with the left hands—4 bars.

Head gentleman and foot lady swing with left hands—4 bars.

Head lady and foot gentleman swing with both hands—4 bars. Both advance four steps, join both hands, make one complete turn, and return to place, moving backward.

Head gentleman and foot lady swing with both hands—4 bars.

Head lady and foot gentleman dos à dos—4 bars. Both advance four steps, passing each other right shoulder to right shoulder, each takes one step to the right side, back to back. Without turning, turn around each other, and move backward to place.

Head gentleman and foot lady *dos à dos*—4 bars.

Head couple down the center—8 bars. They join both hands, chassé down the inside of the set and return to place.

Right arm to partner, all reel—32 bars. The head couple link right arms, and turn once and a half around. The head lady then turns the next gentleman in line with the left arm once around, while her partner turns the next lady with his left. The head couple then turn each other once around, with right arms. The head couple turns the next couple with the left, then turns own partner with the right. This is continued until the head couple has turned each dancer in line, and has reached the foot of the set. There they turn each other half around, so that each is on his respective side. They then join both hands, chassé up the center eight steps to the head of the set. Both are now in their original places.

The idea is that the couple in reeling down the line from one side to the other, link arms and reel each other at each crossing from one side to the other. There will be five crossings, making ten contacts with the linked arms of the other dancers, and five contacts in the center of the set with one's own partner.

March—16 bars. Execute a sharp "about face" toward foot of line. Ladies march to the right, gentlemen to the left. When the head couple reaches the foot of the set, they stop, raise both hands, forming an arch, while the line makes an "about face" toward the head of the line, passing under the arch, up the center to the head.

NOTE.—The couple who started the dance is now at the foot of the set and, of course, foot couple. The new couple now at the head of the set begins the movements and each in turn, until the original couple is back at the head of the set, when the dance is finished. To reel, always turn your own partner with the right arm, and other couples with the left. To end the dance call, "All join hands forward, turn partners, promenade to seats."

Additional Rhythmical Activities

Nuts in May ....Ref. No. 17, p. 73
Sellengers Round (Victor: 20445; Columbia:
   10009D) ....Ref. No. 18, p. 248
Fist Polka ....Ref. No. 26, p. 253
Russian Snowstorm ....Ref. No. 26, p. 212
Troika ....Ref. No. 26, p. 258
Weaving Dance..............................Ref. No. 26, p. 264
Hopi Corn Dances ....Ref. No. 31, p. 83
Janko ....Ref. No. 31, p. 106
Kaca ....Ref. No. 31, p. 97
Nickodickomdij ....Ref. No. 42, p. 47
Soldiers Joy (Victor: 20592; Columbia: 33120F)..Ref. No. 45, p. 6
Strasak ....Ref. No. 54, p. 72
Bummel Schottische (Victor: 20448) ....Ref. No. 95, p. 39

STUNTS

Turk Stand

Cross right foot over left, arms side horizontal; sit down Turk fashion. Stand up again without touching hands to floor.

Heel Click

The heel click should be done by jumping into the air from the side straddle position clicking the heels together more than once if possible. It can also be done from the starting position of standing on either foot with the other extended sideward.

Wooden Man

a. Number one lies on his back on the mat; number two stands at his head, bends forward, clasps both hands behind number one's neck and raises him to a standing position. b. Same as (a) but clasps hands in rear of number one's head instead of his neck. c. As (a) but number one lies face downward and number two clasps his hand under number one's forehead.

Seal Crawl

In push-up position, without sagging the body, walk forward on hands, dragging feet. Keep the knees straight.

Horizontal to Perpendicular

Lie flat on the back and fold the arms. Now get up to standing position without unfolding the arms.

Horizontal Balance

Jump the Stick

Hold a stick with both hands in front of the body. Jump over the stick without letting go of it or touching it with the feet. Jump back. Try to go back and forth rapidly several times. Limber up the legs before trying by pulling them up to the chest several times.

Indian Wrestle

Two players lie on their backs facing in opposite directions, side by side, with adjacent arms locked. At a signal, the adjacent legs are brought to an upright position and interlocked at the knees. The wrestle consists in trying to force the opponent to roll over from his position.

Additional Stunts

Knee and Toe Wrestle .... Ref. No. 19, p. 246
Crane Dive .... Ref. No. 60, p. 103
Eskimo Roll .... Ref. No. 60, p. 127
Front Foot Flip .... Ref. No. 60, p. 130
Hand Jump .... Ref. No. 60, p. 121
Human Bridge .... Ref. No. 60, p. 121
Mule Kick .... Ref. No. 60, p. 97
Solid Ivory .... Ref. No. 60, p. 95

HUNTING GAMES

Ante Over

Two teams are chosen. They stand on opposite sides of a building. A player calls "Ante Over," and throws the ball over the building. Some one on the other team tries to catch it. If he succeeds, he and all his teammates dart around to the other side of the building. There he must throw the ball, trying to hit one of the opponents who are trying to escape around the building. If he succeeds in hitting some one, the player whom he has hit remains on his side. The ball is given to the opponents. If he does not succeed in hitting some one, he joins the other team, and the ball is given to the side he has just left. If no one catches the ball when it is thrown over the building, the side that has failed to catch it calls "Ante Over," and throws it back. The game can also be played by throwing the ball over a curtain stretched in the gymnasium or in a large hall. If the ball fails to go over and rolls back, the side throwing calls out "Pig's tail." The side wins which gains all the players.

Center Catch Touch Ball

All of the players but one stand in a circle, with arms' distance apart. The odd player in the center tries to touch or catch the ball, which is tossed rapidly from one circle player to another. Should he be successful the one who *last* touched the ball before he did, changes places with him. Variation: Add two or three center men. The one who touches the ball first is freed, the others remaining in the center with the new player, until they succeed in being the first to touch the ball.

Circle Kick Ball (5)

Players form a circle, hands joined. A soccer ball is introduced and is kicked from one side to the other. The players should prevent the ball from passing to the outside of the circle, with any part of their body, but must not break hands. The two players between whom the ball passes are eliminated. A player who kicks the ball overhead is eliminated. Those who are eliminated may begin a new game, and play without elimination until the first circle has but five players remaining, when a new game is begun with all the players. Variations: 1. Circle revolves in either direction, instead of remaining stationary. 2. An imaginary line divides the circle into two teams, A and B. Each player endeavors to kick the ball through the opposing side, circle—stationary or revolving. Successful player scores one point for his side; fifteen points make a game. A kick overhead deducts one point; players are not eliminated.

Center Stride Ball

All the players but one form a circle, taking a stride position, their feet touching those of the next player. One player in the center of the circle has a basket or volley ball, and endeavors to throw it between the feet of the players, who may stop the ball only with the hands. The player who permits the ball to pass between his feet, secures the ball and changes places with the center player. If a ball passes to the right side and below the shoulder of a player, that player exchanges places with the center man. A player may pass the ball outside by putting it between the feet of one of his two neighbors. The neighbor then exchanges places with the one in the center. The circle players should try to keep the ball away from the center player by passing it quickly. Two or three center players are permissible.

Bean Bag Target Toss

Draw three concentric circles on the ground. The inner circle should be two feet in diameter; the second four feet; and the third six feet in diameter. Ten or more feet from the outer rim of the largest circle draw a straight line to serve as a throwing line. The thrower stands with the toes of one foot at, and the other foot back of, the throwing line and tosses a bean bag toward the target. If the bag falls within the center circle, it scores fifteen points; if between the center circle and the next larger one, it scores ten points; and if between the middle circle and the outer one, it scores five points. A bag touching a line scores the lower value. The player first making one hundred points wins.

Catch of Fish

A goal is marked off at each end of the field, and the players are divided into two equal groups, which take their positions in the two goals. The players in one goal join hands and stand in line to form the net. The players in the other goal are the fish. At a given signal all the players change goals. The net tries to catch as many of the fish as possible by surrounding them. The fish can escape only through the opening between the ends of the net and can not go under the arms. When the ends close together, all that are within are caught, and must assist that side. The groups go back to their goals. The fish then join hands and become the net. The game continues in this way, each group being alternately fish and net, until all of one side are caught.

Hook On (3)

Players in groups of four, standing behind each other, with arms clasped around the waist of the player in front. An extra player or players, attempt to "hook-on" at the rear of any file, and each file tries, by evading this extra player, to prevent his "hooking on." When the extra player succeeds, the first player in this file becomes the odd man, and tries to "hook on" to a file of players.

Indian Club Guard (16)

Draw a circle fifteen or twenty feet in diameter. All but one of the players stand outside the circle. Indian clubs are placed in the center and the odd player guards them. The players on the outside of the circle endeavor to knock down the Indian clubs with the basket ball. The basket ball is passed swiftly around and across the circle while the guard in the center tries to keep between the clubs and the ball. Whoever succeeds in knocking down the clubs changes places with the center guard. The guard who stays in the center the longest, wins.

FIFTH GRADE

O'Leary (3)

Tune: "One little, two little, three little Indians." The words: "One and two and three O'Leary," ending, "Ten O'Leary postman."

Bat the ball with the flat of the hand to 1-2-3 and do the prescribed movement each time at the word "O'Leary," letting the ball bounce higher by hitting it harder. To "Ten O'Leary postman," give one bounce and catch the "Postman." The ball is never caught until the last. Exercises:

1. Swing right leg outward over the ball on saying "O'Leary."
2. Swing left leg outward over ball on saying "O'Leary."
3. Swing right leg inward over ball on saying "O'Leary."
4. Swing left leg inward over ball on saying "O'Leary."
5. Grasp edge of skirt with left hand and upon saying "O'Leary" make the ball pass upward between the arm and skirt.
6. Same as exercise 5, but let ball pass through from above.
7. Grasp right wrist with left hand, forming circle with arms, and make the ball pass through from below upon saying "O'Leary."
8. Same as exercise 7, letting ball drop over from above.
9. Touch forefingers and thumbs together when saying "O'Leary," and through circle formed let ball drop from above.
10. To the words "One O'Leary," "Two O'Leary," "Three O'Leary" and so on to "Ten O'Leary Postman," bounce ball alternately to right and left of right foot, the foot moving from side to side.
11. Bounce ball to the same words as in exercise 10, keeping foot absolutely still.
12. To same words as in exercise 10, bounce ball, throwing right leg over ball at every bounce.
13. Same as exercise 12, throwing right leg inward over ball.
14. Same as exercise 13, throwing left leg outward at every bounce.
15. Same as exercise 14, throwing left leg inward at every bounce.
16. To the words, "Jack, Jack, Pump the Water, Jack, Jack, Pump the Water, Jack, Jack, Pump the Water so Early in the Morning," go through the same movements of bouncing ball three times and giving it a stronger bat on the word "water," making a complete turn left.
17. Same as exercise 16, making a complete turn right.

Pass and Change

Arrange all of the group but one in a circle forty feet in diameter, players facing in. An extra player, "It," stands in the center of the circle with a ball. At signal, "It" calls the names of two players and at the same time passes the ball to a third. The players whose names are called run to exchange places. The player in the circle who catches the ball immediately throws it back to "It." Upon catching the ball, "It" throws it at one of the players who are exchanging places. If he succeeds in hitting a player before he arrives at his new position that player becomes "It." If he fails to hit a player he remains "It." In either case the ball is recovered and given to "It" and at the signal the game continues.

Vis-a-Vis

Half of group are numbered 1's; other half are numbered 2's; an odd player is "It." Number 1's choose partners from the 2's. Couples scatter over the playground within hearing of the leader's voice. "It" stands in the center of the field and gives directions which the other players must execute. He may say "face to face," "back to back," "kneel on knee," "stand up," "hands on hips," etc. When he calls "vis-a-vis" all the number 1 players run for new partners, while the one who has been "It" tries to get a partner. The number 2 players stand still. The player who fails to get a partner is "It." After a time, have the number 1 players stand still and the number 2 players run, changing the number of the odd player from 1 to 2.

Additional Hunting Games

Going to Jerusalem ....Ref. No. 17, p. 140
Pom Pom Pullaway ....Ref. No. 17, p. 156
Three Deep ....Ref. No. 17, p. 200
Dumbbell Tag ....Ref. No. 19, p. 83
How Many Miles to Babylon ....Ref. No. 19, p. 108
Japanese Tag ....Ref. No. 19, p. 116
Jumping Rope III ....Ref. No. 19, p. 121
Last Man ....Ref. No. 19, p. 126
Leader and Footer ....Ref. No. 19, p. 127
Pebble Chase ....Ref. No. 19, p. 145
Triple Change ....Ref. No. 19, p. 200

MIMETICS

Chopping Wood

Feet apart—jump! Holding ax over left shoulder, strike down and swing back to other shoulder with a twisting of trunk.

Cross-Cut Sawing

Alternate rows face each other. Place left foot forward; reach both arms well forward. Pupils in odd rows sway body forward, bending left knee, and thrust arms forward as if pushing saw. Pupils in even rows sway backward onto right leg, twisting trunk to right and forcibly bring bent arms to right hip. Movements are repeated alternately by rows facing each other.

Pumping Up Bicycle Tire

Vigorous forward, downward bending with decided knee-bending and arm-stretching downward. Keep good posture position with back flat.

Scythe Swinging (4)

Start with the right arm extended sideward, downward and outward; the left forearm held across the front of the body about the waist level, the body twisted to the right. At the command "swing!" the arms are swung vigorously across the body from right to left, the left arm becoming extended downward, sideward and outward; the right forearm held across the front of the body about the waist level, the body twisted to the left. This movement should be done three or four times in each direction.

Signaling

Raise right arm sideward upward and left leg sideward. Return to position. Raise left arm upward and right leg sideward. Return. Continue in rhythm, sixteen counts.

Standing Broad Jump (6B)

In preparing to jump, stand on your toes with arms above head, bring the arms forward, downward, bending the knees and inclining the body forward. Spring from both feet, jump high as well as far, drawing the knees well up. Swing the arms forward and upward as you jump out.

Thread the Needle (13B)

Clasp hands low in front. Step with right foot through ring formed by hands and stand on right foot. Step through ring with left foot, and stand erect.

SIXTH GRADE

	PAGE
Athletic Games	237
Individual Athletic Events	248
Relay Races	251
Stunts	254
Rhythmical Activities	258
Hunting Games	268
Mimetics	271

The teacher should refer frequently to Part I of the book as it contains many suggestions in regard to the various activities. For example—the material presented in Part I under "Posture," "Corrective Physical Education," and "Health Education," applies to all grades and should be reviewed frequently.

The activity classifications in each grade have been arranged in sequence according to judgments of their appeal and importance to the children who will use them. In situations where all the content appearing in this grade can not be taught, the teacher should make selections from each classification rather than attempt to teach all the activities found in any one classification.

ATHLETIC GAMES

Bowl Club Ball

The Field. The shape and size may be the same as a playground baseball diamond.

Equipment. One soccer ball; one Indian club; or substitute, placed on the base. The base is about ten feet to the right of the pitcher's box, and should be at least forty feet from home plate. There is only the one base to which runs are made.

Players. Two teams of one pitcher, one catcher, one baseman, and a limited number of fielders.

The Game. The pitcher bowls the ball to the batter who tries to kick it into the field. Should the pitcher bowl four "balls," i.e., not over the home plate, the kicker places the ball on home plate and kicks it. If fair, he runs; if foul, he is out. A batter is out: (1) If he steps beyond the home plate when kicking the ball; (2) On the third strike missed. The first two strikes count as fouls, as in baseball; (3) On a fly ball caught; (4) If, while running and before reaching the base, a fielder knocks down the club with the ball, or if the batter be tagged with, or be hit by, the ball below the shoulders while running to or from the base. A runner is not safe if he stops at the base; (5) If the trial kick given for "balls" is missed; (6) If he runs out of the lane between home and base. A fielder must throw the ball from where it is fielded. The catcher and the fielders may not hold the ball more than three seconds. Penalty: Runner given the run. The ball may not be passed between any two members of the fielding team more than once. It must then be thrown to a third player who may return the ball to one of the two players, when the two may again pass the ball between them once. Violations of any one of the rules by the fielding team gives a point to the runner. Three men out constitute an inning. Five or more innings shall constitute a match. Four time periods may be used, in which case as many runs as possible are scored during the period regardless of outs made. Teams exchange places alternately.

Circle Strike

This game is recommended for practice in batting, fielding, catching and pitching. Draw a circle sixty feet in diameter. Use a playground baseball and bat. One team of players stand around the circle, and are numbered consecutively. Number one acts as catcher, while the player opposite him in the circle acts as the pitcher. The pitcher steps into a position of about thirty feet from the catcher. The other team lines up in a line and counts off consecutively. Number one of the team is the first batter, and to bat steps in front of the catcher of the other team. Five trial balls are pitched to this batter, and he attempts to bat the ball outside of the circle. Each ball batted outside counts a score for his team. If he bats a fly, however, and a player from the circle is able to run back and catch it, no score is made. When the first batter has had his five trials, the circle shifts one place to the left so that No. 2 is the catcher and the player opposite him is the new pitcher. Batter No. 2 then has his five trials. This continues until all on one team have batted. The teams then change places, and the second team bats as the first one did. The scores are recorded and compared at the end of the game.

Field Ball (14) *

The Game. The game of field ball is played by two teams of eleven players each. The ball is passed from one player to another. Each team tries to get the ball through the opponents' goal, and, at the same time, tries to prevent the other team from securing possession of the ball or scoring. A goal made from the field or from a free throw counts one point.

The Field. The field of play shall be as shown in the diagram. Maximum size—180' x 100'. On school grounds where area is limited, use largest available space.

Goals. Official goals are upright posts placed ten feet apart in the center of the end lines. The cross bars are 8 feet above the ground. On school grounds, in the absence of official goals, portable volley ball standards with a rope stretched between them may serve as goal posts. Jump standards may be used, or width of goal be indicated by baseball bases, hit pins, or similar objects, placed ten feet apart.

Ball. A soccer ball.

Team. Eleven players; i.e., 5 forwards—center forward, right inside, left inside, right outside and left outside; 3 halfbacks—center, right and left; 2 fullbacks—right and left; and a goal keeper. The goal keeper shall be restricted to his own place within the goal area.

Time of Game. Four quarters of five minutes each with two-minute rest periods after first and third quarters and ten-minute rest period between second and third quarters.

Choice of Goal. Captain of side winning toss shall have option of throwing off or choice of goals. Teams change goals at beginning of third quarter.

---

* This is a modified form of the game originated by Dr. Louis R. Burnett, Director of Health and Physical Education, Baltimore, Maryland. The revised rules (1930) for Field Ball may be found in Spaulding's Athletic Activities for Women and Girls, No. 116R, p. 61.

SIXTH GRADE

Start of Play. Team which throws off shall line up at or behind halfway line, and one of their number shall throw ball from center of field into opponents' half of field. Opponents may not block ball within fifteen feet of center line. Penalty: Throw off is repeated. No player on either side shall cross halfway line until ball has crossed line.

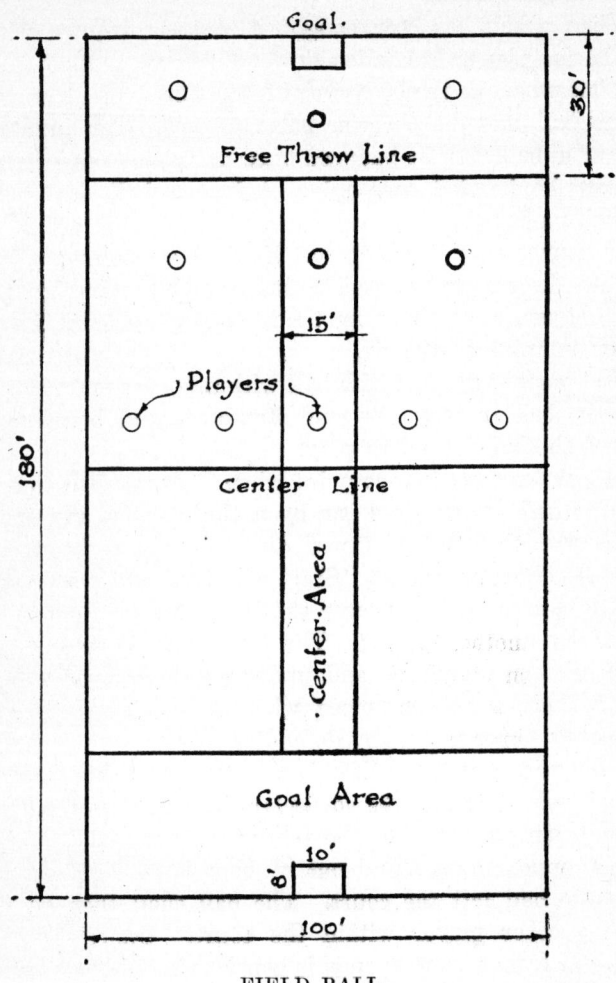

FIELD BALL

Putting Ball in Play. (a) After a goal, ball put in play at center as in "Start of Play." Side which did not make goal shall throw off.

(b) After a successful penalty throw ball put in play at center as in "Start of Play."

(c) At beginning of second and fourth quarters ball put in play at place it was last in play when time was called. It is returned to player in whose possession it was when time was called. Possessor of ball begins play with an unguarded throw—all players five yards away.

(d) If ball is caught simultaneously by two players (four hands) it is tossed up between them as in basket ball. Neither player may catch ball until it has touched ground.

Possession of Ball. (a) When catching a ball, two hands are necessary to secure it; but if caught, it may be legally retained in one hand or thrown with one hand.

(b) When a ball has been caught it must be thrown within three seconds. If the player has fallen down, the three seconds are counted from the time when all the body weight is again on the feet.

(c) The ball may be thrown, batted, bounced or juggled in any direction. The ball may be bounced once only, with one or both hands. The ball may be juggled once only. A bounce ball shall not be used combined with a juggle.

(d) No player may hand or roll the ball to another player. The ball must be thrown or bounced to another player or thrown for the goal. The player, when throwing the ball, must be standing on one or both feet or jumping in the air.

(e) Goal keeper may run with ball within goal area.

(f) If the ball in play hits goal standards and bounces back into playing field the ball is still in play.

Scoring. A team scores one point when it causes ball to go between goal uprights and under cross bar by a throw from any spot in field of play. A goal shall not be scored directly from a throw-in or from a throw from center of field at "Start of Play," or from a free throw outside of goal area. The thrower shall not play again until ball has been played by another player. The team also scores each time the ball passes between standards and under cross-piece, or within 8 feet of ground if there is no cross-piece, whether ball is tossed, bounced or rolled or carried through goal by defending side.

Out of Bounds. If at any time during the game the ball goes out of bounds at the sides, it shall be so declared by the referee, and put in play again by an opponent of the player who caused it to go out of bounds, said opponent to stand out of bounds at right angles to the spot where the ball left the court. The ball shall then be thrown or bounced to another player within the court. Unnecessary delay in recovering ball from out of bounds is considered delaying the game.

Center Area. Center area is a closed area. Two center forwards and two center halfbacks are the only players permitted in this area. It is a foul for any one of them to step over a side boundary line out of center area, or for any other player to step over any boundary line into center area. Penalty: Free throw as for any other foul. Suggested that four center players be marked distinctly, otherwise impossible to tell who is fouling when more than four players appear in center area. Goal area—open area to either team.

Defenders' Ball Out. If the defenders are entitled to the ball beyond the end or goal line, the goal keeper shall take the ball and may throw it into the field from any part of the goal area, with or without a run. The goal keeper may run to the 30-foot line to throw the ball.

Attackers' Ball Out. When attackers are entitled to the ball beyond the goal line, one of them shall throw it in while standing at the corner junction of end and side lines. The defenders must remain 15 feet away until the ball leaves the thrower's hands.

Free Throw. When a foul has been called, the referee shall immediately secure possession of the ball and place it upon the free throw line of the team making the foul. The throw shall be made within ten seconds after the ball has been placed upon the line. The goal shall be guarded only by goal keeper and fullbacks, and every other player, with the exception of the one making the throw, shall stand outside of the goal area. If the goal is made, the ball shall be put in play at the center. If the goal is missed, the ball continues in play. (See "Defenders' Ball Out" above.)

Fouls and Penalties. Fouls:

1. Stepping with both feet while holding ball; i.e., one foot must remain in place when throwing except while feet are in air during jump.

2. Handing ball to another, kicking it or touching it when held by another.

3. Overguarding ball or holder, pushing, striking, or interfering with progress of a player or otherwise using rough tactics (in the judgment of an official).

4. Juggling or bouncing ball twice in succession or combining a bounce with a juggle in same play; holding ball longer than 3 seconds or throwing it while lying down.

5. Center forward or center halfback stepping any part of either foot beyond side boundary line out of center area or any other member of team stepping with either foot within center area.

Penalty for 1, 2, 3, 4, 5, above when these fouls occur outside goal area: Ball given to nearest opponent on the spot for an unguarded throw in any direction; nearest opponent must be 5 yards away.

Penalty when fouls are committed inside goal area: When defenders commit a foul within goal area, a free throw (goal guarded only by goal keeper and fullbacks) awarded attackers. One of attackers shall throw ball from any boundary line of goal area, except the end line. If goal is not made, ball is in play; if goal is made, ball put in play at center as at "Start of Play." This shall include the foul made by a goal keeper who steps out of the goal area while ball is in play.

When attackers commit a foul inside goal area, ball is given to goal keeper for a free throw from anywhere within goal area, with every one five yards away. If two players (one from each team) foul simultaneously in the goal area, the referee shall call "time out" and shall award a free throw to each side, taken on the free throw line. Ball then put in play at center as in "Start of Play." If two players (one from each team) foul simultaneously outside of goal area, the ball is tossed up between the two nearest opposing players, wherever ball is in play on field.

6. Offside: At start of game if a player of side having throw-off at the center crosses halfway line ahead of ball, that player is "offside," and ball shall be called for a second throw from a new line five yards back of halfway line. Same penalty if ball is thrown less than 15 feet into opponents' half of field. When either of foregoing fouls is committed a second time, ball shall be given to opponents for a throw-off at center.

7. Intentional interference: It is a foul to (intentionally) push, hold, strike, or interfere with the progress of a player or otherwise use rough tactics in the judgment of an official.

Penalty: Free throw to side fouled.

Notes on Teaching. Field ball is essentially an open game. Utilize the whole field. Teach players to keep their own positions, and to make their passes fast, short and accurate. Discourage long undirected passes. Outsides and insides should not crowd over to the center. Teach forwards to be fast; to throw swiftly and accurately, and to maintain their relative positions. The function of forward line is attack. The forwards should never fall back into goal to assume defense. This is the province of fullbacks and goal keeper. Halfbacks play partly defense and partly offense. They should keep their position behind the forwards and feed the ball to members of the forward line. The function of fullbacks is entirely defense. They should never advance farther than center line. The goal keeper should be able to get ball quickly and throw it a great distance.

Hit or Out

This is a ball game in which a pitcher stands with his back to a wall or hand ball backstop and pitches to a batter who is twenty, thirty, or forty feet away, according to the grade. The batter tries to hit the ball against the wall or backstop. A twelve-inch playground baseball should be used. Areas are designated on the wall for one base hits, two base hits, three base hits and home runs, which, when struck by the batted ball, enable the batter to progress for a base or run. If the ball misses the wall, or is stopped by the pitcher, an "out" is made. Three "outs" change the sides. Each team keeps its score by innings, but there is no actual base running. Not more than three players should be used on a side.

Net Ball

The rules for net ball are the same as for volley ball, with the exception that the ball is thrown and caught instead of being batted. See "Rules for Volley Ball," page 294. (1) Ball must be thrown from place where it is caught. It is a foul if player walks with ball. (Penalty—one point to serving side, if foul is committed by receivers; loss of serve if foul is committed by serving side.) (2) If impact in catching the ball forces catcher to take one or more steps, he may return the ball from the spot where he stops, whether in or out of the court. Referee shall decide whether player stops as soon as possible; (3) A match may be played on a time instead of point basis; i.e., in quarters or halves of determined length, teams changing courts for second half or for each new quarter. Suggested: Six-minute quarters, one-minute rest period between first and second and third and fourth, five-minute rest period between second and third; or two ten-minute halves, five-minute rest period between halves.

Paddle Tennis (82)

Paddle tennis can be provided on space less expensively maintained than regular tennis, on cement, dirt or grass surface. The game is played on a court marked similar to a tennis court, but with all dimensions halved. The actual area taken is one-quarter that of a regular tennis court. Where space does not permit the official size, the court may be made smaller as long as each dimension is kept proportional. The same rules as lawn tennis apply. See page 291. The court may be marked with chalk, paint, tape, or little grooves in the ground. The net may be attached to posts, railings, chairs, etc., or stands may be ordered or constructed. Height of net from top of ground should be two feet four inches at posts, and two feet two inches at center. First determine the position of your net. Then place in the ground two pegs eighteen feet apart. (See points A and B in the diagram.) Secure a length of non-stretchable cord or rope about fifty feet long. Make a loop in one end and attach to peg B. Now measure off nineteen and one-half feet on this cord from peg B and make a knot—one. Then measure 25½ feet on cord from knot one and make knot two. Attach knot two to peg A. Draw cord taut, holding cord at knot one. This will give you point C. The opposite corner D is found by interchanging the cord on A and B and repeating the process. Place pegs at C and D. Make the same measurements on the other side of the net and place pegs at E and F. Now run your court tapes from E to D, F to C, E to F, and D to C. This will give you the side and base lines. To complete the court, lay the tapes for the two service lines and then the half-court line by following the measurements shown in the diagram. There should be fifteen feet from the base line to the backstop to give room for play.

Equipment. Three-ply, laminated and glued hardwood paddles; a light, solid sponge rubber ball; a net eighteen feet long and two feet high; posts, stakes, and court tape. This equipment may be obtained

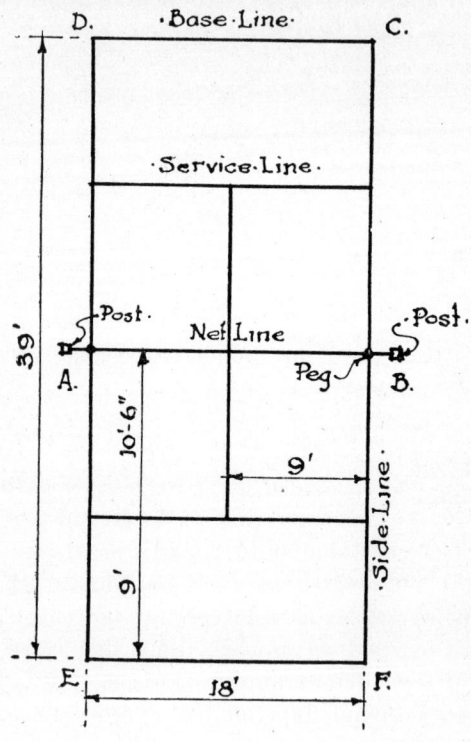

·PADDLE TENNIS·COURT·

from the Paddle Tennis Company, 285 Madison Avenue, New York, New York, or through your dealer.

Pin Basket Ball (14F)

Equipment. Basket ball (or soccer for small children). Two Indian clubs or wooden pins, one in the center of each circle at either end of court. Indian clubs or pins should be fastened upon small wooden bases for greater stability in playing on rough grounds. Usable pins may be made on one-foot lengths of 2 x 4's fastened on bases, or one-foot lengths of 4 x 4's unmounted, or one-foot lengths may be salvaged from broken baseball bats and screwed upon bases, or old ten pins with bases squared off.

Court. Basket ball court or ground of equivalent size marked as for nine-court basket ball with addition of a circle three feet in diameter drawn inside each middle end court, with circumference of circle touching midpoint of end boundary line of court.

Rules. The rules are the same as for nine-court basket ball. See page 282. Exceptions—Ball is thrown to knock down Indian club or pin instead of being thrown through a basket. Upon a free throw for goal, ball is thrown—not rolled—from the regulation free-throw line, fifteen feet from end boundary of court. Should ball touch the ground in a free throw before knocking the club down, a point shall not be counted and the ball shall be in play. In making a free throw, the player may not step past the fifteen-foot free-throw line until the ball has entered the circle. If played on a regulation basket ball court a ball striking the basket ball post and rebounding into the court shall be in play. It is a foul for any player to step inside one of the circles. Penalty—A "free throw" to opposite team.

Score. Two points when pin is knocked over in a "field throw"; one point when pin is knocked over in a "free throw."

Punt Back

This is a game in punting between two teams of from three to ten players, on a field of varying size. A soccer ball is punted back and forth, i.e., held in the hands and then dropped, but kicked while still in the air. A player catching the ball on the fly is allowed three steps forward. The player "marking" the ball, i.e., catching the ball with his heel fixed on the ground, is allowed five steps forward. If not caught on the fly the ball is punted from where it was first touched by a player, or where the ball rests when recovered. To score, it is usually specified that the ball must be "drop-kicked," i.e., held in the hands then dropped and kicked at the instant the ball touches the ground, over the opponents' goal or goal line. Each successful drop kick counts one point. The game may be played in two halves with a definite time limit. The team scoring the largest number of points wins.

Simplified Soccer

Playing Space. Sixty by eighty feet, but may be larger or smaller, if necessary, to suit conditions. The length of the field is divided into four equal sections by lines. Goal posts may be placed at either end of the field, eighteen feet apart and six and one-half feet high. The lines dividing the field are designated as center line, halfback lines and goal lines.

Players. Each team should have eleven players; one goal keeper, two fullbacks, three halfbacks, and five forwards. Number of players may be varied to accommodate a small field, or a small or large group.

Ball. Soccer football.

Time. Two definite periods of not less than five, nor more than fifteen minutes, with a rest of three minutes or more between the periods.

Scoring. Every time the ball is kicked across the goal line between the two goal posts, whether it be on the ground or in the air, one point is scored by the attacking team.

Umpires, Referees, Timekeepers, Scorers. The rules for appointing these and their duties, are the same as those in any match soccer game. Choice of goals and change of goals after each period of play is done in the same manner as in other match games.

Position of Players and Restriction to Playing Space. Five forwards lined up on their own side of the center line facing their opponents' goal. The two taking the outside positions are called "outsides"; the one taking the center position is called "center"; those taking the positions between are called "insides." The words left and right are used to designate the side of the field the player is on when he stands with his back to his goal. These five forwards, after the ball is in play, may go only as far back as the center line, and may go forward to the goal line of their opponents' territory. They must keep to the outside, inside, and center of the field, as their names indicate. Three halfbacks, center, left and right, may play only between the halfback line of their own territory, and the center line. Fullbacks, two, left and right, may play only between the halfback line and the goal line. Goal keeper plays between the goal posts in front of, or to the left or right of the goal. A point is made by the opposing team when a player steps out of his designated playing area. Players constantly leaving their lanes may be required to exchange places with the goal keeper or a fullback.

Duties of the Players. Forwards attack their opponents' goal. Halfbacks keep the ball in the possession of their forwards. Fullbacks and goal keepers protect their own goal and keep their opponents from scoring.

The Start. The ball is placed on the center line between the two center players of each team. When the whistle sounds, these two players touch in unison, the ball and the ground alternately three times with their right foot. At the finish of the third time, each player tries to kick the ball to one of his inside forward men. (The play may be started as in regular soccer or as after a tie ball in speedball.)

Rules. No one may touch the ball with his hands. If he does so, even accidentally, the opposite side is given a free kick at the point where the ball was touched. At any time when a free kick is given, all players must be at least five feet away from person taking a free kick. If the ball goes out of bounds, either at the side or end, the player opposite the one last kicking it is given a free kick from the point on the line where the ball passed out. Holding, pushing, kicking, or tripping of players shall not be allowed. A foul must be called immediately, and a point given to the other side.

Suggestions. Teach the forward players to play the ball to each other rather than straight ahead; also, that it is absolutely necessary for the forwards to be in a nearly straight line across the field when attacking their opponents' goal. When nearing the goal lines, the outside players should begin to close in toward the center and inside players, and always be ready to drop back and get the ball, should it be played out by their opponents' fullbacks or goal keeper. They should also be taught that hard kicks are usually unprofitable ones, and that short, well-placed kicks with every kick followed up, is the idea. Never interfere with the ball if one of your own players is fighting for it—either cover the ground in front of him, or drop a little behind him so that if he loses the ball, you can be ready for it. Weak players may take fullback or goal keepers' positions, as there is comparatively little running to be done. Stronger and more active players should be put into forward and halfback positions.

Two Old Cat

Equipment. Two playground bats, one twelve-inch playground baseball, and two bases thirty feet apart.

Players. There are from four to eight players. Each player keeps his own score.

Game. The object of the game is to keep at bat and make as many runs as possible between bases. The game begins by having one batter and one pitcher-catcher at each base. The remaining players are fielders. The ball is thrown back and forth between bases. When either batter hits a fair ball they exchange bases and thus score a point for each. Foul balls count as strikes. Four balls give a point to the batter, and batters exchange bases.

Fair Ball. Any ball is fair which lands inside the playing area determined by two parallel lines—one drawn through each base. A ball batted beyond the opposite base line is still a fair ball.

Outs. The batter is out when:
1. A fly ball is caught.
2. A third foul is caught.
3. Any foul which goes higher than the head of the batter, if caught.
4. Having had three strikes.

Either batter is out when:
1. Tagged out while running between bases.
2. When the catcher holds the ball with his foot on the base before runner reaches it.

Advancement of Players. When a fly ball is caught, batter and player who caught the ball exchange places. On all other outs the advancement is as follows: catcher to batter; fielders, as numbered, to catcher; and batter to the field.

Additional Athletic Games

Balloon Ball ....Ref. No. 19, p. 325
Battle Ball ....Ref. No. 19, p. 331
Foot Volley Ball ....Ref. No. 33, p. 25

INDIVIDUAL ATHLETIC EVENTS

Alternate Hop Race

The student advances by alternately hopping and stepping on each foot; i.e., a long hop on left foot, a long step on right foot, a long hop on right foot, a long step on left foot, a long hop on left foot, and so on. The race is started and judged as the regular straight-away run. From thirty yards to fifty yards make a good race.

Hand Traveling Events

Equipment. Horizontal ladder.

Hand Over Hand on Rungs. The pupil grasps with both hands an end rung. He hangs facing the opposite end of the ladder. The body must not be allowed to swing. On signal the pupil walks forward hand over hand to the last rung upon which he places both hands, then without turning around he walks backward hand over hand to the first rung from which he hangs with both hands. The pupil must grasp and hang from each rung, both when traveling forward and when traveling backward; i.e., he may not skip a rung.

Double Jumping on Rungs. Hanging position same as above. On signal, the pupil travels forward by jumping both hands simultaneously from rung to rung, until he reaches the last rung; then without turning around he travels backward in the same manner to the first rung.

Walking Sideward on Rail. Facing the center of the ladder the pupil hangs on the extreme end of the rail with hands touching each other. The body should be without motion. On signal the pupil, by moving one hand away and closing the other to it, travels sideward to the extreme end of the rail, at which point both hands must touch each other. The pupil then returns in the same manner to his starting position, where both hands must be together at the finish.

Hand Over Hand on Both Rails. The pupil hangs at the extreme end of the ladder with each hand grasping a rail, facing the opposite end. The body should hang without movement. On signal, the pupil, by swinging the arms alternately forward, travels forward until he reaches and hangs with both hands from the extreme end of the ladder, one hand on each rail. Then without turning around the pupil, traveling in the same manner, moves backward to the starting position, one hand on each rail.

Double Jumping on Both Rails. Hanging position is the same as for "Hand Over Hand on Both Rails." On signal the pupil, by jumping both hands forward simultaneously, travels forward until he reaches and hangs from the extreme end of the ladder. Without turning around he travels in the same manner backward to the starting position.

Scoring. For all five events, failure to travel in the prescribed manner and touching the feet to the floor, each constitutes a trial without record. The time elapsing from the signal to go until the moment both hands return to the starting position, represents the pupil's record.

Ring Travel. Equipment: Traveling rings—straight-away or circular. The pupil, holding a ring in both hands, jumps off an elevated platform, swings and catches the next ring. After this he travels back and forth across the series of rings, or around the circle, in the regular manner without touching the feet to the floor. At the end rings he should swing out and back holding on with either one or both hands. If at any time the pupil touches the floor with his feet, he should be halted and his score taken from this point. Each ring caught and swung on, counts one point. The total number of rings caught and swung on represents the pupil's record.

Heel Grasp Race (59) *

The performer stands behind the starting line, bends both knees and grasps his heels with his hands—left hand on the left heel, right hand on the right heel. Retaining this position he walks forward to the finish line. Any contestant releasing either or both hands from his heels or falling so any part of his body, other than his feet, touches the floor, is eliminated. The race is started and judged as the straight-away run. From ten to twenty yards makes a good race, according to the age and skill of the contestants.

Run (60 Yards)

For explanations, see "Run" for fifth grade, page 209.

Shuttle Broad Jump

Draw a line on the ground. The first jumper from team "A" toes this line and jumps. A mark is placed at this jumper's heels. The first jumper from team "B" toes this mark and jumps in the opposite

---

* From S. C. Staley. "Individual and Mass Athletics." Copyright 1925. By permission of A. S Barnes and Company publishers.

direction. This continues until all on both teams have jumped. If the last jumper from team "B" crosses the original line, his team wins. If he falls short of this line, team "A" wins.

Skipping Race

The performer skips from a starting line to the finish line. To skip, step on right foot, quick hop on right foot, step on left foot, quick hop on left foot, and repeat. Any performer who fails to travel in this manner is eliminated. The race is governed by the same rules as used in any other race. From twenty to forty yards is a satisfactory distance.

Soccer Dribble and Kick for Goal

Draw a line twenty-five yards from and parallel with the goal line. Starting at this line the participant dribbles the ball (running rapidly) toward the goal and before crossing the line defining the penalty area (fifteen yards from the goal line) he kicks for goal. The distance from where the kick is made to the goal line may be varied if desired. If used as a contest, a definite number of trials shall be allowed each student.

Soccer Kick for Distance

Establish a base line. Place the ball on this line. Participant is allowed a run before the kick. Measure from the base line to the point where the ball first hits the ground. Three trials are allowed, the best distance scoring.

Standing Broad Jump (Boys)

The performer stands on both feet toeing a line. He may rock forward and back alternately, but may not lift either foot clear of the ground. The jump is made from both feet to a landing on both feet. After landing, he must fall forward and walk forward, as the measurement is made from the toeing line (or front edge of the take-off board) to the nearest point where the body touches the ground.

Standing Double High Jump (Boys) (59) *

The contestant stands on both feet facing the bar; jumps off of both feet simultaneously; throughout the jump he holds his body square to the front; and he lands on both feet simultaneously with his back toward the bar. Any jump violating these rules constitutes a foul, and is scored as a trial without record. The bar is raised as in the regular high jump.

---

* From S. C. Staley, "Individual and Mass Athletics." Copyright 1925. By permission of A. S. Barnes and Company, publishers.

Standing High Jump (Boys)

The feet of the competitor may be placed in any position, but shall leave the ground one foot at a time (scissors fashion) when making an attempt to jump. When either foot is lifted from the ground twice, or two springs are made in making the attempt, it shall count as one trial jump without result.

Standing Leap and Jump (Boys)

The performer stands on both feet, leaps forward landing on one foot, and then jumps forward landing on both feet. The jump is made without pause after the leap. Measure the distance as in the broad jump.

Three Standing Broad Jumps (Boys) (6B)

This activity consists of three consecutive standing broad jumps without any pause to balance oneself between the individual jumps. It is one continuous forward movement from the beginning of the first to the end of the third broad jump.

Additional Individual Athletic Events

Hand Ball Drill II	Ref. No. 19, p. 381
Standing Double Broad Jump (Boys)	Ref. No. 59, p. 30
Standing Sideward Broad Jump (Boys)	Ref. No. 59, p. 37
Standing Broad Hop (Boys)	Ref. No. 59, p. 32
Running Broad Hop (Boys)	Ref. No. 59, p. 33
Hopping Broad Hop (Boys)	Ref. No. 59, p. 33
Double Hop (Boys)	Ref. No. 59, p. 33
Standing Broad Step (Boys)	Ref. No. 59, p. 37
Elephant Race	Ref. No. 59, p. 17
Squat Jumping Race	Ref. No. 59, p. 14
Toe Grasp Race	Ref. No. 59, p. 13
Double Jumping Race	Ref. No. 59, p. 11

RELAY RACES

Cap Transfer Relay (2)

Arrange the teams in files, ten feet apart behind a common starting line. Give the first three players of each team a stick three feet long. Place one player (the first) from each team at a turning point, thirty or forty feet away, on a line parallel to the starting line. Give the next (second) player a cap which is placed on his stick held upright. At signal, the player runs to the turning point, where he transfers the cap to the stick of the first player. This player runs back to the starting line, places the cap on the stick held by the third player, gives his stick to the fourth player, and takes a position at the rear of his line. The third player runs forward to the turning point and places the cap on the stick held by the second player, who in the meantime has taken the place vacated by the first player. The second player runs back to the starting point and places the cap on the stick held by the fourth player. He then gives his stick to the fifth player and takes a position at the rear of the line. All transfers of the caps should be made without the aid of the hands. If a cap falls, it must be picked up with the stick. This continues until all have run. The team arriving in its original position first, wins.

Double Circle Pass Relay

Divide players into two teams standing in two separate circles. One person in each circle acts as captain. At a signal, each captain passes an object to the player at his right. The passing is continued around the circle until the object comes back to the captain. The captain calls out "one" and continues the passing. The captain announces two, three, etc., each time the object has been passed a complete circle. The team which finishes first the passing of the object a designated number of times, wins the race. Variations: 1. Increase the number of times the object is to be passed. 2. Pass to the left. 3. Pass with right or left hand. 4. Bend over and roll ball on the ground. 5. Pass backward over head, all facing in same direction.

In and Out Relay

Divide the group into two or more teams. Teams stand in file formation behind a starting line. Directly in front of each team, thirty to sixty feet away, place a row of three Indian clubs about two feet apart. On a signal, number 1 of each file runs forward, zigzags between the clubs, without knocking any over, zigzags back, and then makes a straight run back to his team. He touches the next player's hand, and passes to rear end of his line. The second player should be waiting for this "touch off" with toe just back of starting line and hand outstretched. The second player repeats the run of the first and so on until all have run. If a club is knocked over it must be set up immediately by the one who knocked it over. The teams win in order of finishing, plus consideration of their record on fouls. Thus a team finishing fourth with no fouls would get first place if the teams finishing first, second and third all had fouls.

Odd and Even Relay

Players stand in a circle. Players are numbered by ones and twos. Each team has a captain who stands in the center of the circle, holding a ball. At a signal, each captain begins to pass the ball to each member of his team in succession, the ball being returned by each player to the captain. The team whose ball first completes the circle is declared the winner.

Sideward Pass Relay

Players are seated at desks. Those sitting in front seats of all rows constitute a team, those in the second seats another team, etc. A bean bag or substitute is passed from one side of the room to the other and returned. Begin by placing the bean bags on the floor in an outside aisle. On the word "go" those sitting next that aisle pick up the object with the nearest hand, change it to the other hand, and place it on the floor in the next aisle. This picking up, changing from hand to hand, and placing on the floor is continued across the room. The last one (now on the other side from the starting point) instead of placing it on the floor, touches it to the floor, and starts the object on its way back in the same manner. The first player after receiving it touches the floor with the object, then raises it over his head. The first arm going up declares the winning team. Variations: 1. Lengthen the game by passing the object two or three times over and back before declaring a winner. 2. Pass object under seats. changing from hand to hand.

Skip Rope Relay

Arrange the teams in files ten feet apart back of a common starting line. Establish for each team a turning point sixty feet in front of the starting line. Give the first player in each file a rope eight feet long. At a signal, the player jumping the rope skips forward, around the turning point and back to the starting line. Here he gives the rope to the second player who repeats the performance. Any player who stops skipping and starts to run must halt and start skipping again before advancing. Each player skips in his turn until all have skipped. The team having its last player recross the starting line first, wins.

Zigzag Bounce Ball Relay

Divide the players into teams of not more than sixteen children each. Divide each team into two equal groups, which face each other, standing along ground lines drawn at least ten feet apart. A team captain stands at the end of one of his lines with the ball in both hands raised high above his head. At a signal each captain bounces the ball to his opposite team mate, who in turn bounces it in like manner to the next opposite. In this way the ball goes down the line. The team which finishes first scores a point. The winning score may be ten points. On a poor bounce, the ball must be recovered by the receiver who takes his place in the line before bouncing to the next player. Variations: 1. Use more than one ball. 2. Use balls of various types.

Additional Relay Races

Jumping Relay .... Ref. No. 19, p. 117
Line Zigzag I and II .... Ref. No. 19, p. 421
Round Ball .... Ref. No. 19, p. 401

STUNTS

Heel and Toe Spring

Draw a line on the floor. Place the heels against this line, bend down and grasp the toes with the fingers underneath the feet and pointing backward toward the heels. Lean forward slightly to get an impetus, and jump backward over the line. Try jumping forward in the same way.

Ankle Throw (6B)

This feat consists in tossing some object over the head from behind with the feet. A bean bag or basket ball is held firmly between the feet. With a sudden jump the feet are kicked backward so as to jerk the object into an upward throw, which should end in its curving forward over the head. It should be caught as it comes down in front.

Automobiling

Discarded automobile casings are used. Pupil sits inside the casing, places toes inside the casing opening and grips the casing above the head with the fingers. The tire is then rolled about as desired, by a second person.

Sitting Balance

Human Fly (14B)

From push-up position with feet against the wall, walk up wall with feet to a hand-stand facing wall.

Standing High Kick (6B)

A disk or tin pan is suspended from the ceiling, or from an arm projecting from a wall, with facilities for raising and lowering the disk. The disk is lowered to the height of the waist. The pupil stands about a leg's length from the pan. He kicks the pan with either foot. After all have had a chance, raise the pan two or three inches. Two trials are permitted when the first attempt has been unsuccessful. One foot always remains on the ground. It is permitted to rise on the toes, but never to leave the ground.

Elephant Walk

Two students face each other. No. one grasps No. two at the hips. No. two jumps and locks his legs high on the hips of No. one. He then drops backward and works his head, shoulders and arms between the legs of No. one. No. one then drops forward onto his hands. No. two straightens out his arms, lifts his chest as high as possible and looks forward and up. Both persons hold these positions and No. one walks forward rapidly. A small child may be added to enjoy a rolling ride.

Hand Wrestle (6B)

The wrestlers stand with the right foot advanced, clasping right hands. The object is to make one's opponent move a foot from its position on the ground. This constitutes a throw.

Sack of Wheat (5)

Two boys stand facing each other. No. 1 bends forward and places his head against the stomach of No. 2. No. 2 grasps No. 1 around the waist, lifts him up onto his own shoulder, and lets go his hold. No. 1 drops on his feet behind No. 2, facing in the opposite direction.

Knee Spring

"A" lies flat with his knees drawn up but his feet on the floor. "B" runs, and placing his hands on the knees of the one lying down, does a hand spring. As he goes over, "A" assists by bracing the back of the one jumping. This helps to give momentum and also acts as a safety measure.

Triple Roll

Three boys get down on their hands and knees with their sides to each other, and their heads all in the same direction. No. 1 is in the middle and starts rolling sideways to the left toward No. 2 who is about five feet away. As No. 1 rolls up to No. 2 the latter leaps upward, over, and falls on the right side of the first boy, who has rolled under him. No. 2 rolls toward No. 3. In his turn No. 3 leaps upward, falling over No. 2, and rolls toward No. 1, who has stopped his roll and is back on his hands and knees. No. 1 then jumps up and over No. 3, lands on his side and rolls toward No. 2 who repeats his first performance. This process is repeated over and over as rapidly as possible. This is an excellent exhibition event and is strenuous exercise.

Additional Stunts

Rubber Neck	Ref. No. 19, p. 251
Pendulum	Ref. No. 26, p. 365
Back Foot Flip	Ref. No. 60, p. 130
Chair Stand	Ref. No. 60, p. 102
Cock Fight	Ref. No. 60, p. 150
Human Arch	Ref. No. 60, p. 133
Human Ball	Ref. No. 60, p. 94
Stiff Leg Bend	Ref. No. 60, p. 103
Top	Ref. No. 60, p. 95
Twister	Ref. No. 60, p. 122

258   PHYSICAL EDUCATION FOR ELEMENTARY SCHOOLS

RHYTHMICAL ACTIVITIES
The Ace of Diamonds *

(Victor: 20989; Columbia: A3001.)

DESCRIPTION †

Formation: Double circle, partners facing. Numbers one have back to center; numbers two face center.

Part I

Measures 1–4: Four polka steps (R, L, R, L,) with right arm hooked, turning around partner, counts 1–16. As the first polka step is executed to the right, clap hands and stamp right foot on count one; then immediately hook right arms without waiting for count two. Right arms remain hooked throughout the four polka steps.

Measures 5–8: Repeat, starting left; clapping, stamping left foot and hooking left arms.

* From C. Ward Crampton, "The Folk Dance Book." Copyright 1909. By permission of A. S. Barnes and Company, publishers.
† Description contributed by Mrs. Mathilda E. Schuettner, Los Angeles, California.

Part II

Measures 9–12: Numbers one dance backward toward center of circle with four step hops (L, R, L, R), hands at waist. Numbers two follow, dancing forward toward center of circle, with four slide hops (R, L, R, L), arms folded across chest, elbows high, counts 1–8.

Measures 13–16: Repeat, numbers two moving backward and numbers one forward, away from the center of the circle.

Part III

Measures 17–24: Partners face in the line of direction (counter-clockwise), left sides to the center; inner hands joined, outside hands at waist. Eight polka steps in the line of direction, beginning with the outside foot. Turn face to face and back to back on alternate polka steps, swinging inside arms from the shoulder, without bending elbows. Arms are back and at shoulder level when partners are facing; arms are forward at shoulder level when partners are back to back.

Captain Jinks (10)

(American)

(Victor: 20639.)

- A. I'm Captain Jinks of the Horse Marines,
   I feed my horse good corn and beans,
- B. I swing the ladies in their teens,
   For that's the style in the army!
- C. I teach the ladies how to dance, how to dance, how to dance,
   I teach the ladies how to dance,
   For that's the style in the army!
- D. Salute your partner, turn to the right,
   And swing your neighbor with all your might,
   Then promenade with the lady right,
   For that's the style in the army!

Formation: Large single circle, girl in front of boy, facing forward.
A. All march forward—4 measures.

B. Swing partners (join both hands with partner and dance around in a circle with skipping step)—4 measures.

C. Partners join inside hands and skip forward around circle in line of direction—8 measures.

D. Face partner and salute with right hand—1 measure. Make quick military turn one-eighth right—1 measure. Swing your neighbor once around—2 measures. Boy comes to the left side of the girl he has just swung and walks along with her—4 measures.

When the dance is repeated he keeps this partner until D "Swing your neighbor."

Gustaf's Skoal*

Formation: In sets of four couples facing center, two head couples standing opposite and two side couples standing opposite.

Measures 1-2. Head couples walk three steps forward toward center and make a bobbing bow to opposite couple.

Measures 3-4. Same couples—four steps backward to place.

Measures 5-8. Side couples same.

Measures 1-4. Head couples repeat.

Measures 5-8. Side couples repeat.

Measures 9-12. Side couples make arch with inside hands grasped and held high. Head couples skip forward toward center, separate and take hands of opposite, then skip through arch and around to place, meeting own partner.

* From C. Ward Crampton, "The Second Folk Dance Book." Copyright 1916. By permission of A. S. Barnes and Company, publishers.

262   PHYSICAL EDUCATION FOR ELEMENTARY SCHOOLS

Measures 13–16. All clap hands once, take both hands of partner and skip in place turning to the right, pulling away from each other.

Measures 9–16. Repeat—head couples holding arch, side couples skipping around.

Repeat from beginning.

Little Man in a Fix

(Danish)*

(Victor: 20449.)

Formation: An odd number of couples form informally about the room.

Each couple scrambles for another couple with whom to dance. Groups of two couples dance together, and the couple that is left must wait until the first part (a) of the dance is finished before dancing.

(a) The two men link left arms and each places the right arm around his partner's waist; the girl places her left hand on her partner's right shoulder and her right on her own hip, and in this position they run forward in a circle sixteen steps (bars 1 to 8).

(b) Without pausing, the men join left hands and take their partner's left in their right. Simultaneously, the girls run under the men's joined hands, turn left about facing each other, and join right hands above their own and the men's joined hands. Pulling slightly backward, they run to the right in a circle (bars 1 to 8).

(c) The man takes his partner's left hand in his right; he begins with the left foot, the girl begins with the right, and they dance

---

* From Viggo Bovbjerg, "Danish Folk Dances (Description)." Copyright 1917. By permission of author, Recreation Training School of Chicago, 800 S. Halsted street. Hull House, publishers.

the Tyroler waltz which is as follows: Turn away from each other on the first step and face to face on the second (bars 9 and 10); repeat (bars 11 and 12); then take waltz position and dance four waltz steps (bars 13 to 16). Repeat (c).

Instead of waltzing, the step may be simplified. During the reorganization into lines of four, the odd couple try to join another couple.

Lottie Is Dead (Swedish) *

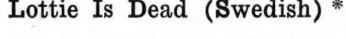

(Victor: 20988.)

Formation: A single circle, partners facing. The hands are joined and the arms raised to shoulder height.

I. Measure 1. Take a slow slide step toward the center. Bend the body toward center. Slide on inside foot and bring the outside foot up to it. Repeat, sliding toward the center. Music of measures 1 and 2 to be played slowly.

Measure 2. Repeat with two more sliding steps toward center.

Measures 3–4. Take eight quick jumps back to place.

Measures 1–4. Repeat entire movement.

II. Measures 5–8. Do hop-waltz about circle. (See Hop-Waltz, page 39.)

---

* From Lydia Clark, "Physical Training for Elementary Schools." Copyright 1918. By permission of Benj. H. Sanborn and Company, publishers.

Norwegian Mountain March *

(Victor: 20151; Columbia: A3041.)

Formation: One man holds a handkerchief by the corner in either hand; two girls stand behind him with adjacent hands joined, and each holds the opposite corner of the handkerchief in her free hand. Thus the man leads the two girls.

(a) The groups of three move to the right round the room with step-hop, the man looking backward first at one girl and then at the other, not in rhythm with the music (bars 1 to 8 and repeat). An accented stamp and two running steps may be used. Bend body as accented step is taken.

(b) Stamping on the first step, the man dances step-hop backward under the joined hands of the girls, who dance in place. The girl on the left then dances step-hop, turning right about under the man's right arm; the other girl then turns left about under her own left arm; then the man turns right about under his own right arm, and all are facing forward again. They repeat (b) twice (three times in all) without stamping (bars 9 to 16 and repeat). All dance continuously.

Polly-Wolly-Doodle (28)

Music: "Polly-Wolly-Doodle."

Formation: Double circle facing partner, both hands joined shoulder height and raised sideways.

---

* From Viggo Bovbjerg, "Danish Folk Dances (Description)." Copyright 1917. By permission of author, Recreation Training School of Chicago, 800 S. Halsted street, Hull House, publishers.

SIXTH GRADE

Measures 1-2. "Oh, I Went Down South for to See My Sal." Four slides clockwise.

Measures 3-4. "Sing Polly-Wolly-Doodle All the Day." Five light stamps, turning once around, starting with outside foot, hands on hips.

Measures 5-6. "My Sally Am a Spunky Gal." Four slides back to place.

Measures 7-8. "Sing Polly-Wolly-Doodle All the Day." Same as measures 3-4.

Measures 9-10. "Fare Thee Well, Fare Thee Well." Make one bow (low) to partner. Hands on hips.

Measures 11-12. "Fare Thee Well, My Fairy Fay." Beginning right foot and facing to right take four skip steps away from partner. During this step the inside partner should be skipping around circle clockwise while outside partner skips contra-clockwise.

Measures 13-14. "For I'm Going to Louisiana, for to See My Susyana." Face about, turning toward other line, and take four skip-steps back to partner.

Measures 15-16. "Singing Polly-Wolly-Doodle all the Day." Join right hands with partner and skip around partner twice with eight skip-steps.

Sicilian Circle *

Metronome 116

(Columbia: 556D.)

---
* From Mr. and Mrs. Henry Ford, "Good Morning; Old Fashioned Dances Revived." Copyright 1926. By permission of Dearborn Publishing Company, Dearborn, Michigan, publishers,

SIXTH GRADE

Any number of couples may take part in this dance and continue as long as desired.

It is performed in a circle formation. The couples in each set face each other, their backs being toward the couple in the next set. Dancers and music begin together.

"All forward and back"—4 bars. Gentleman joins partner's nearest hand and they walk forward four steps and backward four steps.

"Circle four hands around"—4 bars. Both couples join hands in circle and move to the left.

"Ladies chain"—8 bars. See page 40.

"Right and left"—8 bars. Opposite couples advance and pass each other, gentlemen on the outside. Each gentleman separates from his partner so that the opposite lady will pass between him and his partner. Each gentleman touches the right hand of the lady coming toward him. When in the opposite couple's place, the gentleman takes his partner's left hand in his left hand and hands her forward. They turn halfway around. Return to place and turn.

" * Forward and back"—4 bars.

" * Forward again and pass through"—4 bars. In passing through couples drop hands and pass on to meet a new couple. The entire dance is then repeated.

* NOTE.—In some localities the last two calls are omitted and the following calls substituted:

"All stand and balance"—4 bars. Face own partner and each execute a balance step.

"Promenade once and a half around"—4 bars. Cross hands with partner and promenade once and a half around and finish facing the next new couple. Repeat from the beginning.

To end the dance, call: "Join hands forward and back, turn partners, promenade to seats."

Additional Rhythmical Activities

Ribbon Dance	Ref. No. 25, p. 302
We Won't Go Home Till Morning	Ref. No. 25, p. 208
Bounding Heart (Sjalaskuttan)	Ref. No. 26, p. 262
French Reel	Ref. No. 26, p. 249
Minuet II	Ref. No. 26, p. 259
Reap the Flax (Columbia: S3001)	Ref. No. 26, p. 245
Seven Jumps	Ref. No. 26, p. 213
How-Do-You-Do	Ref. No. 31, p. 96
Irish Long Dance	Ref. No. 31, p. 134
Jumping Jack's Jubilee	Ref. No. 31, p. 107
Kerry Dance (Irish)	Ref. No. 31, p. 113
Pear Waltz	Ref. No. 36, p. 67

Three Dance ....Ref. No. 36, p. 48
German Hopping Dance ....Ref. No. 42, p. 21
Lassies' Dance I (Kulldansen)..................Ref. No. 42, p. 11
Cornish May Dance ....Ref. No. 43, p. 32

HUNTING GAMES

Ball Stand (15A)

The players are numbered and stand facing a wall about three feet away. One player throws a large ball against the wall, at the same time calling one of the numbers given to the players. Thereupon all the players except the one whose number has been called run as far away from the ball as they can, keeping within designated boundary lines. He, on the other hand, secures the ball, stands still and calls loudly, "Ball Stand." Then each player must stop running and, without turning his head, stand with his back to the one who has the ball. The latter, without moving forward, after taking time to aim, throws the ball to hit some one on the back. If he is successful, the one who has been struck calls out, "Hit." Upon that the other players run; while the one who has been struck picks up the ball, and calls, "Ball Stand." The game continues as after the previous call of "Ball Stand." If no one has been struck, all the players return to the wall, and the one who failed to hit starts the game as before.

Bowling

Three Indian clubs or erasers, four inches apart and in a triangle formation, apex toward bowler, are made to stand up in front of each aisle. Each player in turn standing with feet behind a line drawn about 20 feet from his own set of clubs tries, by bowling (not throwing) a playground baseball, to knock down the clubs. One point is scored for one club, three for two clubs, and five if all three clubs are knocked down. Individuals or rows may compete against each other.

Club Snatch

A goal is marked off at opposite ends of the play area. A block of wood or Indian club is set up between them, rather nearer one goal than the other. A handkerchief is hung on the top of the object. Half the players take their places back of one goal and half back of the other. In each goal one player stands ready to run at a given signal On this signal the player from the goal nearer the object starts, gets the handkerchief and tries to return to his goal with it before the player running from the opposite side can tag him. The game may also be played that he try to reach his goal before the player from the opposite side can reach it. If he is successful, both players stay in the nearer goal;

if he is not, both go to the farther one. The game is won by the side that brings all the players back of its goal. The right distance for the object from the nearer goal will depend on the skill of the players, and should be changed to suit different classes. All players run in turn.

Cross Tag (17) *

"It" starts after any player he chooses, but must change his course and try to catch any other player who runs between him and the one he is chasing. Thus a fresh runner may at any time turn "It" aside from a tired player. Any one caught becomes "It." In case "It" becomes tired, substitute another player.

Dare Base

A goal line is marked off at each end of the play area, and midway between is drawn a long line that forms the dare base. At each end of this is placed a player who acts as a catcher. The other players stand beyond the goals. After the game has begun, they cross constantly from one goal to the other, and the catchers try to tag them. While they are beyond the goal lines or on the dare base, they are safe from the catcher. They are not allowed to return from the dare base to the goal they have just left, but must continue to the opposite goal. Those who are caught are out of the game. The player who is last caught wins, becomes catcher in the next game, and chooses his assistant.

Duck on the Rock (15A)

When the game is played out-of-doors, a large stone, which represents the duck, is placed on a rock or object which gives elevation. The owner, who is drake, stands to guard it. A line is drawn twenty or thirty feet from the rock. Beyond this each of the other players stand, and, in turn, throws his stone at the duck, which he tries to knock off the rock. If he does not succeed, he may stand back of the line and wait until some one does succeed. If he prefers, he may run in, pick up his stone and try to run back to the goal line before the drake can tag him. If he reaches it in safety, he has a chance to throw again. When some one succeeds in knocking off the duck, all who have thrown, and are back of the line, may run forward, pick up their stones and then run back to the goal line. The drake must replace his duck on the rock each time it is knocked off before he can try to tag any one. Whoever is tagged becomes drake. A player who has missed the duck may run in and try to place his foot on his stone. He is safe in this position, but once he picks up his stone he may not again place it on the ground for safety. To select the first drake all players stand back

---

* From Forbush and Allen, "The Book of Games for Home, School and Playground." Copyright 1927. By permission of John C Winston Company, publishers.

of goal line and throw at the bowlder. The one whose stone is farthest from the bowlder is drake.

Elimination Pass

Players stand in a circle four feet apart facing in. At a signal, a ball is passed from one player to the next about the circle. When the teacher says "change" the direction of the ball is reversed. The players may pass the ball in any manner they choose, but should pass it quickly and accurately. Any pass which the receiving player can touch with both hands is considered a fair pass, if not thrown too hard. Players dropping the ball are eliminated and leave the circle. Players making throws which can not be caught are also eliminated. This continues until only one remains. This player is the champion.

Goal Tag

Have as many goals as players. The game starts with each player touching his goal. Choose one player to be "It." When "It" leaves his goal all other players must leave theirs and find a new one. They must not return to the goal just left. No two players may be at the same goal. "It" tries to tag a player before he reaches a new goal. If he succeeds, that player becomes "It," and the game is repeated.

Hindoo Tag

Players are scattered about in a limited playground area. One player, who is "It," chases about and may tag any one who is not in "safe" position, which is on both knees, forehead on the ground. Players ought not to remain in one place but should move about freely in the limited playing area.

Keep Away

There are two sides. The side that is given a ball at the start throws it about from member to member, and tries to keep it in its own possession. The other side tries to intercept the ball. All the players play for the ball, not for each other. No taking of the ball out of the hands of a player or tackling or rough play is allowed. If an opponent tags the player with the ball in his possession the ball becomes his. This game is fine exercise and excellent practice for basket ball and football.

Last Couple Out (2)

The players form in a line of couples, clasping hands. One player stands about three feet in front of the double line, with his back toward them, and calls, "Last Couple Out." The last two players unclasp hands and run, each on his own side, up the column and try to reclasp hands somewhere in front of "It," without being tagged by him. "It" can not look around to see where the last couple is until they get on a line with him. When on a line, he may try to tag either of the players. If he tags neither, he remains "It." If he tags one of them, he clasps the hand of the other player and they take their place at the head of the line, the player tagged becoming "It."

Additional Hunting Games

Body Guard	Ref. No. 19, p. 56
Jumping Rope IV	Ref. No. 19, p. 121
Pinch-O	Ref. No. 19, p. 146
Prisoner's Base I	Ref. No. 19, p. 156
Prisoner's Base, Forms II, III, IV, V	Ref. No. 19, pp. 157–163
Skin the Goat	Ref. No. 19, p. 176

MIMETICS

Baseball Batting

Face home plate, then turn head toward pitcher. With feet together hold an imaginary bat, parallel to the floor and out in front of the body. Turn trunk to right carrying bat over right shoulder. Stepping left with the left foot, swing bat at ball, transferring weight of body to the left foot. Return to position. For left-handed batters positions would be reversed.

Jump and Clap (4)

With a quarter-turn to the left, jump to a sideward stride position, raising the arms sideward-upward and clapping the hands above the head—1. Jump with feet together, lowering the arms sideward-downward and clap the hands together behind the back—2. Repeat until whole turn is made—3, 4, 5, 6, 7, 8. On 8 come to position by jumping with feet together and lowering the arms. Repeat, starting to the right.

Locomotive (5)

Bend arms to right angles, with closed fists. Stretch right arm forward and bend left knee upward—1. Draw right arm forcibly back, extend left arm, replace left leg and bend right knee upward—2. Continue in rhythm and gradually increase the speed until running in place at the end of 16 counts.

Pulling Up Anchor

With one foot advanced, reach forward, downward, with both hands, bending the forward knee. Pull back with arms, straighten forward knee, bend the other knee and twist the body at the waist. Repeat several times.

Screw-Driver

Hands on neck and feet apart. Trunk twisting to the right. All the way to the left. A vigorous twist all the way from one side to the other emphasizing first the right, then the left turn.

Steamboat

With feet apart and arms raised sideward to shoulder level, bend at the waist to left side, bending left knee, but keeping the right knee straight. Repeat to the other side in the same manner. Keep arms straight in line with shoulders.

Teamster Warming Up (6B)

Spring feet apart and raise arms sideward, palms facing upward. Now jump and cross the feet and at the same time fold arms with a clap, embracing yourself. Spring feet apart again and repeat, alternating crossing the feet. Ten to sixteen times.

SEVENTH GRADE

	PAGE
Athletic Games	274
Individual Athletic Events	297
Rhythmical Activities	300
Stunts	307
Relay Races	312
Hunting Games	315
Mimetics	316

The teacher should refer frequently to Part I of the book, as i contains many suggestions in regard to the various activities. For example—the material presented in Part I under "Posture," "Corrective Physical Education," and "Health Education" applies to all grades and should be reviewed frequently.

The activity classifications in each grade have been arranged in sequence according to judgments of their appeal and importance to the children who will use them. In situations where all the content appearing in this grade can not be taught, the teacher should make selections from each classification rather than attempt to teach all the activities found in any one classification.

ATHLETIC GAMES

Baseball (Boys) (14B)

Size of Diamond. For seventh and eighth grade boys—sixty-foot base lines, forty-foot pitcher's box. For girls—use playground baseball diamond. Order of preference for position of home plate is: (1) N.E. Corner, (2) S.E., (3) N.W., (4) S.W.

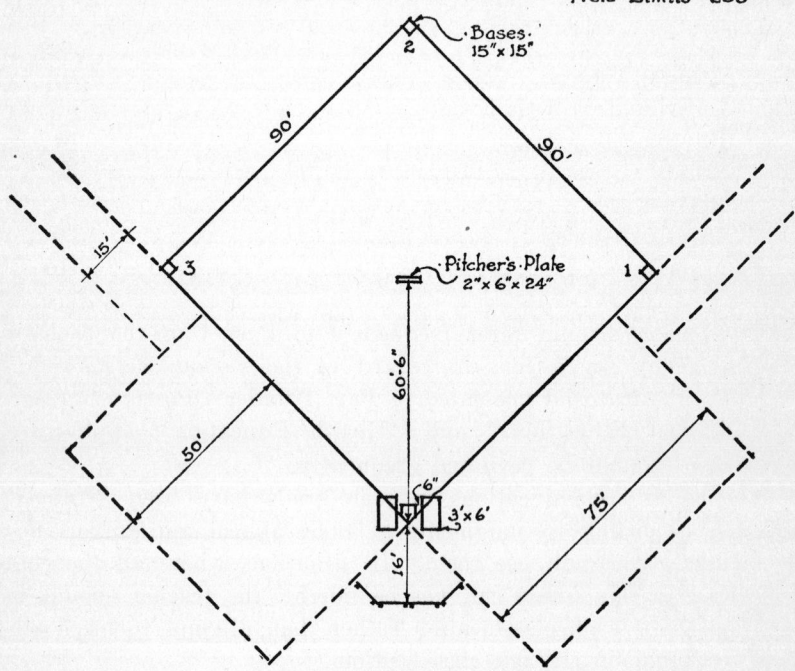

· BASEBALL · DIAMOND ·

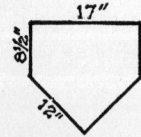

· HOME · PLATE ·
· Four · Pieces · Laminated ·

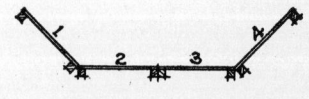

· BACK · STOP ·
Portable ~ Built in Sections ~ Small
Mesh Wire on Inside ~ Each · Section
· 8'-0" · Wide · & · 12'-0" · High ·

Size of Ball. Boys—Official junior baseball; Girls—Use nine-inch or twelve-inch playground baseball with overhand pitching.

Length of Game. The game shall consist of seven (7) innings, except when a game is called off because of rain or closing time. In this case five or more innings shall constitute a legal game, score to be taken when each side has had an equal number of times at the bat.

Fair Ball. A fair ball is a legally batted ball striking and remaining in the infield (between first and third bases) or a ground ball striking into foul territory between home and first, or home and third, and rolling into fair territory. If the ball strikes on fair territory in the outfield and rolls out, it is considered a fair ball.

Foul Ball. A foul ball is a legally batted ball that strikes out of fair territory or rolls out of fair territory inside of first or third base.

Dead Ball. 1. Ball not struck at, which touches batsman's person or clothing.

2. When "ball" is called.

3. An illegal hit—batter hitting the ball while out of batter's box.

Strike. 1. A strike is a legally pitched ball passing over home plate, between the knees and shoulders of the batter.

2. A legally pitched ball struck at and missed.

3. Any foul-strike until the batter has two strikes.

4. A foul-tip caught by catcher.

Balls. 1. A legally pitched ball not a strike.

2. Balk. (Penalty—advance each runner on base one base.)
   a. Any motion to pitch the ball to home plate, first, or third base without completing the throw.
   b. Taking legal position on pitcher's plate without having the ball.
   c. Pitcher delaying the game.

Batter Is Out. 1. On three strikes if catcher catches ball on third strike.

2. On foul-tip legally caught on the third strike.

3. On foul fly legally caught.

4. On intentional interference with the catcher.

5. On being hit with a foul ball before it strikes the ground (third strike only).

6. On a fly ball legally caught.

7. On making an illegal hit. (See *Dead Ball* No. 3.)

8. On making a legal hit when batting out of turn (provided the error is discovered before the ball has been pitched to the next batter).

9. On bunting on third strike (if a foul ball).

Base Runner Is Out. 1. On running three feet out of base line to avoid being tagged.

2. On being hit by a fair ball.

3. On being tagged while off a base (except when returning to base after a foul ball).

4. On failure to reach first base after a fair hit; i.e., if base is tagged before runner reaches it.

5. Failure to touch a base when running bases. In this case the ball must be thrown to the base missed and the base tagged by the baseman with the ball in his possession.

The Batter Becomes a Base Runner. 1. After a fair hit.

2. After four balls have been called.

3. After being hit by a pitched ball.

4. After three strikes, if catcher fails to catch ball on third strike.

5. If interfered with by the catcher.

Suggestions. 1. That captain and umpire decide ground rules before game; i.e., one base on an overthrow to first and third, etc.

2. That both umpires be not stationed together back of pitcher; i.e., base umpire should be stationed back of bases, and ball and strike umpire behind catcher or pitcher.

Basket Ball (Boys) (14D)

Equipment. Basket ball; basket ball court.

Numbers. Two teams of five boys each.

Duration of Game. For seventh and eighth grades—six-minute quarters; if played by fifth and sixth grades—five-minute quarters; two-minute rest between quarters; ten-minute rest between halves; five-minute extra period in case of tie.

Scoring. A goal from field scores two points; a goal from a free throw scores one point.

Ball Put in Play. In center by referee by tossing up between two opposing players: 1. To open game or begin a quarter.

2. After the second of the two free throws following a double foul.

3. When ball lodges in the supports of the basket.

4. When a goal has been made.

Ball Is Dead. 1. When a goal is made (center ball).

2. When held ball is declared (tossed up between opponents).

3. When "time out" is declared (tossed up between opponents where play was stopped).

4. When either a foul or violation has been called.

5. After each of two free throws following a double foul (center ball).

6. At expiration of playing time.

7. When ball lodges in supports of basket (center ball).

8. After first of two free throws awarded to the same team.

Violations and Penalties. A player shall not:

1. Throw for basket when ball is dead.

SEVENTH GRADE

2. While making a free throw for goal (a) touch or cross the free throw line until the ball has touched the basket or backboard; or (b) consume more than ten seconds in making a free throw. Penalty for 1–2: Goal, if made, does not count.
3. Cause the ball to go out of bounds.
4. Carry the ball into court from out of bounds.

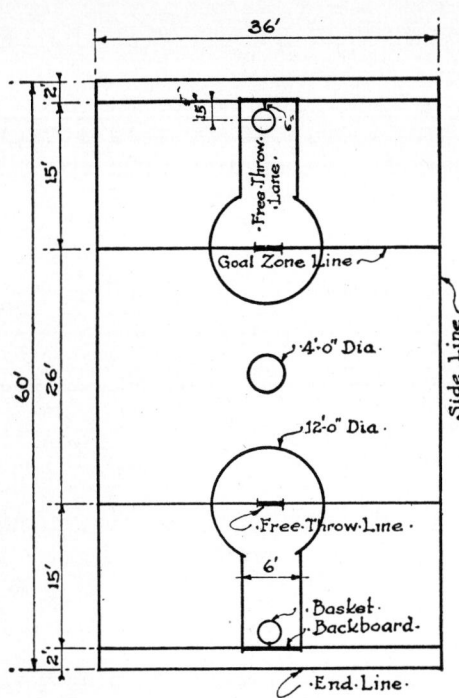

· BASKET-BALL· COURT ·~·BOYS·

~·DATA·~

·1· Length· of· Court· should· be· North· and· South· if· out· doors
·2· Court· should· be· surrounded· by· an· Area· 3'· Wide· for· Out· of· Bounds·
·3· Front· Surface· of· Back· board· should· be   4'-0"· x· 6'-0".
·4· Top· Surface· of· Basket· should· be· 9'-0"· from· the· Ground
·5· Material· for· Back· boards:~   ·2   Posts ~ 6"x 6"x 16'-0"
                                   ·4   Pieces ~ 2"x 4" x 6'-0"
                                   ·4   Pieces ~ 2"x 4" x 4'-0"
                                   ·42· Pieces ~ 1"x 4" x 4'-0" T· &· G· Flooring
·6· All· wood· should· be· Surfaced· and· Painted
·7· Rings· for· Basket· should· have· an· inside· Diameter· of· 18"
·8· Eight· Carriage· Bolts ⅜"x 9½" for· fastening· Backboard· to· Poles

5. Touch ball after putting it in play from out of bounds until it has been touched by another player.

6. Hold ball more than five seconds out of bounds before putting it in play. Penalty for 3-4-5-6: Ball goes to opponent out of bounds.

7. Enter free throw lane or touch free throw lines while a free throw for goal is being made until ball has touched basket or backboard; or attempt to disconcert player who has free throw. Penalty: For violation by team throwing for goal, goal, if made, shall not count, and if missed, ball put in play at center. If violated by player of opposite team, goal, if made, shall count, and if missed, another free throw shall be allowed. If violated by both teams, goal, if made, shall not count and whether made or missed ball put in play at center.

8. Run with ball, kick it, or strike it with fists.

9. Violate jumping rules when the referee throws the ball up between two players.

10. Pass ball to another player while making a free trial for a goal, but must make an honest attempt to cage it.

11. Make a second dribble after having completed a dribble unless the ball when it was out of his possession has touched another player.

Penalty for 8-9-10-11: The ball shall go to an opponent out of bounds on the side of the court nearest the spot where the violation was committed.

12. Interfere with the ball while the ball is on the edge of or within the basket. Penalty for 12: Shall be declared a goal whether made or not (center ball).

Fouls and Penalties

A. *Technical Fouls.* A player shall not:

1. Delay the game; i.e., leave the court, interfere with opponents' ball, take more than three time-out periods, use any unsportsmanlike tactics.

2. Go on court as substitute until he has reported to scorer and referee.

3. Talk to the officials or in any way conduct himself in an unsportsmanlike manner.

4. There shall be no coaching from the side lines by any one officially connected with either team.

5. No person shall go on court during progress of game, except with permission of referee. Penalty for 1-2-3-4-5: Free trial for goal.

B. *Personal Fouls.* A player shall not:

6. Hold, block, trip, charge, or push an opponent whether or not either player has possession of ball.

7. Use unnecessary roughness.

8. Charge in and make bodily contact with an opponent who is one of two opposing players having one or both hands on the ball. Penalty:

SEVENTH GRADE

Two free throws for goal if the offense is committed on a player in his own goal zone. One free throw if offense is committed on a player who is not in his own goal zone.

NOTE.—Four personal fouls shall disqualify a player and require him to leave game. He may not reënter the same game.

Hit Pin Baseball

Equipment. Soccer ball, four Indian clubs fastened to bases six inches square.

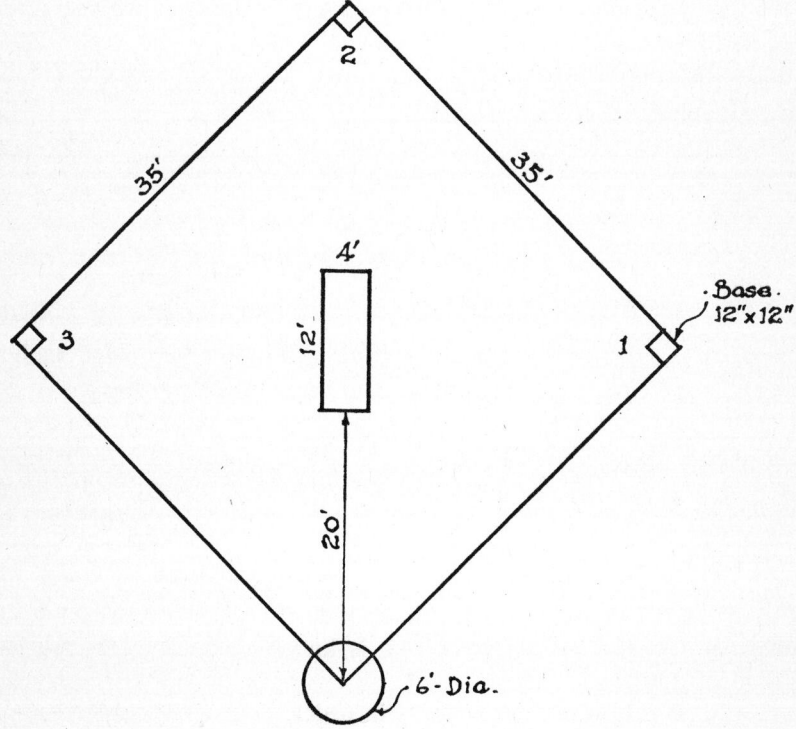

Field. Playground baseball diamond, as shown in the diagram.

Players. There are two teams, with nine players on a side: Catcher, bowler, first baseman, second baseman, third baseman, shortstop, right fielder, center fielder, left fielder. Fewer players may be used.

Object of the Game. To score runs. A run is scored when player kicks a fair ball and makes a home run.

Fair and Foul Balls. As in baseball.

Dead Ball. A ball delivered by bowler which hits kicker. Ball is rebowled.

Rules of Play. 1. Ball, when kicked fair, must be sent to 1st, 2d, 3d, home base, in order.

2. Fielders may not interfere with runner. To do so gives a run to runner's team.

3. To put a runner out, the Indian club at the base must be knocked down with the ball by player covering that base before the runner reaches it.

4. Bowler must have both feet in the box when bowling.

5. Bowler may roll or toss the ball.

6. Baseman must have one foot on the base when passing ball to the next baseman.

Strikes. A strike is called:

1. When a ball which lands on line or inside forward half of home circle is missed by the kicker.

2. If the kicker fails to stand on one foot within the circle when kicking.

3. If the kicker misses a fair bowl.

4. For foul balls until kicker has two strikes.

Outs. Kicker is out at home:

1. Always on third strike.

2. A placed ball kicked foul by kicker. (Note—after four balls have been called on bowler, kicker places the ball in the circle and kicks it.)

3. If Indian club at home is knocked down by kicker or bowler.

4. Foul fly caught.

5. If fair ball knocks down field club before striking ground.

Runner is out:

1. On a caught fly.

2. If hit by fair ball at home before it touches ground.

3. If he knocks down any Indian club.

4. If any club just ahead of him is knocked down by the baseman with the ball.

5. If he does not touch all bases in order.

6. If he runs inside the diamond in front of any club.

7. If he interferes with any player or the ball.

Horseshoes

1. The standard distance shall be forty feet between pegs. This may be varied.

2. The ground shall be as level as possible.

3. The pitcher's box shall extend three feet on either side, to the rear and in front of peg. The ground therein shall consist of clay,

SEVENTH GRADE 281

well damped and dug up to a depth of six inches, leveled and tamped down. A contestant when pitching may stand anywhere inside the pitcher's box. Any pitcher delivering a shoe while outside the pitcher's box shall forfeit the value of that pitch.

4. The pegs shall be of iron, one inch in diameter, lean one inch toward opposite peg, and extend eight inches above level of ground.

5. At the beginning of game the contestants shall toss a coin for first pitch; the winner shall have choice of first or follow.

6. At the beginning of the second game the loser of preceding game shall have first pitch.

7. The shoes to be used must not exceed seven and one-half inches in length or seven inches in width. No toe or heel calks shall be over three-quarters of an inch in height. No opening between heel calks to exceed three and one-half inches inside measurements. No shoe shall exceed two pounds and four ounces in weight.

8. In four-handed games partners shall have the right to coach each other. Those not in the game are forbidden to coach or molest, or in any way to interfere with the pitchers.

9. No contestant shall walk across to the other peg and examine the position of the shoes before making his first or final pitch. All contestants must pitch both shoes from the pitcher's box into the opposite pitching box or forfeit a point to his opponent.

10. Wrapping fingers with tape is allowed.

11. A regulation game shall consist of twenty-one or fifty points, and the contestant first scoring this number shall be declared the winner.

12. The most points that a contestant can score in a single game is twenty-one or fifty points, but all ringers are credited to him.

13. A shoe that does not remain within eight inches of the peg shall not be counted.

14. The closest shoe to the peg shall score one point. If both shoes are closer than either of an opponent's they shall score two points.

15. A ringer shall score three points. To be a ringer a shoe must encircle the peg far enough to allow a straight rule to touch both calks and clear the peg.

16. Two ringers are the highest score a pitcher can make and shall count six points.

17. All equals shall be counted as ties. That is, if both contestants have one shoe each equal distance from the peg or against it, or ringers, they are tied, and the next closest shoe counts.

18. If one contestant should have two ringers, and the other one, the pitcher having the two ringers shall score three points.

19. In case of a tie on all four shoes, such as four ringers, or four shoes each, one inch from the peg, no score shall be recorded, and the contestant who pitched the last shall be awarded the lead.

20. Calipers shall be used for all measurements.

21. In case of any dispute, or where the rules do not specifically cover a disputed point, the referee or committee in charge shall have full and final jurisdiction.

Nine-Court Basket Ball (Girls)

Nine-court basket ball offers unusual opportunities to use large groups of people, eighteen to thirty-six, in playing the game. It is

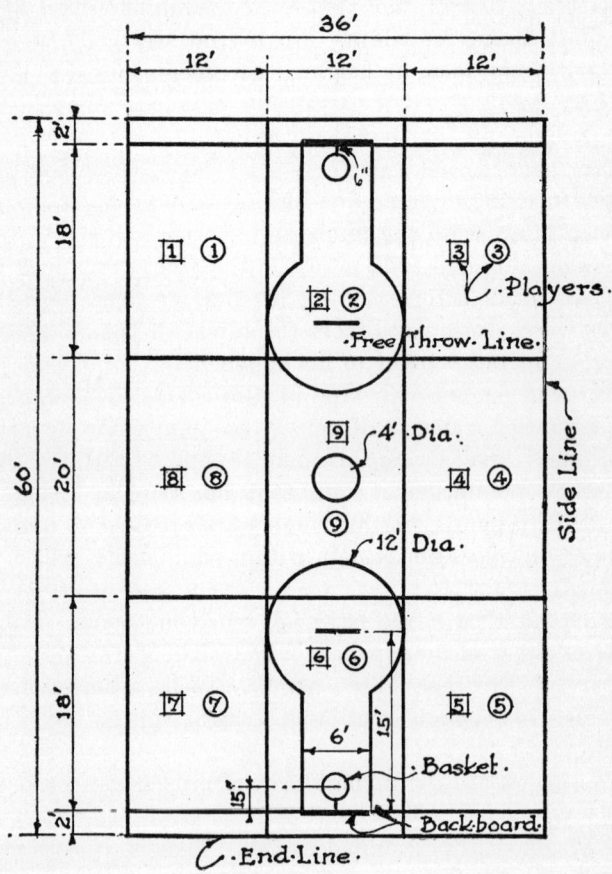

especially suited for the adolescent girl and for mixed groups, as it offers the science of basket ball without the dangers. This game is recommended in preference to the regulation girls' three-court basket ball game, it being safer to use when a thorough medical examination of players is not possible. While not so strenuous as the three-court

SEVENTH GRADE

game, it gives the average girl a more rounded experience in the science of basket ball. In order to utilize space and marking, and to safeguard one of the best features of the game—the small area to be covered by the players—the official size of the court for nine-court basket ball shall be the thirty-six by sixty feet regulation basket ball court. See diagram for the construction of the nine courts.

Teams. Nine on a team shall ordinarily be the official number, but when there is a large group, the number on a team may be increased to as high as eighteen. The object should be to develop the social and recreational features and not "championship material."

Choosing Teams. Players are lined up according to height, strength or playing ability, in two lines, A and B. Both lines are numbered one to nine, the numbering being repeated until all couples playing are numbered. Team A—1, 2, 3 - - - 9. 1, 2, 3, etc.; Team B—1, 2, 3 - - - 9. 1, 2, 3, etc. Players then go to the court which corresponds to their number, and become opponents, playing with their respective teams A and B. When boys and girls are to play together, have boys stand in front of boys, and girls in front of girls. In case there are but eight players on a team number eights are jumping centers, and cover the entire area of courts eight and nine. In case there are but seven players on a team number sevens are centers and cover entire areas of court eight, nine and four. If the above ruling is necessary watch carefully to see that the jumping centers do not overwork. Health comes first of all.

Playing Time. Two ten-minute halves, with a five-minute rest period between shall be the official time for contest games. The game may be played with four six-minute quarters, with rest periods of two minutes between first and second, third and fourth quarters, and a five-minute rest period between halves. The referee may call time whenever she feels it advisable to do so. Practice games may be played with shorter playing periods.

Scoring. Only the forwards in the three end courts shall throw for field goals. Goals so made shall score two points for the side whose basket the ball passed through. When free throws given for fouls are to be tried, one of the center forwards then in court number two or number six shall try for the free throw. If successful, the goal so made shall score one point.

Rotation of Players. Players rotate after each goal made, in the following order: Ones into court two, twos into court three; - - - - - nines into court one.

Rules. Study the rules found in Spalding's No. 17R, "Official Basket Ball Guide for Women." These rules shall govern the game, and are here given in abbreviated form, certain exceptions being noted:

1. Ball is put in play at the center:
    a. At the beginning of each half and each quarter.
    b. After a goal has been made.
    c. After last free throw following a double foul.
2. Ball tossed up between two players:
    a. When ball is put in play at center. Players jumping for the ball at center need not keep one hand behind the back, provided there is no personal contact with the opponent. Players jumping may not catch the ball until it has touched the floor or been played by some other players than those jumping. Penalty—a free throw awarded side that did not commit the foul.
    b. Following a tie ball (when two opponents place both hands on the ball at the same time). If held in a tie ball between center and guard or forward, it shall be tossed up between a center and center opponent.
    c. When ball lodges in supports of basket it is tossed up between two players at the fifteen-foot foul line.
    d. In case of doubt as to who last touched the ball in "out of bounds," a toss is given three feet inside the court. The toss is given at the free throw line, if the ball passed out within six feet of a point on the floor directly under the basket.
    e. Following a double line violation at the spot where the ball is at the time the foul is called.
3. Out of bounds:
    a. If a ball goes out of bounds, it is given to the opponent of the player who last touched it, to be thrown in from outside the court at right angles to the spot where it left the court.
    b. A player may hold the ball no longer than five seconds out of bounds. Penalty—ball given to opponent.
    c. After player has thrown ball in, it may not be retouched by the player until it has been touched by another player.
    d. If ball is batted out of bounds by a center, when jumping, it shall be given to opponent outside.
    e. Player landing with one foot over outside boundary line may withdraw foot immediately and play. However, if inside foot is carried out, ball is given to opponent.
4. Line Violation: Touching the ground in bounds beyond the field division lines, with any part of the body or clothing, shall constitute a line violation. A player may lean over a division line to pick up or receive the ball. Rules for line violations do not refer to outside boundary lines.
    a. If a line violation is made by team in possession of the ball, the referee shall give ball to nearest opponent who is allowed

an unguarded throw. The player can not shoot for the basket.
- b. If line violation is made by the team not in possession of ball, the player who has the ball keeps it and is allowed an unguarded throw.
- c. If two opponents go over the division lines at the same time, the ball is tossed up between the player who has the ball and her opponent in that court.
- d. Foul Line—When taking free throw, player shall not step over foul line until the ball has either gone through or missed the basket. Penalty—goal, if made, shall not count, and whether made or missed, it is followed by a center toss. During the free throw, opponent must be behind the free throw line. If opponent oversteps foul line, as above, goal, if made, counts and if missed, another trial is given.

5. Guarding:
   - a. All guarding must be done in a vertical plane.
   - b. Player shall not guard over opponent or ball.
   - c. Player shall not guard around opponent.

   Penalty (a, b, c)—Free throw for side not committing foul. If an opponent, who is in the act of throwing for basket is overguarded, two free throws shall be awarded.

6. Technical fouls (with the ball): Five technical fouls disqualify a player.
   - a. Failure to throw ball within three seconds after it is caught.
   - b. Double dribble. A dribble is a play in which a player, after giving impetus to the ball by bouncing it, touches it again before it has been touched by another player. (Commonly termed "a bounce.")
   - c. Double juggle.
   - d. Handing or rolling ball to another player.
   - e. Throwing ball from kneeling or lying position.
   - f. More than one player from each team putting hands on the ball.
   - g. Running with ball.
   - h. Batting or snatching ball from opponent's hands.
   - i. Kicking the ball.

   Penalty (a—i)—Free throw for side not committing foul.

7. Personal fouls: Three personal fouls disqualify a player.
   - a. Holding, blocking, tripping, pushing.
   - b. Unnecessary roughness.

   Penalty (a, b)—Free throw for side not committing foul. If player fouls opponent who is in the act of shooting basket, two free throws are awarded.

Suggestions.

1. Keep your eyes on the ball.
2. When you are a guard, keep close to your opponent.
3. When you are a forward, keep away from your opponent.
4. When a player of the opposite team in another court has the ball, stick close to your opponent. When a player on your team in another court has the ball, try to keep away from your opponent.
5. Make short quick passes.
6. Pass the ball through the outer courts as much as possible.
7. Mixed teams of boys and girls of varying ages can be used if the boys play in squares by themsleves and all are matched according to height and weight of players when the playing skill is not known.
8. Adults enjoy the game immensely.

Exceptions to Spalding's Rules.

1. The rule governing the rotation of players.
2. No bouncing of the ball shall be allowed.
3. If, when a free throw is given and there are more than two persons playing in courts two and six, the guards and their forwards shall stand back of the "side dividing lines nearest the basket," and none of the players shall move until the ball has entered or missed the basket.
4. All field goals shall score two points. Goals from free throws score one point.

Pin Football

Play Area: Distance between centers of end circles is seventy feet.

The game is played with a soccer football. Draw two concentric circles of five feet and thirty feet in diameter at each end of a playing area. A circle three feet in diameter is marked out in the center of the playing area. Five Indian clubs are placed at intervals in the inner circle at each end of the playing area. Divide the players into two teams, one team at each end protecting its clubs. The captains may place their players as they see fit. Start the game by tossing up the ball between two players who stand in the center circle and face their opponents' clubs. When the ball has reached its highest point the players jump and bat the ball into their opponents' territory. After this, the ball while outside of the larger circles, must be advanced only by kicking, each team trying to knock over their opponents' Indian clubs. A kick by either team made from outside a larger circle, scores two points for the attacking side, for each club which is knocked down. When a club has been knocked down, the ball is dead and play is resumed at the center. Whenever the ball is kicked into or across the larger circle, without knocking over a club, the attacking side is given a free kick from any point on the larger circle. The defending players remain in the rear half of the larger circle until the ball is kicked, then they may rush forward, and try to prevent the ball from hitting the clubs. The attacking members during this play must remain outside the larger circle until the ball is kicked, when they may enter the circle to secure the ball. One point is given for each club which is knocked down from a free kick. If, after a free kick which does not score, the ball is secured within the larger circle by a member of the attacking side, he may throw it at the Indian clubs, the defending players preventing the throw if possible. The attacking players may also pass the ball to each other in order to make a better throw, but can not advance with the ball. The defending players must pick up the ball and throw it outside the circle toward the opponents' goal. Each club which is knocked down from a throw counts one point. If the ball on a free kick passes through the circle without knocking over a club, play is resumed at the center. The team wins which secures the greatest number of points at the end of a definite period of time.

Schoolroom Volley Ball

Equipment. A volley ball bladder covered with thin cloth covering or the mesh end of a stocking. A net or string is stretched across the schoolroom, dividing it into two equal parts. The top should be six feet from the floor.

Players. The players are divided into two equal teams.

Game. The game consists in batting a volley ball with the open hand back and forth over the string, a point being scored by either team whenever its opponent allows the ball to touch the floor or desks. The ball must be batted (not thrown). The players stand in the aisles, each having a required area to protect. The game starts by number one on either side serving the ball; i.e., tossing it up with the left hand and batting it with the right, trying to get the ball over the net or string to the opposing side.

Rotation of Players. Have the end player of each team in each file serve. When all the end players of a team have served they go to the front of their file. All other players move back one position.

Rules. The same as volley ball. See page 294.

Soccer

The Field. 1. Size—elementary schools, boys and girls, 140 feet by 200 feet.
  2. Center circle—24 feet radius.
  3. Penalty area—108 feet by 45 feet.
  4. Goal area—18 feet by 30 feet.
  5. Goal—24 feet wide by 8 feet high to the cross bar. Ground box 4 feet long.

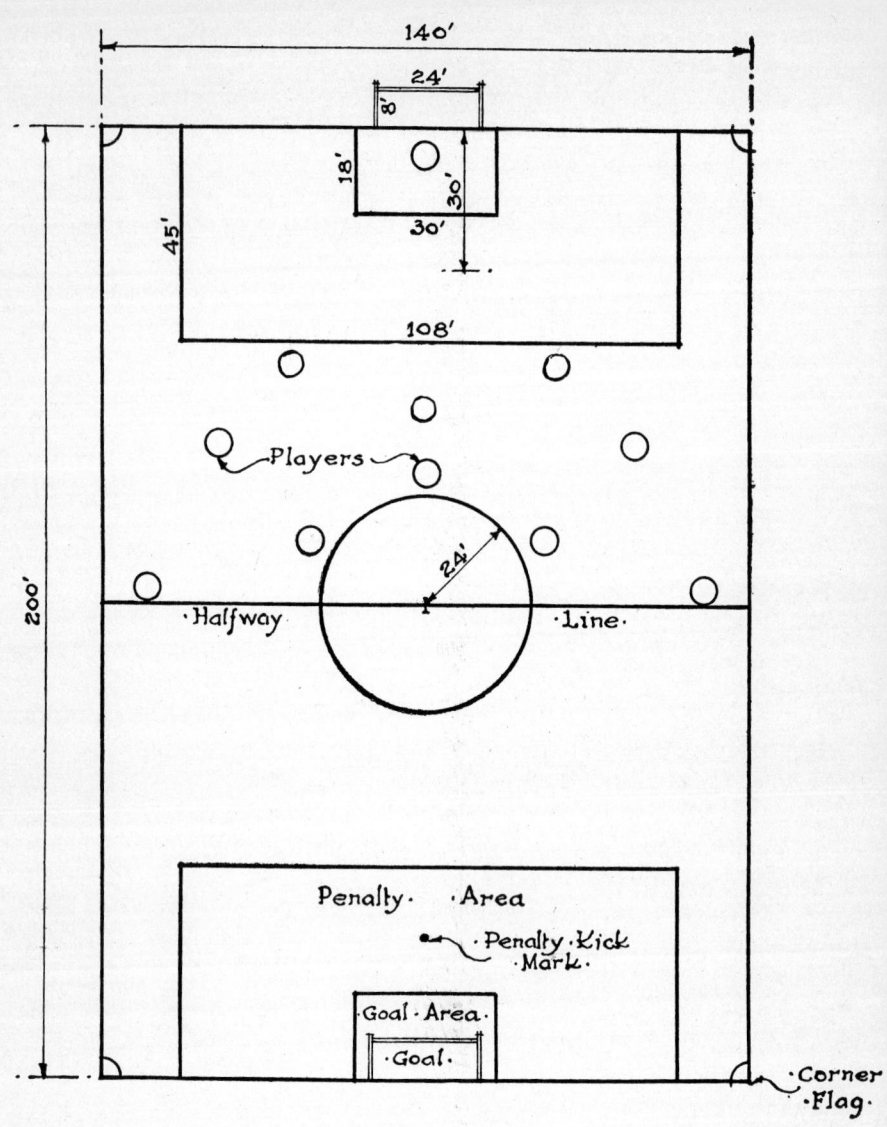

SOCCER FIELD

6. Goal post material—4 Ps 6" x 6" x 12'; 2 Ps 4" x 6" x 26'.

The Game. 1. Number of players: Eleven—five forwards, three halfbacks, two fullbacks and one goal keeper.

2. Duration of game: Boys—Grade 6, six-minute quarters; grade 7, eight-minute quarters; grade 8, ten-minute quarters. Girls—All grades, eight-minute quarters.

SEVENTH GRADE

3. Rest periods: Two-minute rest between first and second; four-minute rest between third and fourth quarters; five to ten-minute rest between second and third quarters.

4. Choice of kick-off or goal shall be made by toss.

5. Substitution allowed in case of injury to player.

6. The kick-off: A place kick from the center of the field of play in the direction of the opponents' goal. Opponents not to be nearer the ball than twenty-four feet. If the kick-off is not properly taken, it should be taken again.

7. Scoring a goal: One point is scored when the ball has passed over the end line between the goal posts and under the bar. Penalty kick—one point if goal is made.

Definitions. 1. Place kick: A kick at the ball toward opponents' goal while it is on the ground in the center of the field of play.

2. Free kick: A kick at the ball in any direction when it is lying on the ground, at any place on the field. Kick must not be made until the referee gives the signal.

3. Handling: Goal keeper taking more than two steps while holding or bouncing the ball on the hand.

4. "Hand": Striking or propelling ball with hands or arms.

5. Holding: Obstruction of a player by the hand or any part of the arm extended from the body.

6. "Touch": That part of the ground outside of the field of play.

Ball Out of Play. 1. After the ball has crossed the goal line or touch line (on the ground or in the air).

2. After a goal is made.

3. Immediately after the referee signals, indicating a foul.

To Put Ball in Play. 1. "Kick-off": The kick-off is from the center of the field in the direction of the opponents' goal line. The opponents must be twenty-four feet away, nor shall players of either side cross the center line until ball has been kicked.

2. Throw in from touch (opposite side throws ball in): Player throwing ball in must stand with both feet together behind or on the touch line, face field of play, throw the ball over his head with both hands in any direction. (A goal can not be made from the throw in.)

3. Referee signals to resume play after a foul.

Offside. If less than two men are between their own goal and the opponent, the opponent is said to be offside. This is a foul with a free kick awarded. If a player is in line with, or behind the ball, he can not be offside.

Goal Kick. If the ball is played over the end line (not between the goal posts) by the attacking side, the defending team (any player) kicks the ball into the field of play from within the half of goal area nearest to the point where the ball left the field. The attacking side is not allowed nearer than thirty feet until the ball is kicked.

Corner Kick. If the ball is played over the end line (not between the goal posts) by the defending team, the attacking team kicks the ball into the field from the corner nearest the point where the ball went out. Opponents are not allowed nearer than thirty feet until after the ball is kicked.

Goal Keeper. 1. The goal keeper may handle the ball within his own penalty area, but shall not carry the ball more than two steps.

2. The goal keeper shall not be charged (except when he is holding the ball, obstructing an opponent or when he is out of his goal area).

3. Goal keeper may be changed, but notice must be given to referee.

Fouls. Penalty—A free kick.

1. A goal may be secured from a free kick awarded for the following fouls: Tripping, kicking, striking, jumping on, "hand," holding or pushing an opponent who is handling the ball.

2. A goal can not be made from a free kick awarded for the following: Offside; carrying by goal keeper; charging goal keeper at wrong time; playing the ball before it has touched the ground after being thrown in; ball not kicked forward from penalty kick; improper throwing in; failure to keep feet behind or on touch line when throwing in; failure to throw ball over head on throw in.

Penalty Area. A foul, made by tripping, kicking, striking, holding or pushing an opponent, or handling the ball while the defending side player is within his own penalty area, results in a penalty kick. This is awarded to the opposing team.

Penalty Kick. The ball is placed thirty feet from the goal line. All players, except the goal keeper, are to remain on the outside of the penalty area, until the ball has been kicked. If the goal is made, a point is scored. If not made, the ball remains in play.

Aids to Referee. 1. Follow closely the ball, and in the case of an expected goal be on the end line in order to judge accurately whether or not the ball goes through the goal.

2. Have lines marked, especially the goal area and the penalty area.

3. Mark players in order to recognize the two teams separately—a loop of bright colored paper cambric slipped over the head and under one arm, making a diagonal of color across back and chest, is most satisfactory marking.

4. Have linesmen watch for balls going out of bounds.

5. Allow and encourage girls to cross arms on chest when playing the ball, as provided for in the speedball rules.

Sponge Ball

Equipment. Volley ball nets; bats similar to paddle tennis racket or tennis rackets. A ball eleven inches in circumference cut from a

SEVENTH GRADE

large sponge (not sponge rubber). The size of the court, the same as for volley ball. When bats are not available use hands.

The Game. The sponge is kept in the air; i.e., is played like volley ball. Volley ball rules apply. The sponge is very light and has an action that is different from any other ball; it remains in the air longer and gives the receivers a better opportunity. It is better for indoor than outdoor use.

Tennis (14D)

The court dimensions are shown in the diagram. The height of the net is three feet six inches at the posts and three feet in the middle. The choice of sides and the right to be server or receiver should be decided by toss (spinning the racket). The winner of the toss shall have the right to choose the side or the serve (but not both). The

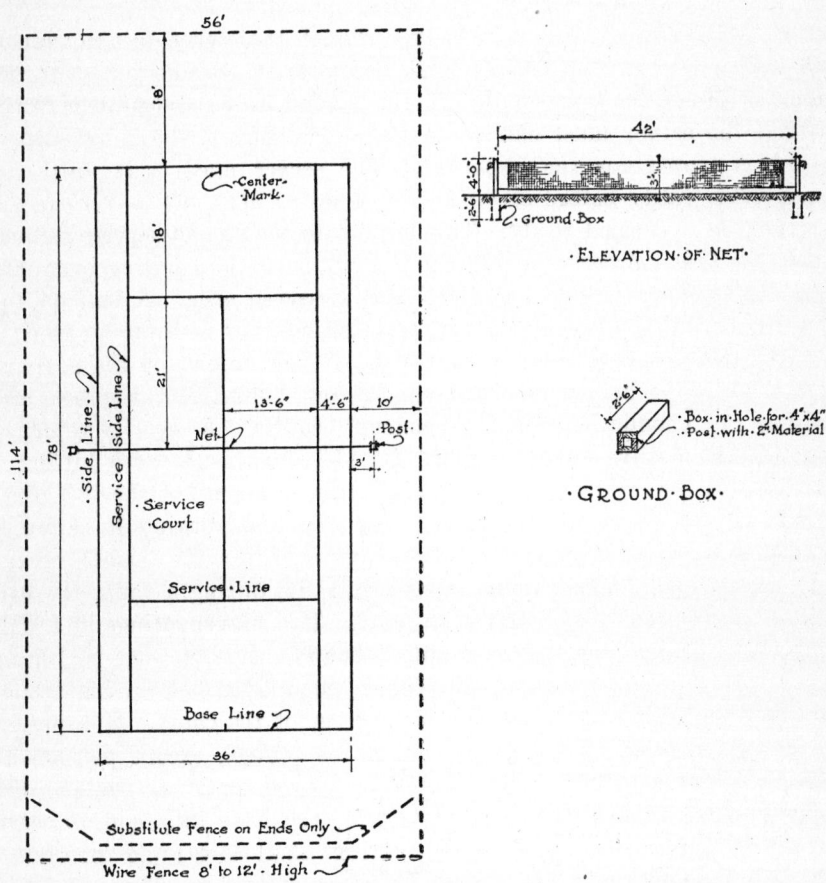

TENNIS·COURT·

players shall be on the opposite sides of the net. The player who first delivers the ball is called the server and the other the receiver. At the end of the first game the receiver becomes server, and the server becomes receiver, and so on alternately during the remaining games of the match or set. The server must stand behind the base line and within the limits of the imaginary continuation of the half court and side lines. He must not step on or across the base line until after the ball is struck. If he does so, a "foot fault" is called, and the receiver is given the point. The service is delivered from the right and left sides of the courts alternately, beginning from the right in every game, and the ball served over the net must strike the ground in the service court diagonally opposite. The server must not touch the ball with any part of his body, or anything he wears or carries, except his racket. A service hitting the receiver before touching the ground is ruled a point to the server. If the server swings at the ball (in his serve) and misses it, it is a fault even though the racket does not touch the ball. If the first ball is incorrectly served the server may try another from the same spot. If the second ball is also incorrectly served the server must change to the other side of the court and a point is scored for the opponent. The server must wait until the receiver is ready before serving; if the latter attempts to return the service, he is deemed ready. This applies to the second service as well as to the first. A serve hitting the top of the net and falling over into the proper court is called a "let" and is served over. A ball on the return hitting the top of the net and falling over is counted as if it cleared the net, and may be returned. A fair return of the serve is made when the ball is returned on the first bound over the net, and within the boundaries of the opponent's courts. A service returned on the volley (fly) counts a point for the server. A serve hitting a ball left in the service court is a good serve. The last of the two players to return the ball over the net correctly, i.e., striking it before it has bounced more than once, and sending it within the bounds of the opposite courts, scores a point for himself. If, during a rally, the ball hits a player, that player loses the point. If a player swings at a ball but misses it, and the ball goes out of bounds, the opposing player or team loses the point; but if the player touches the ball in his swing, he loses the point even if he is standing out of the court. If a player is interfered with by something out of his control, except permanent fixture of the court, the point should be played over. In doubles the players shall serve alternately. The pair who have the right to serve in the first game shall decide which partner shall do so; and the opposing pair shall decide in like manner for the second game. The partner of the player who served first shall serve in the third game, and the partner of the player who served in the second game shall serve in the fourth game; the same order shall be maintained in all the subsequent games of the set. At the beginning of the next set, either partner of the pair who received in the last game of the last set may serve; and the same privilege is given to their opponents in the second game of the new set. The first server is not required to receive in the right court; he may select either side at the beginning of the set, but must hold this side to the end of the set. On either player winning his first stroke the score is called fifteen for that player; on either player winning his second stroke, the score is called thirty for that player; on either player winning his third stroke, the score is called forty for that player; and the fourth stroke won by either player is scored *game* for that player, except as follows: If both players have won three strokes, the score is called *deuce,* and the next stroke won by either player is scored *advantage* for that player. If the same player wins the next stroke, he wins the game; if he loses the stroke the score returns to *deuce,* and so on until one player wins the two strokes immediately following the score of *deuce,* when the game is scored for that player. If a player has scored no points, his score is *love.* In calling the score for any game, the server's score is called first. The player who first wins six games wins the set, except that if both players have won five games or more, either player must gain a lead of two games to win the set.

Tether Ball (82)

Tether ball is an excellent game, especially for the older children. A strong pole thirteen feet long and seven and one-half inches in circumference at its base, is placed three feet in the ground, so as to be steady. A white line is painted around the pole four feet from the top. A circle six feet in diameter is drawn around the pole (as a center) on the ground. A line twenty feet long is drawn passing through this circle, so as to divide the territory into two sections, one for each player. Two spots should be marked six feet from the pole at right angles to the twenty-foot line. These are spots from which the ball is served. A tennis ball covered with a net casing is tied to the end of a piece of heavy cord or fishing line seven and one-half feet long, which is fastened to the top of the pole. The object of the game is to try to bat the ball with a tennis or paddle tennis racket, or any flat wooden paddle, so that it will wind the string and ball around the pole within four feet of the top. The player winning the toss has the choice of ground and direction of winding the ball. The other player has the first serve. The server begins the game by batting the ball. He may hit it during service but once. The other player then tries to bat it in the opposite direction. Each player must keep entirely on his side of the twenty-foot line and outside the six-foot circle. Whenever a player in serving fails to knock the ball outside of his own territory, the opposing player takes the ball and serves it. A player scores a game (1) when he winds the ball completely up within the four-foot mark from the top; (2) when the opposing player steps over his bounds or strikes the pole or ground with his racket. A player has a free serve when the opposing player winds the ball below the four-foot mark, or touches the ball with his hands. Teams may be formed, but only two players play the ball during one game. When there are only two players, the one having the majority of eleven games, wins. Where there are more than two players on a team, the team wins which has the greatest number of games at the end of a definite number of rounds.

Volley Ball

Game. It shall consist of twenty-one points. Practice games may be eleven points. Players exchange courts after each game. The losing side has the first serve. The game may be played with two or four time limits, with short rest periods between. At the end of each playing period, players exchange courts and the player last serving resumes the service.

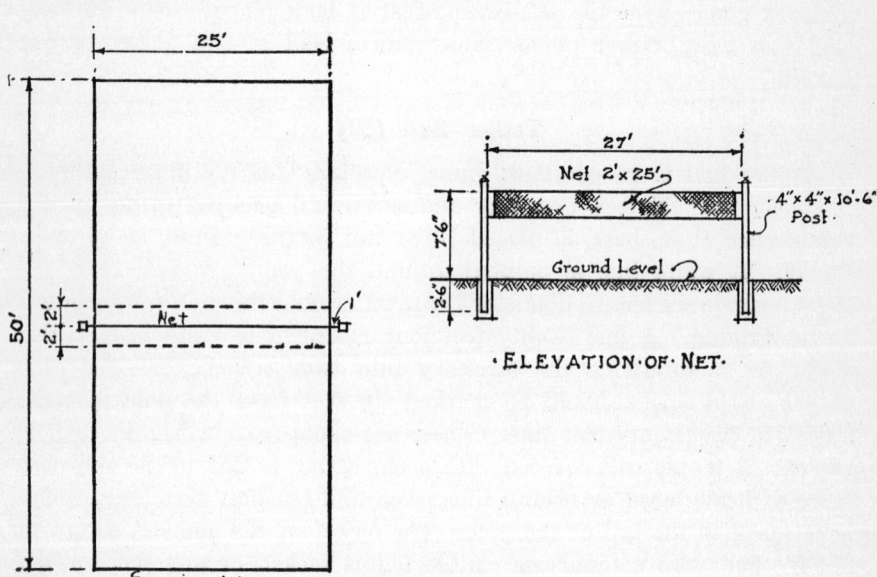

·VOLLEY·BALL· COURT·

Number of Players. Two to eighteen. For match games, six players on each team. The number of players may be increased by mutual agreement to nine on a team.

Size of Court. Court shall be twenty-five feet wide by fifty feet long, divided by the net into two equal courts. When posts are only six feet in height, lines shall be drawn across the court two feet from and parallel to the net on each side. This is known as the neutral territory and may not be entered by either team. For inexperienced players, the service point may be placed fifteen feet from the net in the center of the field. As skill is gained, this point may be moved toward the rear service line. The serving line shall be the rear boundary line. The long dimension of the court should run north and south when outdoors.

Net. The net shall be two feet wide, twenty-five feet long, and shall be suspended from the wall or from uprights placed, when possible, one foot outside the side lines.

Height of Net. The regulation height for the top of the net is seven feet six inches from the ground, but it may be lowered to suit ages of players to six feet six inches in height. If the posts are only six feet in height, the two-foot neutral territory ruling shall be enforced. If the posts allow for the regulation height of seven feet six inches, the ruling may be waived upon agreement of the captains.

Ball. The ball shall be a regulation volley ball.

Object of the Game. It is purely a defensive and batting game. The object of the game is to keep the ball volleying over the net without touching the ground or net. If the ball batted by the server touches the ground of the opponents' court, the serving side scores one point. If the ball is returned by the opponents and touches the ground of the serving side, a point is not scored, but the opponents receive the ball for service and have an opportunity to begin scoring points.

Positions of Players. Number the players and the positions, and have them play the different positions by rotation, so each in turn plays all positions in the field. Rotation of team occurs only when that team receives the ball for service.

Line Ball. A ball striking a boundary line is equivalent to one in court.

The Server. 1. Each member of the team shall serve in turn, as numbered, and may have one trial to get the ball over. If agreed, two trials may be allowed.

2. If the ball on the first service hits the net and then lands on the ground and has not touched or been touched by any member of the team, it shall count as one trial. It is known as a net ball.

3. If a served ball strikes the top of the net and falls into the opponents' court, it shall not score, but shall be called a "let ball," and the server reserves it. Three "let balls" change the service.

4. The server shall stand with both feet back of the rear boundary line.

5. No ball during service may be relayed over the net.

6. The ball must be batted with the open hand, fingers extended. Failure to so serve changes the service.

7. The server may touch the ball but once until it has been returned by the opponents.

After the Service. 1. Members of the teams may touch the ball not more than twice in succession. Skillful players bat the ball but once.

2. If a failure to serve the ball over the net is made, or if the ball strikes any object within the court and falls outside, or if the ball is served out of bounds crossing the net, or if the ball is knocked out of bounds by the serving side, it shall retire the server.

3. A player serving continues to do so until retired by failure in his own service or by loss of the ball caused by his side sending the ball out of bounds, or by failing to return the ball over the net, or by the following fouls made by his side:

(a) Catching the ball; (b) Allowing the ball to rest on the hands; (c) Touching the net; (d) Stepping into the neutral ground, if a neutral ground is used; (e) Fisting the ball; (f) Dribbling or pushing the ball; (g) Serving the ball with bent fingers.

Volleyed Balls. 1. After the service ball, a volleyed ball which touches the top of the net and falls into either court is not in play, but is returned to the server and is served again. No score is made for either side.

2. When a volleyed ball is hit into the net by the serving side, no point is scored—change of service. A volleyed ball hit into the net by the receiving side gives a point to the serving side.

3. After the service, should the volleyed ball strike any player within the playing space and bound back into either court, it is still in play. Striking the ceiling or tree branches within the court causes the ball to be dead. It is re-served or given to the opponents, depending upon who last touched the ball.

4. After the service, during the volleying, if the ball strikes any object other than a player outside the court and bounds back again, it shall not be in play and counts against the side which struck it last. Each good service unreturned by the receiving side, or ball in play unreturned by the receiving side, and each foul made by the receiving side, shall count one point for the side serving.

Fouls. 1. If a player on the serving side touches the net; steps into the neutral territory; fists or pushes; holds and bats; dribbles; or allows the ball to rest on the hands and then bats, it shall change the service.

2. When two or more fouls are made at the same time by the serving side, one of the fouls shall give the ball to the receiving side, and each of the remaining fouls counts as one point for the receiving side.

3. If fouls are made during the volleying by the receiving side, the

play shall continue until one side fails to return the ball, when points made through fouls shall be given to opponents. The serving side may, or may not, have to relinquish the ball.

4. If the receiving side makes any of the fouls it shall count a point for the serving side.

5. If both sides touch the net simultaneously, the ball shall be declared out of play and shall be served again by the serving side.

6. No player may bat the ball more than twice in succession while within the boundaries of the court.

7. No player may serve with the fingers bent.

8. No player may fist the ball.

9. Any player, except the captain, addressing the umpire or making any remarks to or about him or any of the players, or any player kicking the ball may be disqualified and his side compelled to play the game without him.

10. No player shall be allowed to strike the ball while supported by any player or object, but must strike it while on the floor or while jumping up unassisted.

Helps in Playing the Game. 1. In volleying, strike the ball with both hands.

2. Look for uncovered space in the opponents' court and send ball there.

3. Play together; cover your own space.

4. Pass from one to another when possible.

5. Watch the play constantly, especially the opponents' play.

6. Keep your eyes on the ball.

7. With fewer than six on a team, reduce the size of the court.

8. To meet rural conditions children in the third, fourth, fifth and sixth grades may play net ball in the same game with children in the seventh and eighth grades who are playing volley ball. The general rules are the same for both games.

NOTE.—With a few exceptions these rules are similar to the Spalding rules. For the best posture results, keep the net high and taut; no sag should be allowed.

Additional Athletic Games

Captain Ball III .... Ref. No. 19, p. 344
Quadruple Dodge Ball .... Ref. No. 33, p. 51

INDIVIDUAL ATHLETIC EVENTS

Basket Ball One Hand Shot (59) *

The pupil, holding a basket ball, stands on the circle enclosing the free throw line. Running toward the basket, he bounces the ball once

* From S. C. Staley, "Individual and Mass Athletics." Copyright 1925. By permission of A. S. Barnes and Company, publishers.

on the free throw line, catches it in both hands, leaps in the air, and attempts to put the ball into the basket with one hand. Taking more than one step with the ball, shooting with both hands, or running in any direction but straight from the front constitutes a foul, and a trial without record. Five or ten trials are satisfactory for most competitions. The total number of baskets made represents the pupil's score.

Crab Walk Race

The performer supports himself on his hands and feet, with back toward the ground, feet toward the finish line. In this position, traveling with feet foremost, the race is run, without dropping the body to the ground. From fifteen to thirty feet makes a good race. The reverse crab walk race is run by traveling with hands foremost instead of the feet foremost.

Lame Duck Race (59) *

The pupil stands on one leg, raises the other leg forward and grasps the toe of the raised leg with both hands. Keeping this position he hops forward to the finish line. The race is started and judged as any regular race. From fifteen to thirty yards is a satisfactory distance.

Run (70 Yards)

For explanations, see "Run" for fifth grade, page 209.

Seven Jumps (Boys)

The pupil toes the take-off with both feet and makes seven jumps forward without a pause between jumps. Failure to keep the feet together and failure to make the jumps in immediate succession constitute trials without record. The distance between the take-off and the mark drawn at the heels on the last jump represents his record. The record should be taken for both a standing and running start.

Soccer Corner Kick for Accuracy

This event should be performed on a soccer field. Mark an area on the ground five yards wide and eight yards long directly in front of the goal. This area runs from goal post to goal post and extends five yards into the field. A soccer ball is placed in the corner of the field and, with or without a run, the pupil attempts to kick it so it will land within the area. Five or ten kicks may be allowed each student. Balls landing within the area score one point; balls landing outside the area

---

* From S. C. Staley, "Individual and Mass Athletics." Copyright 1925. By permission of A. S. Barnes and Company, publishers.

score nothing. The total number of points made by a pupil gives his score.

Soccer Heading for Distance

The pupil tosses a soccer ball into the air, and drives it as far as possible with his head. He may, or may not, run before heading the ball. Failure to hit the ball with his head counts as a trial without record. A successful trial is measured from the nearest toe of the pupil where he stopped, to the point where the ball first struck the ground.

Soccer Punt for Distance

The pupil stands behind a line. With or without running, he drops the ball, kicking it before it hits the ground. He must be behind the line at the time the ball is kicked. The distance is measured from the point on the line where he kicked it to the point where the ball first struck the ground.

Soccer Throw-in for Distance

The pupil stands with both feet back of a line. Holding the ball overhead with both hands, he throws it as far as possible. The feet may be spread or held together, but both feet must remain back of the line until the ball hits the ground. The distance is measured from the point where the ball was thrown to the point where it first struck the ground.

Standing Hop, Skip and Jump (Boys) (59) *

The pupil stands on one foot at the take-off, hops forward, landing on the same foot, puts the other foot in back of the hopping foot, landing on it, and leaps forward onto both feet. From start to finish the performance is continuous without a pause. The distance is measured as in the standing broad jump.

Standing Hop, Step and Jump (Boys) (59) *

The pupil stands on one foot at the take-off, hops forward on the same foot, steps forward on the other foot and leaps forward, landing on both feet. From start to finish the performance is continuous without a pause. The distance is measured as in the standing broad jump.

Standing Whole Hammon (Boys) (59) *

The student stands on one foot at the take-off, then in continuous succession makes two hops, two steps, and two jumps. The distance covered is measured as in the standing broad jump.

* From S. C. Staley, "Individual and Mass Athletics." Copyright 1925. By permission of A. S. Barnes and Company, publishers.

300   PHYSICAL EDUCATION FOR ELEMENTARY SCHOOLS

Additional Individual Athletic Events

Running Whole Hammon (Boys) ....Ref. No. 59, p. 36
Seven Hops (Boys) ....Ref. No. 59, p. 35
Seven Steps (Boys) ....Ref. No. 59, p. 37
Running Hop, Step and Jump (Boys) ....Ref. No. 59, p. 36
Running Hop, Skip and Jump (Boys) ....Ref. No. 59, p. 35
Soccer Place Kick for Accuracy ....Ref. No. 59, p. 78
Soccer Heading for Accuracy ....Ref. No. 59, p. 81
Soccer Bounce Kick for Distance ....Ref. No. 59, p. 65
Soccer Dribble Kick for Accuracy ....Ref. No. 59, p. 79
Basket Ball Dribble ....Ref. No. 59, p. 24

RHYTHMICAL ACTIVITIES

The Crested Hen (Danish) *

Formation: Sets of one man and two girls form about the room.

(a) They join hands in a circle and, stamping on the first step, dance fast step-hop, moving to the left (bars 1 to 8); stamp, or jump high on first note, and dance the same, moving to the right (bars 1 to 8).

(b) The girls release hands, placing free hand on hip, and dance, one on either side of the man. The girl on the right dances under the arch made by the man and the girl on his left (bars 9 and 10), the man turns under his own left arm (bars 11 and 12), the girl on the left dances under the arch made by the man and the girl on his right (bars 13 and 14), and the man turns under his right arm (bars 15 and 16). They repeat (b) (bars 9 to 16). Throughout (b) all three dance step-hop, moving continuously, which swings the group freely about.

* From Viggo Bovbjerg, "Danish Folk Dances." Copyright 1917. By permission of author. Recreation Training School of Chicago, 800 S. Halsted street, Hull House, publishers.

SEVENTH GRADE

Highland Schottische *

(Columbia: A3039.)

Formation: A double circle, partners facing each other; sides to center; left arm curved high over head; right hand on hip.

Description:

Part I

Very light and snappy. One moves toward the center, the other away.

Measure 1. Hop on the left foot and touch the right toe lightly to the side (one and). Hop on the left foot and swing the right behind the left ankle (two and). Repeat (three and, four and).

Measure 2. Schottische step to right; slide, cut, leap, hop. Slide sideward with the right foot (slide) (one and); swing the left foot up to the right, forcing the right foot off the floor (cut) (two and); spring to the right foot (leap) (three and); hop on the right foot (hop) (four and).

Measures 3 and 4. Repeat to the left, reversing position of arms on first count.

Measures 5–8. Repeat all.

---

* From Caroline Crawford, "Folk Dances and Games." Copyright 1908. By permission of A. S. Barnes and Company, publishers.

Part II

Partners hook right arms, left arms curved over head, and turn around and back with hop steps.

Measure 1. Step with right foot (one and); hop on the right foot and swing the left foot forward, upward (two and); step forward with the left foot (three and); hop on the left foot and swing the right forward, upward (four and).

Measure 2. Like measure 1, but change arms and face about on (four and).

Measures 3 and 4. Repeat, going in the opposite direction.

Measures 5 and 6. Like 1 and 2.

Measures 7 and 8. Like 3 and 4, but instead of turning around, pass forward on the last measure to next partner. The dance repeats until the original partners meet again.

The Mangle (Danish) *

Couples, in waltz position scattered all over the floor. On the first beat of the first bar, the man hops on his left foot swinging right foot sideways, hops on right foot swinging left foot sideways; then hops on his left foot swinging right foot sideways, hops on his right foot swinging left foot sideways (bars 1 and 2). Two polka steps (bars 3 and 4).

The girl does the same, beginning with hop on right foot swinging left foot sideways, etc.

In that way they continue the dance, hop and leg-swinging to repeat of music (bars 1 and 2), polka (bars 3 and 4), repeat hop and leg-swinging (bars 5 and 6) and polka (bars 7 and 8), etc., to the completion of the music.

---

* Fom Viggo Bovbjerg, "Danish Folk Dances (Music)." Copyright 1917. By permission of author, Recreation Training School of Chicago, 800 S. Halsted street, Hull House, publishers.

SEVENTH GRADE

Old Dan Tucker II (12)

"Old Dan Tucker" is a country dance. It is often played by a large group of men and women. It apparently originated in America.

Any number of couples join hands in a single ring around Dan Tucker, who stands in the center. One of the players acts as prompter and calls the figures.

Call: *"All balance to Tucker."* All join hands and walk forward four steps and back four steps (bars 1 and 4). 2 steps to a bar.

Call: *"Allemande left."* Each gentleman turns the lady on his left, both using their left hands. He then turns his own partner, both using their right hands (repeat 1—4).

Call: *"Grand right and left"* (in which Dan Tucker joins). Right hand to partner, left to the next, etc. (bars 5–12).

Call: *"All promenade."* Each crosses hands in skating position with the partner he has when the call is given and walks around to the right (bars 1–4 and repeat). The one who is left without a partner becomes Dan Tucker and goes into the center.

Call: *"All forward and back."* All join hands in a ring, walk forward four steps and back four steps (bar 5–8).

Call: *"Circle to the left."* All gallop to the left (bars 9–12).

Pop Goes the Weasel III *

Music: See page 185.

Metronome 112. Six couples in a set. Call first change before music begins.

---

* From Mr. and Mrs. Henry Ford, "Good Morning; Old Fashioned Dances Revived." Copyright 1926. By permission of Dearborn Publishing Company, Dearborn, Michigan, publishers.

"*Head couple down the outside and back*"—8 bars: Head lady and gentleman walk down the outside of their own line eight steps and return to place.

"*Down the center and back*"—8 bars: The same couple join inside hands and promenade down to the foot of the set, eight steps, then change hands and return to place, eight steps.

"*Circle three hands around*"—8 bars: The same couple join hands with the next lady and circle three hands once and a half around, the second lady stopping opposite and facing her original place. At the word POP in the music the active couples release the hands of the other lady, at the same time raising their own joined hands, forming an arch, under which she passes and returns to her own place.

"*Circle three hands around with gentleman*"—8 bars: Repeat the same with that gentleman. Repeat all, going below one couple each time. The other odd couples 3–5 begin the dance at the same time and continue until the end of the set is reached, when each couple rests one repetition of the dance. The same applies to the head of the set. To end the dance, call: "*Join hands forward, swing partners, promenade to seats.*"

Rye Waltz*

* From Mr. and Mrs. Henry Ford, "Good Morning; Old Fashioned Dances Revived." Copyright 1926. By permission of Dearborn Publishing Company, Dearborn, Michigan, publishers.

I
Waltz Position

Extend left foot to side, toe lightly touching the floor, (1);
Draw left foot just behind right heel, toe lightly touching the floor, (2);
Left toe to side again, (3);
Left toe back, (4) .... 1 bar
Slide close, slide close, (1–2);
Slide close, step to left, (3–4) .... 1 bar
Repeat same right thus:
Right toe to side and toe back, (1–2);
To side and back again, (3–4) .... 1 bar
Slide close, slide close, (1–2);
Slide close, step to right, (3–4) .... 1 bar
Repeat all .... 4 bars

                                                                                                     8 bars

II

Waltz .... 16 bars

Schottische Couple Dance (6B)

Music: Any 2/4 tempo.
Couples in circle formation—inside hands joined.

Step I

1–4. Starting with outside foot, run forward three steps and hop, extending inside foot forward.
5–8. Repeat, starting with inside foot.
9–16. Turn partner with four step-hops, both hands joined.
17–64. Repeat 1–16 three more times.

Step II

1–4. Schottische step forward with outside foot. (Slide forward on outside foot, bring inside foot to 5th rear, step forward with outside foot and hop, swinging inside foot forward.)
5–8. Schottische step forward with inside foot.
9–16. Girl dances around partner with four step-hops, while boy dances 4 step-hops on place.
17–32. Repeat 1–16, boy dancing around partner with four step-hops on counts 9–16. Repeat 1–32.

Step III

1-4. Schottische forward with outside foot.
5-8. Schottische forward with inside foot.
9-14. Walk forward three steps, starting with outside foot.
15-16. Bring heels together and face partner.
17-20. Schottische sideways right.
21-24. Schottische sideways left.
25-32. Join hands with partner and turn with four step-hops.
33-64. Repeat 1-32.

Uncle Sam's Frolic (6B)

Music: "Dixie Land."

Formation: Double circle, facing in sets of fours. Flag on stick is held over right shoulder.

Step I

Measure 1. Slide-hop forward right, extending left foot backward. Flag held horizontally over head with both hands.

Measure 2. Step-hop backward left, with right foot forward.

Measures 3-4. Walking steps (three) forward toward opposite couple, starting with right foot. Heels together on last count. Flag held at right shoulder, left hand at hip.

Measures 5-8. Four step-hops turning right about in place, starting with right foot. Flag is waved overhead.

Measures 9-16. Repeat measures 1-8 walking backwards to original places in measures 11-12.

Step II (Chorus)

Measure 1. Step sideward right and left foot in rear, bend knees slightly.

Measure 2. Repeat step sideward left.

Measure 3. With heels together, wave flag overhead, singing "Hooray."

Measure 4. Sing second "Hooray" while changing flag to left hand and extending it obliquely upward toward center of sets of fours. Turn slightly right.

Measures 5-8. Taking eight skipping steps, each set of four makes a complete circle finishing in original place.

Measures 9-12. Schottische step sideward right and left. Flag is held at right shoulder.

Measures 13-14. Starting with right foot partners take four walking steps forward and pass at left shoulder of opposite girl. Meet new couple.

SEVENTH GRADE

Measure 15. Step sideward right, and with left foot in rear, bend knees slightly.

Measure 16. Repeat measure 15 sideward left.

Repeat dance as many times as desired, meeting new couple each time.

Additional Rhythmical Activities

Sailors' Hornpipe	Ref. No. 18, p. 350
Circle Dance	Ref. No. 25, p. 184
Irish Lilt	Ref. No. 26, p. 279
Tantoli	Ref. No. 26, p. 235
Ball Game, The	Ref. No. 31, p. 123
Bow-Wow (American)	Ref. No. 31, p. 129
Donegal Country Dance (Irish)	Ref. No. 31, p. 131
Hatter, The (Victor: 20449)	Ref. No. 31, p. 132
Lancers, The (American)	Ref. No. 31, p. 135
Russian Scherr	Ref. No. 31, p. 141
Oxcow I (Danish)	Ref. No. 36, p. 26
Three Strand May-Pole-Ka	Ref. No. 39, p. 24
Lassie's Dance II (Kulldansen)	Ref. No. 42, p. 60
Trallen (Fjallnaspolska) (Columbia: A3002)	Ref. No. 42, p. 77
Noriu Miego (Lithuanian)	Ref. No. 95, p. 32

STUNTS

Long Reach (5)

Mark a line on the floor or ground. Toe this mark and with a piece of chalk or stick mark the floor or ground as far as possible from the line rising again to position without having moved the toes from the mark. In returning to position, the hand which has supported the body in stooping to make the mark must not be drawn along the ground or placed a second time to the ground.

Setting Pegs

Use three sharpened pegs. From a mark, hop on one foot as far as possible and set one of the pegs, take a second hop on the same foot and set the second peg, take a third hop and set the third peg. Do not touch the ground with any part of your body other than the foot with which you hop. If balance is lost and the foot moved, hop back to the starting line and begin again. The pegs are left in the ground and each contestant has three trials to set them further out. Indoors this can be carried out by making a chalk mark on the floor in place of setting the pegs.

Chair Vault

With one hand on the seat of the chair and the other on the back, jump through and come back without touching your feet.

Bicycling

Lie on the floor and with an upward throw of the legs stand on shoulders, legs above head. Maintain the balance in this position, and move the legs as if pedaling a bicycle.

Wiggle Walk

The performer stands with heels together and toes pointed outward. Simultaneously he raises the right heel and the left toes, and pivots to the right, thus standing in a pigeon-toed position. Resting on the opposite toes and heel, pivot again to a toeing out position. Continue to progress to the right. Reverse the process and travel to the left.

Finger Feat

Place your hands horizontally across, close to your breast, middle finger tips touching. Another player, by grasping the wrists and with a steady pull, should then try to separate them. Try several times.

Straddle Jump (14D)

Two boys clasp both hands facing each other. Boy No. 1 bends his right knee; boy No. 2 places right foot on the bent thigh, just above the knee, springs, and lands astraddle the neck of No. 1. Both boys are now facing in the same direction. Pupils should have their shoes off.

Shoulder Spring (14D)

This is the same as "Straddle Jump," except that boy No. 2 lands on the shoulders of No. 1, standing in an upright position instead of sitting astraddle of the neck. After getting his balance, boy No. 2 should be able to release his hold on the hands of No. 1 and balance himself upright on the shoulders. Pupils should have their shoes off.

Hand Stand

Place hands on floor; with head back spring from feet, lifting them upward to a perpendicular position. Maintain this position for several seconds.

SEVENTH GRADE

Shoulder Stands

Hand Walk

Come to a hand-stand with the feet above the head. Walk on the hands. Keep the head bent far back, using it as a balance.

Camel Walk

Two boys face in the same direction. No. 1 jumps up backward and locks his legs high up under the arms of No. 2. He then crawls through between the legs of No. 2, and takes hold of his ankles. No. 2 falls over on to his hands and walks on all-fours as in the elephant walk.

Camel Walk

Knee Shoulder Stand

Elbow Roll

Two boys, standing back to back, lock elbows. No. 1 leans forward, pulls No. 2 off his feet and rolls him over his back so that he lands on his feet facing No. 1. Hold No. 2 close to the back, so he will not slip as he comes over.

Additional Stunts

Stooping Push ....Ref. No. 19, p. 252
Merry-Go-Round ....Ref. No. 26, p. 365
Back Toss ....Ref. No. 60, p. 133
Bobbin Ahead ....Ref. No. 60, p. 129
Bobbin Back ....Ref. No. 60, p. 124
Flopper ....Ref. No. 60, p. 124
Front Toss ....Ref. No. 60, p. 132
Through the Stick ....Ref. No. 60, p. 98
Toe Jump ....Ref. No. 60, p. 111

RELAY RACES

Ball Passing Relay

Players are divided into teams and stand in file formation. All players take stride position. The first one in the file passes some object back between the legs to the next player, who passes it on. When the last one in each file receives the object all the players kneel down, and the last man runs forward, straddling the other players, to the head of the column. The others quickly rise and the object is again passed back between the legs. Continue until all have carried it forward. The file which reaches its original position first, wins.

Chariot Race

The children are arranged in groups of three. Two players with joined hands are the "horses," while the third is the "driver" of the chariot. The "driver" uses reins of colored streamers or of rope. The teams race along a straight course between two goals not more than twenty-five or thirty yards apart. They may race around a turning point and return. The first team to cross the starting line is the winner.

Dozen Ways of Getting There, A

Divide group into teams which form files back of a starting line. Sixty feet away establish a goal line. Number the players from front to rear. Each number is then told the manner in which they are to progress. Number one may hop; number two skip; etc. Each player on returning to the starting line touches off the next player and then goes to the rear of the line. The line to finish first, wins.

Goal Throwing Relay (14C)

Divide the players into two equal lines, each line facing its own goal back of a line forty feet away. At a signal, the first runner of each line runs forward with a basket ball and throws it into the basket. The player must not return to his line until he has thrown the ball through the basket. As soon as this is accomplished, the player runs back to his line. He may hand or throw the ball to No. 2, who runs to the goal and throws the ball into the basket. No. 1 passes to the end of the line. The line whose leader reaches his original position first, wins.

Hoop Rolling Relay

Two or more teams are lined up back of a starting line. An Indian club is placed opposite each team and sixty feet distant. At the signal "Go" the first player of each team rolls a hoop around the Indian club and back to the starting line, which thus becomes the finishing line. If the runner knocks over the Indian club, the club must be replaced before proceeding further. Upon crossing the finish line the hoop is given to the next runner who repeats the process. A runner shall not start until the preceding runner has crossed the line. The hoop must at all times be rolled, not carried in the hand. The team wins whose last runner first crosses the finish line.

Jack Rabbit Relay

Players are divided into two or more teams of equal numbers. Each team lines up in single file behind the starting line. There should be about four or five feet between the files and three feet between ranks. The captain of each team has a wand about three feet long cut from a broom handle. Each captain stands toeing the starting line. At a signal the captain turns, gives one end of the wand to the player next behind, retaining his hold on the other end. These two players stoop down, run back to the end of the line, one on each side of the file, holding the wand parallel with and near the floor. Each one in the line jumps over the wand as it reaches him, giving the appearance of jack rabbits. After the last one has jumped, the captain remains at the end of the line. The one who was second in line runs forward to the head of the line and gives the end of the wand to the third player. They in turn carry the wand backward leaving the second player at the rear of the line. This continues until the captain is again at the head of his line. The team wins whose captain is first returned to his original position.

Skin the Snake Relay

Divide players into equal teams. Each team stands in close file formation with feet apart. Each player extends his left hand backward between his legs, and grasps with his right hand the left hand of the player in front of him. At the command "Go" the line moves backward, the rear player lying on his back, still retaining the hand grasp of the player in front. Each player as he lies down should keep his legs close against the body of the one in front, while the players going backward should run with the legs well apart. When all players in the file are lying on their backs, the one at the rear of the line (who headed the file) arises, moves forward, and the others in turn do likewise. Players retain hand grasp until all are up in the starting position. The file to complete this first, wins.

Square Relay

Place four objects or bases from fifteen to thirty feet apart in the form of a square like a baseball diamond. The bases are lettered A, B, C, D around the diamond. Team I lines up single file back of point A. Team II lines up single file back of point C, with sufficient space between the teams and the bases to allow the runners to pass outside of the bases freely. Each leader holds a ball. At a signal, the leader of team I starts running around and outside of points B, C, D back to A and *hands* ball to second runner of his team. Leader of team II starts running around outside of points D, A, B back to C, and *hands* ball to second runner, etc. The team wins whose leader first receives the ball into his hands after all members of the team have run. Variations: (1) A runner of team I may throw the ball to the next runner of his team at any point between D and A, and a runner of team II may throw from any point between B and C. If, however, a wild throw is made by the runner and the ball rolls into or beyond the square between points A, B and C and D, the next runner must secure the ball, return to his starting point and encircle or include points A or C in his run. All four points must be included in the course. Failure to do so constitutes a foul. (2) Walk with ball and hand or throw it to the next runner.

Additional Relay Races

Bend and Stretch Relay.........................Ref. No. 19, p. 50
Line Zigzag III..................................Ref. No. 19, p. 423

HUNTING GAMES

Chain Dodge Ball

A horse "Old Plug" is made up of five players who stand in a file, each firmly holding on to the one in front. The one in front is the head, the one on the end is the tail of the horse. "Old Plug" stands within a circle formed by all other players. The players in the circle have a large ball, or bean bag, and attempt to hit "Old Plug" on the tail. "Old Plug" avoids being hit on the tail by keeping his head toward the ball. The first man in the line may knock the ball with his hands back to the players of the circle. The player who hits "Old Plug's" tail becomes the head. The tail player drops off and joins the circle. In a large circle, there may be two horses.

Chain Tag (14D)

One player is chosen to be "It" and tries to tag the others, who run about as in free tag. As soon as a player is tagged he joins hands with the tagger and both become "It," keeping their hands joined. When they tag another player, he joins hands with them. Thus the line grows at both ends, and the only players who may tag are the end players. To escape being caught the runners may dodge under the arms of the players in the line. Should the chain of taggers be broken no one may be tagged until the players join hands again.

Fox and Geese

One player is to be the fox and one the gander. All the remaining players are geese who line up in single file back of the gander, grasping the shoulders of the one in front. The last goose is eligible to be tagged by the fox. The gander protects his geese by trying to keep in front of the fox, who endeavors to tag the last one in the line. If the fox tags the goose, the goose becomes fox and the fox gander.

Nose and Toe Tag (3)

Players scatter about the playing space. One player is "It," and tries to tag another player, who will then become "It." Players save themselves from being tagged by grasping their nose with one hand and toes with the other hand, standing on one foot.

Poison (4)

Mark a circle on the ground, one-third as large as one formed by the players clasping hands outside it. Each player tries to push or pull the others into the marked circle, but to keep out of it himself. Any one who touches the ground within the circle is said to be poisoned. As soon as this happens, the players cry "Poison" and at once break the circle and run for safety to avoid being tagged by the one who is "poisoned." Safety consists in standing on wood. The merest chip will answer, but growing things are not counted. Any other material may be named as safety. Any one caught before reaching safety becomes a catcher. When "poison" calls "change," players must exchange places and are in danger of being caught by the chasers. When all have become chasers, the circle is once more surrounded and the game repeated.

Whip Tag (15A)

All the players but one stand in a circle, holding their hands open behind them. Players should hold their hands in proper position in order to become chasers. The odd player carries a knotted towel round the outside of the circle and puts it into the hands of one of the players. Whoever receives it becomes chaser and starts, striking his right-hand neighbor with the towel. The neighbor, to escape, runs around the circle back to his own place, while the chaser pursues, striking him whenever near enough. Meanwhile, the player who first had the towel steps between two other nearby players, thus getting out of the way of the runners. After the runner returns to his place the chaser gives the towel to another player in the circle, and the game proceeds as before.

Additional Hunting Games

Dead Ball ....Ref. No. 19, p. 362
Forcing the City Gates......................Ref. No. 19, p. 89
Maze Tag ....Ref. No. 19, p. 131
Odd Man's Cap...............................Ref. No. 19, p. 140
Roley Poley ....Ref. No. 19, p. 399
Third Man ....Ref. No. 19, p. 194

MIMETICS

Windmills

With fists clenched and elbows straight, extend right arm up and left arm down. Left arm swings forward and upward, right arm backward and downward. Continue in complete circles.

Start of Race (13B)

"On your mark": Place right foot back, kneel on right knee (right knee at instep of left foot), rest fingers on line with left foot. "Get Set": Lift body by stretching right knee, head in line with body. "Go": Run twelve quick steps in place and gradually straighten up.

Revolving Light

Fling arms side horizontal and place left foot to side. Twist trunk to left, then all the way over to right. Assume position on count four. Repeat to the right. Continue, alternating left and right.

Jumping Jack

Clap hands in front of thighs, then spring feet apart and clap hands over head. Spring feet together and clap hands in front of thighs. Repeat, jumping in rhythm. Sixteen counts.

Baseball Play (5)

(a) Teacher makes motion of throwing. Class springs up with hands high over head as if catching ball. Repeat reaching to right side, to left side, and stooping to catch a low throw. (b) Pupils throw. Step forward left foot, hold right hand back and over shoulder, left arm extended forward. Make motion of throwing, using body bending in the exercise. Repeat four times. Use left hand four times.

Baseball Pitching

Stretch arms forward, hands together as if holding a ball. Draw back to throw, turning trunk to right and still keep hands together, weight poised over right leg, which should be slightly bent at knee. Throw vigorously, at the same time stepping forward on left foot, and bringing the throwing arm down forcibly across the body. Position.

EIGHTH GRADE

	PAGE
Athletic Games	319
Individual Athletic Events	331
Mimetics	333
Rhythmical Activities	334
Stunts	346
Relay Races	348
Hunting Games	350

The teacher should refer frequently to Part I of the book, as it contains many suggestions in regard to the various activities. For example —the material presented in Part I under "Posture," "Corrective Physical Education," and "Health Education" applies to all grades and should be reviewed frequently.

The activity classifications in each grade have been arranged in sequence according to judgments of their appeal and importance to the children who will use them. In situations where all the content appearing in this grade can not be taught, the teacher should make selections from each classification rather than attempt to teach all the activities found in any one classification.

ATHLETIC GAMES

Advancement

Equipment. Outline a field seventy-five feet by three hundred feet. This may be varied, depending upon the playing space which may be available. The end lines are goal lines. A soccer ball is used.

Object of Game. To drop-kick the ball over the goal line, raising it ten feet into the air. The ball is to land on the other side of the goal line without being touched or caught by a member of the opposing team. When a team is forced backward toward the goal line, it is not permitted to step over it. Teams kick the ball alternately.

Game. The ball is put in play at the center of the field. A coin is tossed to decide which side has the kick-off. After a goal is made, the losing team kicks off. Players are well distributed over the field. Opponents must be ten feet from the person kicking the ball. A place kick is used to start the game. If a ball is caught on the fly by an opponent, he may advance five steps toward his goal and then punt. If the ball is touched, not caught, the ball is kicked back by the player who touched it, from the spot where he touched it.

Out of Bounds. If the ball is kicked out of bounds, it is brought to the place where it crossed the line, and play continues from that point. If the ball is caught out of bounds, no steps are allowed. The ball is brought to where it crossed the line (as before) and punted from that spot. If the ball is kicked out of bounds in trying for goal no score is made.

Fouls. (a) Opponents standing nearer than ten feet from ball when it is kicked. Penalty—Man kicking the ball may advance five steps. (b) There shall be only two hands on the ball when it is caught. This pertains to two or more catching a fly ball. Penalty—The usual five steps are not allowed. Umpire decides who is to kick the ball when two or more catch it.

Scoring. A place kick for goal does not score a point. A punt for goal does not score a point. Players must judge when they are near enough to the goal line and then attempt to score by a drop-kick. A drop-kick scores one point. When a player steps behind his goal line, the opponents score one point.

Field Dodge Ball

Draw a line thirty feet in length. From the center point in this line, and at right angles sixty feet away, make a base. Players are divided into two teams. The team at bat is lined up behind the home line. The other team is in the field. A basket ball, volley ball or soccer ball is thrown into the field of play by a starter, and immediately two runners enter the field. They run toward the base, around it, and return to the home line. The players in the field (they should be well distributed) try to hit the runners with the ball before they can return home. The players in the field may walk or run to get the ball, but must stand still to throw it. They may throw at the runners or pass to another player who is in a better position to throw. When a runner is hit by the ball while in the field of play, he must raise his hand so that the starter may send another runner into the field. When a runner returns home safely, the starter sends in the next runner. After all runners have had a chance, those who return safely indicate the same, and the number of runs scored are credited to that team. The teams then change places and the game continues for a definite number of innings. Infraction of any rule scores a run for the opponents.

Hand Tennis

Equipment. The court is forty feet long and sixteen feet wide, divided in the middle by a taut two-foot net, which at the center is two feet four inches from the ground. Three feet from the net, and on each side of it, a foul line is drawn the full width of the court. The court runs from the net to the base line. Any rubber ball that bounces well may be used.

The Game. The game may be played by two, three or four players. The ball may be hit with either hand. It is permissible to turn the hand so as to cut and curve the ball. The ball is put in play by the server who must stand behind the rear line of the court and drop the ball to the ground, then after the first bounce with an underhand stroke, hit the ball over the net. The receiver must allow a served ball to bounce before returning it. After the ball has been served, it may be returned on the fly or after the first bounce. The only time two serves are allowed is when the first serve hits the net and goes over. If the server serves into the net or out of bounds, he loses his serve and the ball goes to the other side. The server continues to serve so long as he is scoring points. When a server fails to make a good return, he loses the serve. It is a handout, as in hand ball. If during play the ball hits the net and goes over, it is a good ball.

Scoring. Points are scored when a player fails to return the ball over the net or fails to return it so that it strikes the ground inside the opponents' court. Points for play can be scored only by the side that is serving. The winner is the one who first scores fifteen points.

Fouls. If the receiver returns a served ball on the fly, or steps into his foul area during the play, one point is given to the server. If the server steps on or over the end line when serving, or into his foul area during the play, he loses his serve.

Doubles. When playing doubles, the serve alternates between partners every time they win back the serve, which means that both members of a team serve before the serve goes to the other side.

Kickover Ball

Formation. The players are divided into two teams. They sit on the floor or ground in two parallel lines facing each other, and with feet extended. Arms are extended backward supporting the body from the floor. A space of one foot is left free between the feet of the opposing sides. A goal is designated thirty feet away, and equidistant from each team.

The Game. By superior kicking and running, each team endeavors to outscore the other. The instructor stands at the end of the lines farthest from the base. He rolls a soccer ball on the floor between the lines. The players try to kick the ball over the heads of their opponents. Two points may be scored by each play. The first point is given to the team which kicks the ball over the opponents' heads. As soon as the ball is kicked over, two players (one from each team) farthest from the instructor jump up and run around the goal. The first runner to cross the finishing line—a line at right angles to the players' lines and at the instructor's end—will score a point for his team. The runners then sit down at the head of line which has moved down one space.

Duration of Game. There are three methods: (1) Until every player has had a chance to run; (2) Until a given number of points have been scored by a team; (3) Until a given number of minutes of play have expired.

Fouls. The fouls are: (1) Touching ball with hands; (2) Running of players before ball is kicked over head. The opposing team scores one point for each foul committed.

Side Kick (17) *

The object of the game is for a team to kick a soccer ball over a goal line. Two lines called "drivers' lines" are drawn on the ground fifteen feet apart, and parallel to each other. Five feet beyond each driver's line, and parallel to it, two more lines are drawn. These are goal lines. The length of the lines should be about three feet for each player of a team. The players of each team line up in front of their goal line, join hands, and face the opposing team. The first member of each team is driver. The drivers take their positions within the central zone facing each other and facing their own team. When a

---

* From Forbush and Allen, "The Book of Games for Home, School and Playground." Copyright 1927. By permission of John C. Winston Company, publishers.

large number are playing, have four drivers. The referee puts the ball in play at the beginning of the game, after a score has been made, or whenever it rolls out of bounds, by rolling the ball in between the two drivers. The drivers may not kick the ball over the opponent's line, it being their duty to guide the ball with their feet in such a way that their own side may get an opportunity to kick it. If the ball is kicked too high, going over the heads of the opposing team, it counts one point for the opposing team. Teams obstructing the ball may use their legs, bodies, arms or any other part of their bodies, provided they do not use their hands, and do not break the line by letting go of each other's hands. No score can be made by a side if the line of hands is broken at the time the kick is made. On the other hand, if a ball is obstructed by a side while its line is broken, the other side scores a point. When a member of a team steps on or over the driver's line, a point is scored for the opposing team. A kick across the opponent's goal line, if below the heads of the players, scores two points. The team scoring puts in a new driver, the old driver rejoining his team at the other end. An inning consists of twenty points, and a game is made up of three innings. At the end of each inning the teams change goal lines.

Speedball [*]

The game can easily be adapted for use on a small playing area. If size of playing area must be reduced, do not shorten the penalty area, nor width between foul lines. If desired, the penalty zone can be limited to the space between the foul lines and the twenty-yard line that connects them. With this smaller penalty zone the penalties for fouls can be simplified as follows: All personal fouls give one penalty kick; technical fouls by the defense within the penalty area give one penalty kick. These modifications make the game very simple so that beginners can learn it easily. It is also advisable to use a regulation basket ball because the increased size makes it more difficult to throw or kick this ball as far as the regulation speedball or soccer ball, and this restriction helps to offset the limitations of the smaller field.

Playing Field. 1. The entire field outside dimensions shall be 260 feet by 140 feet. The two longer boundaries are called sidelines and the two shorter boundaries the end lines. The field includes two end zones, each twenty feet in width and reaching from sideline to sideline. The outside length of the end zone is the end line of the field and the inside length is called the goal line.

2. The "field of play" shall be that part of the entire playing field which is included between the goal lines and the two sidelines.

---

[*] This game is a combination of soccer and basket ball, and was developed by Elmer D. Mitchell, Athletic Director, University of Michigan, Ann Arbor, Michigan.

EIGHTH GRADE

3. The goal posts shall be placed on the goal line equidistant from the sidelines, twenty-four feet apart, with a crossbar eight feet from the ground. The goal posts shall be twenty feet or more in height.

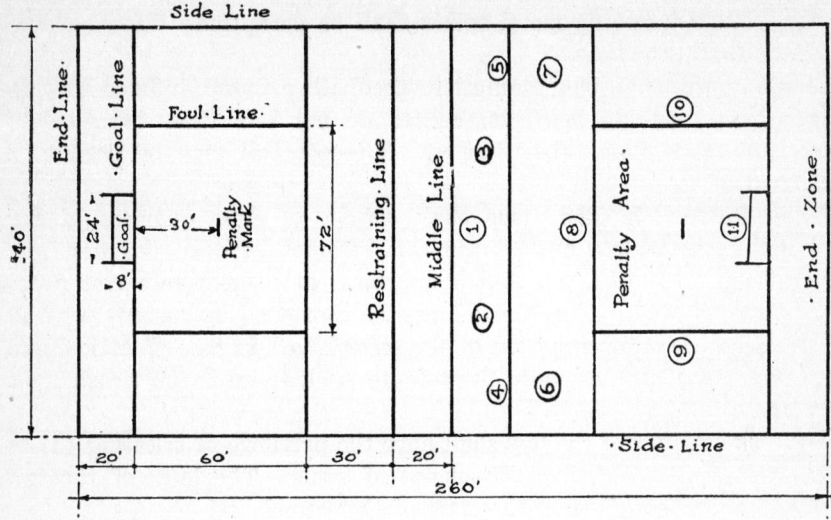

SPEED-BALL FIELD

4. A center line shall be drawn across the field connecting the middle points of the two sidelines. Twenty feet on either side of the halfway line, restraining lines shall be drawn parallel with the halfway line.

5. The penalty area is the space between the goal line and a parallel line, twenty yards distant, which is drawn across the field of play.

6. The penalty mark, one foot in length, is made at a point exactly in front of the middle of the goal posts and thirty feet inward from the goal line.

7. Two foul lines shall be drawn to intersect the goal line and twenty-yard line at a distance of twenty-four feet on each side of the goal posts. These are used only on penalty kicks and on the play following a safety.

8. The goal that a team defends is its "own goal," and the penalty area in front of it shall be termed its "own penalty area." A team also defends its own end zone.

Players and Equipment. 1. A team is made up of eleven players and shall be known as follows: Center, left forward, right forward, left end, right end, left halfback, right halfback, fullback, left guard, right guard, goal guard. For position of players on the field see diagram.

2. A player may be taken out of the game and resubstituted once

during the game. A substitute shall first report to one of the linesmen who shall blow his whistle to allow the change. The linesman shall wait until the ball is dead and the substitute shall remain outside of the field of play in the meantime.

3. No shoes having metal spikes shall be permitted. Teams should wear distinctive colors.

4. The ball shall be a regulation speedball; a round, inflated leather-covered ball having a circumference of not less than twenty-eight inches or more than thirty inches. A soccer ball may be used as a substitute.

The Game. 1. The game shall consist of four quarters of ten minutes each, with a two-minute rest interval between the first and second and the third and fourth quarters; and ten-minute rest interval between halves. The periods may be shortened by mutual consent. "Overtime" is a continuation of the second half in case of a tie score, and consists of one or more five-minute periods until the tie shall be broken.

2. The winner of the toss shall have the privilege of selecting (1) to kick off, or (2) to defend his choice of goals. The loser of the toss shall have this privilege at the start of the second half.

3. Goals shall be changed at quarters, and the side which received at the beginning of the half shall kick off to begin the quarter.

4. In case of overtime, teams shall continue their present goals for the first period, and thereafter shall alternate for each succeeding period. Each overtime period shall commence by the play-off of an imaginary "tie ball" at the center of the field.

5. The game shall be commenced by a place kick from the center of the field of play in the direction of the opponents' goal line. Unless the ball moves forward more than its own circumference it must be kicked over again. The player who has kicked off may not play the ball again until it has first been touched by another player in the game. All the members of his side shall be behind the ball when it is kicked and no opponent shall pass the restraining line until the ball has been kicked.

6. Following a score, the losing side shall kick off.

7. The ball is dead when out of bounds (either at sidelines or goal lines): Following a score, after a foul, after a penalty kick in which no follow-up play is allowed during time out and on a tie ball. In the case of a score, time out, or tie ball, the referee's whistle is needed to start play again; but on out-of-bounds plays and penalty kicks, play can commence without the referee's whistle.

8. "Time out" may be taken by either captain three times during the game. The fourth and succeeding times shall constitute a technical foul for delaying the game. A "time out" is not charged if requested

EIGHTH GRADE

for the purpose of substituting a player. The timekeepers shall take time out after a score has been made, after a penalty kick has been awarded, or whenever "time out" is awarded by the referee. Time shall be resumed when the ball is actually kicked or passed on the next play, with the exception of a penalty kick where no follow-up play is allowed, in which case time shall be resumed at the commencement of the play following the penalty kick. The referee shall not grant a time out while the ball is in play unless the team making the request is in possession of the ball. Time out is taken by the referee on a "double foul" wherein both teams commit a personal foul at the same time. No general play ensues until each team has attempted one penalty kick after which play is resumed by a "tie ball" from the center of the field.

Scoring. Scoring shall be as follows: Field goal, three points; touchdown, two points; penalty kick, one point; drop kick, one point.

1. **Field goal**—A field goal shall be scored, (a) when a ground ball is kicked or legally given impetus with the body (not with the hands) so that it passes over the goal line between the posts and under the crossbar. If such a ball is touched by a defensive player, but goes under the bar without further impetus from the attacking side, the goal shall count; (b) Whenever any ball passes under the crossbar as a result of impetus given by the defending side; (c) If the ball is legally touched by the hands of any player, no member of the attacking side can score a goal until the ball has touched the ground and then been played as a ground ball.

2. **Touchdown**—A touchdown may be scored by the completion of a forward pass from the field of play into the end zone. No part of the receiver's body shall touch the boundary lines of the end zone, or ground outside.

3. **Penalty kick**—This consists of bringing the ball to the penalty mark where, following the referee's whistle, the kicker may attempt to kick the ball between the goal posts under the crossbar. Only one member of the defending side is allowed to guard the goal at this time, and he must stand on the goal line until the ball is kicked. On penalty kicks where no follow-up play is allowed (see Penalties 1a, 2 and 3b) only the kicker and opposing goal guard are concerned. The kicker may not play the ball a second time; if the goal is missed the play shall be considered ended. On penalty kicks where a follow-up play is allowed (see Penalties 1b and 3a) the teammates of the kicker and goal tender shall not encroach upon the end zone or that part of the penalty area that is bounded by the foul lines until the ball is actually kicked. If the ball does not go over the goal line it shall be considered a free ball and played as such. The kicker may not play the ball a second time until it has been touched by another player. The kicker must

make a bona fide attempt to kick the goal, otherwise the referee shall declare a touchback.

4. **Drop kick**—A ball that has been legally caught may be kicked over the crossbar by a drop kick. If the ball passes over the bar between the posts it shall count one for the side making the kick.

Ball Out of Field of Play. 1. **Sidelines**—If a ball goes over the sidelines it shall become the possession of the side opposite that which last touched it and shall be put in play by a pass from the spot where it crossed the line. No score can be made on a direct pass from out of bounds; the ball must first be thrown into the field of play. The player who passes the ball in bounds is restricted from again touching the ball in any way until it has been played by some one other than himself.

2. **Touchback**—Whenever a ball that crosses the goal line without resulting in a score has last been touched by a player of the attacking team, a touchback shall be made. After a touchback the ball shall be put in play by the defensive team at the point where it crossed the goal line by a punt, drop kick, place kick, or pass. The person putting the ball in play is not eligible to touch it again until it has been touched by another player in the game.

3. **Safety**—If a ball which goes over the goal line without scoring was last touched by a player of the defensive side, the ball shall be given to the attacking side and shall be put in play at the point of the foul line and goal line intersection. The player who passes the ball is not eligible to receive it for a touchdown until it has been touched by at least two other players.

4. **Out of bounds**—The ball is out of bounds when (a) it touches the ground on or outside the sidelines; (b) when a player with the ball in his possession touches the sideline or ground outside with any part of his body; (c) when it becomes dead over the goal line without resulting in a score. The player returning the ball from out of bounds is allowed five seconds to make the play; otherwise the ball shall go to the opponents at the same spot. The opponents are required to stand at least three feet inside the boundary line. The player returning the ball from out of bounds must be outside the field of play when he puts the ball in play. A ball hitting the goal posts or crossbar is still in play.

Playing Privileges. 1. **Fly ball**—The ball may be caught, or otherwise played with the hands, whenever it is clearly a "fly ball"; i.e., one that has been raised into the air directly from a kick by one or both feet. A ball thus raised into the air remains a fly ball until it again hits the ground. A fly ball that has been caught may be held, passed, punted, drop-kicked, or played as an overhead dribble, at option. A loose fly ball (not in the possession of a player) may not be kicked or "kneed," but otherwise may be played in any manner by the hands or body. Kicking or kneeing a loose fly ball shall not be construed to include trapping it with the legs below the knees. An overhead dribble shall be considered a loose fly ball. A player kicking a ball into the air is eligible to catch it himself before it hits the ground.

2. **Ground Ball**—A ground ball is one that is stationary, rolling, or bouncing. Even though it may be in the air, as in the case when it is bouncing, the ball is ruled a ground ball until it is in the air from a direct kick. While the ball is a ground ball it can not be played with the hands or any part of the arm below the elbow. Instead, it must be kicked, or "headed," or bounced off the body.

3. **Dribble**—A player may dribble the ball with his feet at will. He may bat or tip a fly ball, or drop a caught ball to the ground and play it as a drop kick or kicking dribble. A player may use one overhead dribble in advancing the ball without the aid of his teammates; i.e., he may throw the ball in any direction and run and catch it before it touches the ground. He may not score a touchdown by this method.

4. **Carrying Ball**—A player who is standing still when catching the ball from a kick or pass may take one step in any direction from the point at which he caught the ball, but must get rid of the ball before a second step is taken. If running, he is allowed two steps, and if at full speed the referee shall decide whether he stops as soon as possible or not. Violations of this rule shall be known as "carrying the ball." A player is prohibited from carrying the ball over the goal line. He must be over the goal line when the ball is caught in order to score a touchdown.

5. **Guarding**—A player may legally guard an opponent who has the ball. He must play to secure the ball and in no way hold the opponent. If two opponents are running for a ball at the same time each must play the ball and not the man. No obstruction shall be made to the progress of any player without the ball.

6. **Tie Ball**—In case a ball is held by two opposing players simultaneously, or where the referee is in doubt which side last played the ball out of bounds, the referee shall declare a "tie ball." The ball shall be placed upon the ground and each player shall stand facing in scoring direction, and with the outside of his left foot against the ball. When the referee's whistle is sounded, they play the ball, using the feet only. A tie ball occurring within five yards of the goal line shall be brought at right angles to a point fifteen feet from the goal line and there put in play. A tie ball at the center of the field shall be used to begin play after a double foul or at the beginning of an overtime period.

7. **Free Kick**—Whenever a free kick is awarded a team they shall have the privilege of putting the ball in play by a place kick, the opposing team being required to stay thirty feet away until the ball is kicked. The ball may be kicked in any direction. The ball must travel its own circumference and the kicker may not play it again until it has been touched by another player. There is no distinction between the goal tender and the other players as regards privileges and restrictions in playing the ball.

Fouls. 1. **Personal fouls shall include:**
    a. Kicking, tripping, charging, pushing, holding, or blocking an opponent. (Charging an opponent from behind is a personal foul in case bodily contact is made.)
    b. Unnecessary roughness of any description.

2. **Major technical fouls shall include:**
    a. Violation of the substitution rule.
    b. More than three time-outs in a game. (See "The Game," No. 8.)
    c. Unsportsmanlike language towards an official or opponent.
    d. Kicking or kneeing a fly ball by player, unless he has first caught it. (If opposing player is kicked or kneed in such an attempt, a personal foul shall be charged against the offender.)
    e. Violating penalty kick rule by defensive team. (See "Scoring," No. 4.)
    f. Delaying the game by illegal interference on out-of-bounds plays. (See "Ball Out of Field of Play," No. 4.)
    g. Violating free kick rule by defensive team. (See "Playing Privileges," No. 7.)
    h. Advancing beyond restraining lines by defensive team on kick-off. (See "The Game," No. 5.)
    i. Having more than eleven men on the field by one team at the same time.

3. **Minor technical fouls shall include:**
    a. Carrying the ball.
    b. Touching a ground ball with the hands or arms below the elbows.
    c. Making two successive overhead dribbles. (See "Playing Privileges," No. 3.)
    d. Violating kick-off rule by offensive team. (See "The Game," No. 5.)
    e. Violating the penalty kick restrictions by offensive team. (See "Scoring," No. 4.)
    f. Violating out-of-bounds rules by offensive player when returning the ball to field of play. (See "Ball Out of Field of Play.")

EIGHTH GRADE

g. Violating free kick restrictions by offensive team. (See "Playing Privileges," No. 7.)

h. Unnecessary delays of the game by the team making a free kick or penalty kick.

Penalties. 1. (a) In case a personal foul is committed by a player within his own penalty area or end zone, the opponents shall be awarded two penalty kicks. The offended player must attempt the kicks. The ball shall be dead after the first attempt in all cases. (b) The ball shall be in play after the second attempt if it is missed.

2. In case a personal foul is committed by a player outside of his own penalty area, the opponents shall be awarded one penalty kick, the ball to be dead if missed. The offended player shall attempt the kick. If missed a touchback shall be declared.

3. (a) In case either a major or minor technical foul is committed by a player within his own penalty area or end zone, one penalty kick shall be awarded. Any member of the offended team may attempt the kick. As soon as the ball is kicked it shall be considered in play. (b) In case a major technical foul is committed by a player outside of his own penalty area, one penalty kick shall be awarded. Any member of the offended team may attempt the kick. The ball shall be dead on this play and no follow-up shall be allowed by either team. If missed, a touchback shall be awarded. (c) In case a minor technical foul is committed by a player within the field of play outside of his own penalty area, a free kick shall be awarded the opponents at the spot of the foul. (d) In case a minor technical foul is committed by a player returning the ball to the field of play, the ball shall go to the opponents out-of-bounds.

4. The referee, on any case not specifically covered by the rules, may declare a technical foul which shall be governed by the penalty rules: (a) Any foul incurred by the defensive team within its own penalty area or end zone shall be governed by "Penalties, 3a"; (b) Any such foul incurred by a team outside its penalty area when it is not in possession of the ball shall be governed by "Penalties, 3b"; (c) Any such foul incurred by a team outside its penalty area when it is in possession of the ball, or has last touched it, shall be governed by "Penalties, 3c."

Forfeitures and Special Rulings. 1. The referee shall have jurisdiction to forfeit a game for refusal of one team to play, or for failure to appear on the field within ten minutes of schedule time. The score of a forfeited game shall be 1 to 0.

2. The referee may suspend any player from the game for unsportsmanlike conduct.

3. A player having three personal fouls charged against him is automatically suspended from the game.

4. (a) If, after a play has been started, the defense commits a technical foul which does not, however, prevent a score from ensuing, the score shall count, providing no further impetus was given to the ball by the attacking team after the foul was committed. (b) If, after a play has been started, the defense commits a personal foul which does not, however, prevent a score from ensuing, the offended side shall be given the score and, in addition, be given one penalty kick without a follow-up. This privilege assumes that no further impetus was given to the ball after the foul was committed.

5. If two fouls are to be shot successively (whether both by the same team, or one by each team), and one involves a follow-up play, but the other does not, the latter penalty shot shall always be attempted first.

Officials. There shall be a referee and two linesmen. The referee shall be in general charge of the game. It shall be the duty of the two linesmen to assist the referee. They shall decide when the ball is out of bounds, and shall blow their whistles to declare it so. The referee shall then award the ball to the proper team, or in case the ball has gone over the goal line, shall declare a score, touchback, or safety, as the case may be. The linesmen have further jurisdiction in aiding the referee to call any foul. The referee shall decide all other questions unless he gives certain specific instructions to the linesmen. He may ask their advice at any time he is in doubt on the proper decision to make. He may detail to them the duties of keeping time and of score. The referee shall officiate within the field and follow the ball. The two linesmen shall be stationed on opposite sides of the field and diagonally apart, so that each of them shall be near a goal line and in a position to judge on out-of-bounds for his respective side and end of the field.

Suggested Changes in Rules for Speedball when Played by Girls.

1. Train girls to fold their arms over their breasts instead of "chesting" the ball.
2. Insist that positions be played, as in hockey.
3. Permit the return of the ball, when out-of-bounds at the goal ends, by the three kicking methods—punt, drop kick, place kick. Do not allow the use of the pass.
4. The ball shall not be played by the hands ("passing") more than three times in succession by members of the same team.
5. The field may be made smaller if desirable.

Additional Athletic Games

War ....Ref. No. 19, p. 417
Bombardment ....Ref. No. 26, p. 59

INDIVIDUAL ATHLETIC EVENTS

Crooked-Man Race (59) *

The pupil advances from the starting line to the finish line as follows: Step forward with the left foot, step the right foot across in back of the left foot, at the same time rocking forward on the left toe, so the right foot is advanced when it is put on the floor; step the left foot across in back of the right foot, at the same time rocking forward on the right foot, and so on attempting to advance two or three inches with each step. From ten to twenty feet makes a good race, depending on the age and skill of the pupils.

Horseshoe Pitch (59) *

For this event horseshoes and a stake rising three inches above the ground are necessary. Establish a throwing line forty-two feet from the stake. The pupil stands on the throwing line and tosses the horseshoe at the stake, attempting to ring it. One foot must be on the throwing line at the time the shoe is released. Each "ringer" scores five points; each "leaner," three points; each "toucher," two points; and each shoe stopping within one foot of the stake, scores one point. Shoes stopping more than a foot from the stake score nothing. The total number of points made by each pupil after throwing twenty individual shoes, constitutes his score.

Lame Dog Race (59) *

The pupil standing back of the starting line, supports himself on both arms and one leg, the other leg being held out behind. Retaining this position with one leg held clear of the floor, he travels forward. From fifteen to thirty yards makes a good race.

Run (80 Yards)

For explanation, see "Run" for fifth grade, page 209.

Standing Three Hops (Boys)

Start from standing position while on one foot. Take three consecutive hops on the same foot. Distance is measured as in the broad jump. The same event may be performed with hopping on the other foot and also with a running start.

Standing Triple Broad Jump (Boys)

The pupil toes the take-off line and makes three successive forward jumps with both feet together and without a pause between jumps. The distance is measured from the take-off to the nearest heel mark

---
* From S. C. Staley, "Individual and Mass Athletics." Copyright 1925. By permission of A. S Barnes and Company, publishers.

made on the last jump. The same event may be carried out with a running start.

Tennis Serve for Accuracy

Upon a wall, mark a space eight feet long and thirty inches wide, the lower line of the rectangle being thirty-six inches from the floor or ground. A line is drawn on the floor or ground thirty-nine feet from the wall and parallel to it. In making the serve the student must stand behind this thirty-nine foot line. The ball may strike the upper line and be good, but must clear the lower line. This event may be given upon a standard tennis court and in this case a second tennis net, or rope, must be stretched above the regular net, leaving a space of thirty inches between the two nets. The serve is then "driven" through this space into the service area. This is designed to prevent an easy "lob" into the service area—no real test of ability to serve. The student's score would be the number of successful serves out of a definite number of trials. The event may be varied by dividing horizontally the wall space into two areas. In this case, count a ball served into the top area as three points and the bottom area as five points.

Volley Ball Serve for Accuracy

A volley ball net or piece of cord shall be stretched across the playing space and at a center height of 7½ feet. Twenty-five feet away draw a line on the ground parallel to the net. The pupil, with volley ball in hand, stands behind the line facing the net. She tosses up the ball with one hand as in tennis and strikes it with the other hand, so that it shall go over the net without touching it and fall within a square fifteen feet by fifteen feet. This square shall be marked on the ground ten feet from the net and at right angles to the center of it. Five or ten trials are allowed. If the contestant steps forward over the line before the ball strikes the ground no score is allowed, but it counts as one trial. The number of times the ball lands within the square is the pupil's score.

Walking Race

The pupil walks as rapidly as possible from the starting line to the finish line. He must place the heel of the advancing foot on the ground before the toe of the trailing foot leaves it. From fifty to three hundred yards may serve as the distance.

Additional Individual Athletic Events

Soccer Accuracy Kick ....Ref. No. 33, p. 112
Bunt and Run.................................Ref. No. 59, p. 26
Catcher's Throw for Accuracy..................Ref. No. 59, p. 71
Hanging Swing Jump (Boys)...................Ref. No. 59, p. 105

EIGHTH GRADE

Sideward Leap (Boys).........................Ref. No. 59, p. 38
Standing High Hop (Boys)....................Ref. No. 59, p. 38

MIMETICS

Basket Ball Goal Throw (6B)

Jump out feet apart and bend trunk forward, extend arms downward to pick up ball—1. Bend arms upward, ball in front of chest—2. Snap ball from chest to basket, arms extended obliquely forward upward—3. Bring arms to sides and jump feet together—4. Ten to twelve times.

Basket Ball Passing

Starting position, feet apart. Bend trunk forward and lower arms to floor, picking up ball—1. Raise trunk and swing arms overhead—2. Suddenly throw arms forward as throwing the ball—3. Position—4. Repeat sixteen counts. Be careful to retain good posture on the throw.

Driving Golf Ball (5)

Jump, feet apart, and place closed hands together on right shoulder, one hand on top of the other. Swing arms downward and then upward to left shoulder; at the same time turn toward the left and sway onto left foot, raising right heel. Swing arms downward and upward to right shoulder, turn toward the right and sway onto right foot, raising left heel. Repeat in rhythm, thirty-two counts.

Kicking Football (6B)

Arms forward, shoulder high, slightly bent at elbows. Step forward with left foot, arms swinging downward and backward (to imitate drop-kick). Carry weight on left foot, swing right leg forward as if kicking football and swing both arms forward at the same time. Position.

Stretching

Stretch and yawn as one does upon getting up in the morning. Repeat several times.

Tennis Serve

With left foot forward take toe touch position, right foot backward. Place right arm slightly forward pointing obliquely forward downward. While swaying backward until weight is on right foot, swing left arm obliquely forward upward as throwing a tennis ball, and let right arm move backward to position obliquely backward downward. Swing left arm forward downward to position obliquely backward downward; carry weight forward onto left foot. Swing right arm upward over right shoulder and follow through as if striking tennis ball.

334 PHYSICAL EDUCATION FOR ELEMENTARY SCHOOLS

RHYTHMICAL ACTIVITIES
Badger Gavotte *
(As danced at Dearborn)

Metronome 96 　　　　　　　　　　　　　　Time: 4/4

* From Mr. and Mrs. Henry Ford, "Good Morning; Old Fashioned Dances Revived." Copyright 1926. By permission of Dearborn Publishing Company, Dearborn, Michigan, publishers.

EIGHTH GRADE

The walking step should be a smooth gliding movement, the ball of the foot touching the floor first, and the heel last, each starting with the outside foot (lady's right and gentleman's left).

First Part

Metronome 96. 4/4 time.

Open position, nearest hands joined; walk forward four steps; count 1, 2, 3, 4—1 bar. Face each other, join both hands, waist high, and slide close; slide close; slide close; step (to gentleman's left); count 5, 6, 7, 8 —1 bar. Turn and repeat all in the opposite direction, starting with outside foot as follows: Walk forward four steps; count 1, 2, 3, 4—1 bar. Turn, face each other, join both hands, waist high, and with right foot take slide close; slide close; slide close; step (to gentleman's right); count 5, 6, 7, 8—1 bar; 4 bars in all.

Second Part

Waltz position: Execute eight slow two-steps, starting with left foot; and repeat all from the beginning—4 bars.

Come, Let Us Be Joyful (13C)

(German)

Arranged by E. B. Gordon.

Come, let us be joyful,
While life is bright and gay;
Gather its roses
Ere they fade away.

We're always making our lives so blue,
We look for thorns, and find them too,
And leave the violets quite unseen
That on our way do grow.

Repeat first stanza.

(Victor: 20448.)

EIGHTH GRADE

Formation: Circle formation. Sets of six—three opposite three. Each three consists of a man in the middle with a girl on each side of him, whose inside hand he holds.

Measures 1-2. Two lines advance toward each other with three walking steps, ending with a bow by the men and a "bob" courtesy by the girls.

Measures 3-4. The lines then walk backward to place, bringing their feet together on the fourth count.

Measures 5-8. Advance and retire again.

Measures 9-16. Hopsa step is used throughout or four walking steps may be substituted for the hopsa (step on the right foot, hop; step on left foot and hop).

Each man hooks right elbow with the girl on his right and turns her with two hopsa steps. Releasing her, he hooks left elbow with the girl on his left and swings her in the same manner.

(While he swings one girl the other performs the hopsa in place and is ready to hook the elbow with the man as soon as he advances.)

Repeat all; finish in two original lines.

Measures 1-8 repeated.

Both lines advance and retire as before in measures 1-8 except the second time they advance and instead of bowing, pass through the opposite line (passing left shoulders) and meet a new line which advances from the opposite direction.

Repeat from the beginning.

Mallebrok *

---

* From Viggo Bovbjerg, "Danish Folk Dances (Description)." Copyright 1917. By permission of author. Recreation Training School of Chicago, 800 S. Halsted street, Hull House, publishers.

Formation: Couples stand informally about the room.

(a) Partners dance polka—bars 1 to 8 and repeat.

(b) Partners face each other and with hands on hips the man dances one change step—slide, change, slide—to his left, then swings his right foot across in front of the left, and claps own hands over his right foot—bars 9 and 10. He dances the same to the right, beginning with the right foot—bars 11 and 12; at the same time the girl dances the same, but uses the right foot when man uses left, and vice versa. Thus both move in the same direction. They then dance eight reel steps in place, partners facing each other—bars 13 to 16. They repeat (b)—bars 9 to 16. Repeat entire dance.

Description for reel step—If the dancer begins with the right foot, he swings the right directly behind the left, places the weight on the right, then hops slightly forward on the right. He does the same with the left, and so on, stepping back and hopping with alternate feet. He dances on place.

May Pole Dance (6B)

Music: "Pop Goes the Weasel." See page 185.

Groups of 16. Square formation, numbering each side A, B, C, D. Four persons on each side. All facing pole. Streamer held in right hand.

Step I

Grasp streamer at half its length. All take four running steps toward center pole.

All take four running steps backward to place.

Leap sideward right and close left foot to right.

Repeat same to left.

Take four running steps in place turning right about under right arm.

Repeat step from the beginning.

Step II

Partners (1-2 and 3-4) face each other. (1 and 3 right side and 2 and 4 left side to pole.)

All take four slides sideward right. Those going away from center will slide to end of streamer.

All take four slides sideward left, coming back to partner.

Leap sideward right and close left foot to right.

Leap sideward left and right foot to left.

Three stamps in place.

Repeat whole step.

EIGHTH GRADE

Step III

Sides A and B take eight skipping steps across, changing places—passing right shoulders.
Sides C and D repeat the same.
This step is continued alternately until streamers are all wound on the pole. A very pretty winding will result.

Step IV

Drop streamers and all join hands in a large circle.
All take eight slides to right.
All skip toward center. (4 counts.)
All skip backward from center. (4 counts.)
All take eight slides to left; grasp hands of partner and take eight step-hops—couples in circle.

Military Schottische (4)

Music: Any good schottische.
Formation: Double circle, partners facing line of direction, inside hands joined, outside hands on hips.

a. (1) Schottische forward outside foot; schottische forward inside foot. (2) Partners face each other and take four step-hops in place, beginning with the foot in the line of direction. (3) Repeat (1) and (2).

b. (1) Same as a (1). (2) Partners drop hands and with hands on hips turn away from each other with four step-hops, making one complete turn. (3) Repeat b (1) and (2).

c. (1) Same as a (1). (2) Partners join both hands and make a complete turn, left shoulder leading, with four step-hops. (3) Repeat c (1) and (2).

d. Same as a (1). (2) Boy takes four step-hops in place, girl turns in under boy's right arm with four step-hops. (3) Repeat d (1) and (2), boy turning under girl's left arm.

e. (1) Same as a (1). (2) Partners take skating position (left hands joined and right hands joined, boy's right arm is under girl's left). Boy takes four step-hops in place, girl takes four step-hops, crossing over in front of boy to his left side. Do not drop hands. (3) Repeat e (1), starting with the inside foot. (4) Repeat e (2), with the girl crossing back to place.

f. (1) Same as a (1). (2) Hands joined in skater's position. Both turn in under the raised arms with four step-hops. Do not drop hands. (3) Repeat f (1) and (2).

g. (1) Same as a (1). This time partners extend arms shoulder high during the schottische steps. (2) Turn away from partner with

340 PHYSICAL EDUCATION FOR ELEMENTARY SCHOOLS

four step-hops, hands on hips, and make a complete turn. (3) Repeat a (1). (4) Take one step in the line of direction with outside foot, swing inside foot in front and behind the outside foot, making a 3/4 turn finishing facing partner; take a step in the line of direction with the foot nearest the line of direction, and bow to partner.

Minuet III (15A)

Music: Minuet rhythm, three counts to each measure, played in a slow courtly manner.

Formation: Circles of four couples, each facing in line of direction. Gentleman on inside of circle on left side of lady, holding hat extended slightly below shoulder level, in left hand. Inside hands joined. When in a square formation couples are numbered around left to right—No. 1, 2, 3, 4.

Description: Introduction—4 measures. May be used as an entrance by repeating enough to bring dancers into circle formation; or, for class work, may be used as follows:

Measure 1. Three light-walking steps, forward in line of direction, beginning with outer foot (gentleman's left, lady's right). Inside hands joined.

Measure 2. Point inner foot diagonally forward, bending slightly toward partner.

Measure 3. Two walking steps forward, beginning inner foot; turn to face partner (ct. 3).

Measure 4. Bow and courtesy. Gentleman bows with heels together, knees straight and hat over heart. Lady courtesies by sliding left foot a short distance behind right and transferring weight to left leg which bends while the right is extended forward. Body is inclined forward and skirts held well out. Sometimes it will be found more convenient to move the right leg backward.

Part I

Measures 1-2. Circle formation. Partners join right hands, beginning with right foot, cross to opposite side with three steps and point.

Measures 3-4. Repeat, continuing back to place, this time beginning with left foot. Right hands still joined.

Measures 5-6. Repeat measures 1 and 2.

Measures 7-8. Repeat measures 3 and 4. End with bow and courtesy instead of pointing foot.

Part II

Measure 9. Partners again join right hands. Step toward each other with right foot, bring up rear foot, rise on toes and look at each other under arms.

Measure 10. Step backward with left foot, pointing right and look at partner over arms. Body slightly bent forward.

Measures 11-12. Repeat measures 9 and 10.

Measures 13-16. Repeat the last four measures of part I. After bow and courtesy partners take position forming and facing the center of a square, lady at right of gentleman.

Part III

Measures 1-2. Opposite couples No. 1 and No. 3, inside hands joined, move toward each other (toward center) beginning with outer foot—three steps and point inner foot.

Measures 3-4. Simultaneously all bow and courtesy as follows: Gentleman No. 1 to lady No. 3; Gentleman No. 3 to lady No. 1; couples No. 2 and No. 4, who have remained in place, bow and courtesy to own partner.

Measures 5-6. Couples No. 1 and No. 3 return to place, moving backwards, beginning with outer foot—three steps and point.

Measures 7-8. Simultaneously all couples bow and courtesy in original square position.

Measures 9-16. The same steps and figure are executed with couples No. 2 and No. 4 leading toward center while No. 1 and No. 3 remain in place.

342 PHYSICAL EDUCATION FOR ELEMENTARY SCHOOLS

Part IV

While the four gentlemen remain in place, the four ladies form a wheel, with right hands joined, and move clockwise as follows:

Measure 1. Ladies leave partners, beginning with right foot, three steps, right hands joined.

Measure 2. Each lady points left foot toward next gentleman to her left.

Measures 3-4. Dropping right hands, step left toward this gentleman and courtesy as he bows.

Measures 5-8. Repeat measures 1-4, continuing on to next gentleman to left.

Measures 9-12. Repeat measures 1-4, continuing on to next gentleman to left.

Measures 13-16. Repeat measures 1-4, lady has now returned to her own partner.

The dance ends with a prolonged bow and courtesy.

NOTE.—For purpose of exit, music may be repeated while the dancers walk off with courtly bearing—lady on gentleman's right.

The Girl I Left Behind Me *
(American)

(Columbia: 33140F.)

---

* From Dorothy LaSalle, "Rhythms and Dances for Elementary Schools." Copyright 1926. By permission of A. S. Barnes and Company, publishers.

This dance comes from the eastern slope of the Adirondack Mountains, not far from Lake George, New York. All calls are in quotation marks. The music for this is Irish. It is not known whether this dance originally came from Ireland, or whether the Americans, having little music of their own, used this Irish tune for their dance.

Formation: Four couples facing in quadrille formation.

I

a. "Hands eight"—All join hands and circle left.

b. "Hands four"—Couples one and two join hands and circle left.

c. "Then pass right through, balance to, and swing the girl behind you"—Couples one and two facing one another, move forward and pass through, the girls passing through the center.

```
   1
X  O      The first man turns and swings the second girl with buzz
↑↓ ↑↓     steps while the second man swings the first girl. Finish with
O  X      second girl beside first man and first girl beside second man.
   2
```

d. "Then go right back on the same old track and swing the girl behind you"—First man takes second girl, second man takes first girl, pass through as before, turn and swing original partner.

e. First couple repeats b, c, and d, with third and fourth couples.

f. "Allemande left"—Swing neighbor.

g. "Grand right and left."

h. "Promenade"—All slide sideways around set each couple in social dancing position.

II

Repeat all of 1, except a, with couple two starting the figures.

III

Repeat all of 1, except a, with couple three starting the figures.

IV

Repeat all of 1, except a, with couple four starting the figures.

344   PHYSICAL EDUCATION FOR ELEMENTARY SCHOOLS

Rheinlander (Swedish)*

(Columbia: A3050.)

Measures 1–8. Sixteen steps walking around circle.

Measures 1–8. Sixteen steps, hop-waltz, or may use running steps around circle.

---

* From Crampton's "Folk Dance Book." Copyright 1909. By permission of A. S. Barnes and Company, publishers.

EIGHTH GRADE

Measures 9-16. Both polka forward two steps, each beginning polka step with his outside foot. Lady then turns under arm of man during two polka steps. Repeat three times.

Measures 9-16. Lady in front of man, man's arms folded, lady's akimbo. Polka forward two steps, then lady whirls with polka steps in line of direction two measures, while man follows with polka, stamping as he follows. Repeat three times.

Measures 17-24. Man kneels, lady with four polka steps goes around him, returning to position. Then both go forward four polka steps. Repeat.

Measures 17-24. Partners take skater's position. Both start step with right foot crossed behind, left foot to the side, turning body toward center; then one running step with right foot, and heel of left foot forward on the ground, toes turned up. Step left foot behind, turn and run outward, ending with right heel forward, partners with backs toward center of the circle. Repeat.

Measures 1-8. Man kneels, lady goes around him—hop-waltz, then both polka forward four steps. Repeat.

Measures 1-8. Polka two steps forward, each starting with outer foot, turn with hop-waltz and lady jumps up as she turns around.

Additional Rhythmical Activities

Harvest Frolic (Russian)	Ref. No. 18, p. 397
Circle Barn Dance	Ref. No. 25, p. 251
Portland Fancy (English)	Ref. No. 25, p. 168
Minuet (IV)	Ref. No. 26, p. 259
Russian Folk Dance	Ref. No. 26, p. 275
Captain Jinks Square Dance	Ref. No. 31, p. 149
Fryksdals Polska	Ref. No. 31, p. 151
Oxcow II (Danish)	Ref. No. 36, p. 60
Highland Fling (Scotch) (Columbia: A3000)	Ref. No. 37, p. 21
Spider Web Maypole Dance	Ref. No. 39, p. 26
Russian Dance (Komarinskaja) (Columbia: A3002)	Ref. No. 42, p. 63
Swedish Polka	Ref. No. 42, p. 74
Varsovienne (Swedish)	Ref. No. 46, p. 10
Jig—"St. Patrick's Day" (Irish) (Columbia: A3000)	Ref. No. 54, p. 76
Oxdansen (Swedish)	Ref. No. 54, p. 26
Tarantella (Italian) (Columbia: A3062)	Ref. No. 54, p. 82
Turn Around Me (Czechoslovakian)	Ref. No. 95, p. 75

STUNTS

Full Squat (5)

Clasp the left wrist with the right hand behind the body. Point the fingers straight down. Bend the knees deeply until you can touch the floor. Keep the head erect and the back flat.

Hand Spring

Use the following procedure for preliminary training: No. 1 is on the ground on his hands and knees. No. 2 takes a short run, places his hands on the ground close up against the body of No. 1, ducks his head, and throws the feet up sharply, keeping the arms rigid until almost the last moment before going over. Then bend the arms slightly at the elbows and straighten them out quickly, thus giving enough spring to force the feet over onto the ground and bring the body upright. If the spring with the arms is given at just the right second, as the feet are traveling at their fastest, one should be able to make a complete turn and come up standing on one's feet. When this is learned, do the hand spring without the aid of a boy on the ground.

Touch Toe Jump (1)

Hold both hands in front horizontal position, jump up and with knees straight, touch both feet at same time to your hands without lowering your hands.

Right Arm Stand

Use an ordinary chair. Grip the back of the chair with the left hand and the seat with the right. Extend the feet over the head, knees straight, heels and toes together. The right arm should be straight. The left arm should be bent and the weight of the body partly shifted to the shoulder that contacts the chair. Repeat the same performance reversing the position of the arms.

Spinning Wheel

Take a squat position, placing both hands on the floor in front with the elbows between the knees. Extend the right leg forward. Swing right leg to the left, under both hands, and hop over it with the left foot. The right leg makes a complete circle. Repeat rapidly. Reverse the direction of the right leg. Repeat, extending the left leg forward.

One Arm Push Up

Place the hands on the floor, shoulder width apart. Extend the legs to the rear, feet together, supporting the body on arms and toes. The body should be straight from head to heels with arms straight. Place one arm along the side of the body, and do a "dip" then a push-up. At the lowest point of the dip pick up a handkerchief with the teeth. At no time should the hips or knees touch the floor. Change arms.

Hand Stand Dip

Face a wall, place the hands near the wall and come to a handstand with the heels touching the wall. Keep the head well back. Now bend the arms until the head touches the floor. Straighten the arms. Repeat.

Duck Fight

Two players grasp their own ankles, and each tries to shoulder the other so as to make him either let go or fall over.

Blindfold Boxing Match

A book is laid on a mat. Two players are blindfolded. Both players get on their knees, placing their left hands on the book. Each player may have on boxing gloves or may hold a long roll of paper in his right hand. Each player has a leader and is permitted to strike only when the leader says "Hit."

Shoulder Dive

Two pupils clasp hands, one standing on the shoulders of the other. The top man turns, as in a forward roll, and lands on his feet. In doing this he must be helped by the supporting man.

Additional Stunts

Dot and Carry Two	Ref. No. 19, p. 249
Stomach Stand	Ref. No. 26, p. 363
Arm Roll	Ref. No. 60, p. 128
Back Straddle	Ref. No. 60, p. 123
Carry Wounded	Ref. No. 60, p. 125
Cork Screw	Ref. No. 60, p. 99
Diving Hand Spring	Ref. No. 60, p. 135
Flying Somersault	Ref. No. 60, p. 137
Front Straddle	Ref. No. 60, p. 122
Giant Roll	Ref. No. 60, p. 133
Head Spring	Ref. No. 60, p. 115
High Dive	Ref. No. 60, p. 107
Human Teeter	Ref. No. 60, p. 136
Rocking Horse	Ref. No. 60, p. 132
Triple Dive	Ref. No. 60, p. 131

RELAY RACES

Hold Hop Relay

Divide players into two or more teams. On signal each player, holding one foot in his hand, hops on the other to a given point. He then changes to the other foot and hops back in the same way, touching off the next player. The team whose last man first crosses the starting line wins.

Human Hurdle Relay

Divide the players into circles of equal number. The players are in single formation facing outward. Players seat themselves with legs extended, feet pointing away from the center of the circle. A space of at least one foot should be between each player. Each circle counts off from left to right. At command, No. 1 stands, immediately faces to the right, runs and jumps over the extended legs of all pupils until he reaches his former position, then sits down and touches off No. 2, the player to his right. No. 2 stands, faces to the right and follows a like procedure. The team wins whose last player is first to reach his original sitting position, with hands raised over head, providing fouls have not been committed. Fouls: 1. Failure to jump over extended legs; 2. Touching off before becoming seated; 3. Jumping over the legs of more than one player at a time. Variation—This game may be varied as follows: As soon as No. 1 has jumped over the feet of No. 2, the latter immediately stands and follows No. 1. In turn, No. 3, 4, etc., follow, continuing the running and jumping. When each player in the circle reaches his original place he must sit down immediately in order that the players following him may jump over his feet. The last player remains standing in his place after jumping over all the extended legs. That team wins, providing no fouls have been committed, whose last player first completes the circuit.

Japanese Crab Relay

At one end of the playground draw a long straight line. Thirty feet from this line draw for each team a circle three feet in diameter. Divide the players into two or more lines. The first player in each line on his feet and hands, facing away from the circle, places his heels on the starting line. At a signal, the first player in each file starts running backward to his circle. On reaching the circle the player stands, then runs forward and touches off the next player. This continues until all have run. The line whose last player first crosses the starting line, wins. Variation: Number players from front to rear. At a signal, number ones run. The player who reaches his circle first scores one point for his team. On signals other numbers run in the same manner.

Obstacle Relay (14D)

The organization is the same as in simple relay, except that each player must overcome some obstacle before he can tag the next runner. The obstacle may be the performance of any gymnastic feat, such as running high jump, climbing a ladder, swinging on rings, or it may be crawling through difficult places, running in and out among ninepins set close together, jumping rope, or carrying a bean bag on the head throughout the race.

Run and Pass Relay

The players are divided into two teams of equal number and stand on two parallel lines about thirty feet apart, facing each other. The ends of the lines should be marked in a definite way and the first and last players must have one foot on the marks when receiving the balls. Each first player at the right end of each line has a basket ball. At the leader's command they run around the opposite line and give their balls to the last players at the end of their team lines; the balls are passed up the lines, all players touching them. The players at the head of the lines run as soon as they receive their ball. The team wins whose first player first receives the ball, after all have run.

Toss, Catch and Pass Relay (6B)

Players are seated with an even number in each row. The first player in each row is the captain and holds a bean bag in his hand. At a signal from the leader the captain of each row leaves his seat, runs forward to the front of the room, faces the members of his team, and toes a starting line. At the same starting signal, members of each row stand in the aisle to the right, facing front. The captain tosses the bag to the first player who throws it back to him, and immediately sits down in his desk. The captain continues passing the bag in the same manner to each member of his team. The last player in the row, upon receiving the bag, calls "stand." The members of his team immediately stand in the aisle to the right and face to the rear of the room. The last player then passes the bag overhead toward the front, the players continuing this passing until the player at the front seat receives it. He becomes the new captain. All turn right about and move forward the distance of one seat, while the first captain runs to the rear of his row in time to receive his throw. The game is continued until each player has become captain. The team which accomplishes this first wins the game.

Wheelbarrow Relay

Couples of about equal size and strength are formed in two or more lines. First man walks on his hands. The second man carries the feet of the first man who keeps his knees straight. On signal they advance and both cross over a line about thirty feet away. The men then change places, second man walking on his hands, first man carrying feet of second man. They return to the starting line. As last man of the couple crosses the starting line, the next couple of the team starts as described.

Additional Relay Races

Circle Relay .... Ref. No. 19, p. 70
Circle Zigzag Relay .... Ref. No. 19, p. 419
Leap-Frog Race .... Ref. No. 19, p. 129
Zigzag Overhead Toss .... Ref. No. 19, p. 424

HUNTING GAMES

Broncho Tag (6B)

Players are scattered about the playground in groups of two. Each group represents a broncho, one player being head; another clasps hands around the waist of the first one and represents the tail. One chaser and one runner are selected. The runner may only escape by seizing the tail of any one of the "bronchos." If he succeeds in doing this the "head" of that broncho immediately becomes the runner. The first one in each group is always the head. The broncho twists and turns in any direction to prevent the runner from seizing it by the tail, but must not use the arms to hinder the runner in any way; therefore it is better for the "head" to fold the arms in front of the body. If the chaser succeeds in tagging the runner before the runner can attach himself to the tail of a broncho, then the runner immediately becomes chaser and tries to tag the other, who has become the runner.

Catch and Pull Tug of War

Draw a line down the middle of the playing area. Divide the players into two equal groups, one group on either side of the line. On a signal players reach over the line, catch hold of an opponent by any part of his body, as hand, arm or foot, and tries to pull him across the boundary. Any number of players may try to secure a hold on an opponent, and any number may come to his rescue, either by pulling him in the opposite direction or by trying to secure a hold on one of the opponents. A player is not captured until his entire body has been pulled over the line. He then joins his captors in trying to secure players. The group wins which has the largest number of players at the end of a time limit, or has secured all of their opponents.

Master of the Ring (15A)

Players stand in a compact group, with their arms folded and held close to their bodies. A circle is then drawn around the group. At a given signal, each player tries to push his neighbor out of the circle. If any player unfolds his arms, or falls down, or gets both feet outside the circle, he is out of the game. The player who is finally left alone in the circle is master of the ring.

Pig in the Hole

Provide a stick about three feet long for each player. A depression is made in the ground somewhat larger than the "pig," (ball or other object to be used). All the players but one form a circle about twelve feet from the depression with five or six feet between each two players. Each player in the circle makes in front of him a small depression about two inches in diameter. Place the "pig" in the center depression. To determine the first driver, and to start the game, *all* the players place the end of their stick in the center depression under the ball. They count "one, two, three," and on "three" all lift the ball into the air, then rush to place the end of their stick in one of the small depressions. The driver, the odd player without a hole, then tries to get the "pig" into the center depression by pushing and striking it only with his stick. The driver also tries at any time to be released from being driver by placing the end of his stick in any vacant hole belonging to a circle player. If successful, the new odd player becomes driver. The circle players try to prevent the "pig" from coming to rest in the center depression, and from leaving the circle, by blocking and striking it with their sticks. The "pig" may not be kicked or be played upon in any other way. The circle players may leave their places at any time to divert the direction of the "pig." While so occupied any player may place his stick in the vacant depression. If the driver succeeds in getting the "pig" to rest in the center depression he wins, all the sticks are placed under the "pig" and the game begins again.

Poison Snake

Players clasp hands to form a circle. Place about seven Indian clubs or substitutes in the center of the circle, with spaces between them in which a player might step. Each player then tries, by pushing or pulling, to make his comrades knock over the clubs. Any player who overturns a club or who unclasps hands must at once leave the circle.

Clubs are replaced when overturned. Players eliminated may start a "scrub" circle, with additional Indian clubs. The player wins who is left in the original circle. Where several circles have been formed, the several winners may form a circle at the close and play to determine the final winner.

Seat Tag (10)

A pupil is chosen to be "It"; another selected to be the runner. At any time the runner may save himself by sitting with some pupil who then becomes "It" and the one who was "It" becomes the runner. Should the pupil who is "It" tag the runner, the runner then becomes "It" and the pupil who was "It" becomes the runner. Thus the game proceeds for any length of time.

Soccer Tag (14D)

Each player has three points at the beginning of the game. The players are scattered about inside a limited play area. One player who is "It" has a soccer ball which he kicks lightly, trying to tag a player by the mere touch of the ball. Any one so touched by the ball loses one of the three points with which he started, and also becomes "It," trying in turn to kick the ball so it will tag one of his fellows. There are no restrictions as to the moving about of players within the play area to evade the ball. The ball must not be touched by the kicker with the hands, nor may it be kicked higher than the chest of the players. Any kicker infringing these rules loses one point for each offense, and remains "It" until he successfully tags some one according to rules. Any player who loses his three points is out of the game as soon as the next player is tagged. The player wins who remains longest in the field.

Additional Hunting Games

Rider Ball .... Ref. No. 17, p. 176
Chinese Wall .... Ref. No. 19, p. 68
Stool Ball .... Ref. No. 19, p. 406

BIBLIOGRAPHY AND REFERENCE CODE

NOTE.—The numbers placed in parentheses after the titles of certain activities in the book refer to the numbers used here.

1. State of Tennessee— Manual of Physical Education. 1926.
2. State of Virginia— State Course of Study, Elementary Schools, Physical and Health Education. 1926.
3. State of North Carolina— Lessons in Physical Education for Elementary Grades. 1924.
4. State of Pennsylvania— Course of Study in School Health. Physical Education, Grades 1 to 8. 1923.
5. State of Connecticut— Manual of Physical Education for Elementary Grades. 1922.
6A. State of New Jersey— Physical Training for Grades 1 to 3. 1926.
6B. State of New Jersey— Physical Training for Grades 4 to 8. 1926.
7. State of Minnesota— Manual of Physical and Health Education. 1924.
8. State of Kentucky— State Course of Study for the Elementary Schools. 1925.
9. State of Massachusetts— Physical Education in the Public Schools. 1922.
9A. State of Massachusetts— Physical Education in the Public Schools, Grades 1 to 3. 1928.
9B. State of Massachusetts— Physical Education in the Elementary Schools, Grades 4 to 6. 1928.
10. State of New York— Syllabus for Physical Training. 1925.
11. State of Ohio— Physical Education and Hygiene Course of Study. 1926.
12. State of Alabama— Manual of Physical Education. 1923.
13A. State of Wisconsin— Manual of Physical Education, Part I, Individual Athletic Activities. 1924.
13B. State of Wisconsin— Manual of Physical Education, Part II, Story Plays and Gymnastics. 1925.
13C. State of Wisconsin— Manual of Physical Education, Part III, Folk and Singing Games. 1924.
13D. State of Wisconsin— Manual of Physical Education, Part IV, Plays and Games. 1924.
14A. City of Oakland— Physical Education Course of Study, Grades 1–2. 1925.
14B. City of Oakland— Physical Education Course of Study, Grades 3–4. 1926.
14C. City of Oakland— Physical Education Course of Study, Grades 5–6. 1922.
14D. City of Oakland— Physical Education Course of Study, Junior High. 1923.
14E. City of Oakland— Physical Education Course of Study, Grades 5–6. 1927.
14F. City of Oakland— Physical Education Course of Study, Rules for Athletic Games, Grades 5–9. 1927.
14G. City of Oakland— Physical Education Course of Study, Grades 7–9. 1927.
15A. State of California— Supplement to Manual in Physical Education. 1918.
15B. State of California— Manual in Physical Education. 1918.
16. Atlantic City, N. J.— Course of Study in Physical Education, Grades 1–8. 1926.
17. Forbush and Allen— The Book of Games for Home, School and Playground, John C. Winston Company. 1927.
18. Clark, Lydia— Physical Training for Elementary Schools, Benj. H. Sanborn and Company. 1918.
19. Bancroft, Jessie— Games for the Playground, Home, School and Gymnasium, Macmillan Company. 1921.
20. Jones-Dorrett— Rhythmic Dances and Dramatic Games, Sherman Clay & Co., San Francisco. 1927.
21. Jones-Dorrett— Rhythmic Stunts and Rhythmic Games, Sherman Clay & Co., San Francisco. 1927.
22. Jones-Dorrett— Rhythmic Songs, Sherman Clay & Co., San Francisco. 1927.
23A. City of Los Angeles— Physical Education Monographs, Grades 1–8.

BIBLIOGRAPHY AND REFERENCE CODE—(Continued)

23B. City of Los Angeles— Athletic Guide, Elementary Schools. 1924.
24. Balch, Ernest— Amateur Circus Life, Macmillan Company. 1916.
25. Elsom and Trilling— Social Games and Group Dances, J. B. Lippincott Co. 1919.
26. Wild and White— Physical Education, Iowa State Teachers' College, Cedar Falls, Iowa. 1924.
27. State of Missouri— Course of Study, Physical Education for Elementary Schools.
28. State of West Virginia— Manual of Physical Education. 1924.
29. State of West Virginia— Manual of Physical Education for Rural Schools. 1928.
30. Kastman and Kohler— Swedish Song Games, Ginn and Company. 1913.
31. La Salle, Dorothy— Rhythms and Dances for Elementary Schools, A. S. Barnes and Company. 1926.
32. La Salle, Dorothy— Play Activities for Elementary Schools, A. S. Barnes and Company. 1926.
33. Andersen, Leonora— An Athletic Program for Elementary Schools, A. S. Barnes and Company. 1927.
34. Ocker, W. A.— Physical Education for Primary Schools, A. S. Barnes and Company. 1926.
35. Burchenal, Elizabeth— Folk Dances of Finland, G. Schirmer. 1915.
36. Burchenal, Elizabeth— Folk Dances of Denmark, G. Schirmer. 1915.
37. Burchenal, Elizabeth— Dances of the People, G. Schirmer. 1913.
38. Hofer, Marie Ruef— Polite and Social Dances, Clayton F. Summy Co. 1917.
39. Lincoln, Jeanette— The Festival Book, A. S. Barnes and Company. 1913.
40. Crawford, Caroline— Dramatic Games and Dances for Little Children, A. S. Barnes and Company. 1914.
41. Crawford, Caroline— Folk Dances and Games, A. S. Barnes and Company. 1908.
42. Crampton, C. Ward— The Folk Dance Book, A. S. Barnes and Company. 1909.
43. Crampton, C. Ward— The Second Folk Dance Book, A. S. Barnes and Company. 1916.
44. Crampton & Wollaston— The Song Play Book, A. S. Barnes and Company. 1917.
45. Burchenal, Elizabeth— American Country Dances, G. Schirmer. 1918.
46. Bergquist, Nils W.— Swedish Folk Dances, A. S. Barnes and Company. 1914.
47. Moses, Irene E. P.— Rhythmic Action Plays and Dances, Milton Bradley Co. 1916.
48. Van Cleve, Cecelia— Folk Dances for Young People, Milton Bradley Co. 1916.
49. Hinman, Mary Wood— Gymnastic and Folk Dances, Group Dances, Vol. IV., A. S. Barnes and Company. 1916.
50. Hinman, Mary Wood— Gymnastic and Folk Dances, Clogs and Jigs, Vol. V., A. S. Barnes and Company. 1922.
51. Cotteral, B. & D.— Tumbling, Pyramid Building and Stunts for Girls, A. S. Barnes and Company. 1926.
52. Bovbjerg, Viggo— Danish Folk Dances (Description), Recreation Training School of Chicago, 800 S. Halsted St., Hull House. 1917.
53. Bovbjerg, Viggo— Danish Folk Dances (Music), Recreation Training School of Chicago, 800 S. Halsted St., Hull House. 1917.
54. Burchenal, Elizabeth— Folk Dances and Singing Games, G. Schirmer, 1909.
55. Davis, Katherine Wallace— Singing Rhymes and Games, Clayton F. Summy Co. 1901.
56. Hofer, Marie Ruef— Popular Folk Games and Dances, A. Flanagan Co. 1907.
57. Hofer, Marie Ruef— Children's Singing Games, Old and New, A. Flanagan Co. 1914.

BIBLIOGRAPHY AND REFERENCE CODE

BIBLIOGRAPHY AND REFERENCE CODE—(Continued)

58. Steiner, Theresa R.— Games in Song for Little Folks, A. S. Barnes and Company. 1921.
59. Staley, S. C.— Individual and Mass Athletics, A. S. Barnes and Company. 1925.
60. Pearl and Brown— Health by Stunts, Macmillan Company. 1921.
61. Bancroft, Jessie— The Posture of School Children, Macmillan Company. 1920.
62. Kennedy and Bemis— Special Day Pageants for Little People, A. S. Barnes and Company. 1927.
63. Drew, Lillian C.— Adapted Group Gymnastics, Lea & Febiger. 1927.
64. Crowninshield, Ethel— Mother Goose Songs for Little Ones, Milton Bradley. 1925.
65. Hinman, Mary Wood— Solo Dances, Vol. I, A. S. Barnes and Company. 1922.
66. Hinman, Mary Wood— Couple Dances, Vol. II, A. S. Barnes and Company. 1918.
67. Hinman, Mary Wood— Ring Games and Dances, Vol. III, A. S. Barnes and Company. 1922.
68. Wood and Cassidy— The New Physical Education, Macmillan Company. 1927.
69. Nash, Jay B.— The Organization and Administration of Playgrounds and Recreation, A. S. Barnes and Company. 1927.
70. Williams, Jesse F.— The Principles of Physical Education, W. B. Saunders Co. 1927.
71. Mitchell, E. D.— Intramural Athletics, A. S. Barnes and Company. 1925.
72. Wayman, Agnes R.— Education Through Physical Education, Lea & Febiger. 1925.
73. LaPorte, William R.— A Handbook of Games and Programs, The Abingdon Press. 1922.
74. Hendy, Lavina M.— Physical Education Complete, News Publishing Company, Sacramento. 1915.
75. Shambaugh, Effie— Folk Dances for Boys and Girls, A. S. Barnes and Company. 1929.
76. LaPorte, William R.— Good Times for Boys, The Methodist Book Concern. 1927.
77. Playground and Recreation Association of America, 315–4th Ave., New York— Eighty-eight Successful Play Activities. 1927.
78. Thomas and Goldthwait— Body Mechanics and Health, Houghton Mifflin Co. 1922.
79. Hetherington, Clark W.— School Program in Physical Education, World Book Co. 1922.
80. Maroney, F. W.— Physical Education Teaching Manual, Lyons & Carnahan. 1928.
81. State of Pennsylvania— Playground Manual, Bulletin No. 30. 1926.
82. Ready, Marie M.— Games and Equipment for Small Rural Schools, Department of Interior, Bureau of Education. 1927.
83. City of Los Angeles— Physical Education Supplies and Equipment for Elementary Schools. 1926.
84. State of California— Scoring Chart for Decathlon, Elementary Boys.
85. State of California— Scoring Chart for Decathlon, Elementary Girls.
86. State of California— Specimen Programs of Physical Training Activities for Use in Small Rural Schools, Bulletin No. 12A. 1923.
87A. Columbia Phonograph Co., New York— Columbia Record Catalog. 1928.
87B. Victor Talking Machine Co., Camden, N. J.— Educational Catalog of Victor Records. 1927.
88. Staley, S. C.— Games, Contests and Relays, A. S. Barnes and Company. 1926.
89. LaPorte, William R.— Recreational Leadership of Boys, Methodist Book Concern. 1927.

BIBLIOGRAPHY AND REFERENCE CODE—(Continued)

90. State of California— Space, Equipment and Supplies for Physical Education in Elementary Schools, Bulletin No. 12C. 1926.
91. Beckley, Fanny E.— Recreative Dances for Classes in Physical Education, Oliver Ditson Co. 1927.
92. Elmore, Emily W.— A Practical Handbook of Games, Macmillan Co. 1922.
93. Acker, Ethel F.— Four Hundred Games for School, Home and Playground, F. A. Owen Co. 1923.
94. Bentley, Alys E.— Play Songs, Laidlaw Brothers. 1912.
95. Burchenal, Elizabeth— Folk Dances from Old Homeland, G. Schirmer. 1922.
96. Sperling, Harry— The Playground Book, A. S. Barnes and Company. 1924.
97. Mr. and Mrs. Henry Ford—"Good Morning, Old Fashioned Dances Revived," Dearborn Publishing Co., Dearborn, Michigan. 1926.
98. Marsh, Chester E.— Singing Games and Drills, A. S. Barnes and Company. 1927.
99. Richards, John N.— Dramatized Rhythm Plays, A. S. Barnes and Company. 1927.
100. Shafter, Mary S.— Dramatic Dances for Small Children. A. S. Barnes and Company. 1927.
101. Shafter, Mary S.— American Indian and Other Folk Dances, A. S. Barnes and Company. 1927.
102. Shafer and Mosher— Rhythms for Children, No. 1. A. S. Barnes and Company. 1921.
103. Reilly, Frederick J.— New Rational Athletics for Boys and Girls, D. C. Heath and Company. 1917.
104. Rodgers, Martin— A Handbook of Stunts, Macmillan Company. 1928.
105. Dunlavy and Boyd— Old Square Dances of America, Recreation Training School of Chicago. 1925.
106. Hofer, Marie Ruef— Music for the Child World, Vols. I, II, III, Clayton F. Summy Company.
107. Colby, Gertrude— Natural Rhythms and Dances, A. S. Barnes and Company. 1922.
108. Elliott, J. W.— Mother Goose Nursery Rhymes, Set to Music by McLoughlin Bros., Inc., Springfield, Mass.
109. Geary, Marjorie— Folk Dances of Czechoslovakia, A. S. Barnes and Company. 1922.
110. Hutchinson, Dorothy— Preparation of School Grounds for Play Fields and Athletic Events, Department of Interior, Bureau of Education, Bulletin No. 1, P. E. Series. 1923.
111. Playground and Recreation Association of America—Athletic Badge Tests for Boys and Girls, Department of Interior, Bureau of Education, Bulletin No. 2, Physical Education Series. 1923.
112. Lowman, Colestock & Cooper— Corrective Physical Education for Groups, A. S. Barnes and Company. 1928.
113. Stafford, George T.— Preventive and Corrective Physical Education, A. S. Barnes and Company. 1928.
114. Smith and Coops— Play Days, A. S. Barnes and Company. 1928.
115. Wright, Louise C.— Story Plays, A. S. Barnes and Company. 1923.
116. Smith, Helen Norman— Natural Dance Studies, A. S. Barnes and Company. 1928.
117. Sheffield, Lyba & Nita— Swimming Simplified, A. S. Barnes and Company. 1927.
118. Andersen and McKinley— An Outline of Physical Education for the First and Second Grades, A. S. Barnes and Company. 1930.

INDEX

A

Ace of Diamonds, The, 258
Achievement Tests, 14
Acknowledgments, v
Advancement, 319
Aëroplanes, 77
Aisle Pass Relay, 120
All Fours Race, 214
All-up Indian Club Relay, 214
Alternate Hop Race, 248
Animal Chase, 171
Animal Imitations, 92
Ankle Throw, 254
Ante Over, 230
Apparatus, Installation of, 62
Arch Ball Relay, 163
Archery, 191
Arch Goal Ball Relay, 215
Arm Roll, 347
Around the Row Relay, 140
Attention Relay, 164
Athletic Games, 27
At the Beach, 79
At the Seashore, 78
Automobile Relay Race, 120
Automobiles, 110
Automobiling, 254
Autumn in the Woods, 69

B

Baa, Baa, Black Sheep, 89
Back Foot Flip, 257
Back Spring, 189
Back Straddle, 347
Back to Back, 95
Back Toss, 312
Backward Roll, 144
Badger Gavotte, 334
Balancing Test, 202
Ball Chase, 126
Ball Game, The, 307
Balloon Ball, 248
Ball Passing, 123
Ball Passing Relay, 312
Ball Puss, 123
Ball Stand, 268
Barley Break, 166

Barnyard Squabble, 140
Baseball, 274
Baseball Batting, 271
Baseball Batting for Accuracy, 203
Baseball Fly Catching, 203
Baseball Pitching, 317
Baseball Play, 317
Baseball Target Throw, 214
Baseball Throw and Catch, 203
Baseball Throw for Accuracy (Boys), 204
Baseball Throw for Accuracy (Girls), 204
Baseball Throw for Distance, 214
Base Running, 204
Basket Ball (Boys), 276
Basket Ball (Nine-Court), 282
Basket Ball Dribble, 300
Basket Ball Foul Throw, 205
Basket Ball Goal Throw, 333
Basket Ball One-Hand Shot, 297
Basket Ball Pass for Accuracy, 205
Basket Ball Passing, 333
Basket Ball Target Throw, 214
Basket Ball Throw for Distance, 205
Basket Ball Throw for Goal, 206
Basket Ball Toss Up, 193
Bat Ball, 151
Batting for Distance, 214
Battle Ball, 248
Bean Bag Board, 126
Bean Bag Box, 123
Bean Bag Circle Toss, 123
Bean Bag Passing Relay, 140
Bean Bag Ring Throw, 140
Bean Bag Target Toss, 231
Bean (Pease) Porridge Hot, 127
Bear Dance, 145
Bear in the Pit, 171
Bears and Cattle, 167
Bell Ringing, 121
Bend and Stretch Relay, 314
Betsy Ross Making the Flag, 76
Bibliography and Reference Code, 353
Bicycling, 145, 308
Bird Catcher, 95
Birds Learning to Fly, 77
Blackboard Relay, 215
Black Tom, 98
Bleking, 218
Blindfold Boxing Match, 347

Bobbin Ahead, 312
Bobbin Back, 312
Body Guard, 271
Boiler Burst, The, 167
Bombardment, 330
Books, Physical Education Minimum List, 66
Bouncing Balls, 145
Boundary Ball, 146
Boundary Lines for Courts and Fields, 52
Bound Ball, 163
Bounding Heart (Sjalaskutan), 267
Bowl Club Ball, 237
Bowling, 268
Bow-Wow, 307
Broncho Tag, 350
Broom Dance, 172
Brownies, 70
Brownies and Fairies, 89
Building a House, 76
Building an Eskimo Home, 114
Building Stone Wall, 93
Bull Frog Relay, 215
Bull in the Ring, 171
Bummel Schottische, 228
Bunt and Run, 332

C

Camel, The, 80
Camel Walk, 309
Captain Ball I, 193
Captain Ball III, 297
Captain Jinks, 260
Captain Jinks Square Dance, 345
Cap Transfer Relay, 251
Carrousel, 128
Carry and Fetch Relay, 164
Carry Wounded, 347
Cart Wheel, 144
Cat and Mice, 89
Cat and Rat, 95
Catch and Pull Tug of War, 350
Catcher's Throw for Accuracy, 332
Catch of Fish, 232
Cats and Rats, 88
Causes of Poor Posture, 33
Center Catch Touch Ball, 231
Center Stride Ball, 231
Centipede, 190
Chain Dance, 187
Chain Dodge Ball, 315
Chain Tag, 315
Chair Stand, 257
Chair Vault, 308

Changing Seats, 96
Chariot Race, 312
Charley Over the Water, 92
Chase the Animal Around the Circle, 89
Children's Books, 43
Children's Polka, 173
Chimes of Dunkirk, 98
Chinese Chicken, 126
Chinese Get Up, 145
Chinese Wall, 352
Choice of Apparatus, 62
Chopping Wood, 234
Christmas Dance, 187
Christmas Toys, 75
Christmas Tree, 75
Circle Ball, 98
Circle Barn Dance, 345
Circle Chase, 167
Circle Dance, 307
Circle Dodge Ball, 163
Circle Kick Ball, 231
Circle Race, 168
Circle Relay, 350
Circle Soccer, 194
Circle Strike, 237
Circle Zigzag Relay, 350
Circus, 69
Classification Chart, 16
Classification of Children for Competition, 15
Cleaning House, 118
Clever Wood Mice, 72
Climbing Ladders, 121
Clown Tricks, 188
Club Organization, 19
Club Snatch, 268
Coasting with New Christmas Sled, 115
Cock Fight, 257
Coffee Grinder, 188
Come Along, 168
Come Let Us Be Joyful, 336
Coming to This Country, 71
Comin' Through the Rye, 174
Commercial Equipment for School Playgrounds, 53
Cork Screw, 347
Corner Kick Ball, 202
Corner Spry Relay, 166
Cornish May Dance, 268
Corrective Physical Education, 27
Countries, 110
Cowboys, 73
Cowboys Throwing Lasso, 145
Crab Walk, 142
Crab Walk Race, 298
Crane Dive, 230

INDEX

Crested Hen, The, 300
Crooked-Man Race, 331
Cross-Cut Sawing, 234
Crossing the Brook, 90
Cross Over Relay, 141
Cross Tag, 269
Csebogar, 220
Cutting the Grass, 71

D

Dance Steps—Names and Descriptions, 38
Danish Dance of Greeting, 99
Dare Base, 269
Day at the Playground, A, 112
Day in the Country, A, 68
Dead Ball, 316
Dear Old Santa, 74
Definition of Physical Education, 6
Did You Ever See a Lassie, 81
Diving Hand Spring, 347
Dodge Ball, 146
Dog Collar, 145
Dog Run, 143
Donegal Country Dance, 307
Dot and Carry Two, 347
Do This, Do That, 92
Double Circle, 96
Double Circle Pass Relay, 252
Double Forward Roll, 188
Double Hop, 251
Double Jumping Race, 251
Double Tag, 124
Dozen Ways of Getting There, A, 312
Drive Ball, 202
Driving Golf Ball, 333
Drop the Handkerchief, 98
Duck Fight, 347
Duck on the Rock, 269
Ducks, 82
Duck Walk, 142
Dumbbell Tag, 234
Dutch Couple Dance, 176

E

Effects of Muscular Activity, 7
Elbow Roll, 312
Elephant Race, 251
Elephants, 108
Elephant Walk, 256
Elevator, 121
Elimination Pass, 270
End Ball, 153

English Harvester's Dance, 187
Entry Blanks, 21
Equipment for Playgrounds, 53
Eraser Relay, 141
Eskimos, The, 114
Eskimo Race, 206
Eskimo Roll, 230
Exchange Tag, 124

F

Fairies, 89
Farm Chores, 111
Farmer and the Crow Relay, 164
Farmer in the Dell, The, 83
Farmer Is Coming, 171
Feather Ball, 195
Fencing, 62
Ferryboat, 93
Field Ball, 238
Field Dodge Ball, 319
Field Events, 22
Finger Feat, 308
Finnish Reel, 221
Fire, The, 109
Fire Cracker, 191
Fire Engine, 124
Firemen, 72
Fish Hawk Dive, 190
Fist Polka, 228
Floor Tag, 124
Flopper, 312
Flower Play, 118
Flowers and the Wind, 96
Flying Dutchman, 124
Flying Somersault, 347
Folk Dances or Games, 37
Follow the Leader, 93, 125
Fongo, 163
Foot Volley Ball, 248
Forcing the City Gates, 316
Forest Lookout, 125
Forward Roll, 143
Fox and Geese, 315
Fox Trail, 126
French Doll, 84
French Reel, 267
Frog Hand Stand, 143
Frog Hop, 187
Frog in the Middle, 92
Front Foot Flip, 230
Front Straddle, 347
Front Toss, 312
Fryksdals Polska, 345
Full Squat, 346
Furling Sail, 145

INDEX

G

Gallop, 143
Gathering Flowers, 78
Gathering Sticks, 168
Gathering Wood for Fire, 76
General Objectives, 6
General Suggestions to Teachers, 64
George Washington, 116
German Hopping Dance, 268
Giant Roll, 347
Giant Stride, 60
Girl I Left Behind Me, The, 342
Girls and Boys, Come Out to Play, 187
Goal Tag, 270
Goal Throwing Relay, 313
Going to Jerusalem, 234
Goosey, Goosey, Gander, 89
Grandmother Will Dance, 187
Gustaf's Skoal, 261
Gymnastic Dancing, 37

H

Half Lever and Toes to Bar, 207
Hallowe'en, 70
Hand Ball, 196
Hand Ball Drill I, 214
Hand Ball Drill II, 251
Hand Jump, 230
Hand Polo, 147
Hand Spring, 346
Hand Stand, 308
Hand Stand Dip, 347
Hand Tennis, 320
Hand Traveling Events, 248
Hand Walk, 309
Hand Wrestle, 257
Hanging Swing Jump, 332
Hansel and Gretel, 178
Harvest Frolic, 345
Hatter, The, 307
Have You Seen My Sheep, 126
Head Spring, 347
Head Stand, 189
Health Education, 29
Heel and Toe Spring, 254
Heel Click, 228
Heel Grasp Race, 249
Heel Run Race, 207
Here We Go on a Merry-Go-Round, 89
Here We Go Round the Christmas Tree, 88
Here We Go Round the Mulberry Bush, 88
Hey Diddle Diddle, 108
Hickory, Dickory, Dock, 89

Hide the Thimble, 92
High Dive, 347
Highland Fling, 345
Highland Schottische, 301
Hill Dill, 126
Hindoo Tag, 270
Hippity Hop to the Barber Shop, 108
Hit or Out, 242
Hit Pin Baseball, 279
Hobble Race, 207
Hobby Horse, The, 140
Hold Hop Relay, 348
Home Base Bean Bag Relay, 165
Home Run Relay, 218
Home Tag, 171
Hook On, 232
Hoop Rolling Relay, 313
Hopi Corn Dances, 228
Hopping Broad Hop, 251
Hopping Race, 214
Hopping Relay, 165
Horizontal Balance, 229
Horizontal Bars, 56
Horizontal Ladder, 58
Horizontal to Perpendicular, 229
Horseshoe Pitch, 331
Horseshoes, 280
Hot Cross Buns, 129
Hound and Rabbit, 96
How Animals Get Ready for Winter, 71
How-Do-You-Do, 267
How D'ye Do, My Partner, 85
How Many Miles to Babylon, 234
Human Arch, 257
Human Ball, 257
Human Bridge, 230
Human Fly, 256
Human Hurdle Relay, 348
Human Rocker, 142
Human Teeter, 347
Human Wheel, 190
Hunting Games, 30
Hunting We Will Go, A, 100
Huntsman, 90
Hurly Burly Bean Bag Relay, 165

I

Ice Play, 116
I'm Very, Very Tall, 89
In and Out Relay, 252
Incentives, 17
Indian Club Guard, 232
Indian Corn Husking Dance, 187
Indian Hunters, 180
Indians, 109
Indian War Dance, 130
Indian Wrestle, 230

INDEX

Individual Athletic Events, 30
Inner Circle Ball, 169
Installation of Apparatus, 62
Instructional Period, 8
Instruction in Use of Apparatus, 62
In the Barn, 110
Intramural Athletics, 18
Introduction, 1
Irish Lilt, 307
Irish Long Dance, 267
I Say "Stoop!", 126
I See You, 108
I Want to Go to London Town, 108

J

Jack Be Nimble, 90
Jack in the Box, 191
Jack Knife Bend, 191
Jack Rabbit Relay, 313
Janko, 228
Japanese Crab Relay, 348
Japanese Tag, 234
Jig—"St. Patrick's Day," 345
John Brown, 187
Jolly Is the Miller, 132
Jump and Clap, 271
Jump and Reach, 207
Jumping Jack, 190, 317
Jumping Jack's Jubilee, 267
Jumping Relay, 254
Jumping Rope, 191
Jumping Rope I, 126
Jumping Rope II, 171
Jumping Rope III, 234
Jumping Rope IV, 271
Jump Jim Crow, 182
Jump the Stick, 230
Junglegym, 54

K

Kaca, 228
Kangaroo Jump, 214
Kangaroo Relay, 215
Keep Away, 270
Kerry Dance, 267
Kick Ball, 147
Kicking Football, 333
Kickover Ball, 321
King of France, 108
Kitty White, 88
Klappdans (Clap Dance), 187
Knee and Toe Wrestle, 230
Knee Dip, 188
Knee Shoulder Stand, 311
Knee Spring, 257

L

Lame Dog Race, 331
Lame Duck Race, 298
Lame Fox and Chickens, 126
Lancers, The, 307
Land of Cotton, The, 222
Lassies' Dance I (Kulldansen), 268
Lassies' Dance II (Kulldansen), 307
Last Couple Out, 270
Last Man, 234
Last One Out, 169
Lath and Plaster, 190
Laying Out Grounds, 49
Leader and Class, 90
Leader and Footer, 234
Leap Frog and Forward Roll, 190
Leap Frog Race, 350
Leg Lifts, 208
Letting Out the Doves, 98
Let Us Wash Our Dolly's Clothes, 108
Line Ball, 142, 202
Line Zigzag I and II, 254
Line Zigzag III, 314
Link Tag, 169
List of Children's Books, 43
List of Physical Education Supplies, 61
List of Play Areas and Equipment, 60
Little Bo-Peep, 133
Little Ducks, 89
Little Jack Horner, 89
Little Man in a Fix, 262
Little Miss Muffet, 89
Locomotive, 271
London Bridge, 108
Long Ball, 155
Long Reach, 307
Looby Loo, 86
Look Out, 89
Lottie is Dead (Lott 'Ist Tod), 263
Lumbering, 117
Lunge and Hop Fight, 190

M

Magic Carpet, 91
Making a Garden, 119
Mallebrok, 337
Mangle, The, 302
Maple Sugar, 111
March Winds, 76
Marusaki, 101
Mass Athletics, 18
Mass Running, 208
Master of the Ring, 351

INDEX

May Pole Dance, 338
May Pole Dance (Bluff King Hal), 187
May Queen, 79
Maze Tag, 316
Measuring Worm, 144
Merry-Go-Round, 312
Merry-Go-Round, The, 139
Methods in Track and Field Events, 23
Midnight, 97
Military Schottische, 339
Mimetics, 31
Minimum List of Recommended Books, 66
Mining Coal, 115
Minuet I (Mozart), 183
Minuet II, 267
Minuet III, 340
Minuet IV, 345
Minuet Bow, 188
Mistress Mary, 140
Modes of Travel, 113
Money Musk, 187
Mother May I Go Out to Play, 98
Motorcycle, 119
Moving Day, 97, 117
Muffin Man, The, 88
Mulberry Bush, 88
Mule Kick, 230
My Dog, 89

N

Names of Steps—Rhythmical Activities, 38
Natural Dancing, 37
Nest Making, 140
Net Ball, 243
Newsboy, 113
Nickodickomdij, 228
Nine-Court Basket Ball, 282
Nixie Polka, 134
Noriu Miego, 307
Norwegian Mountain March, 264
Nose and Toe Tag, 315
Nuts in May, 228
Nutting, 70

O

Oats, Peas, Beans, 102
Objectives, 6
Obstacle Relay, 349
Ocean Is Stormy, The, 125
Odd and Even Relay, 252
Odd Man's Cap, 316
Officials, 21
Oh, Where, Oh, Where Has My Little Dog Gone, 108
Old Dan Tucker I, 135
Old Dan Tucker II, 303
Old Man Tag, 126
Old Roger Is Dead, 103
Old Woman Who Lives in a Shoe, 140
O'Leary, 233
One Arm Push-Up, 346
One Old Cat, 157
Organizing the Program, 22
Otto and the Crow, 108
Our Little Girls, 140
Over and Under Relay, 216
Oyster Shell, 169
Oxcow I, 307
Oxcow II, 345
Oxdansen, 345

P

Paddle Tennis, 243
Pancake Man, 108
Parazontal Bars, 57
Pass and Change, 233
Pass and Squat Relay, 216
Pear Waltz, 267
Pebble Chase, 234
Pendulum, 257
Physical Education Books, 66
Physical Education Periods, 8
Pig in the Hole, 351
Pilgrims, 112
Pin Basket Ball, 244
Pinch-O, 271
Pin Football, 286
Pin Soccer, 157
Play Days, 24
Playground Baseball, 158
Playground, The, 68
Playing in the Wind, 78
Playing Train, 89
Play in the Snow, 73
Play Supervision, 14
Point System, 17
Poison, 315
Poison Seat, 170
Poison Snake, 351
Policeman, 120
Polka, 140
Polly-Wolly-Doodle, 264
Pom Pom Pullaway, 234
Popcorn Magic, 104
Pop Goes the Weasel I, 185
Pop Goes the Weasel II, 222
Pop Goes the Weasel III, 303
Portland Fancy, 345
Posture, 31
Posture Tests, 34
Potato Race, 208

INDEX

Potato Shuttle Relay, 218
Practice Polka, 222
Preface, xiii
Preparing for Thanksgiving, 71
Prisoners' Ball, 161
Prisoners' Base I, 271
Prisoners' Base II, III, IV, V, 271
Progressive Dodge Ball, 198
Protection of Younger Children, 62
Provisions for Safety, 62
Pulling Up Anchor, 271
Pull Up, 209
Pumping Up Bicycle Tire, 235
Punt Back, 245
Pupil Leadership, 17
Push Up, 209
Puss in a Circle, 97
Puss in the Corner, 92
Pussy Cat, Pussy Cat, 105

Q

Quadruple Dodge Ball, 297

R

Rabbit Hop, 142
Rabbit in the Hollow, 89
Railroad Train, 91
Raindrops, 89
Reap the Flax, 267
Relay Race, 141
Relay Races, 35
Relief Periods, 8
Repairing Roads, 116
Rescue Relay, 216
Revolving Light, 317
Rheinlander, 344
Rhythmical Activities, 36
Ribbon Dance, 267
Ride a Cock Horse, 140
Rider Ball, 352
Rig-A-Jig-Jig, 108
Right Arm Stand, 346
Rill, The, I, 187
Rill, The, II, 187
Ring Call Ball, 97
Ritsch, Ratsch, 224
Rocking Horse, 347
Roley Poley, 316
Roman Soldiers, 108
Rooster, 121
Rotation Soccer, 199
Round and Round the Village, 87
Round Ball, 254
Rovenacka, 186

Rubber Neck, 257
Run (40 and 50 yards), 209
Run (60 yards), 249
Run (70 yards), 298
Run (80 yards), 331
Run and Catch, 211
Run and Pass Relay, 349
Running, 108
Running Broad Hop, 251
Running Broad Jump, 210
Running Double Broad Jump, 212
Running Double High Jump, 214
Running High Jump, 212
Running Hop, Skip and Jump, 300
Running Hop, Step and Jump, 300
Running Whole Hammon, 300
Run, Rabbit, Run, 91
Run, Toss and Catch Relay, 217
Russian Dance (Komarinskaja), 345
Russian Folk Dance, 345
Russian Scherr, 307
Russian Snowstorm, 228
Rye Waltz, 304

S

Sack of Wheat, 257
Safety Climbing Tree, 55
Safety Inspection of Apparatus, 62
Safety Platform Slide, 56
Safety Provisions, 62
Sailors' Hornpipe, 307
Sandal Polka, 136
Santa Claus and the Reindeer, 140
Santa Claus' Visit, 115
Santa Claus Will Come To-night, 108
Schoolroom Dodge Ball, 163
Schoolroom Tag, 126
Schoolroom Volley Ball, 287
School Sites, 49
Schottische Couple Dance, 305
Scooping Sand, 93
Score Sheets for Track and Field Meets, 22
Screw Driver, 272
Scythe Swinging, 235
Seal Crawl, 229
Seat Tag, 352
See Saw, 108, 145
Sellengers Round, 228
Setting Pegs, 307
Seven Hops, 300
Seven Jumps, 267, 298
Seven Steps, 300
Sewing Machine, 191
Shinney, 201
Shoemaker's Dance, 88
Shoulder Dive, 347

INDEX

Shoulder Spring, 308
Shoulder Stand, 309
Shuttle Broad Jump, 249
Shuttle Relay, 217
Sicilian Circle, 266
Side Kick, 321
Sideward Leap, 333
Sideward Pass Relay, 253
Signaling, 235
Simon Says, 170
Simplified Soccer, 245
Singing Games, 36
Sitting Balance, 255
Sit Up, 212
Six-Hole Basket Ball, 200
Skating, 74, 146, 191
Skin the Goat, 271
Skin the Snake Relay, 314
Skipping Race, 250
Skip Rope Relay, 253
Skip Tag, 91
Slap Jack, 92
Sleeping Beauty, 106
Sleeping Princess, The, 68
Snowball Game, 108
Snowballing, 121
Snow Fort, 74
Soccer, 287
Soccer Accuracy Kick, 332
Soccer Bounce Kick for Distance, 300
Soccer Corner Kick for Accuracy, 298
Soccer Dodge Ball, 161
Soccer Dribble, 213
Soccer Dribble and Kick for Goal, 250
Soccer Dribble Kick for Accuracy, 300
Soccer Heading for Accuracy, 300
Soccer Heading for Distance, 299
Soccer Keep Away, 201
Soccer Kick for Distance, 250
Soccer Kick for Goal, 213
Soccer Place Kick for Accuracy, 300
Soccer Punt for Distance, 299
Soccer Relay, 166
Soccer Tag, 352
Soccer Throw-in for Distance, 299
Social Dancing, 37
Soldier Boy, 108
Soldier's Joy, 228
Solid Ivory, 230
Specific Objectives, 6
Specimen Programs, 9
Speedball, 322
Spider and Flies, 98
Spider Web Maypole Dance, 345
Spinning Wheel, 346
Sponge Ball, 290
Spring Play, 118
Square Ball, 163

Square Relay, 314
Square Soccer, 202
Squat Jumping Race, 251
Squirrel and Nut, 92
Squirrels in Trees, 91
Standing Broad Hop, 251
Standing Broad Jump, 235, 250
Standing Broad Step, 251
Standing Double Broad Jump, 251
Standing Double High Jump, 250
Standing High Hop, 333
Standing High Jump, 251
Standing High Kick, 256
Standing Hop, Skip and Jump, 299
Standing Hop, Step and Jump, 299
Standing Leap and Jump, 251
Standing Sideward Broad Jump, 251
Standing Three Hops, 331
Standing Triple Broad Jump, 331
Standing Whole Hammon, 299
Start of Race, 316
Stationary Circle Travel Rings, 59
Statues, 125
Steamboat, 272
Step Hop, 143
Steps in Rhythmical Activities, 38
Stiff Leg Bend, 257
Stomach Stand, 347
Stool Ball, 352
Stoop and Stretch Relay, 142
Stooping Push, 312
Stooping Stretch, 187
Stoop Tag, 126
Stop and Start, 92
Story Plays, 46
Straddle Jump, 308
Strasak, 228
Stretching, 333
Stride Ball Relay, 217
Striking the Anvil, 146
Stump Walk, 190
Stunt Relay, 166
Stunts, 47
Suggestions to Teachers, 64
Supervised Play Periods, 8
Surfacing, 49
Swedish Polka, 345
Swedish Ring Dance, 187
Swimming, 109, 214
Swing, The, 107
Swiss May Dance, 140

T

Taffy Was a Welshman, 137
Tag the Wall Relay, 142

INDEX

Tantoli, 307
Tarantella, 345
Target Toss, 171
Teachers, Suggestions to, 64
Teamster Warming Up, 272
Tech Ball, 148
Ten Little Indians, 138
Tennis, 291
Tennis Serve, 333
Tennis Serve for Accuracy, 332
Tether Ball, 293
Thanksgiving, 112
Third Man, 316
This Is the Way My Dolly Walks, 89
Thread the Needle, 235
Three Around, 126
Three Dance, 268
Three Deep, 234
Three Little Girls, 187
Three Little Mice, 140
Three Standing Broad Jumps, 251
Three Strand May-Pole-Ka, 307
Through the Stick, 312
Tip Cat, 170
Toad Jump, 121
To-day Is the First of May, 187
Toe Grasp Race, 251
Toe Jump, 313
Top, 257
Toss, Catch and Pass Relay, 349
Touch Toe Jump, 346
Toy Shop, The, 77
Toys' Jubilee, The, 111
Track and Field Meets, 20
Trallen (Fjallnaspolska), 307
Traveling Ring Outfit, 60
Triangle Ball, 162
Triple Change, 234
Triple Dive, 347
Triple Roll, 257
Troika, 228
Trotting Horses, 89
Turk Stand, 228
Turn Around Me, 345
Twinkle, Twinkle, Little Star, 108
Twister, 257
Two Deep, 171
Two Old Cat, 247

U
Uncle Sam's Frolic, 306

V
Varsovienne, 345
Vineyard Dance, 187
Virginia Reel, 225
Vis-A-Vis, 234
Volley Ball, 294
Volley Ball Serve for Accuracy, 332
Volley-Tennis, 162

W
Walking Race, 332
Walking Relay, 166
Wand and Toe Wrestle, 190
War, 330
Washing Clothes, 114
Washington's Cherry Tree, 75
Weathercock, 126
Weather Vane, 121
Weaving Dance, 228
Wee Bologna Man, 98
Weekly Intramural Program, 10
Weekly Program, 10
Wee Willie Winkle, 89
We Won't Go Home Till Morning, 267
What to Play, 92
Wheelbarrow Relay, 350
Whip Tag, 316
Who Goes Round My Stone Wall, 126
Wicket Walk, 190
Wiggle Walk, 308
Windmills, 316
Windmills at Park, The, 119
Wind, The, 117
Wooden Man, 229
Wood Tag, 126
Work Up, 163

Y
Yankee Doodle, 140
Yearly Program, 9

Z
Zigzag Bounce Ball Relay, 253
Zigzag Overhead Toss, 350